BASE
NATURE

A BILL MURDOCH MYSTERY

BASE NATURE

GED
GILLMORE

deGrevilo
Publishing

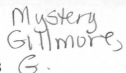

Cataloguing in Publication details are available from the National Library of Australia www.trove.nla.gov.au

Creator: Gillmore, Ged
Title: Base Nature : A Bill Murdoch Mystery / Ged Gillmore.

ISBN: 9780648189008 (paperback)
ISBN: 9780648189015 (ebook)

Subjects: Murder—Abuse—Trafficking—Australia—Fiction.
          Detective and mystery stories, Australian.
          Suspense fiction, Australian.

Editing: Bernadette Kearns, Book Nanny Writing and Editing Services
Additional Proofreading: Ashley Casey, Rachna Verma
Typesetting: Oliver Sands
Cover design: Luke Causby @ Blue Cork
Cover photograph: Matt Mason
Set in Adobe Garamond Pro 11 pt
10 9 8 7 6 5 4 3 2 1

For more information on Ged Gillmore and his books, see his website at: www.gedgillmore.com

For Oliver

Part 1: March

Wednesday, 13th March

Two days before

A dull breeze brings Anita back to her senses. She is standing behind her little Suzuki, the driver-side door hanging open, the engine throbbing eagerly as it helps to bake the afternoon air.

Remembering she is supposed to be checking something, Anita blinks, looks again and sees one of the Suzuki's back wheels is halfway onto the pavement. The tyre is teetering on the concrete kerb, an ugly swell distorting its black rubber and threatening any second to burst. Anita stares at it, until she notices a sharp pain in her hand. She has been clenching her fists so tightly that the broken fingernail of her middle finger has pierced her palm.

She raises her hand to inspect it and sees a tiny drop of blood appear. The drop swells and then – too fat to resist the pull of gravity – starts making its slow way towards her wrist. Under the hard summer sky, Anita fancies she can see her reflection in the shiny claret. She licks her hand clean, keen to understand the meaning of the blood, and immediately wondering if this is what insanity will be like. Empty minutes unexplained, significance given to everyday nothings.

She pulls her sunglasses down onto her face and takes a deep breath that does her no good – the air so hot it scrapes. Her dress is clinging to her sides. The breeze comes again, stronger this time and somehow even drier than before. It is a brickfielder straight from the desert, like opening an oven door: that searing rush you always forget to prepare for. But at least it wakes her up. She regards the deformed tyre once more and sighs. Climbs backs into the Suzuki and edges the car further forwards – the unexploding bump of tyre into gutter a disappointment somehow – then climbs back out, locks the door carefully behind her and sets off along the broken pavement.

They say there is a storm on the way, but, for now, the sky is a pitiless blue. As Anita passes the empty shop windows of Crosley town centre, she wonders why she has parked so far from The Flying Pan. Only an idiot would walk to the café on a day like today. She stops abruptly and turns. Considers hurrying back to the car and driving across the town centre instead. Then, annoyed at her indecision, she tuts loudly. Surely this dithering in the early afternoon heat is the strongest sign yet she is losing her mind? But no. She is *not* losing her mind. She can't – she's got Riya to think of. So she takes a deep breath, turns again and strides purposefully on.

'Anita! Hi! Anita – wait up!'

A man in Stubbies and a PPC work shirt is waving from the shadows of a torn awning on the other side of the road. He hurries towards her, crossing in front of one slow car and waiting for another to pass. He is only metres away before she recognises him. It is Tom Brandle, the PPC warehouse foreman. Anita manages to drag up a smile, grateful for her sunglasses.

'Are you a mad dog, Anita?'

Tom's smile is crooked and yellow, his skin the colour of a summer spent outdoors.

'What?'

'Or an Englishman? Aren't they the only ones who go out in the midday sun? You know, the song?'

Anita doesn't reply and Tom squints at the sky as if looking for confirmation his joke is valid. He is an amber-eyed man, tanned and shaped by a life of hard work, somehow still fair-haired as he approaches retirement.

'Jesus, it's hot,' he says. 'What you doing out here?'

'Getting away from everyone at work.'

She watches him get it.

'Oh. Sorry. Listen, Anita, I'm desperate but. Do you know when Scott's back? I'm not allowed to push out the Hanjin order till he signs it off and he'll be upset if we miss the shipment date. Y'know what he's like about deadlines. Only I can't get hold of 'im.'

Now. Right now. Anita could let it all out. Burst like the tyre had refused to, scream and cry and fall apart. Or she could just close her eyes, fall to the ground and let Tom Brandle call emergency services. Surely, he could be trusted? She could pretend to be unconscious and let Tom put her in the care of strangers, people who could take her to a clean hospital bed where she might remember how to sleep. The thought that those strangers – men – would touch her, handle her, lift and undress her, taints the fantasy. But, again, it is the thought of Riya that kills it. What a burden it is to have a small child. For the rest of her life Anita will have to be strong for Riya's sake; stay alive for Riya's sake; act happy for Riya's sake. No matter how a man might look at her, no matter what thoughts he might have, Anita can never complain. Tom coughs uncertainly.

'Anita?'

'Scott's in the office right now.' She can hear the curtness in her voice but she doesn't care. 'I just left him there. He's got a meeting at three but otherwise he's free all afternoon.'

'But he told me …'

Tom frowns and looks at her with his head slightly tilted. Anita can see he's preparing to ask if she's sure. They both know she's got things wrong in the past. Without another word, she walks past him and further on along the cracked pavement. When she hears him shout after her – 'Thanks! Sorry for bothering you during your break!' – she doesn't respond.

The Flying Pan is busy, a birthday lunch taking up all the tables, the booths so full strangers are being asked to share. Around Ly at the till is a huddle of people and, between there and the door, three young women with improbably straight hair are reading their phones as they wait.

Anita frowns and checks her watch. She has to be back in the office in under an hour – will she really have to return there hungry? Isn't she even allowed to eat? Seeing her in the doorway, Charlie Lam calls out from behind the counter.

'For lovely Ms Patel, we have best seat in house!'

At this, two of the straight-haired women look up, but Anita, safe behind her sunglasses, stares back at them until they remember their screens. Charlie caught her crying in one of the booths once. He didn't ask what was wrong, just patted her arm and told her to take her time finishing her sandwich. He must have said something to the others too because the bill didn't come until long after she had pulled herself together. Now, whenever Anita comes in, they all make a fuss.

'Window seat so you can look at all losers outside on day hot like today!' Charlie points towards a lone free stool at the shelf running along the front window. Someone has left a small metal *Reserved* notice on its seat.

'Bloody hell, Neets,' Mark Lam calls from further along the counter. 'Don't know what you ever did to Dad, but he's smitten. I'm telling Mum!'

The girls on their phones look up again, real life more interesting than Instagram for once, but this time Anita hasn't the strength to stare back. Her mouth is the first to go, loosening as she gasps, then she feels her chin grow weak as tears dampen in her eyes. She turns away out of shock rather than shame that anyone might see her crying. Surely not Charlie? Surely not here? She thinks about the amount of work that would take, everyone in the café in on the plan. There is no birthday party, just an excuse to have the place full, to put her on a stool in full view, her bum visible from wherever he stands.

Mark looks up from his cutting to share his smile. It drops when he sees her face. 'Jesus, Neets, I was only joking. You all right?'

Anita hears Charlie yell at his son in harsher Mandarin than normal and knows she has to leave. She has to get back to the car and lock herself inside before anyone can touch her.

Bronwyn, Mark's tiny mother, appears. 'Come here, Nita,' she says, guiding her towards the stool at the window. 'These stupid men and their stupid jokes. I think Mark isn't too big for me to spank like baby, what you think?'

Anita smiles and says, 'Of course, I mean, of course not, it's fine, sorry.' The light changes and she tells herself it's because she's seated in the huge window now, not because she was dreaming awake again. She is back, she is sane, she is normal. She wants to turn to the straight-haired girls in the queue and ask them what they think they're looking at? To shout over to Mark that he has done nothing wrong. Instead, she lets Bronwyn tell her she is having a bacon roll because that's what she likes. And an iced tea, no argument now.

It is several minutes before Anita is ready to turn and face the café. The girls in the queue are on their phones again, no doubt texting each

4

other about the crazy lady. Mark Lam is cutting another sandwich. When, at last, he looks up, Anita gives him a smile and watches relief light his face, his lovely teeth showing as he smiles in return. And just like that she understands what she has to do. She has to make a sacrifice to her sanity: she has to kill a man.

Later, on her way back through the heat of Macquarie Road, Anita passes a homeless woman, bent over, shouting into a bin. The woman must have been pale-skinned once, before her life got dirty. Now, worn and eaten away, she is rifling through the bin with one hand while flailing about with the other to keep her phantoms at bay. *There,* Anita tells herself, *that's what a mad woman looks like. Not like me at all.* She takes another look to reassure herself and, as she does so, the homeless woman glances up feverishly. The eyes beneath her matted hair are a startling blue, the only surviving part of the girl she once was. Near one blue eye – down a bit, out a bit – she wears a blue teardrop tattoo, the first Anita has ever seen on a woman. In the blistering sunlight it shines as clearly as the woman's eyes and this, Anita knows, this *is* a sign. A sign she must never go to prison. So now the question isn't just how she is going to kill Scott Patterson but how she is going to get away with it.

Saturday, 16th March

One day after

It was only natural Murdoch should bump into Natalie that day. For the first time in months, he actually had somewhere to be, so, of course, there she was: strangely nervous and keen to talk. It was the first real day of autumn, no matter what the calendar said. The previous day there had been a torrential storm and, once its clouds and rain had cleared, it had left behind a new season. Today, for the first time in the year, the breeze had an edge to it, the sun somehow blunted.

Excited by his appointment, Murdoch was taking the shortcut along the beach, hurrying towards the path that climbed through the dunes when, looking up, he saw Natalie. She was on the whale-watching

5

platform at the level of the road but, whatever she was watching, it wasn't whales. She was peering inland, squinting at something hidden from Murdoch's view by the height of the grass-swayed dunes.

In the solid sea breeze, her T-shirt was tight against her torso – her jeans tight enough without any help – and Murdoch remembered the first time he'd seen her. How much he'd fancied her back then, before he'd known she was a copper.

As he trudged through the soft sand, each footstep sucking grains, he tried to remember how long it had been since he'd looked at a woman that way. The answer, when it came, stopped him in his tracks. Stood him staring at his compact shadow as he counted back over the months before admitting, reluctantly, they added up to over a year. He thought about grief and how it sped up time – fifteen months uncounted till now – and, at the same time, slowed things down so a single day had sometimes been too long to bear. Except, he wondered, when was the last time he'd had a day like that? Maybe he really was getting over Amanda, the way everyone had promised he would.

Murdoch had grown used to losing himself in such vague thoughts, so Natalie was only metres away when he heard her.

'It *is* you!'

She must have spotted him from up on the platform. Must have run down between the dunes to where she now stood, panting on the sand and blocking his way as she clipped a chunky two-way radio to the belt of her jeans. Murdoch said hello, nodded at the radio and asked Natalie if she was on duty.

'Me?' She double-checked she had switched off the device. 'Oh, well, you know. Always on duty, one way or another. Where are you off to, then?'

Her smile was less than sincere, a cheerful expression made for someone else's mouth. Murdoch had once told Natalie she looked better when scowling; best of all, when scowling at something he'd done. It was the kind of thing he'd said in those days to wind her up. But then he'd lost Amanda and the old enmity between him and Natalie had softened: a fight run out of fuel. Natalie might be a copper who was always on duty, but, at some point, she had obviously decided that Murdoch was

6

no longer a crook. Or maybe both of them had realised that Montauban was so small – six hundred houses pinned to the coast, half of them empty in winter – that they'd have to get along. Whatever it was, enough nods and smiles across the street, then enough crossing paths at Davie's house, had brought them back to something close to friendship.

Squinting against the bright and gritty air, Murdoch told Natalie she worked too hard. She snorted in agreement – he didn't know the half of it, she was doing two jobs at the same time – then took a step forward, looped her arm through his and turned him away from the path, leading him down to the lapping water. The gesture was such a surprise that Murdoch didn't know how to resist. A few years earlier, when he'd first arrived in Montauban, he and Natalie had had a one-night stand. He wasn't sure they had even touched since then. Now he could smell her: a tiny hint of female sweat adding spice to her deodorant and the soft scent of her hair.

'How have you been, Bill?'

'I'm all right, love.'

'What you up to?'

'Bit busy, actually. I can't hang about, I've—'

'I hear you're learning how to swim?'

That was the last thing he wanted to talk about right there next to the sea. Kildare Public Pool mightn't have much going for it, but at least there was always an edge in sight. Keen to change the subject, Murdoch reached for a flat object floating close to their feet, struggling to keep his trainers dry as he lifted it from the water. It was a wooden bat, one of a pair for hitting a ball back and forth: litter from the overstretched summer.

'Is this, you know, bio-thingy?'

'Do you mean "biodegradable"?' Natalie shrugged. 'Eventually, it would be, I guess.'

Murdoch threw the bat as far as he could. Not that far, as it turned out, not once the breeze had caught the thin wood and angled it back in towards the shore. Natalie laughed and Murdoch managed a defeated smile. The bat looked lonelier than ever, betrayed in its attempt to reach a safe haven.

'So,' Natalie asked again. 'Where are you off to in such a hurry?'

'Just a meeting.'

'Sounds interesting. What's it about?'

'Nothing much.'

'Oh, go on, tell me.'

'Actually, Nat, no. I'm not gonna tell you nothing about it at all.'

Murdoch realised he was rubbing his shorn ginger hair. He pulled his hand down and then stood awkwardly, not knowing how to hold himself. Natalie had planted her hands on her hips and was scowling at him. He'd been right: it was her best look. It took the weakness from her smile, gave a dark glint to the green of her eyes.

'Really?'

'Er ... no. Sorry, love.'

'OK, fine.' She tried a small laugh that didn't work. 'Well, lovely chatting; fuck you too and I'll see you later then.'

'No!' Murdoch reached for her, forgetting he had anyone else to see, embarrassed to find his hand around her wrist. 'I mean, you should be pleased, love. You asked me once, ages ago, never to lie to you no more and, well, I'm not, am I? I'm off to a meeting what I don't want to tell you about; so instead of lying, I'm just gonna not tell you about it. What's wrong with that?'

He'd meant it as a peace offering, something to honour the fact they weren't enemies any more, but somehow it came out as defiance. What was it about Natalie that meant he always wanted to bring her down a peg or two? He took a deep breath, deciding to try again, but before he could, a wave frothed in and chased them up the beach, Natalie's renewed laughter difficult to resist. When Murdoch, soaked to the ankles, sat on the bright sand to peel off his socks and trainers, Natalie detached the radio from her belt and dropped down beside him, leaning back to look at the sky, her top half out of sight.

'Hardly appropriate shoes for an important meeting, Bill.'

'Nat, I'm not telling you where I'm going.'

'Uh huh. So how are you really?'

'I'm fine, love.'

'"Fine" as in Fucked-up, Insecure, Neurotic and Emotionally unstable? Or "fine" as in fine?'

'I'm fine. Why? Do I look sick or something?'

He'd thought this might make her sit up and examine him – lying back as she was, it was difficult to ignore the gap between her T-shirt and the top of her jeans: Natalie's stomach was a soft xylophone, the skin smoothly tanned – but she responded from the sand behind him.

'Since when did looks have anything to do with it? Everyone always looks all right from the outside. That's why we're all jealous of each other – we can't see what's going on under the skin. Look at you with your big house and your fancy car, anyone would think you've got it made. But then I heard you got into a bit of a blue down the surf club the other night.'

Murdoch sighed and shook his head, no sound to compete with the waves, but the brushing of his hands on his feet. Then he said, 'You know, sometimes I reckon you'd hear from half of Montauban if I turned over too often in bed one night.'

'Depends who you were turning over with.'

He twisted around to look at her, but Natalie's eyes were closed against the sun, impossible to know if she'd meant anything by it. Her hair was fluttering in the breeze, a strand teasing her lips until she pulled it away.

'And two speeding tickets in the last four weeks,' she went on. 'I'm a bit worried about you, Bill. It's not like you to … well, you know. Nothing from the old days has come up, has it?'

'Like what?'

'I don't know. The Club?'

Murdoch grimaced and turned back to the sea. The bat had landed on the sand again. It reminded him of pictures of refugees, face down on the beaches of Europe.

'Nothing like that,' he said.

'So why the bad behaviour? What's going on?'

'Jesus Christ, I don't bloody well know, do I?!'

'No need to bite my head off. I just want to make sure you're all right.'

'And why wouldn't I be all right?' He didn't want her to answer that. 'What is this? A formal warning from DC Natalie Conquest or are you the community liaison officer too now?'

'Oh!' She sat up at last, sand scattering the back of his shirt. 'I didn't tell you, Bill! It came through! Signed, sealed and delivered. Not acting, not temporary – the full box and dice.' She was leaning forwards, eyes open now, that intense green gaze checking he had understood. 'My *promotion*, Bill. Detective Sergeant! You know it's two bloody years since I passed the assessment? Not only that, they've put me on the Scott Patterson case. You know, the—'

'Oh shit!'

Murdoch checked his watch, swore again and stood quickly – his turn to spray her with sand. Natalie shielded her eyes too late and sat blinking at the ground between her knees.

'Bloody hell, Bill.'

'Oh shit, sorry. Sorry, Nat, but I've got to … well, you know, I've got to go to that meeting what I'm not telling you about. I'll see you soon and …'

Natalie didn't look up. 'Congratulations?'

'You what? I got to go.'

'Congratulations on your promotion, Natalie?'

She mumbled it, still blinking down at the sand, and by the time the words had sunk in, Murdoch was halfway to the path through the dunes, running with a sock-stuffed trainer in each hand. He slowed for a second, thinking he should turn back, then decided he'd congratulate Natalie next time he saw her. Running on, he was on the path itself when he heard her voice again, shouting, this time, in a tone he recognised.

'Say hello to Davie from me. And to his fancy new client.'

But the breeze did strange things to words on the beach and he decided he must have misheard.

Davie was waiting in line for the beach shower, tapping his hands against his thighs. The temptation not to bother rinsing off, to rush over the road to the office instead, was proving difficult to resist. The angel on his one shoulder might be reminding him that his wetsuit was brand new – that he had promised himself to make this one last by rinsing it properly after every surf – but the devil on his other shoulder kept telling him how sweet it would be, just for once, for Bill to be the one who was late. Hadn't Davie seen Bill down on the beach just now chatting with Natalie at the water's edge? And, besides, didn't Davie need some time to prepare his thoughts before Bill arrived? Even the angel admitted that was true.

Davie decided to wait for one more minute. The guy ahead of him in the shower, Orange, they called him, had his eyes closed under the dribbling water. As soon as he opened them, he'd see Davie was waiting and let him take his place, no worries. After all, it wasn't like Bill had seen Davie come in from the break – he was certain of that – or noticed him jog with his fishtail up to the north end of the beach where the sand climbed to meet the road. And there was no way Bill could have seen him race back along the pavement behind the surf club, past the whale-watching platform to the shower here, where the road was hidden behind the dunes. All Davie needed now was for Orange to hurry up and he'd definitely get to the office first.

'Bleeding hell, you muppet! What you doing there? We had an appointment.'

Davie turned slowly. A few metres down the sandy path that ran to the beach, Bill Murdoch was glowering up at him, out of breath with his trainers in his hands. It was three years since the Englishman had arrived in Montie, but Davie thought you could still tell from a country mile he wasn't from the Coast. Not because of Bill's home-made skinhead or the slightly malnourished look of him, or even the way he walked like a warning. There were, after all, plenty of Coasties who'd survived a hard life. But what marked Bill as different was his refusal to relax now that he *had* survived. To slope to the beach and enjoy the water; to appreciate a beautiful day; to close his eyes in the sunshine. Bill didn't seem to know the meaning of 'No worries' and Davie had once heard him complain that 'She'll be right, mate' was generally a lie.

'Dude.' Davie tested the mood between them. 'What's up?'

'What's up, mate, is you and me have got a meeting about ten minutes ago and a client arriving in half an hour. You was the one what wanted to talk about her first.'

11

'*Potential* client who I deffo want to talk about first. But I only stayed out so long because I could see you were on the beach talking to Nat and, anyway, seeing as I got here first, I'm actually not as late as you are. Oh, watch your back.'

Some of the other boys had come in too – the tide was turning, the swell too full – and were backed up behind Bill on the narrow path. Davie watched the Englishman make as little space as possible and barely respond to their greetings as they squeezed past. How he managed to stay so popular was a mystery: it wasn't as if he liked anyone back.

Noticing Orange had wandered off to the cars parked at the kerb, Davie took his place under the beach shower. Turning under the spray with open eyes – the drops around him sparking the sunlight – he rinsed his face, his wetsuit and his board, relishing the last minutes of being in water. Turning again, he saw Bill had come all the way up the path now, glowering still from just outside the circle of spray.

'Davie.'

'Dude, just one minute more.'

'What'd you say this woman's name was?'

Davie glanced at the guys who'd followed Murdoch up from the beach, but they were out of earshot, chatting with Orange as they admired his new car. At least, Davie assumed it was Orange's new car, he hadn't really—'

'Davie!'

'Oh sorry. What? Yeah, her name's Fran Patterson. Didn't you get the newspapers like I told you to? But it's probably not going to work out. Like I said on the phone, there's a complication.' He frowned towards the surfers at the cars. 'I'll tell you about it upstairs. We should still have time before she arrives.'

'I wouldn't be too sure about that, sunshine.'

Bill gestured towards a fancy blue car parked on the far side of the road, nose to the shops. It was a huge soft-top, roof down to reveal the cream upholstery inside. Davie looked back at Bill.

'What?'

'Davie.'

'What?'

'Davie!'

'What?!'

'The number plate?'

Davie looked back at the car, saw the personalised plate – FRAN 1 – and gasped so hard that shower water hit the back of his throat. When his torso wracked forward to help him cough it out, he banged his head against the rail of his board and had to close his eyes against the pain. By the time he'd opened them again, Bill was already halfway across the road. Still coughing, Davie ran after him, wrestling the key to the office from the tiny pocket on the leg of his wetsuit and trying not to drop his best fishtail which was dragging its leash truculently, as if it hadn't wanted to leave the ocean in the first place.

The Montauban shops huddled under the shade of dilapidated and mismatched awnings, their only common feature, their prime location opposite the beach. There were six businesses now: a pungent chip shop, a dusty bakery, a general store, the estate agents where Davie had worked for years, a filthy café and – the biggest news in town since Murdoch had arrived – a brand new pharmacy. Sitting above most of the shops were short-term rentals: apartments popular with Sydney surfers keen to escape the overcrowded city breaks. But above the bakery sat the offices of Davie Simms Detection Services.

The offices – office singular, unless you counted the toilet – were accessed by an ancient glass door that hung between the bakery and the chip shop, then by a steep and unlit staircase. They ran the full depth of the building, the toilet window overlooking an alley behind the shops, the window at the front overlooking the beach and the ocean. It was a narrow space made narrower still in its dingy back half by the stairs that ran up from the street. Between the bathroom and the roomier front half of the office, a low half-wall was the only thing to stop you falling into the stairwell.

Murdoch had been told that the place had once been a tiny brothel. Then a therapy room, then a beach studio (whatever the hell that was), then a squat, then a storage room. He had never liked it; he reckoned the two rooms still reeked of all their histories and had tried to stop Davie taking them on. What did Davie Simms need an office for, anyway, when he didn't have any customers?

'Clients.' Davie had been adamant. 'I'm going to have lots of clients.'

The muppet had come to his senses somewhere between signing the lease and kitting the place out, the result being the furniture got cheaper the further you progressed inside. At the top of the stairs sat a pair of six-thousand-dollar armchairs: overstuffed bouncers waiting to hold back all those clients. Most of the furniture crowded into the front half of the office – the desk chair, the half-empty bookcase, the glass-topped table and four kitchen chairs – were from Ikea. Davie's desk, under the front window, was a kitchen table he'd found on the street. He'd never got around to repainting the room and there were patches of bare plaster around the power points, the wood of the Ikea shelves still raw. Every time Murdoch walked in, he remembered something he'd once read about new trousers being useless if you couldn't be bothered shining your shoes.

Today, arriving at the top of the stairs – Davie panicking and babbling ahead of him – Murdoch did what he always did: he ignored the over-priced armchairs and doubled back to the front half of the office to sit at the glass-topped table. Davie, meanwhile, rushed into the bathroom with his surfboard before re-emerging minutes later in a crumpled white shirt and jeans. Thirty-four going on fourteen, he never looked comfortable in grown-up clothes.

'What's she doing in Montie so early, Bill? She said ten thirty!'

'Dunno. Maybe she wanted to grab a bag of chips first?'

'I'm sure she said ten thirty.'

Murdoch rolled his eyes. 'You know what, Davie? Whenever anyone says "I'm sure", they normally mean the opposite. You ever noticed that?'

'Aw, man. I wanted to talk to you before she got here. There's a complication, that's why I wanted you to come early.'

Murdoch sighed. There was always a complication; at least, in Davie's head there was. He told the muppet to calm down, to make them a cuppa and tell Uncle Bill all about it. But before Davie had even reached the glass-topped table, they heard the rattle of the street door and quick footsteps on the stairs.

Then, there she was. Pristine in a yellow polo shirt and a white pleated skirt, her tiny gold necklace resisting the gloom. Fran Patterson. Murdoch knew her name all right, he'd been winding Davie up. With nothing better to do, he'd spent the previous day reading all about Fran's husband, Scott, then studying images of the woman herself, swinging golf clubs and holding trophies below her perfect smile. Fran Patterson might not be a famous golfer, but she was good enough, good-looking enough and blonde enough to have her picture on tournament websites. She had golden skin, a pretty nose and a small but full-lipped mouth. In the flesh, she had more lines than in the photos and Murdoch wondered if that was because she was so stressed or if the pictures had been touched up. Neither would have surprised him.

Fran Patterson gave them each a tight smile and walked down the office towards them. She moved like a fighter, Murdoch thought, no superfluous movement anywhere. Not as she gave them each a firm handshake, not as she took the chair offered at the glass-topped table. Not even when she laid her phone and keys gently on the table's surface. No fixing of her thick blonde hair, no looking around the room. No to tea, no to a glass of water, no to Davie's attempts at small talk. Only her honey-coloured eyes struggled to settle until, after a while, she let them focus on the middle distance, staring through the wall behind Murdoch like she was watching a golf ball fly. Up close, he saw, the lines were everywhere and he realised he'd misjudged her age. Scott Patterson's trophy wife wasn't much younger than the missing man himself. Forties, he thought. Fifty?

'Right then,' he said. 'Let's talk about why you're here, shall we, Fran? We've read what it said in the papers, but we need to hear your version.'

Davie was still standing, tapping his hands against his thighs like a little boy wanting a wee-wee but too shy to ask. Murdoch ignored him.

'Just tell it from the top,' he said. 'Like we don't know nothing.'

Fran Patterson looked relieved and did what she was told. As she spoke, her body remained perfectly still: straight-spined with her legs crossed, hands quiet in her pleated lap. She didn't rub her eyes, scratch her nose or look away from the wall, not even when Davie pushed between it and Murdoch to grab a pad and a pen from his messy desk before joining them at the table.

'Yesterday, my husband, Scott, fell asleep at the wheel of his car. He veered off the road and down a steep embankment to a school playing field. He was knocked unconscious, which is probably a good thing, given he broke three ribs and suffered lacerations to his face and neck. I was playing a friendly in the Southern Highlands and didn't pick up the calls from the police until over an hour later. I drove straight home to get some things for him and then to the hospital. When I got there, the place was in chaos. Police, doctors, nurses, everyone running around in a panic. My nephew, Alan – he works with Scott at PPC – was there and he told me what had happened. Scott had disappeared; there were signs of a struggle. The last person who'd spoken to Scott was Dr ...'

She looked down at her hands, her thick hair falling forwards in a veil, as naturally blonde as all the other blonde hair in Australia. Murdoch waited a few seconds, then looked at Davie, who shrugged and said, 'Mrs Patterson? Fran?'

'... Sherezade!' She was back with them, eyes triumphant. 'I knew I'd remember. Dr Sherezade, who said that Scott had been incoherent but had shown no obvious signs of wanting to leave. Well, if you've read the papers, you know the rest. Scott is still missing. The police phone me hourly, I don't know why. They have nothing to tell me.'

There was something unreal about her, like one of those characters in a sci-fi movie who turns out to have been a robot all along. Murdoch imagined Fran Patterson happier receiving police updates via a cable plugged into the back of her neck. He asked how long she and her husband had lived in the area and watched her respond at the same steady pace as she'd adopted from the start. A woman reciting her witness statement.

'We moved to Crosley four years ago. Scott had been through a messy divorce and we wanted to live somewhere neither of us had any history. PPC had a plant here already; it was easy enough to relocate the head office.'

'PPC? Sorry, darling, what's the business?'

She turned her head to Murdoch now, the eyes on him for a startling second, then away to the wall again. 'I didn't say, did I? Maybe I should just check what you've read in the papers?'

'Or we could talk about our terms,' said Davie.

'Nah.' Murdoch tapped the glass tabletop. 'It's better if we hear it in your own words, love. Pretend neither of us has never read a paper.'

'Cardboard,' Fran said without another hesitation. 'Customised cardboard packaging. PPC is the second biggest independent operator in the country. Scott started it up when he was still a teenager. He left school at sixteen but he's very intelligent. Street-smart, you might say. He's good at business.'

'My dad's met him a few times,' said Davie. 'I think they have friends in common.'

Like that alone was a character reference. What a clever and successful man Patterson must be to associate with the great John Simms. Fran was waiting for the next question, but when Davie opened his mouth, presumably to ask one, nothing came out.

Murdoch did the honours instead. 'So you're hiring us to find your old man? You given up on the police already? That was quick.'

Fran's eyebrows creased at the question, a tiny tremor revving beside her lovely mouth. She gave a tiny shake of her head, then reached up and rubbed the back of her neck. It was the first time either hand had left her lap and even Davie seemed to notice the gesture, sitting back in his chair with a curious look on his face. Behind Murdoch, the etched window above the desk rattled as it protected them all from the breeze off the sea. A minute later, it did it again.

'It's not that I've given up on the police,' Fran said slowly. 'It's just that ...'

Her cheeks pinked and her perfect nose crinkled, her eyes forced from the wall to the table. Maybe she caught her reflection there. She certainly seemed to notice her hand rubbing her neck. She bit her lip and returned the hand to its rightful place, took a deep breath and frowned like she'd missed a putt.

'Of course, I've not given up on the police. It's been less than twenty-four hours. But as soon as this happened, I knew I had to involve a ... a

17

private service. It's early, I know, but I've got a tournament in Queensland early next week and I thought I should kick this off before I go. If you're willing to take the case.'

'Yes,' said Davie. 'If we're willing to take the case.'

Murdoch leaned forward. 'You're gonna play golf in Queensland? Ain't you worried that's gonna look a bit funny?'

Fran looked at them each in turn before choosing to answer the wall. 'Why should I worry about what it looks like? I won't be helping just by being here. I've told the police everything I know and now I'm hoping to hire you, so I don't see why anyone should care where I am. I'll be back at the end of next week.'

Davie fidgeted in his seat and Murdoch reminded Fran that she hadn't explained why she wanted a private detective. She gave a tiny nod and narrowed her eyes. When she spoke again, he could tell she'd made a decision.

'It's because there are things I can tell a private detective that I can't tell the police. I'm not sure, but I think these things might help you find Scott. You see, while I make a point of not knowing the details of my husband's business affairs, I do know he has some ... less than entirely legal dealings. As a result, I believe he has some unpleasant connections. If I told the police these things, they might focus their investigations on Scott's business dealings instead of finding him. And if they did that, well, even if they did find Scott, then they might put him in prison. So I'd be no better off, would I?'

She looked at them both again in turn, this time with a tight-lipped smile. Like they were stupid little boys for not having worked it out for themselves. It was a forced expression, as borrowed as the stillness and the calm recounting of events and Murdoch found he wanted to reach across the glass table and shake the woman into a more honest reaction. Behind him, the etched window above the desk did the job instead. When it rattled again, the sea breeze stronger than before, the noise clearly startled Fran Patterson. She glanced towards it sharply, then looked back at Murdoch and Davie, then down to the glass table again. This time she seemed to look through it, staring at Murdoch's bare feet.

'Our contract includes clauses on client confidentiality,' he said.

'Yes,' said Davie. 'About our contract—'

'Is that why you're worried we might not take the case?

Davie pulled his hands down his face. 'We've had our fair share of those, don't you worry.'

Murdoch rolled his eyes. The closest Davie had ever come to an unpleasant connection was when he ran into his old boss from the estate agents. Fran didn't seem to be listening. She had picked up her phone and was scrolling through the screen.

'Scott gave me this information years ago,' she said. 'He told me to keep it in a safe place. That it was important in case anything ever happened to him. And now ... I mean, now, of course, something has ... happened ...'

Wait for it, thought Murdoch. *Here come the tears.* But Fran Patterson had merely found what she was looking for.

She read from the screen. '4720231035509071379.'

She looked up, first at Murdoch, then at Davie, as if expecting a response.

'What's that?' said Murdoch.

'I don't know.'

'Let's see?'

He held out a hand, but Fran Patterson pulled the phone close to the protection of her bosom.

'I can't show you. It was part of a very personal email. Very *romantic*.'

She pronounced the last word like a correction, like it explained things any better. Davie asked her to repeat the numbers so he could write them down, then read them back to her slowly.

'Now,' he said, when that was done, 'about the contract—'

But Fran stood so suddenly that Murdoch flinched. Then, as he and Davie watched, she walked around the glass-topped table and over to the desk beside Murdoch, leaning on it with both hands as she looked out at the view that explained the office's rent. A thin strip of moving green, a thinner one of yellow, then nothing but rolling blue. Davie stood too, like a gent in a black-and-white movie, and asked if she was sure she didn't want tea.

'I'll have one,' said Murdoch. 'Milk, three sugars, thanks.'

19

Murdoch didn't see Davie's reaction to that – although he heard him flick on the kettle – because he was concentrating on the woman a metre to his left. Her face was immobile, the fingers of one hand on the vibrating glass like she was helping it resist the forces of nature. She wasn't wearing a wedding ring.

'This is an unusual situation for me,' she said to the view, breath fogging the window for a second.

'Don't get offered tea too often?'

She turned as suddenly as she had stood and smiled at him, two sets of pearly whites visible for less than a second. Murdoch would have been less surprised if she'd leaned over and slapped him. He watched her walk back to her seat and sit, legs crossed like before, hands in her lap again, the robot back on program. Davie was at the Ikea bookcase behind her, fiddling with cups, while the kettle scratched and scraped itself to a boil.

'No tea,' she said.

The lack of talk which followed was too raw even for Murdoch. This was normally where Davie asked all his stupid questions, but today the muppet seemed to be sulking. Maybe he was upset he hadn't got the smile. The kettle clicked and calmed and Murdoch asked Fran Patterson why the situation was unusual for her. She took a while to compose her answer.

'As I said, I make a point of keeping out of my husband's business affairs. I know some of them may be less than legal, but I know nothing else. We make a point of separating his business life from our personal life. That includes anything to do with … *money*.' She whispered the word like it was the description of a bodily function. 'Scott puts a certain amount in my account on the fifteenth of each month and with that I run the house and live my life. It's generous and I never have to ask for more. We don't discuss finances. I don't really discuss that kind of thing with anybody. It's vulgar. But yesterday's payment didn't arrive. I don't have visibility of Scott's bank accounts and I don't know how to access them. So this conversation presents an unusual situation for me.'

'You can't pay,' said Murdoch. 'You want us to work for a success fee.'

'Bingo.' Davie was talking to the kettle. Nobody else was listening.

'Not quite.' Fran Patterson gave a little victory smile. 'I have a little left over from last month and I'm sure I can persuade my nephew, Alan, to let me have something from the company books. But I can't pay your full rate – not until Scott is back and I can get my cash flow sorted. I am proposing to pay you thirty per cent of your normal rate until then, with the remainder in a lump sum.'

'The thing is—' said Davie.

'And how long can you keep that up for? The thirty per cent?'

Fran Patterson clearly hadn't expected the question. She closed her eyes and Murdoch could see she was calculating the answer. She was like a dummy in a shop window: perfect without being hot. Behind her, Davie had turned, red-faced and frowning. Murdoch gave him a wink.

'Get back to us,' he said. 'You tell us how long you can keep us on at thirty per cent and we'll tell you if we're willing to take the case. Lump sum to be paid whether we find your old man or not, dead or alive. Bonus, if we do find him. There's no point going into this if you can only pay us for a month or so.'

Fran Patterson was human after all. She opened her eyes and stared at Murdoch, her skin patching pink and white. This time she raised both hands to her neck and Murdoch saw why she'd held them so still in her lap. Why, under her fingers, the glass had vibrated in the window.

'A month or so?!' she gasped. 'Scott can't be gone a month or so! We have to find him in three weeks max. He needs his injection. He has to have it or …' But the alternative was clearly too much for her to put into words. She bit her lips and looked at the wall, the window, the table again.

'His injection?' Davie sat beside her again. 'Your husband needs injections?'

Fran Patterson nodded and seemed to make a new decision. 'Scott is HIV positive; nobody knows but me and his doctor. But he hates injections and he can't take pills; he detests them. It's a horrible process for him, trying to get them down. He only manages because he knows if he doesn't, sooner or later, he'll develop AIDS. He's tried everything and the viral rebound is always so strong. But there's a new trial, he just needs one injection every eight weeks and …' She spotted her phone on the table and grabbed it, tapping and swiping hard at the screen until she found what she was looking for. 'Yes, see. The twenty-third of March. Scott's next injection is due on the twenty-third of March – that's only a week away. He can probably manage two weeks after that, but then his CD4 will start declining …'

She went on, staring at her phone and using terms Murdoch barely understood – T-cells, hepatic complications, virological control – talking faster and less clearly, before suddenly interrupting herself and looking up at them. 'You have to find him in the next three weeks, do you understand? He has to have his injection or he—'

'One injection every eight weeks?' said Davie. 'For HIV? I've never heard of that. Are you sure?'

Fran Patterson gave him a stony look. 'Of course, I'm sure. As I said, it's a trial – it's not available to the public yet. It's supposed to be only happening in the States, but Scott heard about it and used his connections to get a supply of the ARVs. He's not supposed to; it's illegal, apparently, but he has a doctor friend here who measures his viral load. It's been working well. He hates getting the shot; won't let anyone else do it for him, won't even let me watch him doing it. I've no idea where he even keeps the injection kit.'

'Did you tell the police?'

'No, I didn't see the point. Scott would hate if it got into the papers. I was going to tell the doctors, but before I got to the hospital, he'd …' She took a deep breath and sat straight again, like that might hide her emotions, but the words continued to tumble from her. 'I've never been away from him for a single night before. Not once since we met. It's why I have to go to Queensland, do you see? I have to get away, distract myself somehow until I know he's safe. I miss him … so … much.'

Davie leaned forward, elbows on the table, a hand towards Fran in case she wanted to take it. She didn't, but still Davie soothed and calmed her, promising, of course they'd help, of course they'd find Scott, everything would be fine. Murdoch watched jealously. He could never work out what to say when someone was unhappy. How to make them feel better when there was rarely good reason to be anything but sad or lonely or scared.

Two days before

At the bang of the blind against the office door, Anita gives a little yelp: the kind of noise a small dog might make. Ever since her near-meltdown at lunchtime, she's been struggling to keep things together. Today is worse than most days and those are bad enough.

As the office door opens, she stands quickly – the main thing is to be on your feet – scratching her left hand badly on the corner of the credenza. She takes two steps into the middle of the room, arms pulled tight across her chest; then she sees it is only Alan Drummond and gives a nervous laugh that lasts a second too long. Alan smiles back awkwardly and Anita can see him trying to work out if he's done something wrong. He's an unattractive man with reddish brown hair, dirty glasses and sad pale skin. His small head does little for him, accentuating the strange shape of his body, tiny at the ends and bulging in the middle, and his clothes are no help either. His suits and shirts are always crumpled or the wrong size or a combination of the two. Anita has never understood why, given Alan's ambitions, he doesn't make more of an effort.

'Sorry, Anita,' he says nervously. 'Did I frighten you? That bloody blind would drive me mad, I don't know how Scott … Oh, you've hurt yourself.'

Anita looks down at the scratch on her hand. It throbs red like a living thing, a sharp animal burrowing into her. Suddenly she understands why people deliberately harm themselves, the relief of something else to focus on. Remembering her fingernail in her palm at lunchtime, she wonders if maybe she did that on purpose? She looks back at Alan and sees he's expecting an answer.

'Sorry. What were you saying?'

'I said, do you want anything for it? There's a first aid kit out in the opening between the offices, isn't there?'

She has a vision of Alan pressing the Band-Aid against the flesh of her hand, of Scott walking in and catching him at it. The vision morphs until she is in a half-lit room, covered in scratches, naked but for the red lines on her brown skin. A crowd of men approaches her with leery smiles, each of them holding a tiny sticking plaster, backing her into a corner. They are countless, getting closer, blocking out what little light there is.

'Anita? Are you sure you're all right?'

The light brightens and she is back again. 'What? No. It's nothing, it'll be fine. I'll be fine. Is there anything you wanted?'

She watches Alan smile again and shrug his soft shoulders. He looks around the office, gives Anita a mischievous grin and walks behind his uncle's desk.

'Oh no, Alan, you shouldn't.'

But it is no use; he is already lowering himself into Scott's chair. The sound of its creaking leather makes Anita want to vomit.

'One day,' Alan says. 'Not long now. I'll fix the blind on that bloody door but I'll keep this chair. I suppose I'd better keep those too.'

He nods at the opposite wall, at the countless framed articles about Patterson Precision Cardboards opening plants in Fremantle, Hervey Bay, Crosley. PPC sponsoring small football teams, supporting local schools, providing boxes for aid. In most of the frames, beside the fading newsprint, Scott Patterson smiles awkwardly, shaking hands or cutting ribbons, his eyes lost in the creases of his face.

'Oh, Alan, really.' Anita forces a little laugh, as if she can play this game too. 'You shouldn't be in here. And, oh, please don't!'

He has picked up Scott's letter opener, a shining blade on an onyx handle, and is twiddling it between the fingers of one hand while he shifts the huge flat pad on the desk to read the numbers scribbled there.

'Who's "Terry H"?'

Anita hurries over, takes the letter opener from Alan and returns it to the correct position. Then she readjusts the desk pad and, on second thoughts, readjusts it again.

'Come on,' she says, annoyed now. 'Out. If you want to talk, we can talk in the opening.'

'Oh, come on, Scott's not going to mind. Besides, he's in Newcastle, isn't he? And *you* were in here.'

'I was filing.'

24

She remembers the papers she has left on the floor beside the knee-high cabinet and walks back to them. But there she stops and forces herself to turn, to think of something else. Behind Alan, through the window that runs the full width of the office, she sees the distant highway, traffic dotting and dashing the horizon like a code she cannot read.

Alan turns the leather chair to follow her gaze. 'God,' he says. 'Isn't it miserable here?'

'I thought you liked it. Isn't that why you want to be the boss?'

'No, I mean the industrial estate. What a miserable bloody place.'

Alan sighs, pulls himself to his feet and steps to the window until his forehead is on the glass, like a child at an aquarium. Anita makes a mental note to clean the window later, then watches one of Alan's shoes kick a black mark onto the skirting board above the carpet; so now she'll have to clean that too.

'Listen, Anita, I don't suppose Scott's given any clues about when he's really going to retire, has he?'

'I'll tell you if you get out of his office. Come on, Alan, let me lock up and we'll have a nice cup of tea.'

He starts to protest, but, catching the look on her face, gives in and lets her usher him into the opening. Locking the door behind them, the blind banging again, Anita turns to find Alan still waiting for an answer.

'Clues?'

'No, Alan, nothing. Frankly, sometimes I wonder if Scott's ever going to retire. He'll be here—'

She stops, unable to put such a hideous future into words. The emotions she has been battling all day rise again stronger than ever and, just as in the café at lunchtime, she turns away, leaning into Scott's office door as if checking she's locked it properly. It is vital she protect Alan from the full force of her tears.

But, try as she might, this time Anita cannot stop herself from crying. Sobs force their way up through her, tapping her head against the doorframe, the wood sharp against her temple. Alan's voice sounds far away even as she feels him put his hand on her shoulder before, at her flinch, withdrawing it again quickly. She has not broken down like this at work before and she knows it is wrong. Knows she needs to stop the tears, no matter the emotions overwhelming her. Awful guttural noises are coming from her throat and she tries to swallow them, to swallow the pain and quieten herself. She puts her hands to her face, but the crying fights back in spluttering coughs until her palms are as wet and flowing as her face.

How strange, she thinks with sudden and startling clarity, that tears are the only thing to come out of the body that isn't considered disgusting. If she vomited, or lost control of her bladder or bowels, or even just broke a sweat, Alan Drummond wouldn't come near. But tears – a woman's tears – are irresistible, it seems. She can see him standing stupidly next to her, his hands worrying the air, no idea what to do. He is apologising and, for a split second, she thinks, *he knows*. But then she watches him step backwards, 'Sorry, sorry,' as he fishes in his pocket for his phone.

'It's the boss,' he says with a grimace, holding up the screen so she can see Scott's silly grin and his puppy-dog eyes.

Her sobbing stops and, immediately, she is divorced from it. Someone else was making that awful noise; it is someone else's mascara all over her hands. Anita checks the door to the stairs is closed – nobody can have heard – then crosses to her desk to find her handbag. Alan takes Scott's call into the sales room, on the far side of the opening from Scott's office, but Anita can hear him clearly enough.

'But that's in *half an hour*. No, no! Of course, I do. Yes, Scott, loud and clear. Yes, I'll get going straight away. Yes. Goodbye.'

Anita finds her compact mirror and checks her eyes. Puffy, blotchy, honest for once. She remembers Pam, the office cleaner, telling her just that morning, how lucky she is, with her own house and a car and a daughter who likes her. Pam should see her now. Everyone should see her now. Alan comes to the door of the sales office.

'Sorry. Listen, are you OK?'

Anita hesitates. Never to trust again, is that what she wants? She nods, wrinkling her nose above an embarrassed smile. 'Time of the month. It's a hormonal thing. Pops up when you're least expecting it. Doesn't Fiona ever get like that?'

She watches Alan think about it, wanting to be convinced, easier than dealing with a crazy lady.

'Erm, maybe. Listen, are you sure you're all right? It's just that Scott's changed his mind about the Hewlett meeting, so now I've got to do it.'

Anita nods again. 'I'm fine. You go. Probably best for me to have a bit of space, anyway.' Oh God, how good she's got at this. Someone could murder her and her last words would be: 'Oh, don't worry about me, I'll be all right.' They could write it on her tombstone – if they ever found her body.

She locks herself in the bathroom, washes and dries her face and is doing her make-up when she hears the door to the stairs bang. As she is packing everything into her handbag, it bangs again. Anita pulls open the bathroom door to ask Alan what he's forgotten this time and finds herself face to face with Scott Patterson.

Saturday, 16th March

One day after

Murdoch was parked with the roof down in the shade of the scrub near the lagoon. Above the car, a thick wattle was wrestling against the lantana, its upper branches so bowed by the vines that they swept the Merc's silver bonnet, scratching the paintwork softly whenever a breeze came through. Murdoch knew he should probably move the car – he'd spent enough bleeding money on it that he ought to treat it right – but his viewpoint was too good to lose.

On this part of Montagne Road – three curves and a hundred metres closer to the shops than Murdoch's own place – all the houses were built on the hill to overlook the thin scrub that separated the street from the lagoon. Davie's shack was no exception. It was a tiny place at the top of a steep grass driveway, partly on the hillside, mostly on stilts. Despite living there for over a decade, Davie had only bought it from his ex-wife the year before. Since then, he'd spent another small fortune renovating the place. Murdoch wasn't sure why he'd bothered. Fair enough, sitting on the shack's balcony to admire the lagoon – and, further away, the ocean – was less frightening than it had been and you could now close most of shack's doors without kicking them. But the place was still a wind instrument.

Murdoch checked his watch. It was a quarter to one, fifteen minutes after he and Davie had agreed to meet, an hour after they'd say goodbye to Fran Patterson. The case, the *potential* case, had reversed their roles. On previous occasions, it had been Davie desperate they should play detective: 'we this' and 'we that', until Murdoch had snapped back that the muppet was on his own. But after their meeting that morning, Davie had been non-committal, rushing home to change for lunch and leaving Murdoch wondering whether he had anything to look forward to. Other than lunch itself, of course – his first social occasion in over twelve months.

In the first few weeks after he'd lost Amanda, Murdoch had done a good job of keeping himself busy, of doing what you were supposed to do and getting out and about. It hadn't lasted. Not once he'd admitted he had no interest in 'moving on'. He had stopped playing tennis, stopped talking to anyone, pretty much stopped leaving the house. He was big enough and ugly enough to know how time healed and had decided Amanda shouldn't become just another bad thing that had happened to him. Spurning the self-discipline that had guided his life until then, Murdoch had turned himself into a hermit, wearing his wounds proudly and forgetting there was any other part of him. It was only in recent weeks that he had woken up and discovered the wounds had scarred into loneliness and – worse than that, somehow – a boredom so hollow it resonated like a drum.

At the sound of footsteps, Murdoch looked up from the newspaper spread across his steering wheel and watched as Davie – one hand in his hair, the other patting the pockets of his trousers – rushed into the dappled green view. He stood where the patchy grass of his steep driveway met the patchier asphalt of the road, his chest heaving, then slowly calming, as he squinted into the trees, no doubt looking for the source of the birdsong above him. Murdoch shook his head but allowed himself a little smile. He took his time finishing the article he'd been reading and, only then, folded the newspaper, started the car and let it roll slowly forwards. Ducking as the wattle and lantana came over the windscreen, he sat up again just in time to see Davie disappearing back up towards his shack.

It was several minutes later – the Merc's humming drowning out the birdsong – before the muppet reappeared. This time he was holding a bunch of flowers that had been treated badly and then, at some point, wrapped even worse. Davie mumbled a vague hello, threw the flowers the into the back of the Merc and himself into the passenger seat.

Murdoch let out an exaggerated sigh. 'D'you reckon, Davie, just once, you could not keep me waiting? Like, just as a favour?'

'What? You were late this morning. We're quits.'

'Once! I'm late once and, even then, I got into the office at the same time as you did.'

'Half a second later, actually.'

'The point is, Davie, it does not make us quits. You keep me waiting every bleeding time we meet. I have just proved, proper scientific, it's impossible to make it work the other way round.'

But with Davie, there was no point complaining. He was barely listening even now, struggling with the seatbelt like he'd not used one before, while examining a spot on his best shirt. Murdoch shook his head again – no smile this time – and drove them through the curves alongside the lagoon, then along the road between the beach and the shops.

'Good to have a pharmacy in town at last.' Davie craned his neck to inspect the new business as they passed. 'By the way, sorry I couldn't hang around to talk before. Seeing as how you've obviously decided we're taking the case. Let me guess; you've got the hots for Fran Patterson?'

Murdoch let the comment slide. It was his own fault no one consoled him any more. When Amanda had first disappeared from his life, he had shrugged off condolences like comments on the weather. Only his friend Suzie Bourne knew the depth of his feelings, but she had gone overseas, joining friends on the world's longest cruise.

'Fran Patterson?' he said, eyes fixed on the road. 'Nah, not my type. All the ingredients, but the wrong recipe, know what I mean? More up your street, I reckon.'

'How do you figure that?'

'Blonde.'

'What makes you think I like blondes?'

'Er … Hannah?'

It was a bad lie. Davie's ex-wife was blonde all right, but only if you'd call Hitler a brunette. Murdoch's assumption had actually been based on photographs he'd found years before in Davie's bedroom. They showed another blonde, all limbs and boobs, in a bikini. One arm around Davie on a yacht somewhere; she was the kind of girl you remembered and Murdoch had always been curious about who she was. Now, though, Davie didn't reply and any chance to move the conversation in that direction flew away in the air rushing over the windscreen. Davie didn't start up about anything else either and, once they had climbed the hill out of Montauban and turned onto the Crown Road, Murdoch stole a look at him.

'Come on, then, Goldilocks. What's wrong?'

'Who says anything's wrong?'

'Davie, we've been driving for more than two minutes and you ain't chewed my ear off about what you've been up to, who's shagging who in Montie or what the waves are like. So, tell me, what's wrong? Is it to do with why you don't want to take the case?'

'Sort of.'

Murdoch slowed the car, then pulled up beside a broken fence.

'What's wrong?'

'Nothing, it's fine.'

'What's wrong, Davie?'

'Nothing. It's just I was hoping for a better rate. PPC went public last year and the share price has been on the up and up since then. The Pattersons must be loaded. When Fran first contacted me, I got excited, thought I could up my prices for the case. I thought you could help me do it – you know you're better at negotiating than I am. I thought we could refuse to even talk to her until we'd agreed the new going rate.'

'Mate, you should of told me.'

'I tried! That's why you were supposed to turn up early, so we could discuss it. But then you took one look at her and all you wanted to do was hear the details and look interested. I've never seen you so excited about a case.'

'Me? Rubbish. You was the one making all the sympathetic noises. I was just trying to help you out. And for your information, I don't fancy Fran Patterson one bit. It'd be like shagging one of them life-size sex dolls instead of ...' For no reason he could explain, an image of Natalie came to mind. Murdoch blinked it away. 'Listen, mate, I'm sorry. We don't have to take the case at all if you don't want to.'

'Well, we do now, don't we? A man's life is at stake. You heard her – if we don't find Scott Patterson within three weeks he going to start getting sick. We have to find him.'

'Right, so we *are* taking the case, then?' Annoyed at how relieved he felt, Murdoch's tone was harsher than he'd intended. 'Listen, Davie, if the Pattersons've got loads of money, what you worried about? Even if you do it at thirty per cent at first, you'll get it all in the end. You can sort out the contract so it says so. And while you're about it, whack a big success fee on top. It's worked before.'

That was an understatement. The previous year, a case they had solved had netted Davie close to a million dollars. Now Davie shrugged and checked his watch while a crow croaked low overhead, bored by its journey.

'We should get going.'

'What else?' said Murdoch.

'Nothing.'

'Out with it.'

Davie sighed and looked away. 'I'm broke.'

'You're always broke.'

'No, Bill, properly broke. I thought this case was going to get me out of a hole and now all I'll get is a third of the normal rate, at least for the foreseeable. Not exactly the cash flow I was looking for.'

'So tap into your savings, pay yourself back later.'

Davie took a deep breath: a teenager confessing a crime. 'Yeah, they're kind of all gone.'

'You what?!'

'Well, the lawyers I had to hire to get that success fee paid last year weren't free. Buying the house took up almost all of the rest, and then I did all that work on it. *Then* I had to pay a year in advance on the office and, well … you know.'

Murdoch didn't know. The cash he'd taken from his previous life wasn't running out any time soon.

'You got a drug problem or something, Davie? Drinking?'

Davie sighed again. 'I can see the appeal, but no. It's just life, you know. Running a business. Advertising and stuff.'

Murdoch thought of the six-thousand-dollar armchairs and said nothing.

Davie was pulling his hands down his face: the only man in the world who could look younger by doing that.

'If the agency goes under, I don't know what I'll do. You know, this is the first time in fourteen years anyone's taken me seriously? I'm running a business, my own business, starting off small like Dad did. I'm remembering what it's like to feel successful and, if this fails too … I just want to make a real go of it.'

'I thought you just wanted to surf and read books all day? You said that's what you was born to do.'

'Well, maybe I was, but maybe I'm going to do something better than what I was born to do. You know, Dad's never forgiven me for not being an accountant or climbing my way up when I was selling houses. I want to show him this is a proper job, a proper business. I want to see his face when he has to admit I've made something of myself.'

Murdoch started the car again and let Davie talk himself out: kilometres of growing the business and franchising nationwide before he came back to the reality of working for a third of his advertised rate. Nothing about this being his first real case in a year.

'Ask for a month in advance,' Murdoch told him as they waited for the lights to let them join the Central Coast Highway. 'Tell Fran Patterson you'll take the case, thirty per cent till she can pay the rest, but you want a month in advance. And do that success fee thing – and make sure it says "dead or alive". You never know, we might even find her old man. Oh Jesus, now what?'

32

Davie was looking at him with narrow eyes.

'Why are you so keen, Bill? What's going on? If you don't fancy Fran Patterson, what's in it for you?'

'Me? Nothing's going on, mate. I'm just looking out for you, aren't I? I reckon this case is a goer and they'll come through with the money. Just stopping you shooting yourself in the foot, that's all.'

They turned off the highway again, the weekend traffic left behind, and wound their way between large houses with meticulously planted gardens. Daisies, schizanthus, calendula: Murdoch had had time to learn all the plants' names. He knew the work it took to keep them tidy too, the constant fight against nature. Not that there was any point – he'd realised that – but gardening was one of those things he'd started up again to prove to himself he was self-disciplined now. That and making sure he shaved every day even if there was no reason to leave the house.

Beside him, Davie was wrestling a slip of paper from a trouser pocket. '472023103509071379,' he read aloud. 'What do you think it means?'

'Beats me. Ain't you got some boffin mate what you can show it to?'

Davie didn't answer, just stared away at the fields that had suddenly replaced the houses and gardens.

'Jesus, now what's wrong?'

'Nothing. Listen, Bill, don't you think it's weird that Fran Patterson's off to Queensland to play golf when her husband's missing?'

'Maybe, maybe not. You heard what she said about not wanting to be home alone. Makes completely bloody sense to me. Besides, didn't she say her nephew, Alan Whatsisname, could tell us more about the business than she could? You should call him up.'

'Yeah, I will.'

'Go on then. Do it now.'

'Now? It's Saturday.'

'Great time to make an arrangement for Sunday morning then, innit?'

Murdoch slowed the car and stared until Davie sighed and started searching his pockets for his phone. Fran Patterson had told them the police thought she had no way of contacting anyone at PPC before Monday. Given how stretched they were for resources, they would struggle to visit the offices before then anyway so, as long as the place was completely locked up, they were willing to wait. Which meant Sunday was Murdoch and Davie's chance to go in and look around for themselves. Accelerating again, Murdoch listened to Davie make the call, cooing sympathetic noises at something Fran Patterson's nephew said. Alan Drummond, that was his name,

'Happy?' said Davie, once he'd hung up on a two-minute exchange that could have taken ten seconds.

'S'pose.'

'And this time you really are going to help me with the case? No disappearing act, Bill? No paranoia you've been found by those blokes you used to work for – what were they called? The Club?'

Murdoch winced. He didn't like anyone mentioning those bastards and now here it was happening again: the second time in one day. The Club thought he was dead and buried and he had a vague superstition that the less he thought of them – the less anyone even mentioned them – the longer things would stay that way.

'Worked *with*,' he said, taking the turning for Bangada Heights faster than it was designed for.

'Crikey, Bill, take it easy.'

'What's wrong?'

'What's wrong? You swung into the opposite lane just then. No wonder you got that speeding ticket the other day.'

The road straightened again, a row of birch along each side like an exercise in perspective. Murdoch hit the accelerator.

'And how would you know about that, then?' He raised his voice over the engine and the rush of air around them. 'Natalie been sharing confidential police information, has she?'

'No, I heard it from Mrs Dunnevirk. She was waiting for the bus when the motorcycle cop pulled you over. Said you were talking to him for ages, wouldn't let him go. Come on, Bill, slow down, really.'

Murdoch gave in and forced himself to drive slower – maybe it wasn't the best way to make life seem more interesting – but even when he was ten below the speed limit, Davie continued to fidget.

'Bleeding hell, what's with you today?!'

'Nothing.' Davie looked away. 'I'm fine, really.'

Murdoch had been to the countryside twice in England, both trips when he was thirteen. Someone had had the bright idea of letting borstal boys experience life on a farm: maybe to teach them the joys of physical labour, maybe to explain where meat came from: it was never clear. The boys from Cookham Wood managed two visits before someone set fire to a pig. There were no more trips after that, but the rolling green landscape had left an impression on Murdoch. He remembered deep winding lanes through hedgerows, chimneyed cottages behind drystone walls, cows and sheep staring back at the wire-meshed windows of the bus. The Australian countryside was different; at least, round here it was. 'Bush' they called it, even when there weren't any bushes in sight. The fields, when they were green, were dry and pale and there were no hedges, just tarmac growing thinner at the edge of the roads until it gave up and let the weeds win again.

The address was Bangada Hill by Bangada Heights, no street name offering further help. Murdoch parked at a quiet junction, horse fences stretching in each direction, while Davie muttered over the map on his phone. Then he said left and left again and, after only one U-turn, they were on the right road, then on the right winding driveway, climbing beside a windbreak of silent poplars. To their left, the land fell steeply away. Then the poplars fell away too and the sky was around them, empty of birds or clouds or anything but the hill they were climbing.

'You didn't tell me you grew up in the country,' said Murdoch. 'I wouldn't of guessed.'

Davie looked around like he hadn't noticed the landscape before. 'I didn't. Mum and Dad only bought this place a few years ago. It's supposed to be a hobby farm but it's going really well. Dad's kind of good at everything.'

'Right. And how come we're here today? I didn't think it was your birthday till Tuesday?'

'Today's the only day Dad's free. He travels a lot for work and, when he is in the country, he stays late in Sydney a lot, entertaining old men in suits.'

'What does he do again?'

Before Davie could answer, Murdoch was whistling at the house that had appeared before them. It was solidly modern, square and red-brick with aluminium windows and a blue Colorbond roof. The tarmac around it had taken the top off the hill.

'Bleeding hell, it's massive.'

'Do us a favour, Bill, park over there. Dad loves fancy cars.'

Murdoch pulled up at the concrete edging furthest from the house. Below them, grazed and mown grass rolled in all directions. At its far edges, scruffy cotoneaster and banksia pressed in against new fences like crowds protesting their land rights. Davie got out of the car and let the door slam behind him. Murdoch raced to undo his seatbelt.

'Here, Davie, wait up. You've got to introduce me. I've not met your folks before.'

Davie turned and walked backwards towards the house with the same pained expression he'd been wearing for the last few miles.

'Oh, don't worry,' he said. 'You'll love them.'

Davie's mother was waiting for them on the curve of brick steps that ran up to the house's mock-Georgian front door. She was trim and lively in a white shirt and fitted black trousers, one of that generation of women who outlive their men because they run around looking after them. Under heavy-framed glasses, there was a sharpness to her face, no surplus weight to soften her.

'Oh,' she said, looking past Davie and giving Murdoch a sweet smile. 'David, you've brought someone.'

'Yes, Mum, I said I was bringing a friend.'

'Oh yes. Yes, you did.'

Davie, two steps below his mother but towering over her, bent dutifully so she could reach up and give him a kiss before pulling him in for a hug.

'I thought you meant a girl,' she whispered. 'You did say you'd try.'

Murdoch turned to the stubby xanthorrhoea planted in concrete pots either side of the steps. Took his time admiring them and looked up only when Davie introduced him, like it was possible he hadn't heard Mrs Simms's comment.

'Pleased to meet you, Mrs Simms.'

'Oh, please call me Penny.'

Penny's hand, once she'd understood what Murdoch's was outstretched for, gave no resistance at all, like it was just another part of her cloud of perfume. She smiled at him again and Murdoch saw Davie had her eyes. Immediately, he found himself wondering – he always did in these situations, he couldn't help himself – what his own mother might have looked like. What perfume she might have worn. He blinked the idea away and followed Davie and Penny into the house.

Inside, everything shone. Pink marble floor tiles stretched between eggshell walls; colour photographs glistened behind glass; ceramic figures stood on well-polished shelves. Even the leather sofas in the lounge room were slightly reflective, like the whole point of the place was to see yourself in it. Murdoch had always liked the phrase 'lounge room'. He liked the way the Aussies called it that because it was where you had your 'lounge', which is what they called a sofa. Everything nice and foreign, different from the shitholes he'd grown up in.

Keen to be polite, Murdoch was determined not to sit down until he was offered a seat. When neither Davie nor his mother offered him one, he wandered over to the huge bay window that curved out behind the world's biggest television set. Stepping over a spaghetti of wires, he looked out at the mown lawns, the wild treetops and, in the middle distance, a shape of flat water. After a while, a black Renault hatchback rolled into sight on the tarmac below the window, parking in a skid next to his car. The woman who climbed out further improved the view. Tall with fair hair in a ponytail, she filled her tight chinos well, the right parts of her tailored shirt too. Murdoch barely glimpsed her face as she disappeared towards the front door, but there was something interesting about the way she walked. Only good-looking women moved like that.

'I'm fine, Mum,' Davie was saying.

'You look like you're not eating enough.'

'Really, I'm fine.'

'But …'

'Nice view,' said Murdoch to the window. 'Anyone else coming?'

'Nicer view from the study! That your car out there?'

Murdoch turned. A tall, pink-faced man with the same smile as Davie was striding towards him, hand held out. Bald on top, grey hair cut short above his ears, he was wearing the same heavy-framed glasses as Davie's mother and a similar outfit of white shirt and black trousers. For a split second, Murdoch wondered if the couple were catering staff and he'd misunderstood who owned the house. Then the man reached him and started shaking his hand, ignoring the wires on the floor between them.

'Welcome to chez Simms,' he said. 'I'm John. David's father, or at least that's what the documents say, ha ha ha. That your car out there?'

'Well, that's what the documents say.'

'Ha ha ha, very good, very good. You've got to give it to the Germans, they know how to build an engine.'

'This is a friend of David's.' Penny Simms had an uncertain hand to her hair, Davie clearly having inherited more than her eyes. 'They came together.'

John Simms clapped Murdoch on the shoulder. 'Well, at least the boy's got friends with nice cars even if he can't afford one himself. Can I offer you a drink?'

Murdoch accepted a beer and, a few minutes later, John Simms's offer of a tour around the grounds. Leaving Davie to fend off his mother's concerns, he followed the man outside, first to look at Murdoch's car, then at the double garage, the terrace overlooking the swimming pool and the view towards some land Simms was hoping to buy. There was no sign of the Renault driver, only the Renault itself.

'Very nice,' said Murdoch, desperate to say the right thing. 'Very *impressive*.'

John Simms seemed satisfied with that and started leading the way back to the front door. But halfway there, beside an empty plastic fountain, he turned so suddenly Murdoch nearly bumped into him.

'Penny said David was bringing a girl,' he said. 'Thought he'd managed to get himself a girlfriend at last.'

'Sorry to disappoint.'

John Simms gave him a matey wink, leaned in and looked away: a man discussing men's business. 'Just wondered if you, well, whether you and David are ... a couple or something?'

Murdoch laughed. 'No mate, we're just friends. I'm not gay; not sure about him though.'

Simms seems disappointed.

'No, you're right,' he said, returning to full height. 'He probably couldn't even manage that.'

Back in the lounge room, Murdoch sat on the lounge opposite Davie and his mother while John Simms lowered himself into a beige leather recliner, tidying away the remote controls perched on its arms. There was a long silence, like this was what they'd all come for, until Davie's father turned his big smile towards Murdoch.

'So, what's your line, then, Bill? How do you make your dollar?'

'Toxins.' Murdoch's favourite response to his least favourite question was both true and false at the same time. 'Dangerous substances, waste removal. Least, it was. I sold up a few years ago and I suppose you could say I've retired.'

'Well, good for you. Nothing wrong with that! If you can afford to stop working, why carry on? Of course, with some people it would be nice if they ever got started.'

'That's meant for me,' said Davie. 'Dad thinks I've never had a job in my life.'

'A *proper* job.' Penny Simms's tone was soothing. 'He means a *proper* job, David.'

'So you don't work at all, eh, Bill? A self-made man of leisure?'

'Well, I do some detecting with Davie sometimes.'

'We're partners, Dad.'

'*Business* partners,' said Murdoch. 'We work together.'

'Not exactly a steady income, though, is it?'

Davie sat up with a smile Murdoch didn't recognise. 'Actually, Dad, we've just taken on a new case. Scott Patterson's wife, Fran, has hired us to find him.'

Interesting. Murdoch made a note to ask Davie about client confidentiality. Was he going to tell his parents Patterson was HIV positive too?

'Oh, Scott Patterson!' Penny Simms was delighted. 'You'd never know to meet him he's a multi-millionaire. He's very down-to-earth, a lovely man. We were so shocked when we read the story in the papers. Whatever can have happened to him? Do you have any ideas?'

'Solid bloke,' said her husband before Davie could respond. 'I met him at a few charity dinners. Great sense of humour. A bit of a larrikin, if you know what I mean. Not very PC – not that that's a bad thing, if you ask me. We got along like a house on fire. Girls played golf together, didn't you, Penny?'

Penny Simms sniffed. Murdoch wondered if it was at being called a girl or at the memory of playing golf with Fran Patterson.

'Scott was so kind helping Jane with references,' she said. 'He offered to do the same for David, I seem to remember. He's wonderfully connected and so generous with his time.'

'Well, you'll both be pleased I'm going to find him then, won't you?' Davie seemed to be struggling with his smile. 'It'll probably make the papers. Imagine the press, the free marketing for my business.' John Simms made a noise in his throat, but Davie pressed on. 'Like you read about our last case in the papers. Do you remember, Dad?'

'David,' said his mother, worried by her rings. 'That was over a year ago.'

'Since when I've been working on the house and setting up the agency. I know I should have jumped on the publicity at the time, I can see that now. Or at least done some marketing. But ... well, I've been busy laying the foundations. Now when we get some publicity, I'll be ready to leverage it.'

'Jane!' John Simms's boom bounced off the shiny surfaces. 'Jane, darling! I saw the car outside. Where's my girl been? What have you been up to?'

She'd been getting changed. Replacing the chinos and work shirt with a flowery dress and high heels, hair released over her shoulders. She was the girl from the photos in Davie's bedroom. Murdoch watched John and Penny Simms jostle for position around the coffee table, Penny getting to their daughter first and pulling her down into the same hug she'd given Davie.

'How was the drive, Jane, darling? Do you want a drink? Come in and sit down, you must be exhausted.'

Murdoch noticed Davie close his eyes and sit back heavily, his face more relaxed than it had looked all morning. Jane Simms, after pulling herself free from her parents, bumped down onto the sofa next to her brother and punched him on the arm. Davie smiled weakly and rubbed the spot where she'd hit him.

'Thanks for coming, after all,' he said. 'I owe you.'

'Davie has a sister,' said Murdoch. 'Nice to meet you.'

Jane stood again and reached a slender arm across the coffee table to shake Murdoch's hand.

'Let me guess,' she said with break-heart smile. 'He's told you all about me?'

'Jane's a lawyer!' Penny placed a hand on her daughter's back. 'She's a partner at Afferchy Uzbian Klein.'

'Bless you,' said Murdoch.

Jane and John Simms laughed at this, but Penny stared at Murdoch blankly while Davie mumbled loudly enough for everyone to hear, 'That's a *proper* job.'

Lunch was a hearty salad. John – explained Penny – had to watch his weight, his cholesterol, his sugar levels and his fat intake.

'Which is why we all have to do the same,' said Jane, moved along the table by Davie so he could sit between her and Murdoch.

'You know, Mum,' Davie said, 'I've got a mate who says salad is what food eats.'

'Don't be rude, David. Now, as it's a special occasion, I thought we could open a bottle of wine.'

Murdoch didn't hear Davie's response to that, but he noticed Jane slap her brother's thigh. Then, at a cough from the head of the table, they all looked up. John Simms had taken his rightful place but now was standing again, showing them all the label of a wine bottle before slowly unscrewing its cap.

It was another half an hour before the fight began. Murdoch missed the start of it. He and Jane had been leaning back in their chairs talking about her life in Sydney. Davie, between them, was leaning forwards, fielding his parents' questions. Murdoch was normally good at having one conversation while listening to another, but today he struggled. *Davie's sister*, he was thinking. *No law against that.* Jane Simms was single, worked too hard and worried about her social life. Murdoch made her laugh twice in a row and was two questions away from discovering something they both liked to do, when Davie sat back suddenly, his knife and fork loud on the table.

'Again?! Why are you doing this all over again?'

'Because I'm your father.' John Simms laid down his own cutlery, calmly but firmly. 'And on a milestone like your birthday, I owe it to you to talk to you about your future. Set you on the right path, so you can achieve things in life. Like your sister and me.'

Murdoch, cut off from his view of Jane, looked at Penny Simms to see what she thought of being left out of this statement. She was staring hard at Davie and nodding. 'Listen to your father,' she said.

'I'm a grown man,' Davie sounded like he was on the edge of tears. 'I don't need constant instruction in what to do and what not to do. I do pay my own way, you know; it's not like I get anything from you.'

Davie's father shook his head. 'Why would we throw good money after bad? When I think of what we spent on your education! Do you know how many kids would give their right arm to get what you got?'

'Has everyone finished eating?' This from Jane, like they were discussing the weather and having a lovely time. 'Shall I clear?'

'I'll help.'

Murdoch stood before anyone could object, picked up Davie's barely touched plate, then his own, and followed Jane across the room towards a small swing door.

The country-style kitchen was surprisingly small after the echoing lounge room. Once Jane had put her plates into the world's cleanest sink, she had to move down a narrow walkway between green and yellow cupboards so Murdoch could take his turn. Behind her, pale light shone through a frosted-glass door, entwining her shadow with Murdoch's on the floor.

'For fuck's sake,' she said quietly. 'You'd think he'd have learned how to play them by now. I work sixty hours a week in a poisonous environment; I could do without this at the weekend.'

'I thought you liked your job?'

Jane snorted and turned to the cupboards, opening and slamming them until she found a glass. Moving down to the fridge, she yanked it open and peered inside.

'What gave you that idea? It's like pushing shit uphill against people who hate you. The whole place is full of arseholes managing morons; idiots who think it's clever to hold meetings on a Saturday. I don't know how I stand it.'

'But your dad said you was really …' Murdoch had been going to say 'successful', but realised it would probably sound rude. '… doing well.'

Jane snorted again. 'He means I earn a lot of money.'

She gave up on the fridge, the door thumping shut like a coffin, and squeezed past Murdoch back to the sink. As she did so, her left breast brushed his arm – a microsecond, but he knew it was the nipple – and the touch ran through him like a current, sparking in his groin and somewhere deep beneath his ribs.

In the other room, everything on the dining table jumped and Penny Simms, shriller than before, shouted, 'Don't talk like that to your father!' Then there were seconds of muffled voices: three people talking at once, until John Simms's tenor voice boomed again, asking why Davie's generation was so obsessed with being 'bloody happy all the time'.

'Fancy a smoke?' said Murdoch.

Jane Simms raised her eyebrows over the rim of her glass, wiped her mouth and came up with a smile.

'A smoke of what?'

'Just a cigarette.'

'Oh. No thanks.' She looked at him sadly. 'Listen, don't take this the wrong way, Bill, but you may as well go. Trust me, this is just Round One. They've got to get through "You never loved me" versus "You've never shown any respect" and Mum running off in tears. They'll be at it for hours and they're always worse when there's an audience.' Another sad look, but with a wink this time. 'That door behind you leads out to the pool. Follow it round to the right and you'll get to the steps by the front door. I'll take Davie home.'

Why don't you take me home instead?

In other lives he said it. In some she said yes, in some no; in others, they just fucked there and then, rattling the kitchen cupboards. This life wasn't that interesting.

Murdoch nodded, checked his pockets for his keys and wallet, then opened the frosted-glass back door near the fridge. The air from outside blew Jane's dress against her and reminded him of Natalie on the whale-watching platform. He allowed himself a long look at Jane's slim back and firm arse, at her calves hiked up by her heels. He could still say it. He just needed to open his mouth and ask her. Instead, he watched her take a deep breath and put a hand to her hair, the same gesture as her mother and brother, then disappear into the lounge room.

It was still light – just about – when he rolled down the hill into Montauban. Nearly six on a Saturday night and the tiny town felt empty. The first hint of autumn had obviously frightened everyone into wrapping themselves up at home. This, Murdoch told himself, was the best news he could have hoped for. The last thing he wanted was an audience.

On the long drive back from Davie's parents, the day crumbling at the edges, the experience of lunch – not to mention the experience of getting lost in the featureless countryside – had dragged him into dark thoughts. He'd been an idiot to get excited about a family meal; nothing was ever as good as you thought it was going to be; he couldn't even find his bleeding way home. The Patterson case – the only other thing he had to look forward to – would be a disappointment too. Scott Patterson would turn up or Fran would change her mind or …

Driving too fast along the country lanes, Murdoch had caught his mood and punched himself in the temple to set it right again. The true disaster of the day had been his own cowardice with Davie's sister. He just needed to grow a pair, remember who he was and start acting like a man again. He was tempted to turn the car around, to drive back and demand to speak to Jane in private. To get her number and sweep her off her feet. He'd even pulled off the road for a while, parking under an ancient gumtree in a mess of shadows and dried tracks, so he could think about how he'd do it. It hadn't taken him long to realise it would never work. Those scenes from the movies: you try them in real life and you always look like a twat. Feeling the self-hatred growing – stronger than it had been in months, as huge and as irresistible as the coming night – he had searched around for something, anything, to resist the abyss. When he had driven on towards Montauban again, he had taken off so fast that his back wheels spun.

Murdoch parked at the shops and, refusing to feel a thing, got out of the Merc, crossed the road and started down the path between the dunes. The only noise, once the dull hum of the new pharmacy's electric sign had faded behind him, was the tiniest swish-swash the ocean knew.

Avoiding a pile of left-behind toys, Murdoch approached the water slowly. He had no towel, but no towel was an excuse. No swimmers either: that was an excuse too. Without looking around to see what other excuses might be watching, he started undressing, balancing awkwardly as he took off his shoes and socks, knowing if he sat on the sand, it wouldn't let him up again. The sky was black at the edges now, the water petrol blue. He didn't think about what was in the blue: that was the last thing you thought about. It was like before a rumble with someone better than you. No point in focusing on what might get broken. Focus on what you have to do, on what you can get away with. On the fact you can swim now – six months of lessons in that bleeding pool – waist-deep will be enough.

Murdoch heard his own voice, pressing and persuading him, in the quiet evening; he blinked and shook his head, not sure if his tunnel vision was from the collapsing light or from something behind his eyes. He dropped his trousers and headed grimly towards the water in his boxers. Turning to make a note of where his clothes were, he saw Montie's streetlights coming on – plinkety-plink – above the rippling banksia at the top of the dunes. Then another light caught his eye.

Months earlier, Davie had had *Davie Simms Detection Services* etched in a curve of capitals into the office window which overlooked the beach. Now the etched letters stood out clearly, catching an inside light differently from the plain glass around them. As Murdoch watched, a few of the letters disappeared, like faults in an ancient neon sign. Then they reappeared as others flickered, gone and then there again, as someone moved around inside Davie's office, blocking them from the inside light.

Two days before

'Wow, it's hot out there.' Scott Patterson beams his famous smile. 'And, is it me, or is it even hotter in here? Any chance we can we crank up the air con?'

He is a small and solid man, keen with energy, a Staffordshire bull terrier in human form. He stands like a Staffie too: legs slightly bowed, biceps away from his body, like he is flexing for show. He has untidy eyebrows flecked with grey above brown button eyes, a mouth that smiles so often you assume it's your fault when it stops. Suddenly and unexpectedly alone with him, Anita realises she will never do anything to harm him. It's a stupid fantasy, her mind trying to convince her she's stronger than she really is. She mumbles that she wasn't expecting to see him today – not mentioning she'd have dressed completely differently if she had been – tells him the air conditioning is at its maximum setting and hurries behind her desk. There she pulls on a grey cardigan and watches as Scott tugs his keys from a trouser pocket and squints to find the right one. When he glances up and smiles at her, Anita looks hurriedly away.

'Listen, Anita, have any of the sales managers forced themselves in?'

'Well, Greg's on holiday, don't forget.'

'And Steph?'

'Melbourne.'

Scott finds the right key, then struggles with his office door, the glass rattling as he pushes against the frame. 'Right. Of course. Just you and me, then, eh?'

He looks up and gives her another smile, eyes bright between the creases of his face. Anita asks him hurriedly if he saw Alan on the way in, like that might somehow protect her.

'I did,' says Scott. 'Really, that bloke! He nags every day about what more he can do, then tries to wriggle out of the next meeting I give him.' Swearing under his breath, he opens the door to his office with a jerk, the venetian blind banging more loudly than normal. When Anita flinches, Scott grins at her. 'You're jumpy! Were you thinking something bad?'

Without waiting for an answer, he walks into his office letting the door bang again behind him. Anita grabs the receiver of her desk phone and wedges it solidly between her ear and her shoulder.

'Yes,' she says to the dial tone. 'Oh yes, absolutely.'

She hits her keyboard and a photograph of her six-year-old daughter fills her screen. Typing so quickly that her first two attempts fail, she enters her login ID and password, wondering why life has to be such a minefield, every moment threatening to explode.

'Oh, I couldn't agree more,' she says.

Pulling up Scott's diary, Anita's fingers quiver down the screen, choosing from that afternoon's appointments, checking her own watch frantically. The venetian blind bangs again and Scott appears in his office doorway.

'Anita …'

'Oh, well, I'll try, but he's very difficult to get hold of at short notice.'

She puts her hand over the mouthpiece and mouths 'Tax Office' at him. She watches him hesitate, on the point of catching her out again, before disappearing behind the banging door. Now she dials, as carefully as she can bear, mouthing the numbers as she reads them from the screen. Her call is answered on the third ring.

'Blister Plastics, John Danson's office; Melanie speaking.'

'Hello Melanie. This is Anita from PPC. Any chance …?'

'Oh hi, Anita, how are you? And how's the lovely Scott?'

'What? Listen, any chance John can come now instead of at four?'

'Are you all right, Anita? You sound in a bit of a state.'

'Please, it's an emergency. Help me out.'

Melanie's silence drags over lazy seconds. Anita has never met the woman, but she knows, just knows, Melanie hasn't a care in the world.

'Hello?'

'Anita, I'm so sorry, darl; he's finishing a meeting in Newcastle. Even if he left now, he wouldn't be there before four.'

Anita hangs up and dials another number. No luck at that one either, or, at least, no inclination to help. She is waiting for her third call to be answered when the venetian blind bangs again. Scott stands in his doorway, clearly frustrated she is still on the phone. He smiles – she can see the effort it costs him – and walks his little Staffie walk over to the bathroom. As the bathroom door swings shut behind him, Anita closes her eyes and prays for someone to answer the phone. She is sweating: the air-conditioning no match for the day outside, the weight of the atmosphere forcing itself through the walls. The ring tone is abruptly interrupted.

'Hullo?'

'Oh! Hello, is that Terry Hatch?'

'Who wants to know?'

'Terry, this is Anita Patel, Scott Patterson's PA at PPC. Is there any chance we can bring your meeting forward? I'm so sorry for the inconvenience, it's just that Scott's diary is a complete mess; it's all my fault.'

There is a hesitation at the other end of the line, then a dull echoing noise as if something heavy has been dropped.

'How soon d'you want me?'

'As soon as possible. How soon can you make it?'

She hears Terry Hatch sniff, then listens to him think about it, as if there is no rush at all.

'I'll leave now; shouldn't be long. No promises but.'

Anita thanks him, hangs up and stands. She listens carefully; then, grabbing a cleaning cloth from her bottom drawer and a file from her desk, runs into Scott's office. As the door swings shut behind her, the venetian blind bangs loudly. In here, the noise is followed by the rattling of the blind's blades, a worse sound somehow: a shimmering laugh at her foolishness. Rushing behind the desk with the file under her arm, she rubs hard at the window where Alan left the mark of his forehead. She is standing back to check the glass, ignoring the letter opener shining at her, when she hears Scott calling her name. Anita gasps, her mouth hanging open, and forces herself towards the office door. But the world has gone into slow motion. It's like trying to run in a nightmare – legs unwilling or unable to help, ideas and reality muddling. The bang of the venetian blind, its cruel laugh, brings her to her senses. Scott is blocking her way, smiling at her curiously.

'Oh, there you are. That's good, I wanted to you do something for me.'

Unable to speak, Anita pulls the file from under her arm and holds it out until Scott takes it. But still he doesn't move out of her way. Instead, he lets the door go again, smiling as it bangs closed behind them.

'OK,' he says, rubbing his hands as the venetian blind laughs. 'Let's get on with it then.'

Sunday, 17th March

Two days after

The green and gold light of morning angled through Davie's bedroom window and woke him too early. Knowing he needed more sleep, he covered his head with a pillow, but it was no use. The arguments that had interrupted his sleep all night were already starting up again. After arriving home from his parents' the previous evening, he'd stayed up late on the internet, reading until the early hours about business plans and growth strategies and social media marketing. Anything to drown out his father's dismissive sneering at anything he had ever tried to—

Davie threw back the covers, dragged on a rashie and a pair of boardies, grabbed the nearest surfboard and ran all the way to the beach. But, of course, there were no waves on offer, just the rare view that, for some reason, had given this ocean its name. Standing above the sand on the whale-watching platform and beginning to wake up properly, Davie realised it wasn't as early as he'd thought. Across the road, the shops were all open, a few tourists even dawdling in the Mon Tea Bon café waiting for their coffees to be made. Only tourists ever made that mistake. Davie shuffled across the road.

The general store was empty but for Anne Lincoln bent intently over a *Sunday Telegraph* spread across her counter. As Davie entered, she stood upright, jewellery clanking at her wrists and throat, a frown drawing lines in her fake tan. Bill had once said Anne looked like a barmaid in a soap opera and now Davie couldn't get the idea out of his head.

'You found him yet?' she said.

'Who?'

'Who? Who d'you think? Scott Patterson. That bloke you's supposed to be finding. For a large amount of money, I shouldn't guess.'

'How do you know about that?'

It was rooky error – one Davie wouldn't have made if he'd been fully awake. Even if Anne hadn't seen Fran Patterson's car herself, someone else would have done and would have mentioned it, leaving the shopkeeper to draw her conclusions. Or maybe Anne really was as telepathic as Bill always claimed. Either way, now she knew.

'Give me a chance,' said Davie, looking around for an excuse to change the subject. 'Got any bananas?'

'Last bunch, next to the lettuce. But you can't go down there, I've just done the floor.'

He could smell the bleach mixing with Anne's perfume, neither of them kind at that time of day. Spotting the cover of *Tracks*, he walked over to the magazine rack instead.

'You should talk to my cousin Karen's neighbour,' Anne went on. 'Wendy thingy. She used to work at PPC years ago.'

'Great.' Davie was already lost in the magazine. 'I'll do that.'

'Make sure you do. That's a lead, that is; you can thank me later. In the meantime, like I keep telling you, this is a shop not a library. You want to read that thing, you buy it.'

'Nothing in it.'

Davie heard Anne tut, but the article she had been reading in the *Telly* must have been about a particularly gruesome crime. Soon her jewellery clattered again as she bent over the counter and the two of them read in a silence unknown to any other visitor to the store. It didn't last.

'Hello there.'

A young man was standing in the shop doorway. He was short and Asian with a round, friendly face, clear skin and thick rough-cut hair. His pupils had the same solid darkness as those of a cartoon character.

'G'day, neighbour.' Anne was upright again, smoothing down the sides of her purple V-neck. 'Have you met Davie yet? Davie, this is Brian Yeow, he's just opened the chemist's next door.'

Davie walked over to shake Yeow's hand, introducing himself hurriedly.

'I'm Davie Simms—'

'Davie Wonder,' said Anne. 'You know, the popstar?'

'Oh yeah,' said Yeow. 'I heard you lived here. My mum was a huge fan of yours. Wait till I tell her I've met you.'

'Your mum?!' Davie checked the tone of his voice. 'Well, anyway, I don't do that any more.'

'Oh, my mum's really young.' Yeow was blushing. 'She still listens to, like, you know, dance music and stuff. She has the radio on all the time. She wants to see Adele next time she's out.' He turned to Anne seeking support. 'Can I get a coffee? I've locked the shop up for a bit – it's not like anyone's going to come in. I thought at least Sunday mornings would be busy around here.'

Clearly disappointed the show was over, Anne walked over to the coffee machine and shouted over her shoulder as she banged the filter clean. 'Give it time,' she said. Then, to Davie, in case he might have missed it, 'Brian's finding business a bit quiet.'

Davie told the pharmacist not to worry. Montie was like that; the locals just needed time. He was about to ask Yeow if he'd ever heard of a trial where HIV patients could be treated with one injection every eight weeks – he'd forgotten to research it on the internet – when Anne called out between spurts of steam.

'Ooh Brian, tell Davie what you told me about Jackson Harper!'

The pharmacist frowned. 'I didn't tell you anything about him.'

'Yeah, you did. I told you how Ruby at the bakery had seen him limping and you said it was easy for foot wounds to get infected.'

'But I didn't tell you anything about *him*.' Yeow was smiling but firm, a man making an important point.

'You said he'd been in for a script!'

'I don't think I said that.'

'Well, he obviously had. Antibiotics, I shouldn't wonder. What do you think had happened to him? You said it was a terrible infection.'

Like Davie, Yeow had yet to learn never to respond to Anne's assumptions. 'I didn't say—'

'Well, you said something like it. You definitely did.'

Bill would have enjoyed the scene: someone else under interrogation for once. But watching the young pharmacist try to work out how he'd got into this mess was like watching a tourist swimming against a rip, the worry growing quickly until it wasn't funny any more.

'Anne,' said Davie. 'It was Phoenix Harper who was limping, and he did it playing touch footie. Jackson Harper had an infected lip from a fight at the surf club a few weeks ago. Everyone was talking about it. That must be what you're thinking of.'

'Yes.' Yeow smiled in unexpected relief. 'Yes, that must be it. You must have been getting the two things mixed up.'

Anne walked back to the counter and banged Yeow's coffee down, a spit of froth spurting through the hole in the lid and dribbling slowly down the side of the cup.

'Three dollars fifty,' she said. 'Davie, isn't there somewhere you should be?'

'I was going to get a banana.'

'Floor's not dry.'

'What about a—'

'You should get going. You being such a busybody detective and all.'

'But it's Sunday. No one— Aw man, what time is it?'

Davie checked the clock on the wall behind Anne, said, 'Aw man' louder than the first time and, after grabbing his surfboard from outside the shop, ran all the way home again.

The road to Bungaree wasn't the ugliest drive in the world, especially on an autumn day. The air temperature at its kindest, sunlight pouring through the stringybarks and the European trees on the turn. But then the trees ran out and Davie found himself at Bungaree Light Industrial Estate. Stranded amongst acres of optimistically cleared land, the estate was six mismatched blocks along an unmarked road. The land around them had reverted to scrub, a jungle of sharp and uneven weeds no prettier than the buildings.

There was no sign of Bill's fancy Mercedes so, once Davie had parked his tatty pink Hyundai in the shadow of the PPC building, he climbed out and arranged himself to look as if he'd been waiting for ages. Arms crossed, leaning against the car's peeling paintwork, admiring the sky. In the warehouse beside him, a huge roller door hung open and, inside, men in blue overalls were bantering in echoes under artificial light. Davie checked his watch – he had to admit it was unusual for Bill to be late – and looked up to see a man in Stubbies and a PPC work shirt approaching from the warehouse. The man was middle-aged with yellowing hair, eyes faded behind his tan. He shouted his opener from a few metres away, like a warning Davie should start running.

'What you doing there?'

'Hi.' Davie stood cautiously. 'I'm waiting for Alan Drummond.'

'Oh yeah? Why's that, then?'

Close up the man was more than middle-aged, greying hair sprouting at the top of his overalls, but he was no less intimidating for that. His hands hung in fists that looked like they'd been used before.

'My name's Davie Simms. I have a nine o'clock appointment with Alan Drummond. Fran Patterson asked us to arrange it.'

The older man softened at the list of names – shoulders down, hands relaxed – but he continued to approach until Davie could smell his Lynx.

'Not a journalist, then?'

'Oh! God no. Not a journalist, don't worry. You can call Alan Drummond, if you want?' Davie fished out his phone like a peace offering. 'Or Fran?'

The man in the overalls sucked on the idea but decided against it. He told Davie his name was Tom Brandle; he was the foreman there, the boys were working overtime to get an important order out. Davie could see he was offering the information to make up for his earlier brusqueness. He smiled at Brandle and tried to look like he'd never been nervous.

'Well,' said the foreman. 'I'll leave you to it, then. I'm sure Alan won't be long'.

As he walked slowly back to the warehouse, Davie saw the other men had gathered beneath the roller door, a row of blue overalls keen to see what was going to happen. Davie checked his watch again – twenty past nine – nodded at the men staring at him and walked down the sloping tarmac to the brightness of the road. His shadow appeared in front of him and he followed it to the overgrown wasteland across the way. Rhus, thistles, boxthorn – it reminded him of clearing his dad's yard as a kid: nothing that didn't scratch or burn. Had that been 'a proper job'?

Davie rubbed his eyes and remembered how tired he was. Around him, the air was silent but for the resumption of echoes in the warehouse and, far away, the rise and fall of highway traffic, so distant you could pretend it was surf. He imagined himself on a tropical beach somewhere, or even at home in Montie. Anywhere but this horrible reminder of the world of 'proper jobs'. He checked his watch again – half past nine – and dialled Bill's number. *Very good, you made me wait, you can come around the corner now.* But Bill's phone rang out to voicemail and there was rarely any point in leaving one of those.

At twenty to ten, after three more dead calls to Bill, Davie was back leaning on his car when a silver Camry drove up fast and scraped to a stop beside him. Its pale driver called an apology before he was fully out of the door.

'Davie Simms?' he said breathlessly as they shook hands. 'I'm Alan Drummond. Sorry to keep you waiting. Hope you don't get the wrong impression.'

There weren't many people in the world Davie could stay angry with and, whilst today Bill Murdoch might be one of them, the man in front of him wasn't. Alan Drummond was too flustered and awkward, his embarrassment too obvious. Davie told him not to worry, told him he knew it was early for a Sunday morning, but Drummond started apologising again.

'It went straight out of my mind. My wife's Irish and we're having people over for St Patrick's Day. I forgot I was even meeting you until Tom called.' Drummond pulled an oversized bunch of keys from his pocket, hurrying through them as he spoke. 'I got here as quickly as I could. Listen, I hope you don't mind, but I'm going to let you in and I'll see you up there in a few minutes. This is the key to Scott's office. I've got to check with Tom on this bloody order and, well, here.'

He detached a key and handed it over with a worried smile, apologising again as he led Davie across the tarmac and past the gaping mouth of the warehouse. They arrived at a smoked-glass door, tiny in the tall brickwork, where *Pa terso Pr ision Card oard* was peeling in faded gold letters. Drummond unlocked the door with a key still attached to the bunch, promised not to be long and hurried back to the warehouse. As soon as he was out of sight, Davie trotted back to the Hyundai and rummaged amongst all the rubbish in his boot until he found his camera. The Canon was worth more than the car, the last purchase he'd made before tipping into the red and he was determined to use it at last.

Inside the smoked-glass door, a blue metal staircase climbed to a blue metal door, turned and climbed out of sight. Halfway up, tugging at the metal door, Davie found himself on more blue metal, inside the echoes of the warehouse. Surprisingly far below, Tom Brandle was remonstrating with Alan Drummond, their voices indistinguishable from the surrounding noise. Davie left them to it and returned to the stairwell. At the top, behind another smoked-glass door, he found a dull anteroom: a stale space between two offices, one at the front of the building, the other at the back. Between their doors, facing him (and facing the door beside him, which it turned out, led to a bathroom), was a strangely tidy desk. There were no pens or paperwork on view, nothing but a monitor and a wireless keyboard. To the right of the desk, stood a green metal cupboard; to its left, a small fridge in an alcove with a tidy tray of mugs and a kettle on its top. Otherwise, the space between the two offices was empty. Nothing on the walls but this year's PPC calendar: a logistics site for every month, nothing marked on the pages.

Davie photographed the space from every angle, then the bathroom that led off it, then the unlocked room at the back of the building. The other room, locked, was obviously Scott Patterson's office, but that could wait. It was called delayed gratification. Davie had started snapping the view out of the back-office window – a few cars parked on a strip of tarmac, the same overgrown scrub as over the road – before he admitted the truth. He was waiting for Bill to arrive before examining the most important room. Waiting for help. He took a few more photos – ten minutes max and he'd do it alone – and was staring down at the parked cars again when he heard a faint voice calling, 'Hello?'

Davie walked into the opening between the offices, the camera bumping heavily against his stomach, and listened hard. Nothing. Just vague bumps from downstairs, a tiny ticking from the metal roof. Then the voice came again.

'Hello?'

'Hello?' said Davie. 'Alan?'

He pulled open the door to the stairwell and went down two steps to look over the blue metal railing, but there was no one there.

The voice called again. 'Hello?!'

It was a man's voice, still faint, but definitely coming from the offices at the top of the stairs. Davie ran back up and pushed into the anteroom again, fishing in his pocket for the key Drummond had given him.

'Is anyone there?' said the voice.

This time Davie was sure. It was coming from inside Patterson's office. Davie fumbled the key, leaning awkwardly to get low enough, then squatting so he was at eye level with the lock. Taking a deep breath, he tried again, but the key's profile was nothing like the one required.

'Hang on,' he said. 'Can you open—'

'Are you coming or what?'

The voice was louder now, angry. Davie rattled at the handle, the venetian on the other side clattering back, but the door hadn't unlocked itself.

'Is that you, Mr Patterson?' He sounded ridiculous, a panicked child at school. 'Scott, is that you?'

A door slammed below him. Davie turned, crossed the room in two strides and tore open the door to the stairwell. Over the railing, Alan Drummond was halfway to the landing. Davie shouted down.

'Someone's locked in Scott Patterson's office! You gave me the wrong key.'

Drummond frowned, then ran awkwardly up the remaining steps, a man not used to moving fast. He took back the key from Davie and was trying the lock himself when the voice inside the office called out again.

'Oh, don't bother. It's too late.'

Drummond looked up at Davie. 'What the hell? That's Scott!'

He pulled the huge set of keys from his pocket and went through them again, reciting their functions under his breath.

'Shit, sorry,' he said at last, putting the key to the lock. 'This one.'

It turned on the first go, the venetian blind banging loudly as he pushed the door open. Davie took a deep breath and followed Drummond into the office, unable to suppress the thought that maybe even thirty per cent of his normal rate had been too much to hope for. He could just picture the look on his father's face when he heard Scott Patterson wasn't missing after all.

Wednesday, 13th March

Two days before

As she sits opposite Scott, Anita remembers the files on the carpet by the credenza. The memory shrinks her stomach and, for a dizzying moment, she thinks she might be sick. Whatever else happens, she mustn't turn around. For then Scott will look too and, if he does that, she'll be lost. She pulls her cardigan closed at the neck, the rough wool against her throat increasing her nausea.

'Did Greg get back about the pamphlets?' Scott asks.

He has a knack for picking the one thing she has forgotten to do. It's like playing chess against a better opponent: a constant barrage of attacks.

'He said he was going to do it before he went on leave.'

'Yes, you told me that yesterday, do you remember? You were going to check with the marketing team that he actually did it.'

'I haven't heard back from them yet.'

Scott gives a resigned smile and Anita's stomach shrinks again. He'll be looking for something else now. The thought occurs to her, not for the first time, that maybe she is already insane. That maybe her overwhelming hatred of Scott is, itself, her madness. She watches him lean forward to read the scribbles on his huge desk pad until he remembers the email he wants her to write. He tells her who it is for and who should see it and who should absolutely not see it. Then he starts to dictate, precise on some words, whole paragraphs vaguely described. He makes her read it back to him, then starts on a second email, standing to look out of the window, then slowly pacing back and forth.

Anita wants to scream. *Write your own bloody emails, lots of dyslexics manage perfectly well.* But she doesn't do it, of course. She'll never do anything, just sit and fantasise uselessly. She tries to make sense of her notes while Scott crosses in front of the window: seven steps to the right-hand wall, a spin on his heels; seven steps to the end of the credenza. Here he only has to turn his head to see the files she has left on the floor but he is watching his little black shoes, deep in thought, that inane perma-smile creasing his face as he tells her what to write. Anita struggles to concentrate. Beyond Scott, the highway is visible in the distance, a hundred lives a minute preferable to her own.

'Anita?'

The snap back to the room is jarring. Scott has stopped to the left of his desk, eyebrows raised in question.

'Sorry,' she says. 'I was just thinking about how to write that bit. What did you say?'

He looks away, struggling to maintain the smile. 'When is Greg back?'

'Er … is it the twenty-ninth? I know it's a Monday. Do you want me to check?'

Scott sighs heavily, no clue as to whether he wants her to check or not, then turns to face her again. 'Really, Anita, I …'

She knows before she understands. Scott's face has frozen, his mouth strangely sullen.

'What are those doing there? Has someone been in here?'

He's as fussy about security as he is about the filing. Nobody but Anita is allowed in his office, not unless he is present. There was a time, when Anita first took this job, that Scott's paranoia about this fascinated her. Waiting until he was on a business trip overseas, she went through the room carefully, telling herself she was looking for something in case she ought to know about it. In reality, she had just been curious and, frustratingly, found nothing much of interest. An injection kit – syringe and needle in a red nylon pouch – in one desk drawer, a hammer and chisel in another. Deep under the credenza, years old and caked in dust, she had found a topless calendar.

Anita remembers this now in a flash, the way they say you remember your life when you're drowning. As Scott repeats his question, she forces herself to turn in her seat, as if she doesn't know what she is looking for. The mess of files sits on the carpet as accusingly as if she has defecated there.

'Oh!' she says in mock surprise. 'I'm so sorry. I was doing the filing earlier when Alan arrived. I went straight out and locked the door behind me. I forgot all about them. I'll do them as soon as we've finished these emails.'

Scott sighs petulantly. 'Oh, Anita, really. You know how I like to keep things tidy. We can't lose control of the filing again. Can you do them now, please?'

He sits with a determined little frown, the leather of his chair creaking in agreement. For the second time that day, someone has opened an oven door. Anita's grey cardigan clings to her underarms, the shirt beneath it part of her skin. She puts her pad down as slowly as she can and lies her pen carefully on top. *Please God, let my desk phone ring. Do that for me, God, and, no matter what Scott says, I will rush out and answer it.* But if there is a God he has abandoned her long ago. Or maybe, in her previous life, she was evil, and this is the hell he has sent her to.

Anita forces herself to stand and straighten her skirt, then to turn and cross the grey-green carpet, head high like a woman condemned. Ignoring the sound of Scott's pencil scratching on the desk pad, she approaches the files and stands over them, as if looking down at a boiling ocean from a cliff top. Then, before she can think again, she squats down to the floor and picks them up, back at full height in a second. But this only brings a new dilemma. To file them in the low credenza, she must either bend or kneel on the floor. Her grey cardigan, plastered to her arms and the sides of her body, can't hide her bum, the back of her legs if her skirt rises up. She stares at the cardboard samples arranged along the top of the credenza, her eyes resting on the last one. It is a sealed square and naked box, left there to highlight how clever the other complex and colourful models are. Anita finds herself jealous of it. She wonders if cutting off her limbs and her breasts, shaving her head too, would make her less of a target.

'Go on, then,' says Scott. 'Then we can carry on with the dictation.'

She turns so that her bum is away from him, then bends to open the drawer. But as she does so, her cardigan falls open and she realises that, from his low angle behind the desk, Scott has a good a view of her hanging breasts. She feels herself flush and smells her own sweat. The worst thing would be to get down on her knees, so again she squats, awkward in the skirt, pulls open a drawer and holds onto it for support. Dropping the files to the carpet, she fingers quickly through the hanging folders. There is no point in dropping the file in anywhere, Scott will check and call her back in, stand over her to show her how to do it properly next time. On and on, she flicks the wrong folders out of the way, panicking and jumping too far forwards, then coming back to remember how far she's progressed. *Arondal, Arncliffe, Assetise, Attriant* – at last she finds *Austripak* and drops the file in, struggling with her balance as she reaches forward. She isn't used to squatting like this, her calf muscles are singing, her shoes pinching her toes.

The next file in her lap is *Bomba*. Hanging onto the drawer for balance again, Anita picks it up and hears Scott's leather chair creak slowly as he stands. Something happens to her vision, some kind of defence that doesn't want to see him approach, but her hearing goes the other way, Scott's breath and his steps filling her ears. She is tearing through the B's, her fingers missing whole folders, then catching heavily on others, when Scott's little black shoes appear on the carpet beside her. Her cardigan is hanging open again, he can look straight down the gap in her shirt. Anita blinks heavily, determined to hold back the tears. *Blackmore, Boane, Boon.*

'Why is the Bomba file out at all?' Scott's voice is close. 'I didn't think they'd ordered in months?'

Another little attack, another diversion to stop her thinking of how to escape. *Why do you have paper copies of anything?* she wants to ask. *Why this stupid filing system?* She finds the *Bomba* hanger at last, then hesitates. Once done, she will have to move on to the next drawer, closer to Scott.

'Anita?'

'They wanted a copy of an invoice,' she snaps, her mouth dry. 'Something to do with being audited.'

She drops the file into its hanger, pushes the drawer shut and stands, struggling with the remaining files. This is what she swore would never happen. She is cornered: the wall of press cuttings and the credenza cutting off her escape.

'What else have you got in there?'

Scott uncurls a thick and hairy finger and pulls the topmost file towards him. He might as well be pulling forward the neck of her shirt, claiming his rights of ownership. Anita wants to protest, wants to push him away, to punch and stab and scream and run, but she finds herself unable to speak, her mouth sucked dry to supply the tears welling behind her eyes.

'Anita? What's wrong?'

He takes the files and lays them onto the low credenza, nudging the naked box to one side. Hands free, Anita grabs at her cardigan and pulls it tighter than ever, but this only makes her feel more naked below the waistline, her thighs and bottom and … she can't bear to think of the places Scott can touch. He is looking at her with his little brown eyes, his head slightly on one side. He takes a tiny step closer and puts a hand on each of her elbows.

'Anita, are you all right?'

They both jump at a harsh rapping on the glass office door. For a tiny second, Anita loses control of her bladder, moistness in her underwear adding to her hell. She sees Scott retreat, sees him turn to the office door and – thinking *now, now, now* – drives herself past him. Before she is halfway to the door, it opens with a bang, the venetian blind rattling its untidy echo.

'You here? Patterson?'

Terry Hatch's weather-beaten face appears, looking around curiously until he spots them. Then his misshapen body follows. Hatch is of a similar height to Scott Patterson and his shoulders appear equally strong, but, at his front he carries a proud beer belly that hides the waistband of his trousers. His nose, similarly distorted by drink, distracts attention from his cruel mouth. He is completely bald.

'G'day, Anita. Look, I made it after all. Not disturbing, am I?'

Thirty seconds, Anita tells herself. In thirty seconds she will be in the bathroom and the tears can flow all they like. She finds a smile for Hatch, easier than she thinks, and asks him into the office.

'I'll bring you both coffee,' she says. 'Won't be a sec.'

She doesn't make it to the bathroom. As soon as the door bangs behind her she loses any semblance of control. With one hand over her mouth to stifle her sobs and the other at her crotch, she hobbles to the bathroom.

Sunday, 17th March

Two days after

Murdoch woke up wondering where he was – on a sofa somewhere, arms and legs entwined in unfamiliar sheets – then, why he was there. He blinked and knew, without moving, that any movement would bring pain. Closing his eyes again, he willed himself to sleep, but whatever had woken him was there still and, when he tuned in to it, sounded like an alarm. Then, for a few unstructured seconds, he really was asleep, warm and dark in stories, until the alarm started up again, revealing itself slowly to be a telephone in a nearby room. Murdoch sat up – pain sloshing in his skull, as he knew it would – looked around and remembered uncertainly that the room next door was a bedroom. Hadn't he fallen asleep in there?

He was halfway towards the bedroom door, naked and stinking of his own acid sweat, when the ringing stopped, like the whole point had been just to move him. He'd made it back to the sofa, one hand over his eyes and the other on the stubble of his scalp, when a new noise came: a hammering on the door. Murdoch shouted, 'Coming!' or something like it: a croak with the remains of a voice. He stood again, too quickly, and the room swung, the orange brown of the floorboards threatening to take him down. Shuffling to the kitchen – a row of cupboards and a sink along one edge of the room – he stuck his head under the tap and turned it on. The water was warm and vaguely salty, but it was still water. He swallowed three mouthfuls, grabbed a sheet from the sofa, wrapped himself and struggled to the door.

In the harsh commercial light of the stairwell stood a petite dark-eyed woman, hair pulled back tight to reveal a determined jaw. She was puckering up for a fight, but, even in his state, Murdoch could see her heart wasn't in it. Her eyes were more used to smiling, her indignity put on for the occasion.

'Mr Murdoch, do you know what time it is?'

Murdoch didn't know what fucking *day* it was. He apologised and shook his head: a big mistake, the world drilling his temples. He watched the woman sigh, watched her look him up and down and see he was in one of her sheets. She shook her own head in return.

'I'm the housekeeper,' she said. 'It's past three o'clock and you're supposed to be out by midday. I've got someone else coming in less than an hour.'

'I'm sorry,' said Murdoch again. 'I'm sick. I was sleeping. I lost track of time.'

'Can I come in?'

It wasn't really a question. The housekeeper took a firm step forward, one hand on the door, a professional foot in the doorframe. Murdoch backed out of her way.

'I just want to check you haven't trashed the place,' she said, answering a question he hadn't asked. 'Otherwise it becomes a police matter. At the Garragula, we always press charges.'

He took another step back, not easy in the tightly-wound sheet, and let the woman all the way into the room. Close up she was thirty-something and pretty in a simple kind of way: clear skin, slightly flushed in the cheeks, dark eyes shining. She looked like she'd gone to bed early the night before, got eight full hours and showered twice before leaving for work. Her blue-and-white striped shirt was as pristine as her black trousers. Murdoch watched her walk halfway towards the kitchen then stop, hands on her hips, to survey the scene. She seemed to be sniffing it as much as looking, like she could smell damage in the air.

Murdoch looked around too, memories of the night arriving incomplete, no idea if there was anything he was supposed to hide. At his feet, playing cards were strewn across the carpet; on the bamboo coffee table glasses stood or lay beside bottles; two ashtrays overflowing beside the dismantled smoke alarm. The sheet Murdoch wasn't wearing lay half on the sofa and half on the floor, like it had tried to make it back to the bedroom but had died along the way.

'Listen,' he said. 'I'm sorry but I really am sick. Can I pay for an extra night? I just need some painkillers and a good sleep. If you could get me some paracetamol and put your other guests somewhere else, I'll give you a hundred bucks on top of the bill to make up for your troubles.'

He'd never learned the trick of making a bribe sound like it was anything else. He'd heard it done all his life, people calling it a tip, or a charitable donation, or a fee of some kind. Like even they didn't think it was a bung and would have been offended if you'd suggested it was. Maybe he was too decent – how's that for a joke? The housekeeper turned and looked at him, the full dry bath – not entirely disgusted by what she saw. She shook her head slowly, but he could see he'd passed a test, the smoker's lines around her mouth only quivering to stop a smile. The housekeeper at the Garragula Hotel might have seen it all, but she wasn't bitter about it yet.

'Two hundred,' she said.

'Do what?'

'Two hundred dollars on top of the bill. I'll get you some paracetamol and a Berocca, change the bed, bring you some food with a cup of tea and you can stay here until midday tomorrow. How does that sound?'

Murdoch forgot not to shake his head. 'I just want to sleep.'

'You want to sleep in clean sheets and wake up to a nice meal. You want to jump in the shower now and, by the time you come out, you want me gone and the bed made up. And you want the air conditioning on in the bedroom so you don't have to sleep out here as naked as the day you were born.'

She wasn't hiding her amusement now. She gave him another long look, hovering halfway down, halfway up, before regaining eye contact with one eyebrow raised. Murdoch could see the possibilities, but she was no competition for his hangover. Behind her, at the dining table, he spotted a chair wearing his jacket, like a guest who'd survived the night and now wasn't sure how to leave. Murdoch shuffled over, swore with relief to find his wallet in a pocket, and pulled out four yellow notes. With them came a business card, thick with glossy writing. It twisted in the air, before landing on the table inside a ring stain the colour of dried blood. Murdoch picked up the card quickly and shoved it back in his wallet. When he handed the money over and asked where the bathroom was, the housekeeper pointed towards a door near the bedroom. She let him get halfway there before she said, 'You need to phone someone.'

'Sorry, love?'

'You need to phone someone. You know what it's like. When you're not expecting to get … sick like this, there's always someone expecting you somewhere the next day to make it even worse. You should phone your wife or work or whoever it is, tell them you're not going to make it.'

Murdoch remembered slowly it was Sunday morning. He swore and looked around vaguely, glancing up as the housekeeper coughed to see her pointing at his phone on the dining table. He shuffled over, grabbed the phone with his free hand, then shuffled back, all the way to the bathroom this time. Two hundred bucks was thanks enough.

In the shower, the memories grew back their missing parts. In the newly crisp bed, Berocca sizzling beside him, he put them in order. The previous afternoon, down on the beach, he'd pulled on his trousers so quickly he'd fallen on the sand, grappling there with his belt and shirt. Then he'd run up the path and across the road, shoes and socks in his hands for the second time that day, wincing at the gravel that littered the tarmac. He'd been angry by then, sort of. Sort of looking forward to the tumble too: in the perfect mood for teaching a little thief a lesson. But at the street door he hesitated, working out how to give the bastard a hiding and get him out of Davie's office without wrecking the place first, what to do if there was two of them. It was then that he noticed the car angled at the kerb: a silver Aston Martin DB9, brand new, by the look of it.

The car was so out of place in Montauban that Murdoch put his head into the chip shop to see if its owner was in there asking for directions. But there was only Hattie behind the counter staring up at the television, her face blue and white and blue again. Behind Murdoch, a breeze came up off the ocean, whispering through the banksia at the top of the dunes and tapping the street door to Davie's office against its fragile frame. *Rat-a-tat-tat. What are you waiting for?*

Pulling the door open silently was easy enough. Letting it close silently behind him again was a slower job. The light Murdoch had seen from the beach was coming from the bathroom at the top of the stairs, the door open to reveal a fat moth buzzing around, banging its head stubbornly against the bulb as it demanded the right to die. Murdoch readied himself to take the stairs, but, before he could move, a voice called down from above him.

'Is somebody there? Mr Simms? Davie?'

It was a man's voice, polite and unsure of itself. Then there were footsteps overhead and a man's face and shoulders appeared over the half-wall at the top of the stairwell. The angle of the light made the face dark, its features lost to their own shadows.

'Sorry,' said the face's owner, seeing Murdoch. 'The door was open, so I let myself in. Are you Davie Simms?'

Murdoch climbed slowly without answering. Had he seen Davie lock the door? At the top of the stairs, the stranger was standing awkwardly outside the bathroom, apologising again. He was still dark, even with the bathroom light in his face: thick lashes crowding middle-eastern eyes, dense curls pushed back from his forehead, a villain's moustache. He was broad-shouldered and tall – six four, at least – long, hairy limbs protruding from shorts and a faded T-shirt. Murdoch told him to sit down and the man complied, walking to the front of the office and taking a seat at the glass-topped table. Like he was reclaiming the chair he'd sat in till now and the shadows Murdoch had seen from the beach hadn't been moving around at all.

'Give us a second,' Murdoch told him.

He checked the belligerent moth was alone in the bathroom, shut the door on its inevitable death, then walked past the stranger in the dark to turn on Davie's desk lamp. He still had his shoes in one hand, the socks hanging out like tired dogs' tongues – any weapon better than none. As he lowered himself into Davie's desk chair, the only light behind him now, the tall man sat back and looked at him quizzically.

'You're not Davie Simms,' he said. 'At least, either you're not, or that photo on your website isn't. You a colleague of his?'

'I'm his partner. Business partner, I mean. Davie's not around right now.'

The stranger unwound his arms and legs – a spider coming out of its hole – stood and took a step forward. If he noticed Murdoch brace, he ignored it, smiling again as he held out a huge hand. Murdoch shook it hard.

'My name's Velis,' the other man said. 'Emre Velis. The name's Turkish, in case you're wondering.'

'I wasn't. What can I do for you, Mr Velis?'

Velis smiled again. 'Listen, I don't mean to be rude, but do you have a business card or something? I didn't notice a partner's name on the sign. Nor on the website.'

Velis remained smiling as he sat back down, eyes friendly but unwavering. *No need to make this unpleasant, but I won't back down if it gets that way.*

Murdoch stood and walked round the table to the half-empty bookshelf. When Davie had first opened the agency, he had over-optimistically printed Murdoch some business cards, some half-arsed idea about Murdoch & Simms. Finding the box of cards behind the kettle, Murdoch wiped it free of dust, unwrapped the cellophane and pulled one out.

'Bill Murdoch?' said Velis, squinting at it in the dull light. 'So now I feel like a bit of a dickhead. Sorry, it's just … you know, empty office, bloke walking in off the street. No hard feelings?'

Murdoch thought about it as he sat down again. 'No hard feelings. Velis, you said?'

'Emre Velis. Turkish mum, Greek dad, true-blue Aussie. You a Pom? I spent some time in London when I was younger.'

'Like it?'

Velis struggled to find the right response. 'Great when you're young,' he said at last. 'Long term, I'm not so sure. Sharpens your elbows a bit, you know what I mean?'

He pronounced it '*u nah ah min*', the overdone accent strange in his face. The Aussie accent too, come to that. Velis looked like something out of *Lawrence of Arabia*, Murdoch thought. Like he should be on a horse with a tea towel on his head. Not that the man was that sure of himself. There was a nervousness about him, an excess energy which kept him pushing back his hair or scratching his chin, tapping a finger or a foot. *Emre Velis, Emre Velis*. The name was something less than new to Murdoch.

'Don't suppose you smoke?' Velis pulled a pack of cigarettes from a pocket, a roll of soft paper ripped at one end, *Samsun* in white letters on red. He looked up and misread Murdoch's curiosity. 'Oh, sorry. No smoking in the office?'

Murdoch stood, reached across the desk and worked open the etched window. The breeze from the ocean filled the room, cooler and damper than the air it replaced, only the darkness left outside. It lifted the top pages of Davie's notepad, the notes of their conversation with Fran Patterson, the numbers written larger than the words. Since Murdoch had seen the pages last, they had been ripped from the pad, then laid back in place.

'You are now in the smoking section,' he said. Then, pointing at the cigarettes, 'What's them?'

Velis smiled his villain's smile again. 'They're Turkish. Here, why don't you try one.'

They sat and smoked like they were listening to music and not the wind rattling the street door downstairs. Murdoch struggled with the dirty strength of the cigarette, but he didn't comment on it. It had been a long time since he'd had met a bloke who knew how to sit in silence.

'So, Mr Velis, what was you after?'

Velis laughed: an advert for his dentist. 'Please, call me Emre. Unless I have to call you "Mr Murdoch" too? Like it's not film noir enough, coming to see a private detective in a small hideaway town.'

Murdoch made a note to look up film 'nwah' later. He asked Velis – Emre – for a second time, how he could help. In response, Velis searched in the pockets of his shorts again before producing a small metal tin. He pushed it halfway across the table to Murdoch, opened its hinged lid and they had an ashtray. Another slow drag on his cigarette and the man was ready to talk.

'I have an interest in a timber yard over at Gumirri. Nothing special, my nephew, Samir, runs the place; favour to his mum more than anything. About a month ago, a casual he'd brought in slipped and fell, hurt himself so badly he didn't come to work for the next few days. Next thing Samir knows, the guy's threatening to sue. And guess what? He's all clued up on the latest health and safety regs. We don't have the right signs up, fire exit lights etc. Reckons it could go badly for us if it got to court.'

'That'll be his solicitor,' said Murdoch. 'No win, no fee.'

'Yeah, you'd think so. But I know a solicitor's letter when I see one, letterhead or not, and this guy's representing himself. I reckon he came in just to set us up.'

Murdoch tapped his cigarette on the edge of the little ashtray. It was ancient, beaten and black inside, real silver he reckoned. 'You want us to follow him?' he said. 'Get photos of him dancing at midnight?'

'I guess. And find out if he's done it before. Find out anything about him, really.'

'Name?'

Velis hesitated, a tiny pause. 'McCaul, Henry McCaul. Bit young for a Henry, can't be many of them around.'

'All right if I talk to your nephew?'

'Of course.'

No hesitation this time and whatever had worried Murdoch floated away in the smoke. He rattled through the fees and Velis shrugged; fine, did they want a deposit? Murdoch pulled out his phone to find Davie's bank details, but Velis beat him to it, producing a wallet from his bottomless pockets and counting jolly green giants onto the glass between them.

'Cash is king,' he said, the moustache making way for the smile again.

'Tell me about it. Just don't tell the tax man.'

'You've got to tell him *something* but.'

'Nice car, by the way.' Murdoch took the hundred-dollar notes and threw them into the drawer of the desk beside him. 'The DB9, I'm guessing it's yours?'

'Aw yeah. Thanks for noticing.'

'Don't sound so pleased about it.'

'You know,' said Velis sadly, 'For a while, I was. I mean, that's the whole point of fancy cars, isn't it? To have them noticed? I'm telling you, mate, I had serious tickets on myself when I bought that thing. Drove it round like I owned the road. Then, after a few weeks, I was out on a date and this gorgeous girl, ten out of ten, gets into it without blinking an eye. I ask her if she likes the car and she's like, *"Yeah, fine, why?"* Like I'd asked if she was feeling all right. Ever since then, I can't help wondering if I'm the drongo who spent two hundred grand on a car when everyone else gets around for a fraction of the price.'

'Not to mention the insurance.'

'Petrol.'

'Luxury car tax.'

Velis stubbed out his cigarette.

'That *was* you in the souped-up Merc.' He nodded at the open window. 'Thought the driver had gone for a swim.'

Murdoch remembered he was barefoot, bent down and started brushing the sand from his feet. Why shouldn't a stranger think he was braver than he was?

'Aha,' said Velis, making him look up. 'You did go down to the beach. But then you saw the light from the office here and came running up, thinking someone was trying to flog the computer.'

'Something like that. You know "flog" in England means selling stuff. Funny how you Aussies use it to mean nicking.'

'Got to nick it before you can sell it.'

There was nothing more than the words. No wink or knowing glance, no eye contact at all. Murdoch went back to his feet, the socks, then the shoes. *Emre Velis.* When he came up for air, the tall man was standing, stifling a yawn.

'I don't suppose there's a pub in town?'

Murdoch snorted. 'I wish. Surf club sells beer, if you don't mind sticking to the floor and explaining your life to the locals. Don't touch the food, though.'

'There's a pub at Garragula. That can't be far, can it? Food's supposed to be good.'

Murdoch nodded. The food at the Garragula Hotel was good. It was the kind of place, every time you went, you wondered why you didn't go more often.

'Don't suppose you fancy a beer?' Velis snapped the ashtray shut and pocketed it with his wallet. 'Or are you already too close to home?'

Murdoch turned to the window, struggling with it for time to think. It was a fair enough assumption he lived in Montauban; it didn't have to mean a thing. As the glass closed, he caught Velis's reflection, hands awkward with his car keys, embarrassed to have asked about the drink.

'Well ...'

'I could race you there,' Velis said quickly. 'How about that? We'll do a time trial so we don't kill anyone coming towards us. Your fancy Mercedes versus my fancy Aston Martin; what do you reckon?'

Murdoch smiled. Velis had to be joking. 'Don't worry about anyone coming towards us?' he said. 'You don't know the Crown Road, mate. In that thing you'll come off it before the third bend. Your family'll be sellotaping flowers to trees for you.'

'Loser buys dinner?'

Murdoch smiled less comfortably this time. He told Velis he was fine, thanks, he should be getting home. Velis shrugged, clear whose loss it was, and handed over a business card. When Murdoch said he'd be in touch about Harry McCale, Velis didn't correct him.

Finding the spare key and walking down the dark stairs to the street, sand between his toes, Murdoch felt the lost opportunities mocking him. Jane, the swim, the car race. Or maybe, outside, the sky did that: bright clouds dodging stars on the way to something more exciting. Velis was at the boot of the Aston Martin, struggling into a huge pullover, face and arms lost in dark wool.

'A time trial,' said Murdoch. 'How would that work?'

Velis's head emerged, teeth a bluey white in the light from the chip shop – the spider dressed up as a bear.

'I start the timer on my phone, drive better than you, stop it when I get there. You set your own timer, leave a couple of minutes later and try not to kill yourself so you can buy me dinner. Safety first though,' he frowned, deadly serious. 'No overtaking on blind bends, no risking other people's safety.'

'Just our own.'

'Isn't that the point?' The grin was infectious.

'And we trust each other not to cheat?'

The smile disappeared again, Velis's whole face a frown: sunshine or rain, nothing in between. 'What would be the point in that? It's just for fun.'

Murdoch was ashamed he'd asked. He turned and, after a struggle, managed to lock the door behind him. Then, before he could post the key back inside, he thought better of it. Upstairs, he crossed the office in the dark and took Velis's money from the desk drawer, glancing down through the window to look at his car, yellow as it reflected the light of the street lamp.

The Crown Road was ten curves to the right, ten to the left, the only way in or out of Montauban. Murdoch drove it so often it bored him. He'd driven it fast a few times – it was the kind of road that made you do it – until, earlier that year, he'd lost control. Only for a second, but it had been enough. Trapped in two tonnes of metal, travelling sideways to a drop, some lessons were easy to learn. Now, as he watched Velis pull away from the chip shop and rumble slowly to the little roundabout, he remembered the feeling of panic. Then – three, two, one, blast off – Velis was up the hill and out of town, his noise filling the streets, the ocean breeze like the DB9's back blast. Before the last echoes of the climb had died, he heard Velis hesitate and choose a gear as he turned onto the Crown Road. Then came the noise Murdoch had rolled his eyes at so many times: too powerful an engine racing on a road deadly for slower cars. He listened to the DB9 take a new breath, explode again, then repeat the cycle further away. Listened until he could be sure the car was fading into the distance, not flying through silence before a violent full stop.

Alone in the sleepy town, Murdoch found his keys and beeped the Merc open. Something moved in his gut, fear or disappointment: he told himself he hadn't decided yet. In a couple of minutes he could be home, warm and safe. Maybe he'd find something on the telly.

'Ooh hoo!' Hattie had come out of the chip shop and was waving, her hair as mad as ever, a brown paper bag in one hand. 'I'm just locking up. You want these last chips?'

Murdoch shrugged and started crossing towards her, blinking away his thoughts.

'What you up to?' she said. 'Anything interesting?'

'No.'

'No, of course not. Nothing interesting's happened round here in years. Never will again, I reckon. Oh, now where you off to?'

He was back at the Merc before he knew the answer, turning it towards the roundabout without checking his mirrors, headlights sweeping across Hattie's printed apron and her last chips. As he took a deep breath and turned left up the hill, Murdoch found his jaws were solid, his torso a fist, his smile in the mirror a rictus. He found his phone and set up the timer, hit start and threw it onto the passenger seat, not caring that it slid across the leather and fell into the passenger door. For now, he was the noise, the escape from a small town on a Saturday night, the only thing of interest for miles around.

Velis was waiting at the bar, foam on his moustache, a head taller than anyone else.

'Jesus,' he said when he saw Murdoch. 'You look like you've seen a ghost.'

'Yeah, my own, several times. Fuck me, that was the stupidest thing what I've done in years.'

Velis gave him his wicked grin. 'How d'you feel?'

Murdoch didn't want to answer that in case it reproduced the remains of Penny Simms's hearty salad. He could still see gumtrees sliding sideways before him, feel the thrust of the Merc sucking him into its seat. He'd never driven the Crown Road that fast. He grimaced.

'Well, you don't ever have to do it again,' Velis told him. 'It's done – tick. Feels good though, doesn't it?'

He wasn't looking at Murdoch. He was watching a leggy redhead stalk across the bar, tight denim helping with her thigh gap.

'It doesn't feel that good,' said Murdoch, one eye on the redhead. 'Just feels stupid.'

Six schooners later, it felt fan-fucking-tastic. Murdoch was gesturing at Velis with a chicken drumstick.

'Nah, that eighth bend, you can see it coming; any fool's gonna slow down on that one. It's the one before it what creeps up on you. Not sure why it didn't kill *you*.'

The pub was loud around them now: people carrying numbers on sticks looking for somewhere to sit; staff carrying food, looking for numbers on sticks. The bar was a scrum, the carpet behind Velis a constant stream of drinkers, the leggy redhead gone, but other women better by the minute. The only space was in front of the fire, too early in the autumn to be comfortable, flames flickering in everyone's beer.

'Aw, yeah, about that,' said Velis. 'Bit of a confession. I used to do a lot of rally driving in Belgium, hundred years ago. Ever been to Belgium? Boring as bat shit, nothing else to do, so I probably got good at it. Studying roads, it gets to be a habit, and I had a good look on the way in. And my tyres aren't exactly standard.'

'So what time did you do?'

Velis gasped. 'Ha! No fucking idea! Forgot all about that. You?'

Murdoch laughed, a proper belly laugh, the first one in months. 'My sodding phone's still in the car. The timer's still on!'

It was funnier than it should have been and Murdoch was still chuckling when Velis went back to the bar. He looked around him at the people shouting and laughing in the beer-coloured light, and wondered where they'd all come from. Then he remembered. They'd always been here: it was only him who'd been hiding in his cave. He checked his watch and realised he could still be at Davie's parents' house, sitting politely and hoping they wouldn't ask him to stay for dinner. Velis came back with four schooners.

'It's like Westfield on a Saturday up there,' he said. 'Thought I'd save us time.'

There was no more talk about driving, just long detours through everything else.

'Do what you're good at,' Velis reckoned. 'All these buggers wanting to ski or surf or ride horses because it looks good, waste of bloody time. Y'know from day one if you're gonna be good at something.'

Murdoch wasn't sure. He told Velis about his swimming lessons, said he was never going to be no good at that, but what was he supposed to do, stay out of the ocean forever? Velis shrugged.

'Why not? Living where you do, you'd have gone in by now, if that's what you wanted. You're old enough to know what you like; so do that and nothing else. You can't beat your base nature.'

The evening grew blurrier after that. Later, Murdoch had memories of laughing a lot but no idea what had been so funny. No idea either at what point he'd decided to get a room for the night; although, hadn't there been argy-bargy with the bar staff who'd wanted to take his car keys? Velis had come to the room, he remembered that. They'd played cards and drunk whisky. Then there'd been a call and Velis had disappeared downstairs. Next thing Murdoch knew, the Garragula housekeeper was banging on his door.

Later still, half-human and driving home, Murdoch found himself struggling with the name again. *Emre Velis*. Something didn't fit.

Wednesday, 13th March

Two days before

Anita sets the alarm on her phone so she can stop checking the clock every few minutes. The trick is to shut down her computer and leave silently before Scott notices the time. But her departure has to be at exactly five o'clock. If it is any earlier, and Scott finds out, he will call her on the mobile with a joke about slacking and a pretext for her return. Any later and she will hit the Crosley traffic and not be home in time to give Riya her bath. The rivalry between Anita and her mother about Riya's bath time is unspoken but intense, each of them seeing the other's right to it but each of them also acutely aware of the effect that missing out has on the little girl's affections. They both agree that bath time should always be at half past five – consistent for Riya's sake – and that, in theory, it is Anita's role. But Scott Patterson has a penchant for end-of-day chats that generally keep Anita back ten minutes into rush hour and Ma has no qualms about starting her granddaughter's baths on time.

Scott's chats can begin at any time between four-fifty and five. His normal tactic is to perch on Anita's desk and ask for a run-through of the next day's diary, or a summary of the emails he hasn't seen. He peppers his conversation with asides about his day: dilemmas with various staff; gossip he normally withholds. Anything to keep her back. The more he catches Anita checking the clock, the more he relaxes and shares his news until, only when Anita has given in and relinquished her daughter's affection, he finally lets her go.

Today, however, there is hope. Scott's wife, Fran, is due to call at four-fifty. She is at a golf tournament in the Southern Highlands and they will be on the phone for at least half an hour. Scott thinks too much time on mobile phones gives people brain cancer, so he will take the call on the landline, stuck behind his desk. Anita is quietly packing up, when her desk phone jangles like a prison alarm. Fran Patterson's number appears on the display.

'Hi Fran, it's Anita. How are you?'

Fran asks coolly after Anita's health, after Riya, after Anita's mother and all the details she always remembers. As she does so, Anita starts to wonder if the other woman represents a potential way out of her hell. Why doesn't she tell Fran everything? The idea is so exciting that Anita stays on the call on mute after she connects Fran to Scott. She knows she is breaking an unbreakable rule, but she tells herself every secretary breaks it and, besides, she needs to know if Fran is really as kind as she appears. It seems so unlikely when she is married to a man as patently evil as Scott.

'Hello, Scott, darling,' she hears Fran Patterson say. 'How has your day been?'

The Pattersons talk about golf, the gas bill and when Fran will be home. As Scott's wife expresses sympathy for his tiredness, support for how disappointing Alan is, tenderness when Scott says he misses her, Anita finds herself smiling. *She doesn't know. Of course, she doesn't know!* For it is Scott who is acting differently from normal. His cocky confidence and his swagger have gone; his voice is that of a little boy. His R's are almost W's, his voice a soft whinge in complaint; his joy at the news of her win at the golf is a Disney-like cheer. Anita tries not to look at the clock, her mind on how to approach Fran and exactly what to say. She is about to disconnect herself from the call, when the sound of her own name stops her.

'How's Anita, darling?' says Fran's voice in her headset. 'Any better?'

'God, no. Worse, if anything.'

She can hear Scott in unbalanced stereo, his transmitted voice clear through her headset, the real him a murmur through the office door, as if the real and fake parts of him have split.

'She's so jumpy,' Scott says. 'Every time I speak to her she's on the verge of tears. I'm nice to her, but it just makes things worse.'

'Well, darling, don't be too nice. You remember her history.'

Her *history*? Of course, he has told her, the bastard! Anita wonders what version Fran has heard. Whichever one it is, she'll have to explain herself before she shares anything else. The *Gazette* was so mean: the whole article full of implications. Anita's eyes sting at the memory, the court case as bad as the incident in Sacramento itself, the bank's lawyers too clever for the one she could afford. Even Ma hadn't believed her.

'I just hate not being polite,' Scott is saying petulantly. 'If political correctness means I can't compliment someone on what they're wearing, then maybe I don't agree with it after all. I thought men and women were supposed to be equal, so why can't I treat them equally?'

Fran's tone softens into something even more soothing than before.

'Scott, darling, how often do you compliment men on their clothes? Now listen to me. As I said at the time, it's admirable that you took her on after everything that happened at that other place she worked, but you have to be careful. Anyone can see the woman's deranged.'

All day the air conditioning has been losing a battle with the humidity outside; now it seems to be working for the enemy. Gasping for air, Anita rips off her headset, kills the call on her desk phone and scrabbles her remaining things together. *Deranged!* She hears Scott's voice raised through the office door but she is so upset she ignores it, shutting down all the applications on her PC, looking for the keys to her drawers. She is halfway to the stairs when Scott's office door bangs open and he is suddenly beside her.

'I got cut off!' He has brought something of the little boy out with him, an angry toddler separated from his mummy. 'How did that happen? It's never happened before.'

The realisation of what she has done crawls slowly up from the floor. Anita has cut the call rather than disconnecting herself. Feeling herself colouring, she uses the clock as an excuse to look away. It is three minutes to five.

'Where are you going?' says Scott. 'What's going on?'

'I …'

'Well, come in here. I'll call Fran back in a minute. I want to show you something.'

She follows him into the office, trying to work out if he could know why the call got cut off. Did she forget to put herself on mute? Is there a light on his desk phone which shows when she is listening? Scott is at the near side of his desk, fiddling with something, until the door bangs behind her and the blind laughs its rattling laugh.

'Look at this, Anita, do you remember my friend here?'

There is a tiny moment between him turning and her seeing, another between her seeing and understanding. Then time stands still. Scott has taken his testicles and his erect penis out of his trousers, the penis pointing at her, its tight foreskin not fully recoiled. The air in the room has been replaced by water. Anita chokes, one hand on her chest, willing herself to scream but unable to make a sound. She forces herself to look away, anywhere but at Scott. At the smudge she's left on the window, at the dark clouds piling up beyond, crawling over one another to enjoy the show. She feels something jab into her back and realises she'd walked backwards into the wall of framed newspaper cuttings. Scott is only metres from her, advancing as she retreats and closing in fast. The softly solid end of his penis reaches her first, nudging against the top of her leg. She tries to turn and, at last, finds a word:

'Please …'

Then Scott's hands arrive, squeezing her breasts so painfully she thinks something might burst, pinning her against the wall.

'No,' she says.

But she can say nothing more, her voice abandoning her as she drowns. Scott stands on tiptoe, his powerful frame pushing his penis into the softness below her stomach, her back into the sharp frames behind her. His mouth is on her ear.

'You know, Anita, the only reason I haven't forced a fuck on you yet is because I don't want to stop looking forward to it. But we're going to have to get on with it in the next week or two. Me and my friend here.'

He fumbles at her breasts, struggling to find her nipples through the thicker bra she has recently bought. Finding them at last, he takes one between each thumb and forefinger and twists so hard the effort shows in his face. Anita gives a sob-choked scream. Scott releases her, takes a step backwards and turns, hands at his fly.

It is another few seconds before she can move, her sobs trapped inside her. Her thoughts are beyond her control, visions of Scott filling her mind, and for a few seconds she forgets where she is. All she can think is *Why can't I find the strength to kill him, why will I never do it?* Scott turns again and she flinches, but his fly is now closed, the vile penis only a bulge.

'You should run along,' he says with a kind smile. 'It's past five and I know you like to get home to Riya on time. Give her my love when you're in the bath together.'

Monday, 18th March

Three days after

Davie had wanted to meet at ten thirty on Monday morning but, Sunday evening on the phone, Murdoch had insisted it should be earlier. He hadn't shared the reason why.

'Come on, mate, let's do it right. I'll bring coffees and we can make it like a proper business meeting. Most people start work at nine on a Monday, don't they?'

Davie snapped back with a rare sourness. 'No, Bill. Not when they have an important appointment the day before. When that happens, believe it or not, they generally start work on the Sunday. As agreed. Especially, when there's an urgent timeline.'

The vein in Murdoch's temples throbbed again – his hangovers always echoed badly in the evening – but he really did feel guilty for not showing up at PPC earlier that morning.

'Here,' he said gently. 'I did a bit of googling and that stuff Fran Patterson was saying about one injection every eight weeks, it looks kosher enough. Not all that new neither.'

'Great. Thanks.'

'But I'm sure what you found out earlier today is much more interesting. So why don't you tell me about it now?'

'Because you don't deserve to know about it now, Bill. Not if you couldn't be bothered turning up.'

'It's not that I couldn't be bothered. Like I said, it's just I couldn't get there. Go on, tell me.'

'No.'

'Go on.'

'I'll tell you tomorrow morning. If you can be bothered turning up.'

There were limits. 'For fuck's sake, Davie, ain't I apologised like a hundred times already? I told you, I was in bits this morning! Even if I had got to PPC, what would of meant driving drunk, I wouldn't of been no good to you. Sorry, sorry, sorry. That enough?'

It ought to be. Davie had known Murdoch long enough to appreciate the word didn't come easily. Then again, Murdoch had known Davie long enough to appreciate it wasn't just his no-show at PPC that Davie was upset about.

'So, where were you exactly?'

'Davie, mate, it's got nothing to do with the case.'

'But where *were* you?'

'Mind your own beeswax. I'm not telling you, all right? I'm allowed some privacy, ain't I?'

Murdoch didn't know why Davie was so worried. It would be a matter of hours before he heard from someone – probably Anne Lincoln in the general store – that Murdoch had been drunk in the Garragula Hotel. Velis, no doubt, would be recognised as someone's cousin's neighbour. The speed and efficiency of the Coast's bush telegraph were a mystery to Murdoch: a game where everyone but him knew the rules and he relished the odd hours when he was winning. Davie, he had decided, would just have to find out the normal way.

Monday at nine, the street door to Davie's office was securely locked again. Murdoch waited across the road on the viewing platform over the dunes. It was a beautiful day, even he had to admit that – nothing in the sky and twenty degrees already. Behind him, cockatoos, magpies and mynas were screaming at each other from the trees. Ahead of him, the ocean lay flat, crystal clear and calling, conspiring with the weather to rob him of excuses. Murdoch stared at it, thinking about his conversation with Velis until, hearing footsteps, he turned and saw Davie sauntering towards him.

'Flat white.' Murdoch handed over a cup. 'Warm ten minutes ago.'

'Oh, sorry, am I late? Still, better late than never, isn't that what they say? Which on recent form makes me *better* than you.'

'Jesus, Davie, are you still sulking about that? What you been doing? Hiding round the corner, having a good laugh at me waiting for you?'

Davie shook his head. 'No, I went for a swim, actually. Then I had a phone call; it was that that made me late. Wish I could have stayed in the ocean, the water's beautiful.'

'Yeah, nineteen degrees. Maybe more. And great vis.'

'Don't tell me you went in?'

'No, I didn't go in. When I go in, mate, you'll read about it in *The Herald*. But so far this morning I've met Anne Lincoln in the general store, Ruby from the bakery, Bob the postie and now you, so it would be a bleeding miracle if I didn't know what the water temperature was, wouldn't it?'

Davie backed off with his hands up, like he could be surprised this was a sore point. Murdoch followed him across the road and watched him struggle with the door to the office.

'This lock's gone weird; I noticed it yesterday,' Davie rattled the key again, then grunted as it suddenly gave way. 'I'm cursed with keys this week. Anyway, guess who called me just now?' He didn't let Murdoch guess, just carried on talking as they climbed the stairs. 'Remember my lawyer friend, Guy? Well, his brother, Glenn, runs this little PR agency. Nothing like Hoxton Harte; smaller, more specialist. Anyway, you know how I really regret not using that press we got off the Harte case? Well, I left Guy's brother, Glenn, a message about getting some publicity when we find Patterson, and he called back and he's interested.

'Jesus,' said Murdoch. 'That's a bit optimistic, innit? What exactly did you find at PPC? A map showing where Scott Patterson is hiding?'

'Not quite.'

'So come on then, what was it?'

But Davie was clearly enjoying himself. He rabbited on about the PR firm's previous successes and what a good bloke Glenn was, not stopping for breath as he turned on his computer and pushed back past Murdoch to the bathroom, calling out from there over the noise of taps as he washed Saturday's cups in the sink. Murdoch said nothing. He wasn't going to play this stupid game. Davie would let him know soon enough what he'd found out at PPC and it wouldn't be anything interesting. Taking his normal place at the glass table, Murdoch looked around and realised he'd never been in the office this early before. At the top of the stairs, it was as dull and boxy as ever, the six-thousand-dollar armchairs hulking and brown. But, closer to the window, the room was sliced by light alive with dust. It caught the edge of the glass table the same way it did the ocean outside – a million tiny suns. Even in here, it was a perfect day for a swim.

Murdoch blinked the idea away and remembered being here with Velis, amazed the dark memory was so recent. *Emre Velis*. The name disturbed him less each time – an echo of a worry rather than a worry itself – but, all the same, he wasn't ready to tell Davie about the man yet. Once Velis confirmed himself as a genuine new client, then Murdoch would share the good news. Spotting Davie's dusty old radio on the shelf below the kettle, he got up and flicked it on. The news was coming to an end – jovial remarks about a local sporting victory – and, after the Easy Coast FM jingle, 'Manic Monday' by The Bangles started up. Even Murdoch knew that one.

Davie must have heard the music too because – still in the bathroom – he raised his voice as he carried on talking, like he could still compete with popstars on the radio. 'Anyway, Glenn's going to drive up from Sydney with a plan of attack. He reckons the old Davie Wonder stuff gives us a pitch for the media. You know, a "where are they now" kind of thing? You see ex-musos doing it all the time.'

'Mate, I thought you was broke? How you going to pay a PR agency?'

'It'll pay for itself! National media coverage, not to mention the *Crosley Gazette* and local radio, the phone will be ringing off the hook. I reckon we'll have to hire some help before the end of the year just to cope with the workload.'

'We?'

Davie leant out of the bathroom door, said, 'Well, I mean, *I* will, of course,' and disappeared again.

'Davie, listen to me. Like I said, I'm gonna help you with this case, I really am. But any publicity, you leave me out of it, yeah? My name doesn't even get mentioned.'

'Of course. I'm not stupid. I know you're still on the run from—'

'You was talking about hiring people?'

'Oh yeah. And then, I reckon next year we, I mean, *I*, could open a second office. In Sydney, maybe.' Davie appeared from the bathroom again, all of him this time, rubbing a mug with a dirty tea towel. 'So what do you think?'

'I think you should tell me what you found out at PPC.'

'Yeah, yeah, I will.' Noticing his satchel on the floor, Davie got rid of the mug and the tea towel and squatted down to rummage through it. 'But first, what do you think about the publicity?'

'I think it sounds like your dad's idea, mate.'

'No, it's my idea. I do have them, you know. I think it'll be great. The trick will be to weed out the crank calls from the serious cases. Bill?'

Murdoch had been checking his watch. 'Nah, I mean it sounds like an idea what you've had to make your dad happy. You know, making the agency a big success, being big in business. What's the point in having ambitions if they ain't your own?' He glanced at his watch again. 'Listen, let's get a move on – you gonna tell me what you found out yesterday or what?'

'It's not just for Dad. I want to be a success too, you know. You think I put all this effort in for nothing?'

Murdoch looked around at the effort. 'Last thing I heard, mate, you wanted a little business what would stop you having to sell houses to wankers from Sydney and let you surf most of the day. "Just enough to keep the wolf from the door." That's what you said. Not sure where all this "growing the business" stuff has come from. I reckon you should try and stop worrying about what your parents think.'

'Yeah, like that's ever possible.' Davie looked down at his satchel, seemed to remember what he was searching for and started rummaging again. It was several minutes before he was seated opposite Murdoch, notepad open on the glass table between them. 'Now look, this is the location of the PPC warehouse and here's a list of who's got which keys.' He dragged through the details slowly until Murdoch sighed through his nose.

'Is this your exciting news what you could only tell me face to face?'

'Hang on, I'm getting there.' Davie looked up with innocent eyes. 'Just giving you details you'd already know if you'd bothered turning up.'

'Sounds like I didn't need to, I knew half that stuff already.'

They looked at each for half a second before Davie returned to reading out his notes about the keys and the warehouse and the offices. Looking up, he caught Murdoch checking his watch again.

'What's up? Are you in a rush?'

'No, mate, no. I'm all ears. Just want you to get to the exciting part you insisted I was here for instead of telling me stuff what I already know.'

'Oh, like you've got something better to do?'

Murdoch stared at him. 'Yeah, I do actually. And I've got to be out of here in forty minutes so I can go and do it.'

'Forty minutes?' Davie coloured, sat back and lifted his feet to the opposite chair, long legs fencing Murdoch in. 'Didn't you say you were going to help?'

'I am. I'm here, aren't I? Doesn't mean I have to hang around all day.'

'Crikey, Bill. I thought you were really into this. For once, you know, I thought you were going to take a case seriously, give it all your attention.'

Murdoch had thought so too. But it was like everything in life: feast or famine, everything or nothing, what did they say about buses? He sighed and leaned forward in his seat, waiting for eye contact before he spoke again.

'Davie, mate, trust me, I do want to work on this case. It's interesting, promise it is. But I have got other things going on too, you know.' It sounded like a lie even to him: it had been so long since it was true. 'Come on. What happened at PPC? The nephew, Alan Drummond, what's he like?'

Davie stuck out his bottom lip. 'Nice, normal, I don't know. He turned up late, let me into the building and then, when we heard Scott Patterson's voice, he let me into Scott's office. I phoned Scott's secretary, Anita Patel, when I got back here, so I could talk to her about it. But she won't speak to me until Fran Patterson gives her the OK in person.'

Davie looked down at his hands and waited. Murdoch gave in and put on a surprised face. It was like working with a child.

'What do you mean, you heard Scott Patterson's voice, Davie?'

'It was coming from his computer. Calling out like he wanted someone to come into the office. He'd recorded his voice to say "Come in here," and "Are you coming or what?" That kind of thing, like he was getting angry.'

'What? How the hell would it do that?!'

Davie smiled like a kid who'd beaten a grown-up at a hand of poker. He took an excited breath and stumbled over his words as he explained how he and Drummond had found speakers wired to Scott Patterson's PC, demanding attention and then suddenly falling silent.

'And Drummond had never heard it before?'

'Nope. I wanted to ask the secretary the same question, that was why I was calling her. It's weird, isn't it? It was so lifelike, it was creepy. Like he was right there in the office. Drummond said it was definitely Scott Patterson's voice.'

'But why would Patterson want someone to think he was in the office?'

'Maybe to stop people coming in when he was giving himself his injections? Oh no, that doesn't work. Maybe … I don't know.'

Murdoch rubbed the stubble of his scalp. 'Talking of injections, d'you find anything to do with that. No syringes or nothing?'

'Nothing at all. I'm sure *you* might have spotted something.'

Murdoch sighed. 'Well, maybe I should go and have a look, then, eh? If only to stop you being so bleeding sarky.'

'Too late. According to Alan Drummond, the police are due round there this morning. They'll probably be there right now. I doubt we'd get within a hundred metres of the place.'

'Oh. Shit. Sorry, mate.'

Davie must have heard the sincerity. He gave his first believable smile of the day and looked down at his notes, reading in silence. Murdoch stood and turned to Davie's desk, leaning forwards and closing his eyes to bathe them in sunlight. *No buses for hours then three come at once* – that was the expression. Where would he have heard that?

'What about them numbers Fran gave us?' he said. 'D'you find anything on them?'

'Yeah, no. I've looked at them so often, I've learned them off by heart. Maybe we should get onto the maths department of some university or something?'

'Nothing on the Google?'

The awkward silence made Murdoch turn, the sun through glass on his neck waking memories of borstal, mucking about at the back of class.

'Davie?'

'Well, who googles numbers?' No one does that. Normally, you put in words when you want to find a number. Here, I'll have a look.'

He stood and came around the table, squinting against the sunlight as he pushed past Murdoch and sat at his desk. Murdoch had always thought it was stupid the way Davie had his computer in the window, an advert to the world the office had something worth nicking. The thought reminded him of Velis again and his assumption the man had been here to steal something.

'Nothing,' said Davie, once he'd brought the internet to life and tapped at it for a while. '"*Your search did not match any documents. Make sure that all words are spelled correctly.*" See?'

Murdoch crouched down and looked at the screen, one hand shielding his eyes against the sun. 'Try just the first few numbers. The first four digits.'

Davie keyed them in. A postcode in Queensland, a model of John Deere tractor.

'Isn't there a geocode thing, like numbers for a location?'

Davie wasn't listening. He was typing again, mumbling, 'Let's try this,' as he entered the first six digits and hit Enter. For a second neither of them said a thing. Then:

'*BSB Number 472-023*,' Murdoch read aloud. '*Central Coast Savings Bank, Crosley Branch*. Click on that.'

Davie didn't click. He turned instead, excitement lighting his face as much as the sun.

'I bet the other numbers are accounts. Or … oh, hang on!'

He turned back to the screen and Murdoch watched him open the Savings Bank's website, scouring the screen with his cursor until he found a yellow button marked *Customer Login*. He entered the next eight digits from Fran Patterson's list into the User Name field, then hesitated.

'No,' Davie mumbled. 'That would be the account number. Let's try this.'

He deleted the digits and brought up the PPC website. Murdoch watched him scroll through the Contact page, noting down on his pad the format of the email addresses listed there, then translating Scott Patterson's name into the same format and, alt-tabbing back to the bank's website, entering it in the User Name field. Murdoch was impressed.

'That's smart,' he said. 'If it works.'

Davie said nothing. He was hovering the cursor over the question mark next to the Password field. 'Eight to twelve digits,' he mumbled, counting on his fingers.

'What you doing?'

'Ssh, watch this.'

Davie typed again, the digits he entered turning into dots in the Password field. He said, 'Cross fingers', hit Enter again and immediately, the blue-and-yellow CCSB logo appeared in the middle of the screen, twirling slowly as the computer and the bank decided if they trusted each other.

'Like dogs sniffing each other's bums,' said Murdoch.

Then the screen flickered again. The CCSB logo had moved to the top left-hand corner and beneath it was written:

Welcome SCOTT. You last logged on at 17:20:29 pm (Sydney/Melbourne time) on 17th February.

Below was a series of menu options and, beside them, an account number, a hyperlink offering a click-through for full transaction details. The mention of the time made Murdoch check his watch again. He swore quietly.

'I know,' said Davie. 'I don't believe it!'

'Nice work, Sherlock. Right, I'll be back as soon as I can.'

'What? Where are you— You can't still be going?!'

Halfway to the top of the stairs, Murdoch hesitated. He knew he should go back to the desk, knew he should sit with Davie and look at Patterson's bank account. He knew it so much, it was like a physical force, pulling him back there. But the pull down to the street was stronger.

The Taradale club room was a place Murdoch remembered as busy and overly loud: kids screaming between the tables, parents discussing what they were watching down on the courts, couples in white with an eager eye on the clock. Today there was none of that, just the Coke fridge and the lights humming at each other across the horrible carpet. Murdoch stood inside the glass doors, thinking maybe it wasn't too late to cancel and go back and help Davie like he ought to do. But then old Bob shuffled out of the racquet room, a folded A4 in his hand like a vague attempt at surrender.

'*Ach, Guten Tag,*' he said, waving the sheet of paper with a laugh. '*Wie geht es Dir?*'

The joke hadn't changed in the missing year. Bob, for some reason, had once thought Murdoch was German and this, for some other reason, was hilarious. In the days when Murdoch had been a regular, it had been impossible for him to walk into Taradale Tennis Club without Bob greeting him in German and everyone falling about. Other than comedy gold, the old man's role at the club was a mystery. Bob played at barista, café manager, receptionist, bookings secretary, racquet stringer or none of the above depending on his unpredictable mood. He was bent and grey with faded eyes, but you could see he'd been a unit in his day.

'Where you been?' he snapped at Murdoch now. 'Thought you'd carked it. Found somewhere better to play?'

'Work. Overseas.'

'Back to Deutschland?'

Bob's croaking laugh turned into a cough and he leaned on a chair to give it full phlegm. Murdoch waited until he'd finished. Then he said, 'I'm meeting a mate here. Booking in the name of Velis?'

'Nah.' Bob shook his head and shuffled over to the noticeboard to pin up the A4 in his hand: a list of singles looking for opponents. 'Someone's been pulling your leg.'

Murdoch swore under his breath: he'd pissed Davie off for nothing. He found his phone and pulled up the text again.

Mate, you said you played tennis. Just been let down for a game at Taradale tmw morning at 11. Any interest? EV.

Murdoch didn't remember giving Velis his number, let alone mentioning anything about tennis.

'No bookings?' he said.

'Plenty of bookings,' Bob shuffled back to the reception desk to study a clipboard lying there. 'No bookings in that name. What time is it? Eleven? So three courts booked ...'

Murdoch crossed the carpet and read over the old man's shoulder searching for 'Velis' amongst the scribbles on the sheet. He felt the nausea of recognition again – bad news in his stomach. Like maybe he hadn't heard Velis's name before meeting the man, but maybe he'd read it somewhere?

Bob grumbled out the sense from his own handwriting. 'Patterson. Haine. Smith. Smith's the only one's not here.'

Traffic noise flooded the room and they both looked up at the heavy glass door to the street. It was like they'd conjured him up by talking about him. Velis, struggling in with an oversized tennis bag, saw them looking and gave them a smile. Bob shouted at him he must be Smith and Velis agreed he was, giving Murdoch a split-second glance to check they were both in on the joke.

They were evenly matched – once they both calmed down and stopped trying to hit the ball too hard. Murdoch, remembering how to play with every stroke, scampered around his end of the court like an animal cleaning its nest. Velis barely moved, constantly too far from the ball until he stretched out a ridiculously long arm and smacked it back again. The points flew back and forth, no faffing around with changing ends until, after almost an hour of occasional cheers, they found themselves at six games apiece. Murdoch was scooting around for the balls, preparing to serve again, when he looked up and found Velis waiting at the net.

'Let's leave it there,' the tall man said. 'That's sweet as it is.'

'You what? We've got a couple of minutes left. Don't we want a winner?'

'Not if the price is a loser.' Velis gave his crocodile smile. 'Let's make it a draw. That way we'll both enjoy it equally. Well, I enjoyed it. But now I've got to shoot.'

'I enjoyed it too, mate.' They shook hands across the net. 'Where you off to then? I didn't think you had to work during the day?'

Murdoch hated it when people asked him the same kind of question: the veiled checking that he really was a man of leisure. Now he understood the curiosity. Velis glanced at his watch with a frown, crossed to the seats beside the court and started gathering his things as he spoke.

'I do, actually – and not only during the day. Listen, we'll play again soon, yeah? How's that case of yours going?'

'Case?'

'The missing guy; what's his name?'

Murdoch had no memory of telling Velis about Scott Patterson. It wasn't the kind of thing he'd normally do. Then again, he had no memory of half the things he and Velis had last spoken about.

'Yeah, fine,' he said. 'Slowly, slowly, catchy monkey, you know.'

Velis nodded vaguely. 'By the way, you ever been canyoning?'

'Canyoning?'

'Yeah, you go up into the mountains, abseil into a creek, follow it through gorges and shit, then float out at the bottom.' He patted his pockets, found his keys and checked his watch again. 'Any interest?'

'Sounds cool,' said Murdoch, who never used the word about anything.

'And, oh, I completely forgot to tell you – what a moron. That's half the reason I wanted to meet up. Mate, that thing with my nephew, that bloke trying it on about health and safety at the timber yard? It's sorted itself out. Turns out Samir's foreman, guy by the name of Cooper, has a kid, right? Anyway, this kid plays touch footie and yesterday morning Cooper's watching the kids at training, and he only recognises the dad doing the coaching. You got it – it's him, the con man! So Cooper whips out his phone to call Samir, then has a better idea and starts videoing, like he's proud of his little kid, you know. A good ten minutes of this so-called health-and-safety victim running around the pitch. Then, because he's that kind of bloke, Cooper just walks up to the bastard, all friendly, introduces himself, reminds our con man who he is and shows him what he's just filmed. Job done! I'm stoked.' Velis remembered too late to control his toothy smile. 'So yeah, sorry about that. Hope I didn't waste

91

your time or nothing with such a furphy? Didn't take you off the Patterson case too much?'

Murdoch told Velis not to worry about it. Told him, 'No worries' and 'You're all good, mate' and 'She'll be right.' He always spoke Australian when he was hiding disappointment: it was like the country had no language for anything but positivity.

'Seriously,' he said, 'I hadn't even raised a finger on it yet. I'll give you that five hundred dollars back.'

Velis looked awkward, the hand from his hair rubbing the back of his neck. 'Aw, well, that was a deposit. My fault, if I lose it.'

'Nah.' Murdoch had his phone out, tapping its screen more gently than he wanted to. 'Give us your account details, I'll transfer it now.'

'It's fine, mate.'

'Not to me, it's not.'

He looked up to find Velis studying him. There was a second or two of silence, dotted by the pock-pock of balls from the other courts and the hum of traffic beyond the club house. When Velis spoke again, he was conciliatory.

'Here's what we'll do. I'll let you give me the money back if you come canyoning with me the day after tomorrow. I was supposed to go with a bunch of guys, but they've decided they want to turn it into a couple of days down in Victoria. I can't do that, but if you come with me I can still do the one-dayer. That way, we're evened out on the favours, eh?'

Murdoch pretended to think about. He spotted a lonely ball near the net, walked over and picked it up.

'Yeah, OK,' he said. 'Why not?'

Velis nodded a firm smile, remembered he was in a hurry and looked around for anything he might have forgotten.

'And don't transfer me the money now. I trust you. I'd prefer cash, anyway. Give my bank details to a private detective, next thing you'll know everything about me!' Velis winked and Murdoch tried to believe he was joking. 'Wednesday, then. I'll call you. Bring an old wetsuit you don't mind getting trashed.' A last glance at his watch and Velis was off the court and into the shadows beneath the club house.

Murdoch took his time getting his things together. Most people he met were bad liars – the truth and bullshit different shapes and colours – but with Velis he had no idea what he was looking at. There was no reason the man should be lying at all, except half the things he said seemed off, shapes that didn't fit together. Would he, Murdoch, really have mentioned that he and Davie were working on the Patterson case? The door in the fence rattled and, looking up, he saw two elderly women in white smiling him politely off the court. Murdoch smiled back and hurried out of the way.

Wednesday, 13th March

Two days before

Halfway home, mired in traffic, something inside Anita changes. It is such a fundamental shift that she can only compare it to childbirth: to the feeling her body has been torn in two to bring someone new into the world. Directly ahead of her little Suzuki, a chugging removalist's lorry mocks her in dirty yellow letters: *We'll get you happily into your home on time!* As the vehicles either side of it move slowly forward, Anita sees she has yet again chosen the slowest lane for the rush hour journey home.

She has never understood why they call it 'rush hour' at all, when rushing is the last thing you can do. The trick, she knows, is to remember you are not in a rush at all. To remember you have nowhere better to be, your daughter already enjoying a bath or, maybe by now, being read a story in bed. To remember that here, right here – alone in a locked car, sweating over the steering wheel – is the safest place you've been in hours. Staring at the back of the removalist's lorry, Anita can still see Scott's vile penis, its slightly open urethra mimicking the panting grin on his face. Fancying she still can smell Scott's breath – or, maybe, something worse – she winds down her window, but the air that breezes in is no fresher than what it replaces.

Ahead of her, the lorry farts out a black cloud that melts surprisingly slowly into the polluted air amongst the traffic. That done, it creeps slowly forward. Anita wonders how many other drivers in this gridlock are here because, like her, their bosses were promising them imminent rape. As the lorry moves further ahead still, Anita wonders what it will take to make her defend herself. To leave another job? To move her family again? To even find the strength to scream aloud when Scott's vice-like hands are on her. *Nothing*, she thinks. *Nothing* will ever make her do it. For she is useless and weak and worthless and, somewhere deep in her gut, she has begun to wonder if this is all her fault. Or if it can really be happening at all?

A loud horn sounds, waking her from her thoughts. Glancing in her rear-view mirror, Anita sees a large white ute is close behind her in the traffic, its small female driver pointing forwards, ahead of Anita's car. Looking back at the road in front of her, Anita notices the lorry is now twenty metres away. She raises a hand to signal sorry and presses on the accelerator but, before she has moved more than a few metres, a car from the left-hand lane nips in front of her without indicating.

'Oh, you bugger!'

Anita brakes suddenly and puts out her left hand instinctively to prevent her handbag, wobbly on the passenger seat, from toppling forwards. But the damned bag is designed to topple, too narrow at the bottom and all its weight in the handles; even as Anita reaches out her hand, she knows she is too late to catch it. The bag falls upside down onto the floor in front of the passenger seat, her purse rolling out, popping itself open and scattering credit cards across the foot mat. Hearing the horn behind again, Anita looks up and sees that, whatever is happening out of sight further down the road, the lane she is in is no longer the slowest. The removalist's lorry is accelerating into the distance, cars from the other two rows pouring into the middle lane behind it, stealing Anita's way home. The horn behind her sounds again. This time, Anita ignores it. Instead she stares down at her purse, open on the floor in front of the passenger seat. From behind the transparent panel of a card holder, her favourite photograph of Riya stares back. Riya is not smiling in the picture. Rather, she is glowering, pulling that face that lets the world know she will get her way.

'I know you like to get home to Riya on time.' Scott Patterson's words ring so clearly in Anita's head, it is as if he is sitting in the back seat. 'Give her my love when you're in the bath together.'

And just like that, Anita knows *nothing* is wrong. For there is something that will drive her to act. She herself might be worthless and useless and deserving to suffer, but Riya is none of those things. Scott's vile implication, the idea he might one day get close to her little girl, the idea that he even knows Riya's name, is more than enough. And so – as the white ute swerves around her Suzuki in a cacophony of horns – a new being is born. Anita will no longer be the weak and flailing victim. Instead, she will inhabit a new kind of loneliness. Instead, she will be—

No. Instead, she already *is* whoever she needs to be to kill Scott Patterson.

Tuesday, 19th March

Four days after

Tuesday arrived too fast and, blinking in the sunlight that slashed his bed, Murdoch regretted his planning. Over the previous year he'd grown used to solitude and now the idea of more chatter was daunting. But he stretched and scratched and reminded himself this was what he wanted. What, underneath it all, he'd always known he needed: to get a life and have some fun. The idea that he was doing just that brought a shadow of guilt. Like surviving the loss of Amanda made his grief less real somehow. He swore aloud, jumped out of bed and tore the curtains fully open. Amanda wouldn't have stood for any of that bullshit.

He was at the top of the house, choosing a shirt in his dressing room, when Davie called. Murdoch answered on the first ring.

'Happy Birthday, Davie Wonder. You looking forward to lunch?'

'Please don't call me that, but, yeah, I can't wait. That's why I'm calling. Can we move it?'

'Move it?' Catching his reflection in the mirror, Murdoch tried a nicer face. 'Sure, I'll call them. What time?'

'No, I mean move it to somewhere else. I'll explain when I see you, but it's good news. It's about the case. We've got an appointment in Crosley at 2 p.m., so I was thinking we could eat somewhere there. I've booked a place.'

Murdoch turned his back on the mirror. He'd done two days' research before booking Brown's in Matilda Bay at high tide.

'Mate, how does that work? I'm taking you out for lunch, I find a nice place, I book it and now you're changing everything. That's like saying you don't like your present.'

'No, it's not,' said Davie. 'It's like you offering me a present and me saying, "No, thanks, I'll have that one instead." Besides, it's my birthday so I choose where we eat, don't I?'

Murdoch scowled. Davie knew he didn't know the answer to that one.

An hour and a half later and Murdoch's mood hadn't improved. The Uber driver hadn't stopped talking – you couldn't tell these people to shut up, they gave you a score – and now it looked like he hadn't even brought Murdoch to the right place. Brown's, his original booking, was an open-fronted restaurant on the edge of a bay, boats bobbing on the water and sunlight in the cutlery and the glasses. This place was a greasy spoon two streets behind Crosley police station. Peering through the huge window, Murdoch saw fifties-style counters and black-and-white tiles, fancy ketchup bottles on check paper tablecloths. Someone had scratched the word '*SLOPES*' into the window, the sun stretching the angry letters across the service counter. The racist scum of Crosley could pollute even the places they couldn't get into.

Murdoch wanted to go in and give the business his support on principle, but it was still a greasy spoon. He was checking Davie's text, regretting his smart jacket, when the birthday boy himself arrived in shorts and an old polo shirt, his tattered satchel over one shoulder.

'Look,' he said, beaming. 'I'm not late! Crikey, Bill, you look smart.'

'Yeah, funny that. Thought I was going somewhere nice, didn't I? What we got on at two, gardening?'

Davie's smile didn't falter. 'I'll tell you all about it inside. Come on, I'm starving.'

'Just tell me this place sells alcohol.'

'What?'

'Davie, I got all dressed up for a nice meal and I got an Uber here so I could have a few glasses of wine.'

'Don't worry. Just remember, it's *my* birthday. Did you get me a present?'

'Yeah, not punching you in the mouth. Go on, then, Goldilocks, after you.'

There had been a time when Murdoch had enjoyed watching the millions grab a hurried bite for lunch. It was a reminder he'd not only survived but thrived, beaten the system that, from birth until then, had squashed him almost flat. But you can get used to anything. Freedom from the daily grind was no longer enough to make him feel special, not when he'd planned an afternoon in a fancy restaurant. He wanted to be the man in a crisp white shirt, knees under a crisper tablecloth, choosing wine like it was important. Over egg and chips, Davie told him about Scott Patterson's bank account.

'So, first of all there's absolutely no connection between the account we found and PPC. I called Alan Drummond and he put me onto the blokes in Finance. They didn't recognise the account number at all; PPC does all its banking with NAB. Secondly, the numbers going through this account are big. Not many transactions, about one credit and one debit every month on average, the credits always much bigger than the debits. Always to and from the same account, it looks like; maybe, but I can't be sure. Some are referenced "Ham Ent", but most aren't referenced at all. The bank wouldn't tell me a thing and they got a bit iffy when I couldn't tell them my phone ID. Then, every so often there are these other transactions, payments to overseas accounts. I'll show you.'

Davie speared too many chips and forced them into his mouth. As he chewed, he searched in the satchel squeezed onto the seat beside him, producing at last a manila file, obviously new, but already dog-eared from its journey. He opened it on the table beside his plate, pushing past a dozen oversized colour photographs as he looked for the bank statements. Murdoch pointed with his fork.

'What's them?'

'The photos I took of Patterson's office. I tried to get every angle so we don't have to go back to remember what it's like.'

Murdoch put down the fork and reached across to lift the topmost image: a strange angle of carpet and skirting board. 'How much did it cost you to get all this lot printed?'

Davie didn't look up. 'Nothing. I bought a printer for the office yesterday. I figure it's easier than running down to Anne at the general store with a USB key every time.'

'So not nothing, then. How d'you afford a printer?'

'You've got to speculate to accumulate. It's like that PR I'm organising. I've already got some interviews arranged and, if they appear at the same time as the press coverage of us finding Patterson, the two can leverage off each other. Got it!' Davie pulled out three pages of figures, each with a few lines highlighted, and looked up to find Murdoch shaking his head. 'What?'

'Mate, do me a favour. Slow down on the PR and, above all, stop spending money what you haven't got.'

Davie passed over the statements, picked up his cutlery and spoke through more chips.

'Trust me, it'll work. Now, see there on the pages, I've highlighted the overseas transactions. That's the name of who it went to. And here' – fork down, another rummage through the manila file – 'are the Google results for them.'

'You're printing out Google results now? What's the point of that?'

'It's for the file. You've got to keep proper files, everyone knows that.'

Murdoch sighed and looked at the search engine results, every page in a foreign language. Inside he'd known plenty of blokes who couldn't read and had often wondered what that would be like.

'That one's Cambodian,' said Davie, his ketchupy knife spattering the pages like a murder scene. 'That's Vietnamese and that's Chinese.'

'Maybe that's where Patterson gets his ARVs from.'

'His what?'

'Antiretrovirals. HIV drugs.'

A young waitress walked over to take Murdoch's plate and asked him if he wanted anything else.

'Yeah,' he said. 'Can you read Chinese, love?'

The waitress nodded like it was a normal order. 'My dad can. I'll go and get him.'

As soon as she'd gone Davie hissed across the table. 'Bill, for goodness sake, that's so culturally insensitive. She might have been Vietnamese or Filipina or something.'

'Davie, mate, she looks about as Vietnamese as you do. And, trust me, she's not hot enough to be from the Philippines.' Davie, clearly struggling between reasons to disapprove, sat shaking his head in silence, so Murdoch went on. 'Listen, what do you know about canyoning? You ever done it?'

'Canyoning? Once, yeah. It's OK, depends where you go. Generally involves hanging around with a bunch of macho dils desperate to prove how tough they are.'

'Right. Not too dangerous, then?'

'Of course, it is, I think that's what's supposed to make it fun. You just have to make sure you go with a pro. Hey, we should get the bill. We've got to be down the road soon.'

A short man in a black T-shirt appeared at the table beside them, a dirty apron around his waist. He had a severe expression under unruly eyebrows, his face covered in a thin sheen of kitchen sweat.

'This your place?' said Murdoch. 'Nicely done. Bit too nice for Crosley.'

The older man stared and Murdoch felt himself blush. He'd seen protection done often enough to know how he sounded. He held up the sheet of paper in his hand.

'Yeah, so I was just asking your daughter if you could help us understand this? If you don't mind …'

The man reached out, snatched the paper and read it quickly.

'This about newspaper in Lanzhou,' he said. 'Different things like website, articles from newspaper. You go to Lanzhou? Try Guangzhou instead.'

'We're just curious about it,' said Davie. 'What does this word "*bàozhǐ*" mean?'

He was reading a transaction detail from Patterson's bank statement. The old man corrected his pronunciation.

'Newspaper,' he said. 'But this local newspaper. Nothing big. Like *Gazette* round here.'

He produced a yellow-toothed smile, put it away again, turned and walked back to the kitchen, shouting at his daughter on the way. She laughed and walked over to the table.

'Dad says not to go to Lanzhou. It's a shithole. Can I get you guys anything else?'

Davie asked for the bill, hurrying the statements and photos back into the manila folder.

'So you gonna tell me where we going?' said Murdoch. 'And that they serve alcohol?'

'Natalie's asked to see us at the police station.'

Murdoch had started shuffling out of the booth. Now he sat down again.

'You're fucking kidding me.'

Davie only ever looked this wide-eyed when he knew he'd done something wrong. 'No, it's all right. She said it was good news.'

'Yeah, she's just saying that to get us down the nick. What's the bet she'll produce someone too important to wear a uniform what'll give us a bollocking and tell us to mind our own business?'

'She wouldn't do that.'

Davie stood and lifted his bag, knocking over the ketchup and salt in the process.

'Davie, she does that every time.'

'Not this time. She said she had a birthday present for me.'

With his shorts and his satchel, Davie looked like an eight-year-old waiting to be taken to his party. Murdoch said nothing. Natalie could be the one to disappoint him.

The previous time Detective Constable Natalie Conquest had pulled them into the station for a bollocking, she had led them past reception, through a heavy security door and down a cold corridor to the interview rooms. The first sign that anything was different today was the plain-clothes officer waiting for them behind the desk. He was slim and bearded with pockmarked skin and a faint English accent. Natalie had obviously given him a good description of Murdoch and Davie because, as soon as they walked into the station, the bearded officer shouted something back to a colleague – a blurred silhouette behind a frosted glass partition – then told them to wait for a second so he could take them upstairs.

'DC Conquest not here?' asked Murdoch.

'It's DS Conquest now. Liaison to the Serious Crime Squad.'

'Right. So, basically, too important to come and fetch us herself?'

Murdoch had meant it as a joke, but the officer behind the counter didn't laugh. He told them to hang on, then walked behind the frosted glass so he too became a blurred silhouette. Davie didn't laugh either. He nudged Murdoch in the ribs and reminded him he was going to be nice.

'You're lucky it's your bleeding birthday, mate, else I wouldn't be here at all.'

Davie looked around, like he'd only just cottoned on they were in a police station. Like the crime posters and the dirty yellow floor, and the attitude behind the desk, could have had them anywhere else. 'You need to move on, Bill,' he said, whispering for some reason. 'You're a good guy now, remember? This is probably the safest place for you.'

Murdoch said nothing. He felt vaguely sick, uncertain whether to blame his surroundings or the hurried egg and chips. Nowhere was that safe. The Club was like a cockroach infestation – you only ever controlled it for a while. The previous year, Ibrahim Hussein had reminded him of that. Murdoch was frowning the memory shut again when the security door rattled and swung towards them, revealing the bearded copper. He was shorter than he had been behind the counter and even slimmer somehow, but the skin and the attitude were no better.

'Right then,' he said. 'Shall we?'

The meeting room was on the third floor, halfway along a peeling corridor that, even after a smoke-free decade, still stank of cigarettes. It reminded Murdoch of a seaside hotel he'd once hidden in out of season. The smell of other people's fun, he remembered, was never a good thing. They crossed an empty common room: cheap chairs around a tea-stained table, a fragile fern waiting for water, then pushed through a swing door into a second corridor. It was as empty as the first but for the odd smug uniform strolling past, happy not to be on the beat.

While Davie made small talk with the bearded copper, Murdoch trailed behind and read the signs on the thin wooden doors. He was on the point of asking a question about them when their guide stopped and told them they'd arrived. Room 3.17: a yellow-ceilinged box with a table, four chairs, a scarred whiteboard and a greying clock. The only light came through a thickly stippled window: the outside world an abstract concept.

'Won't be long,' said the beard – obviously a guess – and left them with the door open.

'Crikey.' Davie rubbed his hands together as he walked round the table. 'It's freezing in here.'

'Must be all the demons.' Murdoch pulled out a chair, turned it the wrong way and straddled it. Not exactly comfortable in his smartest trousers, but the point was clear enough. 'It's these buildings what make most coppers wankers, I reckon. Bit of nice décor and they might chill out a bit. Reckon I could get away with a smoke?'

Davie's face froze in an awkward smile. Murdoch turned and saw a man in a shirt and tie had appeared in the doorway behind him. He had the heavy, tired skin of all senior coppers: too much time at work and not enough fresh air. A broad flat nose and a wide mouth pushed his cheeks into jowls; dark circles sat under his smiling eyes.

'Detective Inspector Pete Mackintosh,' he said, crossing the threadbare carpet with a hand out to shake. 'But you can call me Chief Wanker. You must be Stereotypically Surly Ex-Con?'

Even Murdoch had to smile at that. He stood to shake Mackintosh's hand and was watching Davie do the same when the plain-clothes beard returned, followed by Natalie in her normal uniform: white T-shirt and tight jeans, hair back in a ponytail. She was carrying a heavy stack of papers and forced a smile when she saw the happy family scene. She suggested they all sit down, and Murdoch turned his chair round the right way.

'So,' Detective Inspector Mackintosh said to Davie, 'you're the famous detective. Natalie tells me it's your birthday today. Many happy returns.'

Davie went red and made some simpering reply that the DI turned into small talk. Murdoch sat back to wait until it was done, ignoring the scowls from the beard beside him and wondering what they were all doing there. He wanted a fag, wanted to read up on canyoning and have those few glasses of wine. Natalie nodded him in towards her.

'Listen,' she said quietly. 'You giving Davie a lift home after this?'

Murdoch shook his head.

'Good. Hang back, if you can. I want to ask you something in private.'

'So let's get down to business, shall we?' Detective Inspector Mackintosh checked his watch against the clock on the wall. 'Conquest, do you want to explain why we're all here?'

Natalie sat up straight and Murdoch looked at his hands, across the table, at Davie and past him to the window. Anywhere but at what Natalie's nipples were doing to the fabric of her T-shirt. None of the other men seemed to have noticed.

'Yes, sir. Bill, Davie, I've been appointed the OIC on the Scott Patterson case and I've proposed an idea which is a little unconventional, but which Detective Inspector Mackintosh here is far-sighted and brave enough to give a go.'

Mackintosh laughed. 'Quit the suck-up, Conquest, and get on with it before I change my mind.'

The beard – yet to be introduced – snorted quietly at this. Natalie blushed, a thing Murdoch wasn't aware she was capable of, frowned and bit her lip. Her boss's comment had kicked her off-rhythm and Murdoch felt an urge to tell her everything was OK.

'As you both know,' she said, 'Broadwater detectives have not previously been welcoming of your ... or, well ... any private investigators' involvement in ... well, investigating criminal activity. But a recent change in leadership has given us an opportunity to review the situation as regards to, well ... co-operation with external parties.'

'Jesus, Conquest! You're not in court. Just spit it out.'

'Er … well, the thing is …'

Natalie consulted her notes, her mouth worried by what she read, while the DI sighed and looked at the clock again.

'Don't tell me you want to hire us?' Murdoch offered.

It did the trick. 'No,' said Natalie with a challenging look. 'We suspect someone's already done that. As I said, I'm the OIC on the Scott Patterson case. On Saturday morning we trailed Patterson's wife, Fran, to Montauban. There she paid a visit to Davie Simms Detection Services.'

Murdoch remembered the clunky walkie-talkie on Natalie's belt, her rush down to the beach to question him. There must have been another cop or two in plain clothes up on the street. He looked at the bearded officer beside him, trying to remember if he'd seen him there. When the beard smirked in return, Murdoch turned back to Natalie with a flat-eyed grin.

'Don't know what you're talking about,' he said. 'I was chatting with you. The perfect alibi.'

Natalie rolled her eyes. 'The perfect witness, you mean. I followed Davie's surf mates up the path, I saw you two run across the road and enter Davie's office. I saw Fran Patterson enter a minute or two later. Let me guess, she was lost and looking for directions? Was that why she was gazing out the window for a while? Don't try and deny it, Bill. Anyway, I'm not sure if you heard what I was trying to say before: we don't actually mind. What we're looking for is co-operation.'

'Really?!' said Davie excitedly. 'You want us to work together? Share what we find out about Scott Patterson?'

Murdoch shook his head. Davie obviously hadn't twigged that maybe, on Sunday, he'd been followed too. Maybe Natalie and her team had seen him visiting the offices of PPC, proving Fran had misled the police and helped him contaminate a potential crime scene. Beside him, the bearded copper snorted again and Murdoch wondered what the man would look like with a fist in his face. Natalie, meanwhile, was telling Davie that she always wanted him to share anything he discovered in the course of an investigation.

'But the difference is, this time, we're willing to share what we know with you. You two have been successful in the past, and given we could better direct our resources elsewhere, there doesn't seem any reason for us to be in competition. For the first time, we're willing to share our case file with you.'

She made eye contact with Davie as she emphasised *for the first time*, but Murdoch thought she was taking a hell of a risk. He wouldn't put it past Davie to forget that the previous time she'd let them see a file had been a breach that could have ended her career. But Davie had either cottoned on fast or, more likely, forgotten there had been a previous time.

'Really?!' he said again. 'Brilliant! That's fantastic news. When can we see it?'

Natalie pulled out the bottom half of the papers in front of her: a small pile of papers in a manila folder similar to the one Davie had in his satchel.

'Naturally, you will need to keep in regular contact with us. Weekly updates to DC Burran here.' She looked at the plain-clothes man expectantly, but he gave nothing in return. 'Immediate notification of anything material you uncover.'

'Well, then,' said Mackintosh standing suddenly. 'I'll leave you to it. Not sure why I was here in the first place.'

With no further comment he left the room, closing the door gently behind him.

'You need me for this bit?' DC Burran said, standing like he already had his answer.

Natalie shook her head and they watched him leave too.

'They seem nice,' said Davie. 'Let's see the file.'

'They seem like a right pair of tossers,' said Murdoch. 'What d'you bring the big cheese in for?

Natalie sighed, something like a smile teasing her mouth. 'That's what we in the job call an ACE. An Arse Covering Exercise. I wanted to make sure the DI was in the room when I showed you the file. Just so, later on, he can't deny he approved your involvement.'

'Why would he do that?' Davie asked the question vaguely, his attention on the papers under Natalie's hand. A dog waiting for its bone.

'In case we cock things up,' said Murdoch. 'Or get caught being naughty boys.'

'Which you're not going to do.' Natalie gave them a stern look, one after the other. 'That's part of the deal. We share information with you and you don't do anything illegal.'

'No problem,' said Davie. 'Promise. Let's look at the file.'

'Bill?'

When Murdoch said nothing, Natalie sighed and pulled the file towards her.

'Come on, Bill,' whined Davie. 'If the police are helping us, we probably won't need to do anything naughty. Besides, now that we know how urgent it is we find Pat—'

Murdoch's kick wasn't meant to be subtle, not from a pain point of view, but he didn't mean Natalie to see either. Davie went puce and had the sense to stop talking, but Natalie was unimpressed.

'Great,' she said. 'So glad you're getting into the new spirit of things. Sharing information so we can all move forward.'

Murdoch scowled at her. 'And you are? Bringing us in and pretending you don't want us to do nothing what you lot can't do yourselves. You know what that bloke downstairs told us? He said you was helping out the Serious Crime Squad. But every office on this floor is highway patrol, traffic services, public prosecution. What we doing here? What's going on what you're not telling us, Nat? Wouldn't be anything life-threatening for me, would it?'

Natalie shook her head and studied her hands. When she looked up again she was smiling.

'It was tough enough getting the DI to this floor, I'd never have got him down to the interview rooms. Yes, Bill, very good. There is potentially another element to this and we'd like to keep it at arm's length from the rest of the team. Just a person of interest who might be involved, that's all. I suspect this same person of interest is why Fran Patterson has brought you two in. She probably … Actually, that's confidential. The point is, this person of interest is no one from your past. Nothing to do with the Club or their suppliers, otherwise I wouldn't have involved you. But, in case this person of interest *is* involved, we want to keep the case away from … other things I'm working on. I can't tell you any more than that.'

'Really?' he said. 'Nothing to do with the Club? You sure? That's not what you wanted to tell me in private later?'

Natalie blushed and said 'No' so quietly that Murdoch almost regretted asking.

'Can we see the file now?' said Davie, eager to unwrap his present. 'Come on, what's in it?'

Natalie pushed the papers roughly across the table, more annoyed with the two of them or with herself, it wasn't clear.

'Nothing in there gets copied or goes off the premises,' she said, her in-charge face back on. 'I've got this room booked for two hours. If you need longer than that, I can move you somewhere else.'

Davie mumbled, 'OK', but he was barely listening. He was already pushing a finger along the opening lines of the first page in the file. Murdoch was curious to see what was in there too. He wanted to read the witness statements, check for descriptions of anyone he might want to avoid. First things first, though; he stood and stretched and told the room he needed a fag.

'Outside,' said Natalie. 'But not within twenty metres of the building.'

Murdoch held her eye and asked if she'd keep him company. She nodded and was standing up – Davie already in another world – when there was a tap on the door. A spherical woman in a muumuu wheezed into the room.

'Boss wants you on the T7 conference call,' she told Natalie. 'You're late.'

She looked at Murdoch like it was his fault, turned and wheezed away again. Natalie gave him a smile and put a hand on his forearm.

'We'll talk later.'

Murdoch had his cigarette in the beer garden of a pub that was dying on Macquarie Road. It was a concrete space like a prison yard, plastic chairs between high walls that made you wonder who was supposed to be hidden: the smokers behind the pub or the smackheads in the alley beyond. It wasn't the afternoon he'd planned but he told himself it was more interesting than most had been of late. Hadn't he been excited about a case to work on? Hadn't he told himself this would be a chance to help people out? To do some good and balance all the bad he'd ever done? Not to mention making it up to Davie for the cases in the past when he'd only taken part begrudgingly. The ideas were the same as when he'd first thought them – when Davie had called on Friday evening to say they had a case – but for some reason the feeling had gone. Instead, he found himself smiling at the memory of his race along the Crown Road and wondering exactly how dangerous canyoning would be.

Back in 3.17 – where Davie had progressed to page three of the file – Murdoch had to threaten physical violence before the birthday boy agreed to share his present. He soon regretted asking. The amount of information was daunting, the level of detail a long joke, bad from the beginning. Beneath still-blank templates for suspect interviews were pages full of language that reminded Murdoch of time spent in courtrooms: *I-proceeded-to*–this and *the-witness-confirmed*–that.

Several motorists had seen Patterson swerve off the road shortly after 10 a.m. on Friday morning (three paragraphs of precise location and estimated speed). Between ten and fifteen minutes later, an ambulance crew had arrived to find Patterson unconscious in his vehicle (four paragraphs of precise medical assistance provided on-site). At 10.40 a.m., an emergency physician at Crosley General – his arrogance wafting off the page – had averted further disaster by checking what was already in Patterson's system, discovering indications of 'enough benzos to bring down a water buffalo'. Murdoch flipped to a reference note. 'Benzos', or 'benzodiazepine receptor agonists' were, apparently, commonly found in sleeping tablets.

'Here,' he said, turning the page so Davie could see. 'Fran Patterson never told us her old man had drugs in his system, did she?'

Davie shook his head as he read the note slowly. 'No. Makes sense about him falling asleep at the wheel, though. Maybe she didn't know?'

Murdoch turned the page back and read on. At 11 a.m. the police, who had arrived at the scene of the accident to find the ambulance had already left (nearly two pages justifying that), arrived at the hospital. At

11.20 a.m. they called Fran Patterson as Scott's next of kin. Shortly before 1 p.m., after initial treatment of his wounds, Patterson was taken to a private room. There, another doctor, a Beneshte Sherezade – having confirmed the patient was in a semi-conscious but stable condition – organised monitoring of his vital parameters. The last time anyone in the hospital had seen Patterson was when a Zoe Cushing, described as an Enrolled Nurse, had passed the open door of his room. That had been close to the start of her shift, estimated between 1.30 p.m. and 1.45 p.m. The patient, Nurse Cushing confirmed, had been asleep. It was shortly after 2 p.m. that anyone noticed anything wrong. Dr Sherezade had returned to check a few things: haemodynamics, pulse oximetry, cardiac rhythm – no mention Murdoch could see of anything relating to HIV – but had found Patterson's room in a mess. A table on its side, bedclothes on the floor, sensor wires and the IV tube hanging loose. The monitor Patterson had been wired up to had been turned off.

Murdoch moved on to statements from more doctors and nurses. From orderlies, catering staff, the hospital receptionists, patients in nearby rooms. But whether Patterson had left the hospital of his own accord, or was taken by force, no one who worked there had seen a thing.

Next were the statements of Alan Drummond and Fran Patterson who, one after the other, had rushed to the hospital. They had nothing to add but their worries. The police had asked if there was anyone who might wish Patterson harm, then about Patterson's frame of mind, his feelings about hospitals, if he'd expressed any suicidal intent.

'CCTV.'

Murdoch blinked himself up from the pages in front of him. 'You what?'

'CCTV,' said Davie again. 'There's a plan here of level three of the hospital with all the cameras. The one covering Patterson's room was smashed, but it would be good to look at the others, don't you think?'

Murdoch studied the plan. The private room Patterson had been in was only a few doors away from an unmonitored stairwell. With the right CCTV camera smashed, it wouldn't have been difficult to get the man away unseen. But that implied a professional job, the involvement of someone smart enough to think things through in advance.

Remembering Davie had asked him a question, he rifled through the pages in front of him.

'Yeah,' he said, pulling out a report by DC Burran. 'The cops already did that. According to this, Burran watched every second of every working camera in the vicinity from two hours before Patterson was found to be missing until one hour afterwards. Nothing suspicious, except some unidentified feet in one corner of a shot during the time when Patterson could have been taken.' He found the relevant paragraph. 'Burran says there's no way anyone could "ascertain the likelihood of this being material". And that's it, nothing else.'

'Let me see.'

Murdoch handed the page over without asking why and went back to his reading.

An hour later, back from his next cigarette with takeaway coffees, he found the floor covered with Davie's colour photographs. Davie was kneeling beside them, his laptop retrieved from his satchel and displaying, as Davie clicked through them, a series of black-and-white images.

'What's this?'

Davie didn't look up. 'Those are my photos and these, on the laptop, are the ones the police took yesterday morning when they went in. There was a USB key in the file. I'm just seeing if there's anything I forgot to get a picture of.'

Murdoch rolled his eyes. 'I notice they don't waste money printing stuff out.'

Davie ignored the comment, took his coffee without saying thank you, and went back to learning how to photograph a crime scene. Murdoch forced himself back to the file, picking up the pages Davie had already read. They detailed garage reports, phone record research warrants, known offenders in the local area. Submissions to major banks asking for alerts in the case of ATM or other withdrawals. Similar submissions to Medicare and Centrelink, and others to police organisations across Australia. Even one to the Department of Immigration and Border Protection in case Patterson's passport was used. All of it in mind-numbing detail. Murdoch rubbed his eyes and sat up to stretch. He was staring at the whiteboard, half his brain deciphering the rubbed-out writing there, the other half thinking what he might have for his tea, when, beside him on the floor, Davie gasped and sat up, eyes and mouth open wide.

'Oh man!'

'Pins and needles?'

'No, look at this.' Davie held up a photograph, then tilted his laptop so Murdoch could see the screen. 'See, this is the one the police took. It's Scott Patterson's office from the inside corner facing back to the window onto the road. And this is the one I took from the same angle. See?'

Murdoch didn't see. He got off his chair, squatted down and made Davie show him again.

'So?'

'You tell me.'

Murdoch stared at the two images, one on paper, one on the screen: a tidily-arranged desk top, an office chair dark against the windows. 'Sorry, Davie, mate, I'm not getting it.'

'Look at the stuff on the desk.'

Murdoch stared again, shaking his head until Davie pointed at a specific part of each photograph.

'Nah. It's just the different light. The angle or something.'

He pulled the laptop and the photograph from Davie's hands and stood, legs aching from the awkward crouch. Davie stood too, breathing too close as he peered excitedly at the pictures. Murdoch gestured with the laptop.

'When was this taken?'

'I told you, yesterday. And that one was from Sunday, one day before, when I was there by myself.'

'And who had access to the office between then?'

'Alan Drummond has a key and the secretary might have one. I'm not sure who else, Fran Patterson, maybe? But they say no one went in.'

Murdoch looked at the photographs again. Heavy in his left hand, the laptop showed a police photograph of a pen, a stapler and a Canterbury Bulldogs mug tidily arranged on a desk. In his right hand was the same desk the day before. Shiny on Davie's high-quality paper, the pen, stapler and mug were all still there. But the mug stood at a slightly different angle and it was emblazoned with a different logo.

'Oh!'

Davie found his satchel and, after some digging, produced an oversized magnifying glass. They passed it back and forth, until even Murdoch was convinced the mug in the Davie's photo was different from the one on the laptop screen. It had what looked like a Central Coast Mariners' logo. Natalie found them playing spot the difference.

'Time's up,' she said. 'At least for this room. What are you two up to?'

At the expression on their faces she barked an angry laugh.

'Oh, don't bother, pretend I didn't ask. Listen, one of the interview rooms downstairs is free if you want to carry on for a while?'

Murdoch rubbed his back and said he'd rather stick pins in his eyes. Davie said, 'Yes please, definitely,' snapped his laptop shut and squatted down to gather his photographs together, meticulously rearranging them in their original order. After a minute of watching him, Murdoch sighed and raised his eyebrows at Natalie.

'Tell you what, Davie,' she said. 'How about, when you've done that, you go back down to reception and ask Bethany on the desk to show you to an interview room?'

Davie barely nodded. He shuffled the laptop and his photographs into his satchel like a kid late for school, then turned his attention to the police file, still splayed across the table. Murdoch and Natalie left him to it.

They walked along the corridors, down the stairs and through reception in silence. Murdoch's head was still full of the information in the file, the professionalism of the job. He had no idea what was keeping Natalie so quiet. Outside it was later than he had realised, the dirty autumn sun heading for the hills and the breeze whispering of the cold night to come. He stopped at the first corner and Natalie stood close beside him, rubbing her bare arms and avoiding the commuters who filled the pavements around them. Murdoch rubbed his eyes with his knuckles.

'You tired, Bill?'

'Bit. My brain's not used to taking so much in, or I've got lazy or something. Mind you, I had a big weekend – they take longer to get over these days.'

Natalie shook her head slowly. 'Please, you're breaking my heart. Meanwhile, I'm working two jobs. They only let me take this DS gig if I promised to finish that other piece I'm working on. I reckon they thought I'd say no, the whole thing's so under-resourced. It's got to the point where, every time I go to my Local Area Manager to ask him for more people, he says 'no' before I open my mouth. I got here at seven thirty this morning and I'll be here till eight tonight.'

Murdoch didn't respond. He was curious about 'that other piece' she was working on: the person of interest linking it to the Patterson case. But Natalie clearly felt she'd told him enough. They stood in an awkward silence until Murdoch checked his watch and said he better get going. Natalie frowned and nodded and said nothing, but still he didn't go. Instead they stood again, unspeaking, the crowds of Crosley pushing past, half a minute or more until an irritated car horn on the road beside them broke whatever the moment had been. They spoke at the same time – 'Listen' and 'Did you want to tell me something?' – and laughed like it was funny not embarrassing. Murdoch took Natalie by the elbow and guided her to the doorway of an abandoned shop where he made a show of finding his cigarettes and, slower still, his lighter, like he could somehow magic the silence back.

'It's nothing,' Natalie said suddenly. 'Well, it sounded better in my head when I thought it last night, but that was after a glass of wine.'

'Just say it.' He lit up and held the cigarette at arm's length out of the doorway, like it didn't deserve the secret she was about to share. When Natalie crinkled her nose, he said, 'Actually, tell you what, I'll put this out and—'

'No, don't. I'm going to say this and then I'm going to go, so you may as well smoke it. I was just going to say that normally, when you and Davie are on a case … well, you find an excuse to have a drink with me or a meal or something because you need some information. But now I've persuaded the DI to share the file with you, so you won't have a chance to do that. So I'm going to invite you to dinner instead. At my house.'

'Right.'

'But you don't have to, not if you don't want to. I won't be offended.'

He looked at her and knew she would be. It was an invitation to more than dinner.

'It's fine,' Natalie said, pushing her hair out of her eyes and trying a smile that didn't work. 'Maybe another time. Look, I better get back.'

'No.'

'No?'

'No, not another time. I mean, yeah, I'd like to come to dinner. That'd be nice.' *Nice?* He took a drag he wasn't ready for. 'When exactly?'

Maybe she hadn't thought they'd get this far. She pushed her hair away again, bit her lip and frowned. Told him it couldn't be before the weekend – like she'd said, she was working all hours. What about Saturday?

Murdoch pretended to check the calendar on his phone, unsure what he thought about the whole idea. It could only mean complications. But, conscious of Natalie's nervousness beside him, he told her sure, why not, he'd bring a bottle of wine. Which meant now they had to say goodbye. Murdoch thought he should reach in for a kiss on the cheek, but Natalie must have seen him coming. She checked her wrist like she was wearing a watch, made an excuse and ran back towards the police station. Watching her go, Murdoch wondered if, somehow this week, Natalie had become more attractive. How the hell else could he have lived in the same small town as the woman and not noticed her for so long?

But the answers to that question were easy enough. Anger, Amanda, grief – either in that order or whatever order you wanted. There had even been a time, in the darkest of days, when he had wondered if Natalie wasn't secretly pleased Amanda was out of the way. After all, hadn't Natalie been the one, all those years ago, who'd been so pissed off when their one-night stand hadn't turned into anything else? Maybe he was remembering that wrong, maybe not; either way, it was a long time ago. More important was now and now she was inviting him to dinner.

A long-forgotten discomfort twisted his face – smoke in his eyes, one cheek too hot – and Murdoch remembered, the first time in a long time, what it was like to smile with a fag stuck in your mouth.

Thursday, 14th March

One day before

Early in the morning, groggy after another night of terrible sleep, Anita calls Alan Drummond. She is sick, she tells him, she is not coming to work and it's up to him to tell Scott.

'You know what he's like, Alan – he doesn't believe in illness. If I tell him, he'll find a way to make me come in.'

Alan is unsure – she can picture him squinting behind his dirty glasses – but today Anita is not taking no for an answer. She moves from asking Alan to telling him. He has to inform Scott because she won't. Scott's calendar is up-to-date and she'll be back in tomorrow. She's sure everyone can cope until then.

Hanging up on Alan gives Anita further strength. During the lonely quiet of the previous night, she has worried that daylight will drag her back to reason, morning revealing her new plans as yet more waking dreams. She is, after all, no stranger to the desolate hours between midnight and dawn when everything seems possible because you don't have to do it yet. Equally, she is no stranger to fantasies. How could she be when there nothing else that lulls her to sleep? Not even her mother's sleeping pills can do that any more, not since Ma noticed her dwindling supply and started hiding the tablets.

At the thought of the sleeping pills, Anita finds herself smiling. How sadly typical it is of her mother to vanish away the plastic bottle containing six or seven remaining tablets, and yet leave the repeat prescription – good for another fifty – in the hall drawer. Anita has spent countless nights fantasising how to get that prescription made up. Now she has a plan.

First, though, she has to deal with her mother, a far more formidable opponent than Alan Drummond. Once she has killed Scott on Friday, Anita knows she will need to come back to an empty house. She knows herself – knows the limitless depths her nerves can sink her to – and she will need a day or two to bring herself back to strength. Her mother will have to go away for the weekend. But, watching Anita hurrying her breakfast, Ma informs her daughter she has absolutely no intention of going away. Her friend, Mrs Shah in Cronulla, might not be free and, even if she was, she hasn't repeated her invitation in weeks. Who is going to look after Riya? What is Anita planning? Is there a man involved? Something in Ma's face quickens at this last suggestion and Anita sees her advantage. She looks away, as if trying to hide her blushes when, really, she is trying to summon them. Then, through a last corner of toast, she confesses: yes, there is a man involved. A nice man from a good Gujarati family with a large house and a very impressive job. It doesn't make her task too easy – her mother demands photographs and family trees – but, in the end, it does the trick. Ma will go to Cronulla early the following morning.

After that, everything seems easy. Or maybe life really is easy when you ignore everyone else's feelings. Riya is already due at a sleepover on Friday night and a birthday party on Saturday, with most of the same friends. With deaf insensitivity, Anita persuades the mother hosting the sleepover to pick up Riya straight from school on Friday and take her to the birthday party on Saturday too. Sitting on the stairs once she's hung up – pretending not to know Ma has been eavesdropping from the lounge room – Anita realises she has no plan for after that. How to get herself into a fit state for caring for Riya when she returns on Saturday afternoon. But that, she decides, is a bridge to be crossed if she makes it that far. Who knows, maybe she'll be in prison by then? Finding she is smiling again, she realises it is because, even in that scenario, Scott Patterson will be dead. But then she remembers the teardrop tattoo on the crazy lady going through the bin and decides no: whatever else happens, she must get away with this. She must act like a professional and ensure there is nothing to link Scott's death back to her.

'Professional.'

There is a rustle of sari in the lounge room – a sound Anita recognises as her mother leaning in to hear better – and she realises she has spoken the word aloud. The irony of this is not lost on her and she makes a note to keep herself in check over the coming days. If she's going to be a professional, she needs to be silent about it. Still, she cannot resist playing with the word in her head. *Professional, professionally, professionalism.* It is a talisman for success and against discovery and Anita convinces herself that, if she does everything as carefully and precisely as a professional would, she can only succeed.

She leaves the house on time as if going to work – there's no need for her mother to know any differently – and drives to a petrol station. Good planning should take account of everything and, through the long night, Anita has had time to make good plans. Imagine if she got distracted and ran out of petrol somewhere she isn't supposed to be?

Next, she drives through the morning's humidity to the doctor's surgery – a low-ceilinged prefab next to the Kildare shops – and sits in the line of people waiting for the practice to open. Here, again, she finds herself smiling. For every time she has been here in the past she has either been worried (for Riya), resentful (of her mother) or sick. Today, she feels wonderful. A dozen witnesses look at each other – including her – because there is little else to look at. Then her name is recorded on a computer and, when at last she leaves, she holds in her hand a script for migraine tablets that she will get made up at her normal pharmacy, before flushing two away and leaving the rest beside her bed. Everything nice and provable.

The problem of where to get her mother's repeat prescription made up is more complex. Clearly, it cannot be at Anita's normal pharmacy, nor at any she has visited before, nor any where her mother might have been. Along with the script for fifty sleeping tablets, Anita has taken from the hall drawer her mother's Medicare card and a bank statement showing proof of address. But the first pharmacist Anita feels it is safe to visit, on the far side of Taradale, asks for a driving licence too. The pharmacist is very nice about it. He ignores Anita's panic (that maybe her mother's date of birth has flashed up on his screen) and apologises so profusely that Anita wonders if he's frightened she'll accuse him of racism or sexism or some other 'ism' that's big these days. She remembers only slowly that some people are just nice and, forcing herself to be nice back, says she doesn't have her licence on her right now, she'll have to come back with it later. The lie is utterly believable for, out of luck rather than good planning, Anita has parked a good distance away and the sheen that covers her skin is ample proof she has had to walk through the damp and cloying day.

As she is leaving the Taradale pharmacy, Anita notices the *Out of Hours Assistance* sign sellotaped to the store's glass door. The sign lists other local pharmacists with their addresses, phone numbers and opening hours. Below the printed information someone has scribbled in red biro: *New! Pharmacy now open in Montauban!*

Determined to resist the idea that the blood red of the biro has special meaning – that the sign on the door is more of a sign for her than anyone else – Anita drives calmly and slowly to Montauban. But parking outside the Montauban shops, her logic starts to fail her. The new pharmacy looks less than real. It is too clean and shining and perfect, as if magicked into existence just for her. Inside, it feels no less like a fiction of her imagination. The goods on the shelves are perfectly aligned, their colours and corners precise. When Anita reaches out to touch the boxes and sachets, they feel real enough, but there are no other people in the pharmacy, no music playing, no noise at all. Behind the counter stands a young man of Chinese heritage in a pristine white coat. He smiles at Anita as if he is delighted to see her and she realises he is the character in a story that guides you into another land. The white rabbit, Mr Tumnus, the Yamadutas. Anita hears her footsteps on the reflective floor tiles and realises she is walking towards the man, drawn as if beyond her will.

When she presents her mother's script and her mother's Medicare card and offers her mother's bank statement, the pharmacist looks at her lovingly. He barely glances at the bank statement before giving Anita a beautiful smile – his teeth as unnaturally perfect as everything else in sight – and disappearing between high shelves to one side of the space behind the counter. Anita waits to wake up and find herself on the sand or sweating beside her open car door, the Suzuki's engine throbbing away.

When that doesn't happen, she walks to the front of the shop to look out at the street but instead she catches her reflection in the plate glass window. She looks relaxed and happy, better than she has looked in years. She looks, she thinks, as nature intended her and she takes that as a sign that what she is doing is right. That this is who Anita Patel really is, underneath all the stress and worry and fear. She is strong and fearless: a tiger mother protecting her young. Maybe, she thinks, it's who anyone is if you push them so far that they consider murder. *Murder.* It's the first time she's allowed herself to think the word. She imagines herself a murderer and remembers a school reunion that has been rumoured for years. All her old classmates will arrive as doctors and dentists and accountants and she will be there as a *murderer.* Her mirror image smiles again, encouraging her on, and behind it she sees the pharmacist's reflection, returning to the counter with her pills.

The rest of the day feels more like reality. Upon leaving the pharmacy, the humidity a shock after the air conditioning, a woman waves at Anita from the doorway of a chip shop further along the street. Anita barely nods in return before scurrying to her car and driving quickly away. Before she has reached Crosley, the sky, doubtful all morning, has turned decidedly grey, clouds amassing from nowhere to press their dampness into the dirty town. Anita's car radio talks of a storm, optimistic it will break the humidity at last, but it fails to warn her of the dire Crosley traffic.

This, it turns out, is not restricted to rush hour after all. It takes Anita almost half an hour to find a suitably inconspicuous park. Leaving the Suzuki there at last, then moving it again to be sure she won't get a ticket, Anita gets to the souvenir shop at Crosley Stadium to find it closed until 2 p.m. Anita takes a deep breath and reminds herself she is now a professional and a professional need not be fazed by this. Instead, the professional will take the opportunity to find something to eat, no matter how little she feels like it.

Struggling to find anywhere she won't bump into someone from work, Anita buys a sandwich from a rancid café behind the stadium. The shapeless sandwich, despite its unprepossessing origins, still manages to disappoint, but a professional eats when she has decided to eat and Anita forces it down.

When the souvenir shop opens at last, Anita searches the shelves for a Central Coast Mariners mug. If she is going to drug Scott Patterson, she will need to replace his mug with a replica free of any forensic traces – she has seen enough *CSI* to be sure of that. But, as far as she can tell, the souvenir shop has no mugs that look like the one Scott normally uses. In the end she asks a shop assistant who, in turn, asks two other shop assistants, all of whom take a good look at her. The professional looks back at them with a patient smile and gives them no reason to remember her face. There is, after all, nothing else she can do: she's not going to stop now.

The right mug is found at last, paid for – in cash, of course – and safely stowed in Anita's handbag. But upon leaving the souvenir shop, Anita discovers she has no idea where she has left the Suzuki. Panic storms in: the professional exhausted after her first day at work, the sucking humidity insufferable, the grey air sticking her dress to her sides. When, after twenty horrible minutes, Anita finds her car in the next side street – remembering how she moved it from its original spot – she wants to cry with relief. But a professional does not cry. A professional simply remembers the rage powering her every move. A professional remembers her daughter.

It is only later, when everything has gone horribly wrong, that Anita realises even her rage was a fiction and it was something far more powerful that was blinding her.

Friday, 22nd March

Seven days after

Murdoch came from a world where weakness got you killed; his education from the School of Hard Knocks, the earliest lesson: Trust No One. And yet there was one thing he never learned. A trick the gods

played on him again and again – those evil bastards sitting up there nothing to do but throw shit.

Canyoning on Wednesday hadn't been as bad as he'd thought until the moment it was far worse. But, like Davie had said, that was what made it fun.

'You can abseil, can't you?'

Velis had asked it like he was talking about driving, shrugging off his backpack after they'd walked through the bush for an hour and a half. The day had been fully formed by then: warm enough to silence the birds and for a thick sheen to be sticking Murdoch's shirt to his back. After the long drive into the Blue Mountains, then the slow and dusty walk uphill, it was easy to believe they were the only living things out there. Them and the endless gum trees: a forest the size of Belgium, according to Velis. Then, suddenly, the eucalypts were only behind them, or in the blue distance ahead. Flat sandstone stretched from under their feet towards the view, then disappeared, no path away from the cliff top except the one they'd come in on.

Murdoch had seen abseiling on telly: a few window cleaners in Sydney CBD; he knew no more about it than that. A short while later, he was in a wetsuit, over the side of the cliff and bouncing twelve metres down a rope. After that, everything seemed normal. Wading through icy water at the bottom of ravines, the sky a distant blue scratch; floating through shallow caves blind but for fireflies; squeezing between rocks to jump to a lower level of water. Fear hit when he was abseiling again, down the face of an underground waterfall, his ropes knotting, a tonne of water a second boxing him back and forth. It was every drowning nightmare he'd ever had with some bondage thrown in for fun. This, he was certain, was where he would die: in a cold wet cave far from home. Then the knots slipped and he was abseiling again, Velis's toothy smile bright above him, only his eyes betraying his concern.

Later, he discovered Velis had been on the way down to cut his rope, preferring Murdoch to break his legs than drown in his harness. Weirdly, knowing that helped and, after it, nothing fazed Murdoch. It was like surviving the waterfall, neither drowning nor breaking his legs, had freed

him from a level of fear. Like the caves and canyons were in a different world and he was a different man for having been there.

But what surprised him most about the whole day was Velis's attitude towards what they were doing. There was no machismo in the man. If he saw Murdoch unsure about anything, he was reassuring, but only as much as he needed to be. When he had to give instructions, he wasn't patronising about it. He behaved like he and Murdoch were equals and it just happened Velis was the one who'd done this stuff before. Or like he was showing Murdoch something he thought was interesting, nothing he had reason to be proud of.

The next day, Thursday, they had played tennis again. The invitation to that, Murdoch noticed, was as casual as Velis's first text. No pressure, no implication Murdoch should decide one way or the other. If the invitation had come from Davie, it would have been followed with an argument Murdoch *had* to come, an insistence he should *want* to, a pleading he couldn't help resist. Velis didn't even ask.

I can do tennis in the morning. Let me know if you're interested.

A nice easy way out in case Murdoch wanted to sit at home and watch the dust settle instead.

More impressive still, Velis continued to prove he didn't need to fill every minute with words. Inevitably, he showed interest in the life of a private detective – how the Patterson case was progressing – but when there was nothing to say, Velis didn't say it. For Murdoch, the silence was like clean air. For months, he had known only his own stale company or the stifling noise of talk. Now he remembered, with stupid surprise, how you only survived in the clink by sharing silences. How, inside, men quickly judged and punished the talkers. He found himself enjoying male company for the first time in years – looked forward to Velis calling.

Except: *Emre Velis.* Whenever the name appeared on the screen of his phone, Murdoch felt as uncomfortable as the first time he'd heard it. He wasn't used to his memory failing him but, after googling Velis and finding nothing, he refused to look any further. It was normal, he told himself, not to remember every little detail when your life no longer depended on it. There were plenty of reasons to recognise a name you

didn't know. Still though: *Emre Velis, Emre Velis*. He'd get over it soon enough.

On Friday, empowered by everything he'd recently done, or maybe just bored of his own excuses, Murdoch drove himself north to Laguna. He spent no more than half an hour there, frightening himself far more than on the waterfall earlier in the week, then drove back to Montauban in a new skin, the old one itching as it fell away. He was speeding through a tiny suburb – what every other country in the world calls a village – when his phone started to ring. Murdoch braked hard, reversed into the entrance of a lonely garden centre and caught the call on its last ring.

'Davie, me old cauliflower, how are you mate?'

'Bill? Are you all right? Have you been drinking?'

Murdoch turned off the engine. 'Yes, I am all right. In fact, I'm bleeding marvellous. And no, I haven't been drinking. Well, not alcohol.'

'Oh, good. Listen, I wondered if you'd have any more thoughts about the case? Fran Patterson keeps calling me and I haven't seen you in days.'

'Ain't you gonna ask me why I'm in such a good mood?'

There was a silence at the other end of the line and Murdoch was about to repeat the question when Davie's voice came again, less certain than a second before.

'Oh, yeah, OK. Why are you in such a good mood?'

'Actually, don't ask me that. Ask me how the water is today.'

'The water?'

'The ocean.'

There was another hesitation and Murdoch knew Davie was at his desk, eyes on the computer like he could multitask.

'What? Sorry, how's the ocean?'

'Beautiful.' That's what Aussies always said. *Byooodiful*. 'Just beautiful. Crystal clear, warmest time of the year.'

'Great,' said Davie. 'So, anyway, I've sent the information about those Asian companies off to a language agency. They're *all* newspapers, apparently, one in each country. Anyway, the agency's going to get in touch with the papers and ask them what the payments were for. Should only take them a couple of days, although, of course, they can't promise how long the papers will take to get back to them.'

'Davie, the water is beautiful.'

'Yeah, you said.'

Murdoch ran his free hand over his scalp and down his neck. He wasn't used to the sensation of salt water drying. A cold thrill ran through him, not just the joy of knowing he'd done it, more the relief from worrying he never would.

'I went swimming, Davie. Swimming in the sea!'

'Oh, good, yeah. How's the water?'

'Ain't you impressed?'

'What? Oh, yeah, great.'

Murdoch swore under his breath and asked Davie how much the language agency was charging. Was it more than the gratis the bloke in greasy spoon would of done it for? Now he had Davie's attention.

'This is serious business, Bill, a real case, and I'm going to give it all the professionalism it deserves. I am not going to rely on a man in a café to provide critical evidence.'

They went back and forth until Davie confessed to the amount he'd paid and Murdoch swore again, louder this time.

'I thought you had a cash flow problem?'

'It's an *investment*, I put it on the credit card. We have to find Patterson within a few weeks and the press about that will fit in perfectly with the PR I'm organising. Then the money will be flowing in.'

Murdoch looked at the sky. It was English summer weather: clouds like a badly painted ceiling, no clue where the sun might be.

'So, you still doing that publicity stuff then?'

'Yeah, why not?'

'You want me to answer that?'

'Oh, and listen, Bill, Anne in the general store knows someone whose cousin used to work for Patterson years ago. Her name's Wendy something, she lives in Montie and Anne wondered if we'd like to meet her?'

Murdoch was about to make a comment about professionalism and critical evidence when, across the road, something caught his eye. On a slip of tarmac behind a wooden bus shelter, sat a scruffy row of shops, two of them with the name of the suburb in their title: Gumirri Mixed Business and The Gumirri Café.

'Bill?'

'I'm listening. You want us to go and meet Anne's friend's cousin cos she worked at PPC a hundred years ago.'

Davie rattled on about checking every detail, talking to everyone they could. 'Then there's the warehouse manager, Tom Brandle,' he said, running out of steam. 'And, of course, Patterson's secretary, Anita Patel.'

Murdoch asked when they were going to meet her then, half-listening as Davie explained how the secretary was still waiting for the OK from Fran Patterson. With the phone tight against his ear, Murdoch climbed out of the Mercedes and walked into the quiet road. Invisible birds were losing a competition against a distant power tool: the kind of thing that only stops so it can disappoint you when it starts up again. To his right, a hundred metres away, was the back of a speed limit sign. Murdoch turned and looked in the other direction. Another sign, further away, gave permission to return to 100 kph. That was Gumirri, its only houses climbing the hill behind the shops.

'Davie, I've got to go, speak to you later.'

'But—'

Murdoch killed the call.

The mixed business was closed, but, in the café, Murdoch found an oily teenager hunched behind the counter, his face reflecting the light from his phone.

'This Gumirri?' Murdoch asked him.

The boy looked up and pulled a face, looking for the trick in the question. 'Yeah …?'

'I'm looking for the timber yard.'

He pulled another face, equally confused, and shook his lank hair.

'No timber yard here, mate. Nothing but the shops and … aw, gotcha. The garden centre used to be a wood shop, years ago. Timber yard thing, yeah.' He turned on his stool and yelled to a strip curtain in the back wall. 'Here, Uncle Wozzer! When did the garden centre open?'

A short man with a pink face appeared among the strips of curtain, large black eyes above a Fred Flintstone five o'clock shadow. He said g'day to Murdoch and wiped his hands on his jeans, thinking slowly about the answer.

'The Chilsons sold it … aw, I reckon that would be about three years back. Yeah, cos the site was empty for a year, and the Smiths have been in there for two. Just before Christmas when they opened up. Stupid time of year to open a garden centre, I told 'em, but what can you do?'

'No other timber yard around here?'

Murdoch saw them react to his tone, apologised and said he was looking for an old friend. A guy called Samir had run the place, he'd appreciate any help finding him.

'Nah,' said the man. 'No other timber yards near here. No money in it, see. The big warehouse chains undercut them every time. Bunnings and that, you can't beat them for wood. I'm surprised the Chilsons managed as long as they did.'

'Do you remember if a guy called Samir used to work there?'

This time Fred Flintstone didn't have to think. 'Doubt it! Chilsons was a family business, that lot would rather cut their throats than pay anyone outside the clan – that kind of people. Now, the Smiths, much nicer. They'd have Zachary here, if he was willing to get off his arse.'

Back in the car, Murdoch pulled up the notes on his phone.

Gumirri Timber Yard

Samir

Henry McCaul

He remembered getting the name wrong deliberately, saying 'Harry McCale' and Velis not correcting him. Then how, when canning the case on the tennis court, Velis had avoided using the compo conman's name at all. Murdoch dialled up a map and searched for other Gumirris, other suburbs that might sound like that. He googled for timber yards too, but, like the man in the café had said, there were few outside the DIY chains on the whole Central Coast. Those that he found were near Crosley or further inland, nowhere near Gumirri. Staring at his phone, the nausea *Emre Velis* had always given him started to spread, tightening his skin more than the ocean had done.

The bastard gods had tricked him again.

Saturday, 23rd March

Eight days after

The morning ran hot and cold, bright and shaded by turns. Ragged clouds cooled the air the moment they greyed it, then let the sun splash gold, teasing for minutes before hiding it away again. Davie called Bill hourly, leaving increasingly desperate voicemails. He went to Bill's house and leant on the bell, even crept round the back and looked in through the French windows. It didn't matter if Bill had hung up on him the day before, Davie was willing to forgive him for that, if only now he would show himself. But it was always when Bill most needed forgiveness that he went and annoyed you all the more and now he had done a Gandalf – vanishing exactly when he was needed most. At lunchtime, Davie gave up and drove to Kildare alone.

Anita Patel's house was in the wide streets that had been laid down at the same time the Kildare shops had been built. The land had been bush when Davie was a kid; now, every time he came here, he wondered who mowed all the grass. There was so much of it: wide expanses of buffalo green, running between the roads and the houses and stretching between the well-spaced driveways – these days, they'd put up twice the number of houses on the same plot. It wasn't a particularly well-off suburb and the properties, though big, were as well lived-in as anywhere else on the Coast. But there was something soulless about the place. It was the lack of trees, Davie decided – he was driving slowly along the empty streets, looking for the secretary's house – especially here, where there had once been so many. It would have been better for everyone if the developers had left a few eucalypts to give some shade and laid a bit less grass to be mown. Better for everyone but the developers, that was. Instead, the suburb was bare and flat, even the best-tended gardens barely reaching knee height. On a day like today, the weather unable to decide between shade and sunlight, it felt like a stage during a lighting rehearsal.

Anita Patel had phoned Davie the previous evening, an hour or so after Bill had hung up on him. She was, at last, able to talk because, after days of trying, Fran Patterson had got back to her. *Half your luck*, Davie had thought. Fran phoned him twice a day. Her attempt to play at the tournament in Queensland had been scuppered by the press, fascinated by a woman showing so little concern for her missing husband. Journalists and photographers had chased her to Gold Coast airport, then from Kingsford Smith to the Pattersons' home in West Crosley. Now she was besieged there with nothing to do but call Davie for status reports. At least now she had also called the secretary.

'I'm sorry for being so cautious,' Anita had explained on the phone. 'It's just that with all those horrible things written in the papers about Fran, I need to know who I'm talking to. But, now that she's confirmed it's all right, please come and talk. Would tomorrow morning be OK?'

Unable to get hold of Bill, Davie had phoned Natalie to ask for pointers on how to handle this key suspect. Natalie, obviously at work, had been less than excited. Her new trick, Davie noticed, was to turn herself into DS Conquest with no more than a tut and a sigh, her voice barely louder than the echoes around her, her interest on something else.

'She's not a chief suspect, Davie. She's just the missing man's secretary. Ask her what you want, just don't let her know we're collaborating with you guys on this. The press would have a field day.'

'But it said in the police file she looked nervous. "Suspiciously nervous." I copied it out.'

'Davie, she's a twitchy character, there's plenty of them about. Look at the worldwide sales of Valium. Besides, tell me how a nervous overweight woman managed to wrestle a man from his bed and out of hospital single-handed?'

Bill would have had an answer for that. And Bill would know how to put the same question to Anita Patel and how to tell if her answer was less than truthful. Davie might be good at the details, but it was always Bill who spotted when someone was lying. It was, Davie had often thought, as if the Englishman didn't trust anyone. As if he thought the whole world was trying to trick him and he was just waiting to be proven right. Not that Bill's scepticism was of any use right now, because Bill, of course, wasn't around to help.

Anita Patel opened her front door almost before Davie had finished ringing the bell. She was a plump Indian woman with a kind open face, a nervous smile and huge brown eyes. She asked Davie in, then remembered she wanted to check he really was who he said he was. Then, once he'd shown his ID, she apologised for asking to see it, insisting on shaking his hand so that Davie stood awkwardly half-in and half-out of her front door.

'Nice place,' he said, once he was in at last. The house, in fact, was nothing special. A plain manila hallway, a standard brown carpet: Davie recognised a rental property when he saw one. But Anita seemed touched by the compliment. She thanked him and gave him a soft smile before, seeming to remember something, she put the smile away and gestured him along the hallway with fluttering hands.

In her flowery living room, overly full of over-stuffed furniture, she offered him a seat with the same busy gesture. In a corner on the carpet, a little girl in a *Frozen* dress – a miniature of her mother with the same big eyes and a wealth of eyelashes – was playing with a stuffed toy, making it dance up and down. Davie said hello, but the child ignored him the way children always did, the stuffed toy far more interesting. Also in the room, on the far end of the sofa where Anita indicated Davie should sit, was an old lady in a sari, thin, milky-eyed and grey. Anita introduced the woman as her mother so hurriedly that Davie wasn't sure if he'd heard correctly, especially when the secretary sharply dispatched the woman to go and get them tea.

'So,' said Anita, with another smile, as she sat in a faded armchair. 'What can I do for you?'

Davie started with what he thought were probably standard opening questions. How long had Anita been in Crosley? How long at PPC? What her duties as a secretary were. In return, Anita answered in so much detail that he struggled to take notes. What, where, who, how, why, when, which way. She talked without pause, ignoring his attempts to interrupt, then filling in the further details he'd wanted to interrupt for anyway. Her husband had died of cancer two years earlier – Riya had been four – he had gone very quickly. Anita had moved with her mother and daughter from Sacramento to take this job. She enjoyed her role at PPC, it wasn't exactly demanding. Scott Patterson was very private about his business dealings, even with her. He had dyslexia, so sometimes she wrote his emails and did his filing, but otherwise it was mostly looking after his diary and answering the phones. She didn't know anyone who knew him other than the people in the contact list on her computer. She'd never seen anything suspicious, she couldn't imagine what had happened to him.

Davie could see why the police had described Anita Patel as nervous. The woman barely took a breath – not even to acknowledge the return of her mother with a mismatched tray of tea. She just kept her huge eyes fixed on Davie, as if her only concern was that he should understand. Her hands were constantly moving: something always needed rearranging, checking, tucking, smoothing, scratching. Anita's mother, meanwhile, sat quietly in the same spot as before, so still Davie almost forgot she was there, her eyes fixed on her granddaughter as she listened to what her daughter had to say.

It was only when Anita spoke about Scott Patterson – what he was like to work for, how popular he was, how doting on his wife – that Davie thought he saw a change in the woman. There was moisture in her eyes that she struggled to blink away, a tiny vibration near her upper lip, and he realised how worried this dutiful secretary must be about her boss. She was frail, he realised, on edge. The last thing he wanted was to make her cry.

'What about his nephew?' Davie asked. 'Alan Drummond? Would he have any reason to want Scott out of the way?'

Anita looked at Davie as if he had suggested Drummond was a paedophile from Mars. She opened her eyes wide and told him she really had no idea, shrugging her shoulders extravagantly. The gesture seemed to bring her relief – her hands suddenly calm in her lap – and she used it again and again after that. Any bank accounts the PPC finance team might be unaware of? Any unpleasant connections Scott Patterson had? Any medical conditions she was aware of requiring regular treatment? Who could possibly want to harm him? Each question was answered only by Anita's shrug, accompanied, after a while, by a pout of her full lips, as if she needed to taste the question before deciding, no, really, she didn't know. She apologised several times for this and, frightened and helpless as she obviously was, Davie took pains to reassure her. He would find

Scott Patterson, he promised, no matter what it took. And Anita wasn't to worry. Scott would be back in the office before she knew it.

Once the secretary had shown him out again – as politely nervous as on his arrival – Davie drove around the corner and parked beside a broad verge, its grass flashing bright and dull under the changing sky. He closed his eyes, sighed and rested his forehead on the steering wheel.

On the way to Kildare he had tried to convince himself Anita Patel had to be guilty, or, at least, somehow complicit with the guilty party. That she and her stalling tactics were the only things between him and full payment of his invoice and, equally importantly, some healthy exposure in the press. He had told himself he was going to be tough. He was going to question the secretary into a corner where she broke down and confessed to everything. He would 'totally own her' (Davie was never quite sure what this expression meant, but it sounded about right). But now Anita Patel had turned out to be a lovely lady, supporting a family and as worried for her boss as everyone else.

Alone and hot in the quiet car, Davie realised the case had barely progressed. The payments from the secret bank account, the voice recording on Patterson's computer, the changed mug on the man's desk – they were just further mysteries, not leads. There was no way Davie was going to solve the case in time for— He knew he should be thinking 'in time to get Scott Patterson his next injection'. But why shouldn't that also be in time for the PR he had planned? *You've overreached yourself, Davie*, he thought. *You must've been dreaming.* It was exactly the kind of thing his father would say.

At that idea, Davie sat up, opened his eyes and took a deep breath. 'You're going to do this,' he said aloud. He said it again, trying to deepen his voice to sound more like Dad. 'You've done it before and you can do it again. With or without Bill bloody Murdoch. You just need to put your mind to it.'

He put his mind to it all the way back to Montauban. So much so that, by the time he was rolling down the hill into town – trying to ignore how inviting the ocean looked – he'd given himself a headache. Deciding he was hungry, he pulled up outside the chip shop and parked at an angle across two bays.

Hattie Thornton was as delighted to see him as ever. Leaving his chips to overcook, she leant on the greasy counter and asked after his parents and what was Bill up to and wasn't it exciting about Davie investigating a real case at last – who'd have ever thought?

'I've had real cases before, you know, Hattie.' Davie always regretted buying chips, but he normally got to eat them first. 'And solved them.'

'Ooh, you know what I mean. This one's in the papers and everything. My cousin Tom works up at PPC, I've been up there to see him a few times. I even met Scott Patterson's secretary, that Indian lady, Anita Patel's her name. I saw her again the other day, coming out of the chemist, and I gave her a wave, but she pretended not to see me. Must be the worry.'

'You saw her coming out of the chemist? Here?'

'Yes. And Anne told me that when Brian Yeow –the Chinese fella what works in the chemist – well, when he heard us talking about Scott Patterson going missing, he said Fran Patterson wasn't the only person losing sleep over it. Anne asked him what did he mean, did he mean that the secretary woman was buying sleeping tablets? And he blushed such a funny colour and wouldn't say a thing; so it has to be true.'

'No, it doesn't. I mean, not really, it doesn't.'

'And I know from Tom that Anita Patel lives in Kildare behind the shops. So why would she come all the way to Montie to get a script made up, when there's a chemist up there? Looks dodgy to me.'

Davie ate his chips on the whale-watching platform, deliberately digging through the paper from one end in a way that, as a teenager, had always driven his father crazy. As he ate he leant against the coastal regeneration sign and studied the shops. Brian Yeow's *Pharmacy* sign was the newest thing in town, not to mention the cleanest. Just by hanging there, humming lightly, it seemed to make Montie less grotty. Davie stared at it, knowing what he needed to do and knowing he didn't want to do it. But, as Bill had once said to him, 'This is what it takes, mate.' Davie had often repeated the phrase to himself, normally as an excuse for spending money, but this, he knew, was what it really meant. Forcing yourself to do things that went against your better nature. He told himself a man's life was at stake and it was the urgency of that – nothing to do with timing of his planned publicity – that justified what he was about to do.

He finished his chips, forced the paper into the overflowing bin and watched Jackson Harper's ute roll down the hill and park in front of the shops. As soon as Jackson had climbed out and limped into the general store, Davie hurried up to the roundabout and approached the shops from a direction neither Anne Lincoln nor Hattie Thornton would be able to see.

Brian Yeow was in a white coat, taller on the platform behind the counter. His round face lit up when he recognised Davie. He greeted him by name and gave a friendly smile.

'You need a sign on your window,' Davie told him, walking up to the spotless counter. 'To let the kids round here know there's no cash kept on the premises overnight and nothing they can make ice out of.'

'You mean pseudoephedrine? So I can't sell Lemsip?'

'You can't leave it in here overnight, and you need to let the locals know that you know that. No sign and they won't find out until they've driven through your window. And, listen to me, you need to stop talking to Anne Lincoln about anything but the weather. Even a vague reference about anyone is enough for her to draw her own conclusions. You breathe another word about anyone and you're through. They don't call her Montie FM for nothing. Mates of mine used to drive to Crosley to buy their condoms. Don't tell Hattie in the chip shop anything either. Oh, and you're better off opening at ten and closing at seven, no point doing nine to six around here.'

Brian laughed. 'Got it. Thanks. That's good of you.'

'No, it's not.' This is was what Bill would have said.

'Isn't it?'

'No, it isn't. This is what's going to happen. I'm going to tell everyone how Anne and Hattie were drilling you for gossip and you weren't having a bar of it. How Anne was ropeable about it; they'll love that and repeat it. And I'll say the same, how I wanted some information for the case, but you gave me nothing. Clear?'

'Oh, thanks. That's great.'

'But in reality, you are going to tell me something. You're going to tell me if you sold prescribed sleeping tablets to a woman called Anita Patel. And, if you did, whether they contained a type of ...' Davie checked the photograph on his phone and spelled it slowly into words, '... benzodiazepine receptor agonist called, er ... zolpidem?'

He looked up to find Yeow's smile had disappeared.

'No, I'm not.'

'Or I walk out of here now, straight into the general store and tell Anne you've confirmed what she suspected. That Jackson Harper needed antibiotics for his foot and the script you made up for Anita Patel was for sleeping tablets.'

Davie had made people dislike him before – generally unintentionally – but it had never bothered him so much. He'd have felt better if Brian Yeow had shouted at him or thrown him out. Instead the young pharmacist frowned and started playing distractedly with an earlobe. He was caught in a rip again.

'I'm sorry,' said Davie. 'Dude, I really am. But this is for a case which I've got to solve. A man's life is at stake. If you don't tell me, I'll get the police to ask you and once you've told them anything, you'll be bust within six months. My office is in this same strip, I know what the rents are. Come on, man, help me out and I promise to never ask you again. And I will send you lots of customers. Please.'

Yeow crinkled his already surly brow.

'You have to hurry,' said Davie. 'Before Hattie starts to wonder why my car's still out the front of the chip shop. Just yes or no. Did you prescribe a plumpish Indian lady sleeping tablets? And did they contain this zoplidem stuff?'

Bill would have said something else here, something to make the pharmacist's decision easier, but Davie had no idea what it might be. Should he offer money?

'Yes,' said Yeow, his face colouring. 'She was one of the few customers I've had, it's not difficult to remember. I gave her some Stilnox: main ingredient zolpidem. Exactly like you said. Now fuck off.'

'Dude,' said Davie, 'I promise to see you right.'

134

He was going to say more, anything to remove the hatred from the young pharmacist's face, but, before he could, Yeow told him to fuck off again. And never to come back.

It was later that evening that Murdoch eventually forced himself out of his cave. In Gumirri the previous day, discovering Velis had lied to him, he had felt a sickness deep in his core, a sudden lurch that had made him want to puke. It was, he thought later, like discovering your opponent was better armed than you or realising you had been spotted on enemy turf. Or, maybe – who knew? – like being stabbed in the back. On the drive home he had tried talking himself calmer, telling himself there would be an easy explanation. Velis would have got the name wrong, that was all.

Over the following twenty-four hours, his unease had only intensified. *Emre Velis.* For hours on end Murdoch had typed the man's name, until, when he closed his eyes, he could see it scratched brightly in the darkness. He could no longer remember if the name had always made him feel sick or if he was making that up. Holed up behind drawn curtains, he studied every reference to *Emre Velis* he could find on the internet and came up with a grand total of not very much. There were a few Greeks or Turks with that name on Facebook, but they were all back in Greece or Turkey, as far as Murdoch could tell. Other results were for either Emre or Velis, nothing for both. Not that that meant much; Murdoch could search for himself and find a blank. But then Murdoch had a lot to hide.

So on Saturday evening, he forced himself out. Not because he thought fresh air might help his ever-tightening nausea. Just there was only one possible lead to the secret of Emre Velis and, short of going to the general store, only one way of following up on it. Murdoch was in the middle of the creaking stairs that ran from Davie's grass driveway up to his shack, when Davie himself yanked open the front door.

'Bill!' he said breathlessly, one hand on the door frame. 'Of course, you're back. Just when I don't need you.'

'What you talking about? Back from where? And why're you out of breath? You been wanking at your computer or something?'

Davie told him he was just in the door himself. He'd been busy running around seeing people, given *one* of them had to work on the case. Murdoch ignored the overdone emphasis and asked if Davie was going to ask him in for a beer.

'Not really. Seeing as you haven't even apologised for hanging up on me and then disappearing.'

'Mate, that's what I'm here for, innit? To apologise.'

'Well, go on then.'

Murdoch gave Davie the stare he normally saved for loud children. 'I'm sorry. Honestly, I am and I wanna make it up to you. So, you gonna let me in?'

'What, now? But it's nearly six o'clock.'

'So? You free?

'Well, *I* am, but ... is that what you're wearing?'

'You what? What's it to you what I'm wearing? You want me in a special apologisation outfit or something?'

Murdoch looked down at his T-shirt and dirty jeans. True, he'd been wearing them for twenty-four hours, but since when did Davie care about that kind of thing? The muppet was in nothing but an old T-shirt and board shorts himself. It wasn't like they needed to dress up nice to drink beer on his stupid balcony.

Davie mumbled, 'Never mind,' and gestured him inside.

'Little bastards,' said Murdoch when he'd taken his normal seat on the balcony and was studying the view. 'It was bloody lovely at the bottom of my garden this week, grass running into the water, swans everywhere. Now it stinks.'

Overnight, some kids had let out the lagoon again. Digging a trench through the sand that separated the fresh water from the ocean, then surfing its emptying brown wave, was a local rite of passage: extra points if the police turned up and chased you along the beach. The game turned a wide lake into an ugly mudflat in less than twenty minutes, a million dead reeds and huge rotting trunks littering the battlefield. Things stayed that way until there was proper rain again or a king tide or a combination of the two.

'Weird, isn't it?' Davie was leaning against the railing that Murdoch still didn't trust. 'Why are trees and water nicer to look at than logs and mud? It's all nature.'

'So's puke and shit, doesn't mean you want to look at it.'

The comparison was too good, the browns of the mud flat streaked with the orange of the setting sun. Murdoch closed his eyes and asked Davie what was happening with the case. He could tell Davie must have found something out and, despite everything else going on, was curious about it what it could be. As Davie explained about Anita Patel and Brian Yeow, Murdoch watched the sun crash into the wooded hills, the air around them dimming.

'And it's definitely the same sedatives what was found in Patterson's bloodstream?' he asked at last.

'Definitely.'

'But the secretary didn't flinch when you asked her about the mug? Didn't spill her tea or nothing?'

'Er, no. I mean, she didn't flinch at any point. Didn't touch her tea at all.'

'Didn't seem bothered?'

'Not really.'

'You didn't ask her, did you, Davie?'

Davie turned, his back to the dregs of the sunset, his features half-hidden in shadow. 'OK. No, I didn't think I should. I thought we should keep our cards close to our chest about all that. And yes, you would have done. But you weren't there, were you, Bill?'

Murdoch had no answer for that. He'd seen Davie's calls coming in and had heard him at the door. Had even guessed more or less what Davie might want. 'Tell you what,' he said after a while. 'Why don't we go round and see her in the morning? Ask her about the mug and the pills at the same time?'

'I thought of that. I tried phoning her to arrange it, but she's not answering.'

'Well, maybe we'll just turn up at her house, then?'

'Maybe we should. And maybe this time, you could come too. You know, Bill, it's the twenty-third today – the day Patterson's due his shot.

From now on, every day we don't find him, he's another day closer to getting ill. I could really do with some help.'

Murdoch didn't know what to say to that either. 'You done well with the chemist,' he tried at last. 'Good thinking, mate, I'm impressed.'

Davie turned back to the darkened view. 'Yes, well, I'm not exactly proud of that. That guy, Brian, he seems all right. Just trying to make a living, you know, provide an important service to the local community and here I am blackmailing him with bankruptcy.'

'Well, you'll just have to make it up to him, won't you? Tell you what, I'll go in tomorrow and buy a couple of condoms, say it's on your recommendation.'

Davie didn't laugh.

'Davie, mate, you're the one what said you was desperate to be successful. You need to toughen up, you can't make an omelette without breaking eggs. All them big business men, you think they didn't tread on people to get where they are? It's why most people what drive nice cars are such arseholes. You can't be successful and nice.'

The truth of the statement reminded Murdoch of Velis. He hoiked a greenie and spat it through the railings. Worrying was like a wound: you forgot about for a while and then it hurt all the more.

'Anyway,' he said – the reason for his visit – 'what's the gossip round town, then, eh?'

'What? I don't know. Nothing. You know what, though, Bill? I'm trying not to jump to conclusions, but you have to admit things do point to Anita Patel being the culprit.'

'Nah. All you've got is circumstantial evidence. It's weak and that's why it's no good in court. Well, not often. So she had a key to the office, so what? Anyone could of picked the lock. You said it was a standard Chubb, yeah? Easy done. And didn't you say them sleeping tablets was easy to get hold of?'

'The most widely prescribed in Australia. And the sedatives mentioned in the police file are in half the other brands too.'

'Exactly. And don't try and tell me a woman by herself could of wrestled Patterson out of his hospital bed, off all them machines and away to wherever he is. There's not a lawyer on earth what could get the DPP to fly with that.'

Davie's broad back rose and fell with a heavy sigh. 'That's what Natalie said.'

'Well, then, there you go. Cheer up, mate, we'll work it out soon enough.' Murdoch caught the lack of response. 'Now what?'

'Oh nothing. It's just, well, I really wanted to have the case wrapped up by the end of the month.'

'Course you do. To get Patterson his injection, if he's still alive.'

'Oh yeah. For that, of course. But also, I know you'll think this is stupid, but I wanted to tie it in with that publicity stuff I told you about. Glenn's got me an interview with *The Sydney Morning Herald* next week. Imagine that got published at the same time as the news of us solving the case?'

Murdoch clapped at a mosquito. 'Jesus,' he said, examining the corpse on his palms. 'Talk about being business-minded rather than worrying about saving a bloke's life. Maybe you're learning after all. Anyway, mate, let's talk about something what's not work. What's Montie FM been chatting about?'

Davie shrugged at the blackening view.

'C'mon, Davie, humour me. I bet Anne knows someone what knows someone what's seen me doing something I shouldn't of been doing. Bet she saw me in the Garragula Hotel a few weeks ago.'

'No.'

'Really? You telling me it's possible to go out round here without Anne knowing about it?'

'Oh, well, yeah, she did mention something. Said she heard you were very drunk.'

'And let me guess, her source recognised the bloke I was with. Anne had an affair with his dad in the seventies or something? I bet you could even tell me his name.'

Davie didn't need to think about it. 'No, she was asking me who he might be, actually. Her friend, Trudy, who works weekends at the Garragula said he was tall and foreign-looking. I think she fancied him. Who was he?'

Murdoch forced himself to sound as cheery as a second before. 'No one important. Bloody amazing – I thought the Montauban grapevine never missed a trick.'

Davie shook his head. 'It's not infallible. I heard from three different sources you were having dinner at Natalie's tonight. Denise at the supermarket in Kildare told me Nat was buying lamb shanks for two. Apparently …'

Murdoch stood so quickly the deck wobbled beneath them.

'Shit! Shit, shit! Why didn't you tell me? What's the bleeding time?!'

Before Davie could answer either question, Murdoch was back in the brightness of the shack and tearing across the living room towards the front door. On the creaking steps and down the steep driveway he swore again – a single syllable for every step – cursing his flip-flops for slowing him. The bleeding Montauban grapevine had let him down yet again.

Natalie lived in the half of Montauban that lay north of the beach. The ridge that surrounded the tiny town formed a bowl there, most houses climbing the hill to get a view of the ocean, others so crowded by canopy that all they saw was green. Three years in town and this half of Montie was still a mystery to Murdoch: a maze where he still had to check the street signs. In certain places, steps cut up from one road to the next – it could be quicker to walk up the hill than to drive – but you had to know the steps were there and, even then, they weren't easy to find. Ash, sassafras, satinwood, eucalypts – the trees conspired with undergrowth to blur the borders between one property and the next; or property at all and unclaimed bush. Whenever he ventured this side of the shops, Murdoch found himself thinking it would take the greenery a year, maybe two, to reclaim the whole place if the people disappeared. After that you'd never know it had been civilised.

When he rang the bell, Natalie unlocked her front door, but she didn't open it to say hello. Instead, she ran back down her hallway, shouting at him to come inside before disappearing into her kitchen. Murdoch checked his watch for the third time in as many minutes and stuck another mint in his mouth. He'd smoked two cigarettes while getting changed and another on the walk over.

'Sorry I'm late,' he said, following her into the clammy kitchen, steam on the windows like they were holed up in a car. 'I brought you these.'

She turned from the stove and saw the flowers and the wine.

'I got them at the general store,' he said, gesturing with the lurid gerberas. 'Sorry.'

He'd never seen Natalie in a dress before, let alone a pretty one that clung in all the right places. She was wearing high heels too, her legs better than ever. In comparison, the dyed flowers were like a bad joke, but one which Natalie seemed to find funny, at least for a second. She tore herself away from the cooking – her face and neck spotted with red sauce – grabbed the flowers and the bottle by their necks and put them on the table with a smile.

'I'll put those in a vase later,' she said. 'Open the wine if you want. Sorry, but I'm a terrible cook. I hope you like lamb.'

'Just as long as it's not shanks.'

He said it with a grin so she'd know he was joking, but she'd already turned back to the stove, hands at three saucepans like she was learning the drums. Now she swung back forlorn.

'Joke!' he said, hands up. 'I'm joking. I love lamb, you know I do. Lamb shanks best of all.'

'You don't have to eat it if you don't want to.'

'No, really, I was joking. I knew we was having shanks.'

'Really? How?'

Shit. Murdoch struggled with some half-lies and ended up with the truth. It sounded like he'd been talking behind her back.

'Jesus, Bill, you really have gone native. Will everyone in Montie know how our evening went too?' She heard her own words and turned quickly back to the saucepans. 'Open the wine, pour yourself a glass.'

'That's all right,' he said. 'I had a beer at Davie's. You want one?'

He watched the back of her shoulders shrug and remained awkwardly in the doorway, no idea what to say next. The only local gossip he knew was about the new chemist. He'd popped in on the way over, telling the Chinese bloke it was Davie what had sent him there, but he didn't want to mention that. On the fridge, he noticed a photo of Natalie with Davie, the two of them looking about sixteen, but Murdoch didn't want to talk about Davie either.

'Nice dress,' he managed at last.

'Thanks. You know, I don't normally wear them.'

'Yeah, I can see why. I mean, I can't imagine you, like, wanting all the attention you'd get in that … dress. So maybe that's why you wouldn't wear one. Cos it's so nice.'

Natalie turned off one of the gas rings and Murdoch heard her swear as she examined the saucepan above it. It was weird to be in her kitchen again. The only other time had been years before, the first month he'd arrived in Montie. Davie had brought him to Natalie to get some stitches put in: she'd been a nurse once, apparently. The two of them had sat at the table where his flowers now lay, managing less than five minutes before building a fight. He'd been in her house only once since then, in her bed, both of them drunk. Sober, the next morning, there had been another fight.

'All right if I sit down?'

'Of course.' Natalie turned again, biting her lip the way that always made him smile. 'And I'll have a wine, even if you won't.'

They managed a bit of small talk while he found a glass and opened the bottle. The weather, mutual acquaintances, town planning. Then she asked him if he'd ever heard any more from the Club.

'Why d'you always bring that up? I wouldn't be here to tell you about it if I had, would I?'

It came out more abruptly than he'd meant it to, days of worry tumbling out with the words. The last thing he'd had to do with the Club had been a year earlier, when an ex-Club heavy, Ibrahim Hussein, had threatened to tell the organisation that Murdoch was still alive. Murdoch had managed to turn the tables, Hussein last seen from a distance bundled into the back of a van. Murdoch blinked the memory away, the same way he always shut down that kind of memory. Keen to get the small talk back, not thinking too clearly, he told Natalie of Davie's thoughts about the case, too late moving on to the weather, what he'd been up to, the wine that he'd bought.

'The secretary?' Natalie lifted a saucepan like an unexploded bomb and carried it towards the sink. 'I can't see it; no motive. What makes him think that?'

Murdoch studied the label on the wine bottle. '*McLaren Vale*,' he said. 'Where's that?'

He looked up to find her with her hands on her hips, the steam from whatever she'd drained bothering her eyes.

'What?'

'Bill, are you seriously going to close up when I ask a single question about the case? After everything I've done for you guys? You're the one who brought it up.'

'I thought we was just having dinner.'

'We are just having dinner. And we're just making conversation. Different from that old crook–copper dynamic we used to have, you know?'

'Oh, right then, fair enough. So, who's the person of interest in the Patterson case what you lot don't want your own people to know about?'

She dropped the saucepan onto the draining board, the bang making him jump. 'You know I can't tell you that!'

'Well, then, it's quits, innit?'

They stared at each other, until they both smelled burning. Natalie spun round to the stove, then swore again, louder this time. 'Oh fantastic,' she said bitterly. 'Now look what you've made me do. You're a major pain in the arse, do you know that?'

Murdoch put the wine bottle back on the table.

'Don't worry about it,' he said, getting up. 'Suddenly I'm not so hungry, anyway.'

At the front door he hesitated, one hand on the lock, the other rubbing the tiny spikes of his hair. All week he'd been looking forward to the evening with Natalie until Gumirri had happened and made him forget. If the twenty-four hours following that discovery had taught him anything, it was knowing who his friends were. Back in the kitchen, Natalie was still at the stove.

'You know what,' he said to her back, to the nape of her beautiful neck. 'Davie told me once I always pick fights. Not like argy-bargy, but arguments, you know. But it's only with you, Nat. I dunno what it is. Anyone else, I'd deflect, but I see you coming at me and I feel like I've got to bring you down a peg or two. Remind you that you're not better than me. But it's only cos you are. You're great. It's so stupid, I like you, and you like me, but we always do this.'

She nodded her head but made no other movement, any agreement weaker than the smell of burning. For one minute, maybe more, they remained silent.

'Listen,' he said, at last. 'Don't move, right? Don't move till you hear the bell.'

He grabbed the gerberas and the wine and walked to the front door, went outside and shut it gently behind him. Then he turned and used the hand with the flowers to press the doorbell. Had to do it three times before she answered.

'Ta-da,' he said. 'Look, I went down Sydney and got you some top-notch flowers and fancy wine. Please tell me we've got burned lamb shanks for tea. Let's get pissed and have a laugh.'

Natalie put one hand to her mouth. Tears filled her eyes and the black around them smudged.

'Oh shit,' he said. 'Oh fuck. I didn't mean to—'

Before he could say anything else, she'd grabbed him by the wrists and pulled him into the hallway, kicking the door closed behind him.

'You made me cry, you bastard. No one does that.'

'Nat, I'm so sorry. I'm a twat.'

She held up a hand, fingers splayed.

'Your turn to not move, OK? Stay there.'

She was back in a minute, face pink and eyes dry. She came close, between the flowers and the wine, one hand on his chest, the other on a shoulder. It was over a year since a woman's face had been so close to his.

'Let's never talk about work,' she said. 'Not unless we're down at the station. Or somewhere official, I mean; it doesn't have to be there. But we never discuss it in our own time, right?'

'Right.'

'And we admit we like each other, right?'

'Yeah, right.'

'Like each other so much that maybe we can't be friends.'

She gave him a smile that made him hold up the bottle in defence.

'We gonna finish this off, then?'

Natalie shook her head slowly.

'Why not?'

'Because I don't want you blaming what happens next on alcohol.'

She leaned in and kissed him, slowly at first, then, at his response, more fervently. One of her hands cupped his jaw, the other pulling the waistband of his trousers towards her as her tongue worked its way into his mouth.

Friday, 15th March

The day itself

During the night, the sky breaks under the weight of its own humidity, thunderous rain driving deep into Anita's dreams. Scott comes too, his horrible erection leading the way. He is chasing her across the overgrown field opposite the warehouse, the two of them naked under the downpour. Anita has to run, but her legs are heavy, the field a sea of mud, every step a fight against the sucking dirt. Behind her, Scott is catching up fast while policemen, judges and prison wardens cheer him on. The nightmare twists and repeats itself, dark figures in a darker world, until Anita's alarm finds her covered in sweat and twisted in the doona, more tired than before she went to bed. The old Anita would have been terrified by the nightmare. She would have taken it as a sign not to push on with her crazy scheme. The professional takes it as a useful warning and determines to do everything exactly as planned.

Arriving at work, Anita waves through the pouring rain to the men in the warehouse because that's what she always does. Then she climbs the metal stairs slowly before confirming the offices are empty, turning on her computer and checking her emails. Everything, the professional tells her, must appear like any other day. That way no one will suspect Scott Patterson is driving to his ten thirty meeting with Blister Plastics – after his obligatory morning coffee – with the contents of fifty sleeping pills in his stomach. And, even when they find out, there will be nothing to link his overdose to Anita. The police will find a coffee-stained Central Coast Mariners mug on Scott's desk, in the same spot as he always leaves it. They will then test that mug and confirm it is utterly clean of sedatives. Nobody, least of all dead Scott Patterson, will be able to point the finger at Anita. She is tempted to check her handbag for the hundredth time that morning – to confirm the mug she purchased the day before is in there – but, instead, she listens to the professional, who tells her there is no need to check. Everything is on track.

What happens in the following minutes remains a mystery. All Anita knows is that at twenty past nine – when Scott Patterson and Alan Drummond start clattering up the stairs – she is staring blankly at her computer screen. High overhead, the rain is hammering on the Colorbond, drowning out the murmurs from the radio. Anita checks her clock instinctively and is shocked by the lost minutes, furious at the professional for having abandoned her so soon. Alan pushes through the door from the stairwell first, his hair and shoulders dark with moisture, a familiar frown on his face. '... long-term view with Blister,' he is saying. 'It's not going to get any easier. We need to keep them sweet. Morning, Anita.'

Anita smiles and even manages a comment on the weather. Then Scott appears behind Alan. He too says hello, adding a wink only she can see.

'Feeling better are we, Anita?'

'Much better, thanks.'

'Mm. Has Tom been up?'

'No.'

'What about Terry Hatch? Has he called?'

'No.'

'Good. If he does, I'm out of the country, yeah?' Scott turns to his nephew. 'Listen, Alan, bird in the hand, that's always been my policy. Get the money in now and let the future worry about itself. At least for these small players. You've finished the proposal, haven't you?'

Alan removes his rain-spattered glasses and starts drying them on his tie, blinking like an animal not used to the light. Above, the rain ramps up its efforts and Anita remembers how, two days earlier in the office with Scott, she had the feeling she was drowning.

'Yes?' says Alan. 'I think so.'

'Good.' Scott clearly believes he's caught his nephew out. 'Bring it into my office, we'll look at it now. Bring us some coffees, would you, Anita? And a pad, in case there's anything we want you to take down. Oops, that sounds a bit rude, doesn't it? Take some dictation, I mean.'

He leaves the tiniest pause before 'tation': a secret just for her. Anita turns to Alan. Surely, he can hear it too? But Alan simply replaces his tie-smudged glasses and frowns, noticing for the first time how wet he's got.

'Is there a towel in the office?' he asks, brushing at his shoulders.

'I don't know, do I?'

Anita's hands are shaking, barely able to type. She understands why they say rage is white, the pure heat of it burning her inside. Staring at her screen, she still catches the look that passes between the two men.

'O–K,' says Alan slowly before disappearing into the sales office. Scott rattles through his keys, but when his office door opens with a bang, Anita doesn't flinch. The professional has reappeared from nowhere and is berating Anita for her rudeness. She must appear calm, as smiling and as harmless as ever: nobody must notice a thing. When Alan returns, flipping through a file as he crosses the opening, Anita waits until he looks up and gives him an apologetic smile, checking he wants a coffee too, in a tone designed to let him know things are fine between them. Alan looks relieved, seems to remember where he is going and, frowning once more, continues on to Scott's office.

As soon as he is inside, Anita stands and turns to the tray on top of the little fridge in the alcove. She flicks on the kettle and takes three mugs – two plain blue, the other Scott's Central Coast Mariners mug – and throws coffee into each. Then she takes from her pocket a wrap of paper. The previous evening, after she put Riya to bed, the professional emptied the fifty capsules bought in the magical pharmacy into this paper, folding it carefully. Anita had wanted to google how long fifty capsules would take to work, the impact they would have on Scott, how to fold the paper to avoid spillage, but the professional reminded her that the police might check her search history. It is better to gamble on killing Scott too soon – or perhaps a little too late – than to risk detection.

Now, as the kettle surges and gurgles, then settles down to boil, Anita empties the dirty white powder into Scott's mug. She has already set an alarm to remind herself to burn the wrap of paper in the bathroom sink as soon as he has left for Blister Plastics. Next the professional applies milk and sugar to the mugs according to Scott's and Alan's tastes, using a separate spoon to stir the one containing the sedatives. Her hands, Anita notices, are not shaking. She stares at them, turning them over and back as if trying on a pair gloves. For the first time in weeks there is not a tremor and, again, she has the sense of having found her true self: the woman previously buried beneath fear and worry. It occurs to her, the first time in years, that she is far too clever and far too well-educated to work at PPC. When this is all over, as soon as it no longer looks suspicious, she will find a better job.

Kicking open the door to Scott's office, proud to be the one to make it bang and the evil blind rattle, Anita sees Alan is sitting upright with his back to the door, trying to defy the lowliness of the chair that faces his uncle. Neither he nor Scott acknowledge her arrival, but, as Anita sits the tray of coffee between them, Alan reaches distractedly mid-sentence – 'Come on Scott, you're deliberately missing the point' – and grabs the mug closest to him without looking at it properly. It is the Central Coast Mariners mug.

'That's got full fat milk and two sugars,' the professional says calmly, leaning across to take the mug from Alan and place it on the desk in front of Scott. Then, grabbing a plain blue mug and turning back to Alan, she says: 'This one's for you.' For the professional has had the good sense to ensure the two plain blue mugs are identically prepared, both with skim milk and no sugar, the way Alan likes it. One less thing to worry about.

'I don't know,' says Scott. 'I'd quite like to see Alan drinking from a Mariners mug.'

Alan is not a soccer fan. He prefers League and even has a Canterbury Bulldogs mug sitting by the kettle. Anita glances at it as she walks into the opening to fetch her chair, wondering if she should have given Alan that to drink from instead. But the professional isn't concerned. Not even when she rolls Anita's chair into Scott's office and sees he hasn't yet touched his coffee.

But then, as the conversation about the Blister proposal drags on – Scott pretending Alan is allowed an opinion – the professional slips quietly away again. Suddenly alone, Anita struggles to concentrate on what is being said. She struggles even to sit still, the truth of what she has done clutching at her like a fever, energy infecting her every limb. She calculates how to spill Scott's coffee or what excuse she can use for throwing it away. Outside the rain changes direction, rattling against the window behind Scott, and they all look, Scott turning in his creaking chair. *Now!* thinks Anita. *Grab his coffee now!* Instead, she remembers the last time she was in this room – Scott's words about Riya. The memory calls the professional back.

'Your coffee's getting cold,' she says.

Scott turns to find Anita is talking to Alan.

'You don't want to get a chill,' she says. 'You got drenched out there.'

Alan nods agreement and drinks, but Scott leaves his mug untouched. He repeats his arguments about the proposal and checks his watch.

'What time's the meeting?'

'Ten thirty,' says the professional. 'You should probably get going.'

Scott picks up his coffee and drinks half the cup. 'No. I think Alan's got this one wrapped up. No need for me to get wet too. As long as he's clear what I want?'

Alan hesitates, catches Scott's expression and nods. Anita finds herself staring at the two men, no idea what the professional would do now. The bloody woman's disappeared again.

'You're the boss,' says Alan.

'Yep, and don't you forget it.' Scott downs the rest of his coffee and plonks the empty mug onto his desk with a satisfied smile. 'Just you and me, then, Anita. We can bed down those plans.'

Anita stands so suddenly that her chair makes a break for the door: rolling fast and threatening to topple. She forces her eyes away from Scott's empty mug, follows her chair, turns it and wheels it out of the room. A few minutes later, the rain as heavy as ever, Alan leaves for the

Blister meeting. Anita's desk phone rings eight times before she thinks to answer it.

'Patterson Precision Cardboards, Scott Patterson's office.'

Because no matter what else happens, she'll always answer his damned phone. Just like she'll always get his coffee and even lie down and let him rape her when the time comes.

'This is Terry Hatch. Can I talk to Scott?'

'No, Terry, I'm very sorry, but Scott's in a meeting. Can I take a message?'

Hatch swears brutally and hangs up. It's the last straw. Anita feels a shift inside herself, similar to the one in rush hour traffic on Wednesday night. The door to Scott's office bangs open.

'Who was that? Was that Hatch?'

Anita rearranges her face. She has to do this herself: the professional is too unreliable.

'Oh my God, Scott, I don't know how to tell you. That was a doctor at a hospital in the Southern Highlands. Fran's been in an accident. They want you to go straight there.'

She watches the blood drain from his face, everything but his eyes shrinking. His fingers are white on the edge of her desk.

'What?! Which hospital? What did they say? What kind of accident?'

'Stay calm,' she says, as if talking to him. 'This is what we're going to do. I'm going to get them on the line, then I'll put them through to your mobile. But you get on the road straightaway, put the phone on hands-free. That's the quickest way for you to have all the information you need and also get to Fran.'

Scott appears to be barely listening. He is swaying slightly – Anita wonders which of her contributions have led to that – one hand on his head, the other rummaging in his pockets until he discovers his keys aren't there. He bangs his office door open and yells to her from inside.

'Where's Alan?'

'He's gone,' she says, leaning forwards to see him through the open door. 'Why?'

But Scott is pressed against the window, staring down through the blurs.

'No,' he says. 'He's still there. I can't drive like this, I'll get him to take me.'

He turns, grabs his jacket, checks all he needs is in his pockets, and races out past her desk. Before she can stop him, he is across the opening and gone, the door to the stairwell swinging slowly behind him.

Monday, 25th March

Ten days after

The bottom of Murdoch's garden wasn't the worst place to be on a gentle autumn morning. The air a soft blanket, butcher-birds and lorikeets flitting between the trees, sun rays visible where branches broke them gold. There was an indecisive breeze playing and, every so often, it brought up the stink from the empty lagoon. Each time it did, Murdoch remembered he was supposed to be inspecting his hedge. He would bend to poke at the red robin's leaves or squat to look at its holes before, less than a minute later, losing himself in his thoughts again: smiling at the weekend behind him; grimacing at the afternoon to come.

Murdoch had once read that lagoons can only support a very specific type of life. Tiny slugs or insects or something: creatures that can live in salt water and fresh water and no water at all, adapting to the sudden shifts between the three. He was beginning to think he needed the same talent himself. The amazing events of the previous days: the worry that wouldn't go away; Natalie, the good news, Velis, the bad. He kept forgetting how to feel, struggling with the sweetness of life when there was salt in his wounds.

Getting together with Nat had been a long time coming – he could see that now – but it had been a surprise to find it happening. But even that was a good thing. Murdoch hadn't had many women in his life – very few he hadn't paid for – and with advance notice he'd have worried about how he was going to perform. He would have presumed he and Natalie would struggle for control, both of them wanting to lead the dance. But on Friday night their push and pull to a common middle ground had been a good part of its own reward. Murdoch had always thought sex was supposed to be feverishly silent, nothing but breath and body delaying the inevitable. But Natalie had kept being funny, joking with him, then teasing him further until neither of them were laughing. It was good and then, after smokes and some talk in the dark, the second time was better, more intimate and knowing: a raw physicality that took him somewhere new. He had never known anything like it, not even with Amanda.

Natalie and he had spent the whole weekend together, not a cross word between them. On Sunday evening, unshaven and sore, he hadn't cared who'd seen him leaving her house. As he picked his way home through the barely lit streets, bats giggling overhead, he kept thinking of that scene from *Singin' in the Rain*. He was at his front door when the text came in. He'd pulled his phone out with a smile, thinking it would be from Natalie, missing him already as much as he was missing her. The effect of the name *Emre Velis*, shining from his screen, had been no better than ever.

Monday morning in his garden, Murdoch was grimacing again – at the remembered disappointment, not the sad the state of his hedge – when Davie's voice dragged him too slowly from his thoughts. Too slowly because, by the time Murdoch came to his senses, he no longer had time to make it to the she-oaks on his neighbour, Mr Minter's land. The leaning trees provided the perfect cover for observing his own house or, at times when his brain was already full, for hiding from Davie and his eagerness. Today, though, by the time he'd turned, Davie was already above him, shouting down from the patio and waving papers like a newspaper boy in a vintage poster. Then Davie had taken the jagged garden steps two at a time and was on the lawn opposite him, peering at him closely.

'Dude, what's wrong?'

'Who says anything's wrong?'

'You look so worried.'

'Shut up, I'm fine. What you doing here?'

Davie held out the papers, the kid in the poster sharing his news. 'The language agency got back to me. They're very thorough, I knew they

152

would be. They got in touch with all the newspapers and heard back from all but one of them. Look!'

Murdoch didn't want to look. He wanted to be alone with his cigarette while he inspected his hedge. Then, suitably calm, he wanted to sit and plan how, later that day, he was going to deal with Emre Velis. He checked his watch. He'd been in the garden for over an hour.

'Not sure I've got time for this,' he said, snatching the papers. 'I'm off out later, should be getting ready.'

'Where are you—'

Murdoch must have pulled a face because, instead of finishing the question, Davie gave a girlish sigh, pulled a sizeable twig off the hedge beside them and started plucking sulkily at its leaves. The first of the papers, Murdoch saw, was a letter from the language agency, a reminder of their ridiculous fees, excuses about the newspaper that hadn't got back to them. The rest were different versions of the same advertisement, all of them featuring Huntingdon's Golf and Country Club.

'Huntingdon's,' said Murdoch. 'Weird.'

'What do you think it means?'

'I think it means you're going to Huntingdon's Golf and Country Club, mate. Wave these adverts under their nose and see what they've got to say about it.'

Davie looked crestfallen. 'I thought you might come with me.'

Murdoch had to laugh at that. 'You're joking, right?'

'Well, it's been a while. The people there might not remember you.'

'Who gives a shit about what *they* remember? *I* remember. I remember them turfing me out on my arse and every bloke there helping them do it. What I don't remember is an apology in the post when they found out I was right. I wouldn't go back there if they gave me a lifetime membership for free.'

Neither of them believed that. Huntingdon's had grass tennis courts and views to the ocean. Murdoch checked his watch again and looked up to find Davie scowling.

'You said you'd help.'

'Davie, mate, I am helping. Trust me, I go in there with you, it'll blow any chances of them talking. Go by yourself, they might just open up.'

Davie pulled another twig from the hedge and yelped when Murdoch jumped forward to slap his hand.

'Mate, will you leave my fucking hedge alone; it's got enough problems as it is. Listen, this is what you have to do. Dress up smart, park your little shit-box of a car out of sight of the office, put your posh on and butter them up. Drop in the fact you went to that school you went to. If that don't work, try the Davie Wonder act or something. And if that's no good, threaten them with the police and the press. You know what they're like about their bleeding reputation.'

He looked at the papers again like he was reading them more carefully. The quickest way to get rid of Davie was not to hurt his feelings.

'When you heading up there?'

Davie shrugged. 'I don't know. Now?'

'Good lad. Sooner the better. Call me as soon as you're out – let me know how you went.'

The car park at the Roseville Bridge boat ramp was deserted, its scruffy grey concrete empty but for faded boxes that, at first glance, looked out of perspective. At second glance, they turned out to be parking spaces big enough for 4x4s pulling trailers, a rich man's car park where everything was bigger than normal.

The parking meter, a grey box at an inconvenient height, stubbornly contradicted the sign at the entrance. The price per hour in these months at those times was this unless the weather was that. In recent times, someone had stuck a laminated A4 to its base. *Boaties!* it said cheerfully, before explaining properly what the sign at the entrance and the instructions on the meter had refused to make clear. It reminded Murdoch of Velis. How the previous time they'd parted, he'd watched the man stop his car and wind down the window to give his unexpired parking ticket to the woman taking his spot. It was the Aussie way: honest people conspiring to beat the system, a gentle and permanent rebellion. Honest? Some fucking joke that was.

Lost in his thoughts, Murdoch found the right coins and fed them methodically into the meter, as rational as an addict at a fruit machine.

Maybe he didn't need to confront Velis at all? Maybe he could leave well alone and everything would come out in the wash? Why should he know everything about everyone he met? It wasn't like he didn't have secrets of his own. As the coins dropped and the meter reluctantly printed his ticket, he remembered what those secrets were. Remembered who he was still hiding from and why he had to know who the hell Velis really was. His feeling he'd heard – or at least read – Velis's name before, his inability to find out anything about him: none of it was good. You could forget about a tumour if you wanted to, but it would only kill you all the quicker.

Back in his car, he sat smoking with the roof down, a laughable attempt at enjoying the day. Five minutes, ten, fifteen. Velis had never been late before and Murdoch wondered whether his internet searches had alerted the man. The idea that Velis might have turned into smoke as suddenly as he'd appeared – the man kosher but offended that Murdoch was researching him – felt strangely like disappointment. Maybe Velis was all right, perhaps Murdoch was paranoid. Maybe, perhaps, might, could, possibly. Hope had a tenuous grip: like the fruit machine might pay out after all. But a good mate to hang out with *and* now a girlfriend too? The gods had never liked Murdoch that much.

At twenty past he started up the Merc, cursing the dollars wasted on the meter, and drove slowly back across the car park. He was nearly at the slip road to the bridge when, through a shading pair of rosewoods, he saw Velis's DB9 dragging a twenty-one-foot Trophy in the other direction. Murdoch hesitated – his last chance to let Velis fade into the past. Then he sighed, turned the car and paralleled Velis back to the car park.

'Sorry, mate!' Velis was out of the Aston Martin as soon as he saw him, his full height cringing in apology. 'I didn't know whether to stop and text you or just keep pushing on. That bloody trailer is a nightmare, I was stuck in the slow lane all the way here.'

The technicalities of reversing the trailer down the ramp, floating the boat and motoring off gave them more than enough to talk about – no need for Murdoch's mood to show. Then, once they had chugged through the intricacies of Middle Harbour and were sitting in Sailors Bay, there were fishing rods, baits and currents to discuss. It was a good hour after Velis arrived that Murdoch found the appropriate time. Or maybe it found him, like he had no say in it at all, his only role to slip the Trophy's ignition key silently into his pocket.

It was the warmest part of the afternoon. In January, it would have been stinking hot, water and sun conspiring to make you sweat, but on an autumn day, diluted by breezes, the temperature was close to perfect.

'Yeah, perfect for burning', Velis told him. 'You're not brown like me, you know.'

He insisted Murdoch slather himself in factor thirty and keep his cap and shirt on. Maybe it was this that got Murdoch's guard down; or maybe it was the life jacket Velis also insisted upon, the same snug fit as a bulletproof vest: that constant reassuring hug. They fished in a silence, only broken by the burr of a boat they couldn't see, until Velis told Murdoch he was smoking a lot.

'What's wrong, Bill? No progress on the Patterson case? You worried about something?'

'Yeah, I am.'

But Velis was taking as much bait as the fish of Middle Harbour. After a slow minute, Murdoch coughed and carried on.

'I was up Laguna way the other day. Went for a swim.'

'What? In the ocean? Mate, that's bloody fantastic. Good for you.'

Murdoch frowned away the comparison to Davie's reaction. 'Yeah, anyway, so on the way back I drove through Gumirri.'

'Right.'

Velis moved slowly, leaning forwards to scratch a shin and then deciding to stay there, hands close to his fishing bag. A sudden movement would have worried Murdoch less. If there was anything in the bag, Velis's readjustment was professional. Murdoch himself had no weapon.

'Yeah, so I thought I'd drop in on your nephew.'

Velis turned his head to give him the full crocodile. 'How is Sufjan?'

'Samir,' said Murdoch. 'Your nephew's name was Samir. And the guy causing the trouble was Henry McCaul, not Harry McCale. You're bad with names, you want to watch that.'

156

Velis gave a lazy look over his shoulder towards the front of the boat: the empty pilot's seat, the empty ignition. When he looked back, reflections of water swimming in his sunglasses, his smile had changed to something gentler.

'I'm sorry,' he said. 'Really, mate, I am so sorry. You caught me on the hop, I had to make up a lie there and then. I'm a planner, very cautious, never been that good at thinking on my feet. So it was a bad story and, yeah, I'm shit with names, so, sorry again. You deserved better, I know that now.'

He turned to his fishing rod, pulled it from its holder and sat back in his seat. It was Murdoch's turn to lean forward.

'Oh well, that's all right then, innit? Sorry for a bad story, let's all be mates, tra la la. But not sorry for bullshitting me in the first place. Who the fuck are you?'

Velis scratched the underside of his chin, a gesture Murdoch hadn't seen on him before. Like even the way the man held himself was a lie.

'I'm going to tell you everything,' the tall man said. 'But you've got to let me tell you something else first. I mean you no harm, you got that?' Murdoch stared at him until Velis coughed awkwardly and carried on. 'I'm sorry, mate, really I am. But I honestly mean you no harm and whatever you do now, however you react to what I'm going to tell you, that will stay the same. You got it? Bill? Mate, you've got to acknowledge that or I'm not going on. I'll swim home, it wouldn't be the first time.'

'So what's in the fishing bag?'

'A little Beretta my wife gave me years ago. Strictly defence only. Take it if you want.'

Velis knew not to move the bag himself. He sat and watched as Murdoch dragged it across the floor of the boat with a foot, lifting it carefully and rifling through until he found the semi-automatic in a sandwich box. It was loaded.

'Go on,' said Murdoch.

'You haven't acknowledged what I said.' Velis took off his sunglasses and smiled again, no fleck of aggression. 'Please?'

'Got it,' said Murdoch. 'You're a bullshit merchant but you don't mean me no harm. Like you'd know where to start.'

'And no matter what happens, things will stay that way.'

'Got it. Talk.'

'Ibrahim Hussein.'

Velis said it like he was breaking bad news: that copper on your doorstep you never want to see. He said no more, trusting the two words to be enough. Murdoch didn't get it at first, not all of it, just the understanding the name was in the wrong scene. He was used to suppressing memories of Hussein, proactively not thinking about what he'd done to him. When Hussein had threatened to tell the Club Murdoch was still alive, Murdoch had turned the fat man's blackmail back on himself. And how had he done that? Something moved in his stomach: a violent contraction that made him lean on the side of the boat, confident he was going to vomit.

The smell of his sun cream combined with the stale water in the bottom of the boat, the reek from the bait box and the fust of his life jacket. The light dimmed, like the sun had found a cloud in the empty blue sky. The local Club executive had thought Hussein was blackmailing him because Murdoch had stolen Hussein's phone and called the man. Henry Wallis was his name. Except Hussein was so fucking stupid that he'd spelled it wrong, Murdoch had struggled to find it in his contact list. Henry spelled 'Hemry', Wallis with a 'V'. Spew from his stomach hit the water, the loudest thing in the bay, the violence of it wrestling with his life jacket. Murdoch pulled at the jacket's toggles, punching at Velis's hands as he leaned over to help. Velis deflected with one hand and opened the toggles with the other, only sitting back when Murdoch could shrug the thing off.

'Breathe,' he said.

'You fucking breathe, you cunt.'

Murdoch stood, the world unsure under his feet.

'I mean you no harm, remember that.'

'Yeah, right, the Club means me no harm. Not sure I ever noticed that.'

Velis shook his head, picked up his fishing rod and sat back in his chair. Sunglasses on, hat low, he was a man gone fishing again.

'I'm not here on behalf of the Club, Bill. I'm here on behalf of myself. The Club thinks you're dead, remember?'

He let the question hang there, fishing silently until Murdoch sat again, the life jacket splayed on the floor, the loaded Beretta cocked and unlocked in his hand. Velis ducked his head forward to look over his sunglasses, a smile in his Middle Eastern eyes.

'Mate.'

'So what do you want?' Murdoch realised his free hand was rubbing his scalp; he pulled it down and used it to steady the Beretta.

'Well, it would be nice if you could stop pointing that thing at me, or at least put the lock on, but that's probably not what you mean. What I want Bill is not the same as what the Club wants, let's get that clear. The Club thinks you're dead. When Hussein started screaming that you'd set him up, my boys just laughed and asked for a better story. Which, needless to say, they didn't get. Poor Ibrahim. But I can tell when a dying man is telling the truth, so I did a little digging. Of my own – I tell you again – just me. None of the team on it, no one. I thought the best place to start was at your last known address. Nothing there and, by the way, your mate really needs to start locking the door to his little shack. His office looked more promising but. You know, I'd only been there ten minutes when you showed up. Easy pickings, you have to say.'

Murdoch was struggling to concentrate. Velis's body could go overboard. Murdoch could get the boat back to shore, Velis had shown him how to drive it. But the shot would be heard by every millionaire at home around the harbour. The police would be at the boat ramp before he was.

'I mean you no harm.'

'Yeah, Emre, so you keep saying. So what *do* you want?'

'Well, again, not having my own gun in my face would be nice for a start. But what I really want is this. I want to know if you'd be interested in a little side venture? Something the Club doesn't know about.'

'Of course!' Murdoch tried a fake laugh, the resulting croak more like a sob. 'This is the bit where you offer me a job and I say no and you say: "You might want to reconsider that," and next thing I know I'm back with the fucking animals I spent half my life getting away from. Go on,

159

your turn. Tell me you can never escape your past, then threaten me subtly with your fucking Turkish charm.'

'Aw, mate, do you think I'm charming?'

'Don't call me "mate". We're not mates; you're just a Club exec and I'm one of your bleeding ex-employees.'

Velis flushed and looked away. There were empty seconds before he spoke again, the harbour slapping the hull.

'Listen, it's a fifty–fifty deal. No one is anyone's employee. And, at the risk of repeating myself, nothing you say will make me do you any harm. You can say no and it's fine with me. I have no interest in the Club knowing you're still alive.'

'Yeah, right.'

'For fuck's sake, Bill, do you honestly think I haven't got to know you by now? Do you think I don't remember what happened to the last Club exec who tried strong-arming you into something you didn't want to do? The only reason Harris died of natural causes is because we didn't get to him first. Bill, listen to me, I want us to be mates. This offer is between you and me, even terms.'

'Except all you need to do is change your mind, call the Club and I'm a dead man.'

'Mate, we work together and either one of us calls the Club and we're dead men.'

They had both raised their voices. Now the silence between them spread and filled the bay, even the breeze keeping its distance until a gang of cockatoos, invisible on the shore, took up the cause and started screaming abuse in turn. Murdoch spat viciously at the water. He locked the Beretta, but kept it cocked on the leg furthest from Velis.

'I thought we was mates.'

'Yeah, well, I didn't exactly plan on liking you either. Let's face it, Bill, going dead on the Club and getting away with it? Bringing down an exec. Seriously damaging the Sydney Metro area for a good twelve months? Mate, I thought you'd be some kind of mad genius psycho and I wouldn't want to work with you. But I do. So, if you're up for it, let's do it. If not, no harm done. We'll go fishing instead.'

Murdoch watched as Velis reeled in slowly, checked his bait and cast again. Beside him, his own rod twitched in its holder, paused and twitched again, stronger this time.

'Whoa,' said Velis. 'Check it out.'

Murdoch held up the Beretta. 'Your wife really give you this?'

Velis grimaced. 'She thinks I'm an accountant.'

Putting his fear and fury into his right arm, Murdoch launched the gun through the air, the splash bigger than he'd have thought. He picked up the rod beside him and passed it to Velis.

'Your fish,' the other man said.

'You fucking have it; I need to think.'

'Tell you what,' Velis took the rod and pushed Murdoch out of the way like there'd never been a bad word between them, 'why don't you just say "No thanks" and we'll leave it at that?'

'Right. And why should I trust you for one second to accept that?'

Struggling with the line, Velis managed a grimace into a grin.

'Oh, that's easy,' he said. 'You should trust me because you want to. Because you like me. Because I'm so fucking charming.'

Friday, 15th March

The day itself

Alone in the office, Anita stands for minutes staring. She imagines the scene in Alan's car. First Scott will insist Alan drive him to the Southern Highlands, but, then, before they even reach the motorway, he will fall asleep in the passenger seat. Alan will struggle to rouse him until, panicked, he will give up on the route south and instead drive to Crosley General. The two men will almost certainly get there in time for Scott to have his stomach pumped. Scott will survive and, shortly after that, he will discover Anita was lying about Fran having had an accident. Her plan will have failed – no, she realises, her plan has already failed – and Scott will soon work out what has happened. Anita imagines him threatening her with prison, making her do whatever he wants if she ever hopes to see Riya again. And, of course, because Riya is her entire world, she will do it. Glimpses of what 'whatever he wants' might mean confuse themselves with memories of Scott's erect penis and the previous night's dream of being stuck in the mud.

Her desk phone wakes her slowly. It goes to voicemail twice, twelve rings each time, and is starting up for a third go when at last Anita moves. She bangs Scott's door open and walks into his office, knowing only she has to follow through with her plan to replace the Central Coast Mariners mug. Without it, she can deny anything Scott might accuse her of. But at the sight of the mug she realises its irrelevance. Scott will not tell the police; he will not need forensic evidence. He will be accuser, judge and enforcer of the sentence and she will not have the strength to resist. Outside, the rain smatters harshly against the window, eager to attract her attention. Looking over the desk, Anita sees Scott has left its top drawer open. Anita feels herself pulled around the desk and, sure enough, when she opens the drawer fully, she sees Scott's injection kit is in there. Its bright red nylon and fat white cross are the surest signs she has seen in days.

Back in the opening, Anita turns on her desk lamp so she can read the tiny writing in the kit's instruction pamphlet. She reads the words aloud with her fingers on the black-and-white diagrams – cartoons to make injections less fearful. It's like reading a book with Riya.

Remove cap as shown in A, insert needle into solution as shown in B.

The words and pictures swim in front of her until she realises, with fury, that she is crying. Snatching a tissue from the box on her desk, she pushes the tears away, snapping at herself to get a move on. Any minute now the door to the stairs will open and Alan will be standing there confused. Then there will be police, but not for long; Scott will see to that. Because to prosecute her, to send her to prison, will remove her from his grasp. Her desk phone rings again, its severe trill cutting through the noise from the roof: Alan's number flashing as if she has thought him into her presence. The previous three calls were from him too.

Anita stands slowly and walks to the cupboard that occupies the wall next to the sales office. On its lowest shelf, next to a box of rags, is a mismatch of cleaning products. Mr Sheen, Windowlene, Ajax. She pushes through them and finds the bleach. Back at her desk, the phone now silent, she pushes and twists to remove the lid from the bleach bottle, then holds it at an angle between her knees. Picking up the syringe from the kit, she removes its cap as shown in image A and puts its tip into the stinking bleach B. Then she pulls back the plunger as shown in C. That is the easy part. Rolling back the sleeve of her shirt, it is the sight of her bare inner arm that makes her pause.

She thinks of Sandeep. The sight of him in his last days, tubes going in and out of his skin, the man she'd married barely there, everyone but her waiting for things to be over. She remembers the tiny moments when the morphine and the cancer both let him go and he saw her and told her he loved her. Then he'd be gone again, slurring and blurred, a dying man abandoning her.

A crescendo in the rain on the roof above her brings Anita back to her senses. The rain, she decides, is too heavy to last. As soon as the Colorbond grows quiet above her, she will pick up the needle and push it in. A few moments of pain and then peace for ever; it's not too bad a bargain. Her only request is a moment's peace in this world first. Surely that's not too much to ask? She lays the needle back on her desk and phones home, but, of course, there is no one there. Maybe it's better that way. Riya is never cute and loving on the phone, she's too interested in the person next to her. Or maybe she simply prefers her grandmother? Maybe that excuses what Anita is about to do, if such an act can ever be excused? Anita consoles herself with the knowledge that Riya will never be told her mother killed herself; not if her grandmother has anything to do with it. Anita's death will be retold as tragic and romantic, like the story of her rebellious cousin who 'died of a broken heart'. Ma will talk of her as a hard-working heroine, not a pathetic victim who died at her desk.

Grabbing a pen, Anita writes out a hurried suicide note, all the details of what Scott has done to her and when: she knows the dates off by heart. He'll talk his way out of it, of course, he will, but the least she can do is make him work for it. She is reading the note through when the phone rings again and, lost in her thoughts, she answers it.

'Hello? Anita? Are you there?'

Alan is short-breathed and talking too fast. Anita stares at the bare skin of her inner arm. If only the deafening rain would stop.

'Anita, I can't hear you. You have to help me. Promise you won't breathe a word of this to Scott. He mustn't know.'

'Alan?'

'Oh, thank God. Listen, Anita, I forgot to bring the proposal with me. Can you email it to John Danson's secretary at Blister, what's her name …?'

'Melanie.'

'That's it. Email it to Melanie and ask her to print out two copies for me so they're ready when I get there. And whatever you do, don't tell Scott.'

'But Scott's with you.'

'What?'

'Scott's with you. Isn't he?'

'No, you heard him. Please, Anita, just email the proposal and tell Melanie I'll be late.'

'Scott went with you.' Anita's realises she is repeating herself, but she struggles to find any other words, the smell of bleach overwhelming her. Above, the rain intensifies further, ten thousand nails dropped every second. Suddenly Anita is talking fast, so loud she is almost shouting. 'He ran after you, Alan! He said you hadn't left yet!'

'Was he actually going to come with me? God, that man! I thought I saw him waving after I drove off; thought he was going to tell me how to do my job again. Bloody typical. Oh God, needless to say, please don't tell him I saw. And, please, Anita, just send the proposal through. I'll owe you a huge favour.'

She taps at her keyboard and gasps at the screensaver of Riya in the park. Then – password, contacts, the right file attached to an email – she tells him it's done and Alan is off the phone, leaving her alone with the stink of bleach, the syringe pointing accusingly. Leaving everything where it lies, she runs downstairs. Outside, the air is saturated, water thrown in every direction. After the metal-roofed offices, it is surprisingly quiet, the rain dull on the tarmac, the noises from the warehouse muted.

Anita leans out to check in all directions, her hair immediately soaking, her shirt thirsty, clinging, but there is nothing to see. Scott's car is gone.

'Oh!'

The sound of her own voice – the exclamation of utter joy – surprises Anita. She pulls her head back inside, clatters up the metal stairs and, at the top, locks the door to the stairwell behind her. Forcing the cap back onto the needle, she bundles the syringe and its accompanying paraphernalia of cloths and folded instructions back into the red nylon pouch, everything squeezed in so quickly the zip won't fully close. Her desk phone rings again, Fran Patterson's number on the screen. Fran who never calls more than once a week, even when she's away. Anita stares at the phone until it has rung out, then walks slowly around her desk and lowers herself into her seat. She is freezing, the wet of her shirt complaining at the air-conditioning, but all she wants to do is laugh. Then she notices she still has one sleeve rolled up. Anita pulls it down hurriedly, the skin of her arm a shameful thing. She is buttoning the cuff with uncooperative fingers when the phone rings again. Fran Patterson again.

'Patterson Precision Cardboards, Scott Patterson's office, Anita speaking. How can I help you?'

'Anita, it's Fran. Oh my God. I've just had a call from the police. Scott's been in an accident.'

'What kind of accident?'

'The car. He came off the road, apparently. Oh my God, they said another few minutes and he might have been on the highway. He could have died!' Fran is crying. 'He's on the way to hospital, or there by now, I don't know. Oh, Anita.'

'Which hospital?'

'What? Oh … erm, Crosley General, the private wing. You know, the new building?'

'Will he be OK?'

'Oh, I hope so. I mean, yes, they say it's just broken bones and concussion, but, oh Anita, they said he's still unconscious! Can you let Alan and everyone know? Tell them I'm on my way; I'll be there as soon as I can.'

Anita tells Fran to drive carefully. There are other words she should use, surprise or sympathy, questions she should ask, but she can think of nothing. Instead, she hangs up and stares at her desk. Her suicide note stares back at her, the words of a woman willing to give up too soon. Anita reaches forward and rips the note into tiny pieces, then shoves the torn paper into her mouth and chews on it until she nearly chokes. Turning to the fridge, she pulls out a bottle of milk and drinks from it so quickly that half the liquid dribbles down her chin. Anita wipes the spillage away with the back of her hand, takes another gulp and eats the rest of the paper, chewing hard it until she can swallow what she has nearly done.

Her senses seem to be on overdrive. All at once she can hear a noise downstairs, smell the bleach and, from the corner of her eye, see her computer click back to its screensaver, the bright colours of Riya's photograph in competition with her desk lamp. Returning the milk to the fridge, she walks around her desk and clicks off the lamp. Then she finds her handbag and her car keys and picks up the injection kit. The red of its lumpish nylon pouch, the glaring white of its cross, really were signs – it's simply that she misread them. After all, it is not she who deserves to die, and she knows the way to Crosley General.

She is outside the door to the stairs, looking back in to confirm she's left nothing behind, when a familiar male voice echoes in the dark stairwell behind her.

'Hello, Anita. Where are you off to then?'

Monday, 25th March

Ten days after

Davie's phone rang as he was crunching his Hyundai Excel along the driveway of Huntingdon's Golf and Country Club. The name that flashed on the phone's tiny screen made him wince but, knowing he had to answer, he pulled over and parked up, making sure he'd left plenty of space for any other driver to pass. The chances of such conscientiousness being necessary at ten thirty on a Monday morning were slim, but, still reeling from the interaction with Brian Yeow, Davie was determined to prove you could be a good detective and a considerate person at the same time.

'DC Burran,' he said, answering the phone with more enthusiasm than he felt. 'How are you? I was going to call you tomorrow for our first weekly update.'

'Yeah, right.' The policeman said each of the words as if he was suppressing laughter. 'Got a lot to report have you? Solved the case?'

Davie sat up straight. He wished he'd left the Excel sitting in the middle of the driveway. 'Actually, nothing that needs sharing, now that you mention it. But Natalie, I mean, Detective Sergeant Conquest, said I should call you weekly.'

'Well, I wouldn't lose sleep over it, mate. She might be getting her knickers in a knot about us working together, but I'm not expecting much from you.'

'Are you telling me I don't need to phone you? I don't suppose you'd like to confirm that in writing?'

DC Burran's snort came clearly down the line and Davie thought of Natalie's words to Bill. *So glad to see you're getting into the new spirit of things.* He waited for the detective constable to continue – Bill said you always got the upper hand on people if you made them talk first. But maybe DC Burran knew that game too. It was Davie who gave in.

'So why are you phoning me? Are the police aware of a development in the case?'

'Yeah, right.' DC Burran put the same amusement into the same two words. 'Nah, the boss just said I should let you know: Anita Patel's gone to Fiji.'

'What?! When?'

'Dunno. Yesterday I reckon. She phoned us from Nadi airport, said she'll be away till the fifth.'

'But I spoke to her on Saturday – she didn't mention she was going anywhere.'

'Spend a lot of time talking about your holiday plans, did you?'

'No, but—'

'Not sure what the big deal is, but the boss said I should let you know. So now I've done that. See ya later.'

'Hang on. Aren't the police going to start extradition procedures or something?'

Davie hated the way his voice went high when he was surprised. It echoed around his tinny car and, in response, he heard, actually *heard*, DC Burran shrug.

'Not sure what the point of that is,' the policeman said. 'Takes ages to get the forms signed off and the woman and her family will be back by then. It's not like she's even a suspect.'

'So you're not going to do it?'

Burran didn't reply and Davie knew that Natalie had told him to start up the necessary process. He smiled at the tiny victory – over DC Burran, not Anita Patel – and listened to the phone find a new kind of silence as the policeman hung up on him.

Anita Patel. Davie's first instinct had been right: the woman must be guilty. Why else would she leave the country? Then, remembering what she had been like in her cosy living room, he asked himself the same question Natalie and Bill had asked: how a woman her size could have wrestled Patterson out of his hospital bed and spirited him away by herself. Or if, Patterson – paranoid about hiding his HIV status – had maybe left of his own free will? Davie sat pondering the question, then noticing the scenery outside the car, remembered where he was and why.

Driving on, Davie saw that the grounds of Huntingdon's Golf and Country Club were similar to the grounds of his old school. Everything in sight had been tamed and trained until it might as well have been man-made. The lawns were trimmed, the hedges squared off, the lilly-pillies fully pollarded until they did what they were told. Grimacing at the memories the view provoked, Davie took Bill's advice and parked out of sight of the main buildings.

The path that took him up to reception ran past the tennis courts – obedient agapanthus lining the way – and he watched two silhouettes warming up behind the sponsored gauze that hid the wire fence. He listened to them too, the way they bellowed their conversation the length of the court. Again, it was just like school: boys proud of themselves just for being there, as if luck and their parents had had nothing to do with it. Then, at the top of the path, he turned and caught sight of the ocean, a distant blue line beyond the courts and the golf course further down the hill. Overnight, he knew, the swell had picked up again, the first good surf day in weeks, the water at its warmest. And here he was twenty kilometres inland in a place that reminded him of school. He forced a smile, told himself this was what hard work felt like, and pressed on towards the buildings.

The club house at Huntingdon's was a grand Federation property: verandas on each sandstone storey, three-sixty-degree views over what had once had been rolling paddocks. The renos were first-class, the woodwork on the veranda faultless, the paintwork too. Being an estate agent, no matter how much you hated it, left a lasting legacy and Davie could guess how many millions someone had gambled on the idea of a country club on the Central Coast. But despite all the money spent, there was something missing in the building now and it reminded him of some of his mother's friends: the original beauty somehow lost in the attempt to hang on to youth.

Inside, he found a high-ceilinged hallway, the air dull and a little too cool after the perfect day outside. A vase of overblown lilies, their scent too sweet, blocked his view and, for a second or two, Davie thought he was alone. He stood looking around, tapping the translations nervously against his thigh.

'Can I help you?'

Stepping to one side, Davie saw a small reception counter tucked beside a flight of stairs that ran up one wall, then out of view. At the counter was a tight-haired woman in head-to-toe black and a professional smile. Behind her, a man sat hunched over a desk tucked under the angle of the stairs, a lamp helping with his paperwork.

'Hello,' said Davie. 'I hope so. I was wondering if I could speak to the manager?'

At this, the man at the desk turned. He was pale under bushy little eyebrows, at the early end of middle-age. Seeing Davie, he stood quickly, avoiding the stairs above him with the instinct of a man hurt before.

'If it's about membership, I can help you,' said the woman.

'It's fine, Irene,' said the small man, now beside her.

'But …'

'I said, it's fine. And, anyway, weren't you going to check on the housekeeping schedule?'

The woman called Irene gave the man a strange look and echoed 'fine' in a way that meant the opposite. Then she turned, opened a folding panel in the counter and, without another word, walked past Davie and jogged up the stairs. The little man she left behind beamed at Davie.

'How can I help you?'

'My name's Davie Simms.'

'Yes, I know your name. I'm Jonathan Hughes, the manager here and I'm very excited to meet you.'

This happened so rarely these days that Davie forgot to prepare for it. There had been a time when it had been normal, then a much longer period when it happened often enough for him to hold out hope. Now when it happened it was a surprise and Davie's bumbling, humble reaction came almost naturally.

'Oh,' he said, looking at his hands, folding the translations awkwardly. 'Really?'

'Oh yes.' Hughes leaned forward, elbows on the desk. He was wearing a suit too small for him, the shoulder pads struggling. 'I bought both your albums and saw you live four times.'

'There were three albums,' said Davie, before he could stop himself. 'But don't worry, no one bought the third one.'

'Oh?' Hughes seemed dismayed. 'But I suppose that's show business, isn't it? You're a superstar one day and then it's all over.'

'Quicker than you'd think.'

Hughes gave him a kind smile. 'It's not just you superstars, you know. I sometimes think we all achieve our best when we're young and then spend the rest of our lives pining after it.'

He looked so wistful that Davie was momentarily lost for words. He wondered if Hughes was about to share too much information.

'Well, it's nice to know someone remembers me,' he said. 'I'm being interviewed by the *SMH* next week and I was wondering if anyone reading the article would even know my name.'

'Of course, they will!' said Hughes excitedly, his English accent breaking for cover. 'You did have a lot of fans "Up Around Here" you know.'

Davie pretended to consult the papers in his hand. It wasn't only Hughes's excitement that was unnerving. There was something wrong, he knew, with how much pleasure he got from people remembering the names of his songs.

'Did you want membership?' Hughes asked. 'I'm sure it wouldn't be a problem. You'll like it here. You're probably free all day so you can come at the quiet times. Are you a tenniser or a golfer? Everyone seems to be one or the other, never both. It's the temperament, I suppose.'

Hughes seemed to realised he was babbling. He coloured and stood straight, pulling at his shirt cuffs.

'I don't mind a bit of tennis,' said Davie, sorry for the little man. 'I hate golf. Even when I'm old, I think I'll hate it. My real love is surfing.'

'Surfing?' Hughes pronounced the word as if he might have heard of it, but he wasn't quite sure.

'Yes. You see, I'm not actually here about membership at all. And I'm not free during the days, I'm quite busy actually. I'm a private detective now. That's what the *SMH* story's about.'

Hughes laughed, too much eye contact for comfort.

'No. I mean it, really.' Davie fished out a business card and slid it across the counter. 'I am a private detective. I'm here about a case.'

'A case?'

'You've probably heard about Scott Patterson going missing?'

The manager looked warily at Davie's card but didn't touch it. He sniffed and worked at his cuffs again, properly this time.

'I am unable to reveal any information about our members.'

'Oh, is Patterson a member here? I didn't know that. Did he look after recruitment for you?'

'As I said, I can reveal no information. This is a private club and we pride ourselves on our discretion. I'm sure you understand.'

Hughes had pulled his shoulders back and was jutting out his chin with the hurt pride of the betrayed.

'Oh, go on,' said Davie. 'Help out a former popstar, eh?'

'Really,' the manager said. 'I must ask you to leave.'

'So you don't know why Patterson paid for these job ads to appear in papers overseas?'

It was called a puppy-dog sale. You put the little animal into their arms and, before they knew it, they couldn't say no. With houses you let people sit in the lounge room and drink their takeaway coffees, or left them to wander around upstairs, opening the cupboards without you watching. Before Hughes could protest further, Davie had lain the translated newspaper advertisements on the counter in a row. Hughes crossed his arms and stared straight ahead: a man used to resisting temptation.

'No,' he said, his pale eyes cold. 'Please leave.'

'But Scott Patterson, a member here, is missing and we need to find him urgently. It's his wife who's asked me to find him and the police are co-operating with us. It's fair dinkum.'

'Please leave.'

Davie cursed Bill for not being there. He wouldn't be pushed around by a terrier like Hughes. Mind you, he'd probably reach across the counter and punch him and that wouldn't help either.

'Listen,' he said quietly. 'You're a fan, so I'll help you out. As soon as the police find out about this, they're going to be crawling all over this place. There'll be a blue flashing light outside, uniformed officers in here, stories in the press. Your members aren't going to like that.'

Hughes shifted his weight from one hip to the other. 'I'm sure they'll prefer it to knowing I shared confidential information with a *private detective*. Besides, Chief Superintendent Hamilton is on our committee and I'm sure he'll manage things through the proper channels.'

'Oh,' said Davie. 'The committee, of course. Is Mal Butler still Chair?'

Hughes seemed to struggle with whether this, too, was confidential information.

'What's that got to do with anything?'

'Oh, well, Mal's my godfather, that's all. He's got a bit of a soft spot for me; asks after me every time he plays golf with my dad. John Simms, know him? He's on the committee too, isn't he? It would be a real shame if they both found out the police were called unnecessarily when you could have answered my questions nice and quietly on a Monday morning with no one around. Has Uncle Mal still got that dreadful temper? He fired the last manager, didn't he?'

Two blackmails in one week: Davie wondered if he'd start getting used to it. Hughes glared at him, unfolded his arms shakily and grabbed his side of the counter. Instinctively, Davie turned to calculate the distance he'd have to cover if Hughes came out from behind the counter. Turning back, he found the little man frozen. Hughes's eyes were glazed over and the colour had drained from his face. Davie remembered Jane, his sister, on a fairground ride when she was ten. It was how they'd discovered her fear of heights.

'Mr Hughes?'

Hughes didn't answer and Davie wondered if the little man was holding on to the desk to keep himself upright.

'Listen,' he said. 'Mr Hughes, listen. It's going to be fine. I'm not going to tell Dad or Uncle Mal anything. But look at this.' He slid one of the recruitment adverts between Hughes's hands. 'All you have to do is confirm Patterson was recruiting for Huntingdon's in Indonesia, China, Vietnam, Thailand and Cambodia. Just nod and I'll know this is a false lead and we're all done. Mr Hughes? Jonathan?'

Hughes jolted and shook his head jerkily: an actor in a film with frames missing.

'No.'

'No?' said Davie. 'No, you won't help me?'

Hughes looked at him with the same hatred Davie had seen in the pharmacy.

'No, Scott Patterson doesn't do our recruitment. These, I can't explain. They didn't come from here.'

He pushed away the articles with more disgust than he had reserved for the words 'private detective', shoving at them with such emotion that Davie couldn't help but stare at the little man. He remembered Jane on the rollercoaster ride again – what fear had done to her features. Then Hughes shoved the papers again so that they lifted and floated to the edge of the counter. Davie snatched at them before they fell to the floor.

'You're sure?' he said.

'Of course, I'm sure. This is a reputable establishment. We certainly wouldn't recruit in the third world.'

'And this contact address mentioned in the article, the PO box, that's not correct?'

'No.' Hughes barely glanced at it. 'I've never seen that address in my life. I told you, these are nothing to do with Huntingdon's. Now, please leave.'

They both looked up at the sound of feet on the stairs: Irene coming slowly into view.

'Oh,' she said uncertainly. 'I'll just check the laundry.'

'No,' said Hughes quickly. 'I'll do that. You can see Mr Simms here out to his car. He's decided there's nothing for him here after all.'

Davie smiled at Hughes sadly and said he could see himself out. Another fan lost, nothing new there.

Wednesday, 27th March

Twelve days after

Natalie had reminded Murdoch she was doing two jobs at the same time: he mustn't take it the wrong way if she was never free. But maybe the old job was taken off her, or maybe she got the extra staff she needed. Either way, Murdoch saw her every night in the first half of that week and she didn't mention work once, not even when he joked it had been years since the police had shown so much interest in him.

Murdoch went to her house each time, arriving after dark out of coincidence rather than any sense of secrecy, too keen to be in her bed to care who saw him come and go. The erotic hold Natalie had over him was complete: any single sense enough to make him hard. The touch of her hand on the back of his neck, the smell of her skin. The sight of her returning to the bedroom naked but for a T-shirt was a memory he would take to the grave. But, of the two of them, Natalie was the more demanding. Murdoch wanted her so greedily, so needily, he instinctively

174

reined himself in. Over the phone, he would suggest dinner or a walk, then feel his soul soaring as she suggested sex instead. On the Monday night, when he had said they should go to his house sometime, that he didn't want her thinking he was being secretive, she rolled over and looked him in the eye.

'All my cycling stuff's here and I've got to be at work early in the morning. But thank you.' She kissed him slowly, both their eyes open and Murdoch realised with horror and joy that he'd never been in trouble like this before.

Wednesday lunchtime, suddenly free in the daytime now – 'Don't get excited, it won't last' – Natalie phoned to ask what he was up to that afternoon. Murdoch grimaced. He was supposed to be driving south with Davie, helping him follow up some unlikely leads. But what was the point in resisting? When he spoke to Natalie, even his voice was different, like a man trying not to sing.

'Nothing,' he said. 'I'm free all afternoon. What were you thinking?'

'You ever been to the Drop Off?'

'What is it? A pub?'

'No, it's a— You know what, I'll surprise you. Get into your swimmers, I'll pick you up in half an hour.'

Murdoch nearly called her back. He wanted to warn her he wouldn't cope with a gap in the rocks, a loud and surging swell. He'd seen blow holes and cauldrons on the telly – some fundamental kind of hell – and he didn't want to bottle in front of her. All he needed to say was that he had to help Davie on the case and she'd be sure to understand. But not calling her back felt better. He could swim now, after all. He was, in fact, a man who swam in the ocean alone. Remembering this to be true, Murdoch felt a rush like the first time on a good drug – pride or relief or maybe just joy at the idea of Natalie and him swimming together. Whatever it was, he walked himself to the hall mirror and told himself to calm the fuck down. When that didn't work, he reminded himself of Emre Velis and watched his reflection remember what life was really like.

Natalie, it turned out, was the proud new owner of a shiny black Mazda MX-5. Murdoch nearly asked her if she'd been robbing banks before remembering they weren't quite there yet.

'I got it the day my promotion came through,' Natalie beamed. 'I've been promising it to myself long enough. You've walked past it every day for the last few days. I keep it under a cover or it would be filthy in minutes from the all the leaves and the birds hanging over my place.'

Murdoch wanted to take her out in *his* car, the wind in her hair and his hand on her leg, but Natalie wasn't stupid: she knew how he'd paid for it. He gave her his impressed face, threw his towel in the boot and climbed in.

She drove the Crown Road like it was Brands Hatch, her lifelong experience more than a match for his daring in the Merc. Murdoch tried to relax and enjoy himself but inevitably kept thinking of his time trial against Velis. Every time he thought of the bloke it was like a cloud had come over him: anger and something else. Disappointment and – why not admit it? – *sadness*. Fucking sadness that someone he respected, someone he liked, didn't like him back just for himself. It didn't matter what Velis had said, Murdoch knew the Club and its type well enough to know Velis was only interested in what he could get out of the arrangement. Murdoch sighed, rested his head back and looked at the kaleidoscope overhead, the sun catching and sparkling through the trees. The weather had been heating up all week, even in autumn, when it was supposed to be going the other way. Global warming, Armageddon, Murdoch didn't care – he was going swimming. He turned to Natalie and asked her where they were going. In return, she grinned and told him he'd see soon enough. It didn't help him relax.

The Wurra Wurra Road was the scenic route to the highway but only because it avoided Crosley. There was a lookout point on it somewhere, a clear view across the bays and inlets of Broadwater, but, apart from that it snaked through the same twiggy bushes that covered half of New South Wales: thick scrub just tall enough to hide the view. You could get lost in it for days, Natalie told him, no idea if the road was ten metres away until something drove past. Murdoch thought that sounded comforting. Then, slowing on a bend that looked like all the others, Natalie turned onto a rocky fire trail blocked after a few metres by a heavy triangular gate. She parked in a spray of dirt and laughed at the confusion on his face.

'Hope you don't mind a walk,' she said. 'Most people do, thank God.'

They strolled along the fire trail for forty minutes, the sun warm on their backs, until, at an ancient wooden arrow – a worn-away 'D' above a pale 'ff' - they found a narrow path. Here the scrub was close and scratchy and the way was always down, the steepness soon twisting them back on themselves until, at yet another corner, Murdoch suddenly heard thick and rushing water. Ignoring his stomach and the idea that he should be with Davie in the Southern Highlands right now – that this was the world getting its revenge – he told himself it would be fine and concentrated on nothing but Natalie's little rucksack bobbing along ahead of him and taking the springy branches she held patiently out of his way. Then the path ran under a huge overhang, a cave with no bottom, the way down just steps now, uncovered rocks and dry earth held by rotting planks until, surrounded by tree fern trees, they were level with flat water, staring at the source of the noise.

'Bleeding hell,' said Murdoch. 'It's like a Timotei advert.'

Twenty feet ahead of them, a waterfall tumbled down a high rock face before dropping the last centimetres into the pool. The air around them was green mist: light diffused by a million leaves, then caught in ten times that number of droplets. Murdoch watched Natalie pull off her small rucksack and squat down to rummage inside. She pulled out a black bin liner, shook it open and reached down to the wet earth at her feet. A Magnum wrapper lay caught in a finger-wide stream snaking from the pool into the scrub. She found another three pieces of litter before she looked up and caught his eye.

'What?'

'Nothing.' He had to shout to make himself heard. 'It's nice. The way you don't mind fixing the mess other people make.'

'Someone's got to. Otherwise it wouldn't be paradise, would it?'

She spotted something further round the pool, a flash of grubby white amongst wet brown leaves, then came back with a smile he recognised. After tying the bag and hanging it on a young gum tree, she crossed her arms to the waist of her T-shirt and pulled it off over her head. She wasn't wearing a bra. Maintaining full eye-contact, she pulled off her trainers, socks, trousers and knickers. Murdoch looked around nervously, trying to spot the steps to the path.

'I thought you said to bring my swimmers,' he said.

'Just in case. But there's no one here is there?'

'Yeah, but what if someone comes?'

'That's generally how it works.'

Not today it didn't. Murdoch had never been naked outdoors before: it felt like being locked out of somewhere. He wasn't used to places with no people and knew the noise of the waterfall would hide the footsteps of anyone who might arrive. Then they struggled to find a suitable place to sit, stand or lie. The idea of doing it in the water deflated him completely. It was a first for him, a failure to perform, but Natalie didn't seem to mind. It was normal, she said; lots of guys couldn't do it outside.

She jumped into the water with a whoop, but Murdoch edged himself in more slowly, shocked at the cold. Fully in, he gasped again and tried a few strokes, mouth clear of the water, like he was keeping a cigarette dry. Then, from nowhere, he saw the purity of where they were. Following Natalie's example, he opened his mouth to drink what they were swimming in. He trod water, laughed at nothing and watched Natalie climb out and lie on a flat rock: the only spot in the hollow where the sun shone through. Doggy-paddling over, he climbed out and lay beside her, the rock less comfortable than it looked.

'And all of this is natural?' he said, up on his elbows. 'It all just happened by itself, like?'

She shook with laughter, eyes closed, tiny droplets falling from her nipples.

'Of course.'

'I didn't know there was places like this. Not any more.'

'Yeah, well, we keep them secret, but the further you get from the city, the more of them there are.'

He whistled slowly. There would never be an end to the stuff he didn't know.

'Imagine the whole world was like this. Just plants and water and stuff. No people making a mess of things.'

'Oh, come on, people aren't so bad. They just need telling how to be good. Even the bad ones can be rehabilitated.'

She elbowed him in the ribs and he smiled despite himself.

'You really believe that don't you, Nat? You really believe bad people can turn good. Overcome their base nature?'

The last two words were from Velis and Murdoch regretted them immediately – the man didn't belong here. But his memory wasn't easy to shake.

'You can't change who you are,' Velis had told him. 'You're a crook, an adventurer. You're bored in the normal world, same as me. Why do you think we've been doing all those crazy things these last few weeks? We need the thrill. And what I'm proposing, mate, you know full well there's no thrill like it.'

Murdoch blinked the memory away. Natalie had opened her eyes and rolled onto to one side, her head in one hand, the other on his stomach.

'I think everybody wants to be good,' she said, 'even if they don't know what it means.' She caught his expression. 'It's like the people who drop litter round here. They don't know that what they're doing will ruin this place and, most times, when someone sees me picking rubbish up, they want to help. Or, on a different scale, it's like when you introduce a bank robber to a woman whose life he's ruined by sticking a gun in her face.' He flinched and knew that she felt it. She started talking faster than before. 'He normally wants to make it right. Or when you take shoplifters to the rough part of town. Show them what life is like where no one can be trusted. Cages over the windows, alarms under doormats, shopkeepers staring as you walk down the aisles. You tell them that this is what they're creating and sometimes they get it.'

'You do all that?'

'Well, no, actually, but I'd like to. That's what they should spend money on instead of just banging youngsters up.'

Murdoch snorted. 'I don't think your average bank robber is going to pass on an easy hundred grand just cos he feels guilty about some nice lady having nightmares.'

'It's more than nightmares, Bill. It can lead to a complete nervous breakdown.'

'Doesn't matter. Trust me, most crims are not that nice.'

'You mean the "animals"?'

Murdoch didn't want to be having this conversation, not here. He stood quickly – Natalie's turn to flinch – and threw himself into the water. He'd hadn't remembered how cold it was and, for a moment, his limbs forgot how to swim. Swearing in his head, he came up into the noise and pushed his panic into a shape between breast stroke and treading water, taking a slow minute to breathe himself calm. Natalie was on her back again, eyes closed to the sun. It was like being a kid, staring at a picture because it had a naked lady in it. Murdoch pushed against the water for a while longer, enjoying the sensation of everything floating, then climbed out and stood astride her. Watched her frown at the cold water dropping onto her breasts, then smile as she shaded her eyes and looked up at what he had for her.

Friday, 15th March

The day itself

At the sound of the man's voice, Anita turns so suddenly that she loses her balance. Using the hand holding her keys, she grabs at the door frame, pinching her fingers painfully between the metal and the wood. Over-compensating with her weight in the other direction, one of her feet twists painfully away from its shoe and her handbag slips from under her elbow. She catches the bag at the last second, but something else falls too and, in her pain and confusion, Anita can't understand what it might have been.

'Oh, Terry,' she says. 'I didn't hear you come in.'

Terry Hatch stares at her in the gloom of the stairwell, eyes narrowed and calculating. He is wearing a pale blue polo shirt that stretches across his belly, its shoulders and chest soaked and moulded around his hairy frame. As Anita watches, Hatch bends down to pick up the injection kit from the metal landing between them. Overhead the rain intensifies, its hammering faster than ever, a continuous blur of metallic noise.

'You all right, Anita? Why you so jumpy?'

'I'm not!' She laughs at the tremble in her voice. 'Oh, thank you, I'll take that. Are you looking for Scott?'

'Your foot,' Hatch gestures with the kit in the half-light. 'You hurt yourself?'

She can feel every pulse passing through her ankle and she knows already it will swell.

'I'm fine,' she says. 'It's these silly shoes.'

Hatch inclines his head to one side and gives Anita a strange look as she forces her foot back into her shoe. The pain makes her start to sweat, salt water mixing with the rain in her still-damp shirt.

'This is a bit lumpy.' Hatch is squeezing the injection kit with both hands, like a child working out a Christmas present. 'Whoever packed it didn't do a good job. What is it?'

'It's Scott's.' Anita, the discreet and loyal secretary, tugs the kit gently from Hatch's hands. 'Were you looking for him?'

It's unpleasant here on the dark landing with Hatch, his belly almost touching hers. Anita has often wondered if the man buys his polo shirts to fit his biceps, forgetting they have to accommodate the rest of him too. She wants to move away from him but she doesn't trust her ankle to get her down the metal staircase.

'You all right, Anita?'

Before she can answer, there are footsteps below them and Tom Brandle, the foreman from the warehouse, appears at the turn of the stairs. He seems surprised to see anyone there.

'G'day,' he says, squinting uncertainly up at them. 'Anita, there's two blokes in a car downstairs blocking the entry—'

'They're with me.' Hatch says it in a tone that doesn't invite questions, but maybe Tom Brandle doesn't hear it over the noise of the rain. Or maybe he chooses to ignore it.

'Sorry, mate,' he says. 'You a client of ours?'

Anita wants to scream at the two men to get the hell out of her way. Instead, the professional tells Tom, yes, this is Terry Hatch, an important client, and pushes open the door beside her again, testing the carpet in the opening as if climbing into hot water. The pain in her ankle is acute, but she manages to limp back to her desk. Hatch follows her in, asking once more if she is all right.

'I'm fine!' she laughs, leaning heavily on her desk. 'But if you're looking for Scott, you're out of luck. He's had an accident, he's in hospital.'

Dropping her handbag and the injection kit onto the desk, she uses both hands to guide herself around the desk's edge to her chair.

'Really?' says Hatch, the question mark barely there. 'Badly injured, I'm guessing.'

'I think I just twisted it.'

'No, I mean what happened to your boss?'

'Oh. A traffic accident, apparently. He fell asleep at the wheel. I mean, they think he did. I mean, it's awful. Just terrible.'

Did Fran tell her Scott had fallen asleep at the wheel? Anita forces herself to believe she did, swallowing hard against the blushes crawling up her neck.

'Right. OK.' Hatch is clearly only now beginning to believe her. 'For real? Which hospital did they take him to?'

Anita forces a helpful smile – more effective than the words she wants to yell. Then Tom Brandle is in the doorway too, asking what's going on, who's in hospital, and she has to repeat her lies. Except, she remembers slowly, they're not lies at all.

'He's in Crosley General,' she tells the two men. 'The private wing. Do you want me to find the number?'

Tom Brandle doesn't move. He is a man who does things in order, Anita remembers. First, listen; second, think; third, make a decision. Hatch is faster. He nods at Scott's office door.

'You sure he's not in there?'

'Absolutely.'

'Mind if I take a look?'

Tom starts to protest, but Hatch ignores him. Waddling across the damp carpet, he pushes at Scott's office door, then pushes again, harder, until it bangs open. His fat frame immediately fills the gap, his head disappearing around the door.

'You can't go in there!' Tom is clearly furious, so Anita gives him a soft look to tell him everything is fine. A gentle rolling of the eyes that this is nothing unusual, she can manage this man herself.

'I told you, Terry,' she says, maintaining eye contact with Tom. 'He's not here.'

Hatch turns, no happier than before, and walks back to her desk, ignoring the foreman entirely but annoyed by the bang of the office door behind him. Above, the rain falters, weakens and suddenly stops, the abrupt silence making them all look up. When Anita looks back down, Hatch is quietly assessing her. His eyes move to the red nylon pouch, lumpy on the desk between them. But it is Tom Brandle who speaks.

'When did this happen?'

He is still standing in the doorway to the stairwell, as if afraid Hatch might escape. As she responds, Anita is unsure which of the two men to look at: Tom asking the questions, or Hatch, uncomfortably close.

'He left for an appointment just before ten,' she says, 'and then I got a call from Fran. The police had contacted her. That's all I know.'

Tom makes the right noises, offering to call people or help in any way, insisting the reason for his visit is no longer important. Hatch, still ignoring the foreman, twists his mouth unpleasantly as he watches Anita fend him off. He only speaks when Tom has been reassured there is nothing he can do and, at last, has gone.

'Right,' he says, rapping his knuckles on her desk. 'Well, let's hope for the best. But you remind Scott he owes me a call, yeah? It's important. The moment you talk to him, you tell him to get in touch with me.'

Hatch walks to the door to the stairs and gives her a last curious look before disappearing into the stairwell, footsteps fading down the metal steps.

Anita waits for her resolve to crumble. To remember she is not a professional at all but a bumbling amateur making mistakes at every turn. To cry in despair and wake up to the madness of what she was planning to do. How can she possibly go through with it now when two witnesses have seen her with Scott's injection kit in her hands?

But her resolve does not crumble. She does not cry and she does not wake up. Instead, the professional voice inside her head points out that, whatever happens now, she must replace the apparatus in the red nylon pouch with a clean syringe and needle. And, if she's going to do that anyway, she might as well get on and finish the job at hand. The kit can be replaced, everything can be explained away, but only if Scott Patterson dies. Otherwise …

But 'otherwise' is more than enough.

Anita stands suddenly, gasping at the pain in her ankle, and hobbles to the cleaning cupboard. There she fishes out the office's ancient first aid kit. It doesn't contain a syringe and needle but it does hold a bandage long enough to wrap up her foot and ankle. She takes her time over the job, lost in her own thoughts, still waiting to wake up and remember she doesn't want to kill Scott Patterson. When she walks again, her ankle doesn't hurt much less than before, but it makes her feel better to know she has done something about it. Mind over matter, strength over pain, top teeth over her bottom lip, Anita picks up her handbag and the injection kit once more – remembering this time to grab an umbrella too – and leaves for the hospital. Second time lucky.

Progress, however, is slow. The rain has returned more intensely than ever; the blurred traffic is crowded and crawling; puddles stretch across entire roads. Lost in thoughts of where the hell she's going to find a clean syringe and needle, Anita nearly runs down a pedestrian on a zebra crossing. The pedestrian – male or female, it's impossible to tell – is dressed for the weather, completely hidden by black Gore-Tex and gumboots until a pink fist is shaken in Anita's direction. Anita's reaction, a surprise to herself, is to laugh a loud and derisive laugh – the sound of a woman who has finally shed her fears. She is tempted to drive after the Gore-Tex figure, already barely visible through the insistent rain, and show her what a car can really do to a pedestrian. Instead, she presses on to Crosley Hospital, passing uncounted minutes in frowning over the steering wheel until, at last, she must admit she is lost. She knows only that she's in the confusion of streets behind the football stadium. But even this does not faze her. With more determination than ever, Anita tells herself she is a professional. An unstoppable professional. Pulling up

Google maps, she finds she is laughing again: at herself now, perhaps. Or maybe just at the world for thinking it can thwart her.

Shortly after two o'clock, she parks in the car park of the hospital's private wing.

Wednesday, 27th March

Twelve days after

Even after navigating the right motorways around Sydney, it took Davie four hours and almost a whole tank of petrol to get to the Southern Highlands. This was definitely Bill's fault. It had been a fair assumption they would drive down together in Bill's Mercedes, which had to be twice as fast and three times as fuel-efficient as Davie's own car. And it had been a fair assumption that—

Davie corrected himself. The only fair assumption with Bill was that he'd let you down. Over the phone at lunchtime the Englishman had explained his last-minute change of heart by complaining the journey would be a waste of time. That there was no point in travelling so far when the police had already done their bleeding job. But Davie knew Bill well enough to know that wouldn't be the real reason. He didn't know what the real reason was, but he'd bet fifty dollars it wasn't that.

The day got worse at a busy servo outside Berry. When Davie tried to pay for a full tank of petrol, none of his cards – not even the one he'd promised himself to only ever use in emergencies – managed to persuade the little payment machine to say 'Approved'. The woman behind the service station counter, beefy arms in a well-ironed work shirt, was years past caring, but the motorists queuing behind Davie were fascinated.

'Have you not got another card?'

'Fuck 'em, what they gonna do, syphon it out again?'

'What about EFTPOS, has you no money in your bank account neither?'

Davie smiled his way backwards from the competing suggestions and stood next to the ready-meal microwave so he could work out what to do. He was due a payment from Fran Patterson in four days but he could hardly ask for an advance. Any call to her would involve a thirty-minute explanation of what progress he'd made since their previous conversation and he wasn't sure he had enough credit on his phone for that, let alone the mental energy required. Asking Bill for a loan was equally unappealing, but at least the call would be short. And besides, Bill owed him.

'Eighty bucks?' Bill puffed when Davie explained the situation. He sounded like he was walking uphill. 'That's more than your bleeding old banger's worth. What you putting in it – gold? I told you not to bother going down there.'

Bill repeated the argument he'd given earlier in the day when explaining why he wasn't coming along: why would hospital staff who'd told the police they knew nothing tell Davie a different story?

'Maybe they won't,' Davie said. 'But maybe they will. And, do I need to remind you, there is a level of urgency here, after all? It's like exams, Bill, you have to work as hard as you can, so that no matter what results you get, you'll know you did your best.'

'You what? What do you know about exams? The way I remember it, you've got about as many qualifythingies as I have, despite that posh school you went to.'

'Exactly, and I don't want to make the same mistake again. So now I'm going to do things properly. Follow up every lead, dot the i's and tick the boxes. I refuse to lose faith.'

'You can't afford to lose faith, mate. You're like a gambler doubling down to cover your losses, throwing good money after bad.'

Davie was tempted to hang up, but he knew he had no other line of credit. Instead, he listened to Bill repeat his arguments. *'I told you not to go'* and *'I said you was spending too much'* and *'Don't expect me to bail you out.'* But maybe Bill was feeling guilty, or maybe he was in a rare mood of generosity. Either way it was only a few minutes before Davie was allowed to carry the call to the woman behind the counter so she could enter Bill's credit card details into the fussy little payment machine. When Davie insisted she add on the cost of a pie and a chocolate milk, she raised her scratchy eyebrows and gave him an evil smile.

And Bill was right, of course. The staff at Southern Highlands Private, and then at Robertson Public, could tell him nothing. Scott Patterson's phone records – as detailed in the police file – might show he'd called each hospital just before crashing his car, but, as he'd dialled the general enquiries lines and not triple zero, the calls had not been recorded. No one at Robertson Public could explain to Davie why Patterson might have called them and the staff at the private hospital refused to even talk to him. Neither hospital, as far as Davie could tell, offered any specialist HIV support services. But, at least, Davie had gone down there; at least, he'd checked. And wasn't hard work its own reward? Or was that optimism?

On the way back to Sydney, stewing in solidified traffic, Davie fiddled with the radio and found the local news: bushfires and pet rescues topped off with a surf report. The swell had grown again, coinciding, for once, with an offshore breeze. 'Get out there, folks,' the reporter demanded cheerily. 'This will be the best day of the season!' Davie's phone rang in welcome relief and he answered it without checking the number.

Jacqui Russell was a small overly tanned woman who, as Davie's regional manager at Deutsch & Bowler Estate Agents, had terrified him on a monthly basis.

'How are ya?' she demanded now with a voice like a kookaburra. 'How's the detectivin'?'

Davie grimaced. He might as well still be working for her. Any answer he gave would only elicit more questions until he ended up contradicting himself. He was tempted to hang up, to pretend he was out of range. Instead, he took a deep breath and told Jacqui he was fine.

'Where are ya?' she demanded, her chewing gum loud. 'Ya sound tired.'

Davie looked around. He no idea where he was and, momentarily, no idea what he was doing there.

'How are you, Jacqui?'

'I'm good, yeah. Very good, in fact. Too good. Work's going nuts; that dil who took over from you can't cope and I was wondering if ya wanted a bit of work. Just weekends, but a full share of commission on anything ya show. Plus, auctions, of course.'

'Oh, thanks, Jacqui, but I'd rather roast in hell.'

He didn't say it; he would *never* say it. There had been a time when he'd spent hours on end fantasising about how one day he'd tell Jacqui exactly what he thought of her. How, on the day he left Deutsch & Bowler, he'd humiliate her in public to repay the countless times she'd humiliated him in the office. In the event, he'd shaken her hand and thanked her for her support over the years. There had been an awkward kiss on the cheek.

'That's very kind, Jacqui. I'll give it some thought. But the agency is going quite well and I'm rushed off my feet.'

'Well, work out how much money you're turning ya nose up at and if ya change ya mind, give me a call.'

Davie resisted Jacqui's attempts to do the maths for him, made more polite noises and hung up. A minute later, the traffic started moving again and, for the rest of the journey north, he scratched between stations, sang out loud, counted backwards in French; anything to avoid calculating how much money he'd just turned down. When he parked in busy North Sydney, he found he'd landed on the same number twice. He could earn more in six weekends than he had in the previous twelve months.

North Sydney was as bad as ever. Sydney itself was bad enough, but at least it had some history to it: the occasional old building. North Sydney was nothing but office blocks over cafés, full of people who worked in office blocks. Streets too wide and pavements too narrow; a thousand companies too tight to pay the rents across the harbour. Davie sweltered for a hundred metres along Miller Street trying to find the right tower, dodging the suits and the funereal women, telling himself he was freer than all of them. But the pie and chocolate milk had put cottonwool in his mouth, the baking traffic had left him dirty and slow and everyone else's life seemed more attractive.

CenSecCo Tower had a marble lobby, empty but for a white marble desk overseen by a white marbled security guard who hated Davie on sight.

'Name?'

'Davie Simms.'

'Here to see?'

'Ben Thisten, CenSecCo.'

'Appointment?'

'Yes.'

'Tenth floor.'

In the lift, Davie tried to focus on the changing floor numbers – the urgency of the case he was trying to solve – and not the dollar amount he'd calculated in the car. But the knowledge of the money he was turning down refused to be denied. It overwhelmed him, confusing his thoughts, weighing on his eyelids and weakening his limbs as if he hadn't eaten in days. Davie hadn't often fainted in his life, but he remembered the feeling as similar to this. As if standing up was too much to expect of your body. He needed time to think, needed to be in bed, alone in the dark, so he could sort out the mess in his head. Ten storeys up, when he forced himself out of the lift and found he was facing a receptionist, he struggled to understand what she was asking him.

'Sorry,' he said at last. 'Simms. Davie Simms.'

'Are you all right, darling? You look like you've seen a ghost.'

The girl behind the reception desk was ridiculously pretty: long hair framing her pale Asian face, full lips the same red as her dress. Davie told her he was fine – it had been a long day – but agreed with her suggestion he should probably sit down. On the far side of the lobby's shining floor was an oblong lounge of studded black leather. Davie recognised it as the model he'd nearly bought for his own office before realising he couldn't afford it. He walked across and sat himself down cautiously.

'Ben will be with you in a sec,' the receptionist called over. 'You're here to see footage, aren't you? He's already pulled it from the archives. You just need to sign some forms and Ben'll take you to the viewing room. But are you sure you're OK?'

Davie said he'd be fine, closed his eyes and rested his head against the wall behind the lounge. Immediately, there were footsteps and a new voice: 'Dave, I'm Ben. Shall we?'

Ben Thisten, so sensible and cautious on the phone, was twenty-something and skinny. He had thick black hair in a severe side-parting, horn-rimmed glasses and a too-busy-to-be-here look on his face. After an unconvincing handshake and a severe glance at the receptionist, Thisten led Davie through a glass door and down a flesh-coloured corridor. It reminded Davie of Crosley Police Station – but maybe if you walked along enough corridors they all began to look alike? The bland walls, the growing sense of claustrophobia, the obligatory palm dying in its pot, like a warning to get out while you can. Then he and Thisten turned a corner into a wide space bare of both carpet and paint: a long low wooden box. Ben Thisten crossed it and opened a door in the opposite wall.

'You're in here,' he said. 'The lights aren't working, I'm afraid, but you'd probably want them off anyway. I've prepared the forms for you to sign and I'll need to see your ID.'

As if Davie might have forgotten. Ben Thisten had made it abundantly clear over the phone how much CenSecCo prided itself on protecting the security assets of its clients. A faxed letter from Crosley General hadn't been enough to secure this viewing. Natalie had had to send something on police letterhead and follow it up with a call. Davie handed over his driving licence and, as Thisten copied its details onto a form, stepped into the tiny room. Looking around in the gloom he saw red and blue wires curling from the walls where the light switches should have been; in the ceiling, one of the panels was missing. Davie couldn't help but wonder if further comforts were stripped away as you continued into CenSecCo's corporate belly. If Thisten's own office was no more than a phone in a bare concrete cell?

'Dave?'

Thisten was holding out his driving licence. Davie took it, then dutifully gave the four signatures required, fixing his smile while Thisten checked them – against what, it wasn't clear. It was another ten minutes before the young man had fetched a box of tapes and shown Davie how the monitors worked, innocent of the fact there had been a time when normal people knew how to operate videos.

'Hang on.' Davie was rifling through the tapes before Thisten could disappear again. 'The police file mentions three cameras.' He pulled a crumpled A4 from his pocket, tilting it to catch the light from the corridor. 'CCS CCTV 190973 was vandalised, so I need to see CCS

CCTV 190972 and CCS CCTV 190974. These tapes are all from 972. I need to see both sets of tapes.'

Thisten did a bad impression of checking his clipboard, his own body shadowing it from the light outside the room.

'I believe you're investigating the disappearance of Scott Patterson from Crosley General, Room 1347? The best view of the corridor outside that room is from camera 190973 but someone had the foresight to damage that camera shortly before—'

'Yeah, thanks. Like I said, I've seen the police file. But both 972 and 974 show potential routes to and from the area covered by 973. I'd like to see 974 too, please.'

Thisten's face changed colour, his shadowed features less distinct than they had been.

'974 is not available.'

'Why not?'

'Well, as clearly stated in the service level agreements of CenSecCo, we guarantee that, at any time, ninety per cent of our closed-circuit cameras are functioning at peak performance. However, given the size of our network and the need to constantly update technology …' The young man hesitated, the requisite comms failing him. He made another show of checking his clipboard in case the words he needed were there.

'974 was broken?' said Davie. 'For real?'

'We made the police fully aware of the fact and cannot be held liable for any … malfunctions within the limits of our SLA's, to which – along with our other terms and conditions – all clients are signatories.'

'Really? Broken?' Davie realised he was repeating himself. 'I don't remember seeing that in the police file. My bad, I'll go back and check.'

Thisten looked less comfortable still. He was as young as his years, after all – learning what life was like when you did whatever the boss told you to do.

'Well,' he said swiftly. 'I'll leave you to it, then. Enjoy.'

For half an hour or so, the footage was interesting. White coats gathered in small groups and went their separate ways; small children and inflated balloons were dragged one way, then another; a doctor wept alone. When the time on the tape was showing as 15/05 – 13:52:26, Davie spotted a confusion of feet in the top right-hand corner of the screen. Nothing more than that. Two or three pairs of feet: shadowy and out of focus and moving fast. He remembered reading what DC Burran had put in the police file: *Unable to ascertain likelihood of this being material.* Davie could just imagine Burran shrugging his shoulders and curling his lip as he typed it. He wound the footage back and forth – the time on the tape fell right into the gap between a nurse seeing Patterson asleep and Doctor Sherezade finding his room empty – but eventually Davie had to agree: it was impossible to tell if it meant anything.

After that, he struggled to concentrate. With no sound to give life to the black-and-white figures on the screen – the scenery behind them bland and unchanging – Davie started making up stories as to why they might be there. Sensible stories at first, then strange and mismatched, their details mingling with his long day.

It was his own noise that woke him. The cheap office chair he was sitting in had rolled slightly further from the wall, allowing his head to tip back and give his snoring full throttle. Wiping his chin, Davie pulled himself upright and remembered slowly where he was. He crept to the door and cracked it open to wince and blink at the overlit space outside, but there was no one there who might have heard Davie Simms, professional detective, asleep on the job.

Back at reception, the gorgeous girl in the red dress was alone. She was applying a new coat of lipstick and seemed embarrassed to be caught in the act, as if maybe people were supposed to believe the effect was natural. To make her feel better, Davie complimented the shade and told her how well it matched her dress. It never failed to amaze him how much women responded to the tiniest compliment given honestly and free of any pervy undertone. The receptionist brightened immediately and sat up straight, telling Davie he was looking much better than before. Suspecting it was the sleep that had done the trick, Davie felt himself blush and asked for directions to the bathroom. Once he was back – the memories of Jacqui Russell's offer leaving him weak again – he gave the receptionist the best smile he could muster.

'Is it always this quiet around here?'

'Yep.' She popped the syllable like bubble gum. 'Boring as bat shit. I'm only just back from overseas. I don't think I've ever had the return-to-work blues so bad.'

'Tell me about it. Work schemer. Still, only another forty years, eh?'

The receptionist laughed at that – her teeth as beautiful as the rest of her – then gave him a complicit look.

'Here, darling, listen.' She nodded him in closer and continued in a whisper. 'Did Ben feed you some bullshit about any of the cameras not working?'

'Er, yes, he did. I mean, I'm not sure it was bullshit—'

'It probably was. They always say that when they can't find the tapes. The girl who was here before me, she completely fucked up the filing system. I'm working my way through it when I can find the time, but it's still pretty shithouse. Do you want me look for a tape for you?'

'Well, wouldn't you have looked already? I mean, the police would have asked for all the footage from the cameras I'm interested in. I don't want to sound ungrateful or anything, but I'd hate to waste your time.'

'Oh, trust me, darl, it wouldn't be a waste of time. I've been overseas, see – went to Bali for two weeks with my boyfriend. I only got back yesterday. Jesus, I wish I was still there. Anyway, the police would have asked Ben for the tapes, but little Mr Thisten is far too important to get his hands dirty in the filing rooms. I reckon the dipstick would have looked for a whole two minutes, then hid behind his precious … what does he call it? Some service contract thing.'

'Service level agreement?'

'That's the one. Sorry, my brain's still on holiday. So, you want me to have a look?'

Davie didn't believe the receptionist's cynicism. This was a police matter, after all and wasn't there something about obstructing the course of justice? Even the Ben Thistens of the world had to understand the seriousness of that. Still, Davie could see the girl in red was enjoying her moment of power and he didn't want to bring her down. Returning from Bali to a corporate town in North Sydney had to be almost as bad as sitting in an estate agent's office opposite a beach.

'Sure,' he said, with his best grateful smile. 'As long as you don't think it will be a waste of time. It's the most recent one from camera 190974.'

'974, got it.'

She stood quickly, smoothed her red dress, gave him a wink and her mobile number, told him to call her if either of her desk phones rang or if anyone came out of the lift and – without giving Davie a chance to protest further – clicked her red high heels in the direction Ben Thisten had led him an hour earlier. Once through the glass door and into the flesh-coloured corridor, she disappeared through the first door on the right.

Davie crossed to the oblong lounge again, dropping into it less cautiously than before and banging his head on the wall behind it. Rubbing the back of his hair absent-mindedly, he let out a deep sigh. Now he was going to have to sit here like a dil for half hour until, knowing his luck, he'd have to explain to Ben Thisten or some other employee of CenSecCo what the hell he was doing. Not only that, he was going to have to try and do it without getting the receptionist into trouble.

But there was no sign of Ben Thisten, nor of anyone else. Neither of the desk phones rang, nobody came out of the lifts, no employees came strolling down the corridor. Remembering the undecorated passage around the corner and the unfinished viewing room, Davie wondered if the whole building was empty but for the space around him. Maybe even the receptionist had escaped and the whole thing was a joke – like when he was a little boy and all his friends had gone home when it was his turn to be the blind man in blind man's bluff.

Sighing again, Davie tried to resist the tiredness. He had no idea how long he'd been trying to resist it, when a knee against his shook him awake. The pretty receptionist was seated on the black leather lounge beside him, her fingers filthy but her face glowing. She was holding a video tape.

This time, Davie remained on his feet. Hands behind his back, feet wide apart, he wouldn't even allow himself to lean against the wall as he watched the new tape. When his focus wandered in the dark room, he clenched his thighs and his buttocks, lifting his toes until his calves hurt. Once upon a time, the excitement of viewing footage unseen by the police would have been enough to keep him awake. These days there was probably nothing to be excited about. This would be, no doubt, yet another thrilling discovery that led to precisely nothing.

On the monitor, he soon began to recognise people he'd seen in the recording from camera 190972, although the two sets of footage were more disjointed than he had expected. The doctor who had been crying alone was now walking quickly as he wiped his face. A child who had been dragged along truculently with his balloon now strolled alone, until an adult appeared, picked him up and carried him away, screaming. The huddle of white coats, who had been showing each other their clipboards and nodding, were now in two separate groups. Davie pulled up photographs on his phone that he'd taken of the plans of the hospital and the positions of the CCTV cameras. Sure enough, the camera that had been smashed – 190973 – covered all of the area between the corridors surveyed by the camera he had viewed before and the one he watching now. There was no sign of the feet Davie had viewed in the corner of the other camera. Nothing, in fact, of any use at all.

Davie let the video play on longer than he needed to, refusing to listen to the voice in his head that said nothing could come from watching it. The day's efforts and bad food were seeking escape through his pores and, refusing to let himself think of the ocean, he found he was suddenly desperate for a shower. Still, he continued to stare at the screen, bending only to fast forward through empty minutes before slowing the tape again to stare hard at everyone who walked in and out of this new angle. Patients, visitors, doctors, cleaners. Two nurses greeted each other like long-lost friends, then huddled close in conspiracy. Davie wondered whether they were discussing a patient or their private lives; whether the one on the left was crying or laughing or just jiggling about as she spoke. Behind them, a woman limped furtively along, sticking to the wall like a frightened insect, while a third nurse joined the conversation with a laugh. Davie could never get his head around how many centres of the universe there were; how irrelevant billions of people were to all the other billions on the planet. He caught himself swaying, shook himself awake and – deciding he'd finally watched enough – leaned forward to eject the tape.

Halfway there he stopped, hovered for a second in the darkness, then stood suddenly straight again. The nurses had gone off together, the corridor empty. White numbers running in a corner of the screen were the only proof time was passing. Davie bent again and fiddled under the screen until he found the rewind button. He waited until the nurses appeared again, walking backwards in jilting comedy, until he saw he'd spooled too far. He hit Play and stood in eager silence, hands clenched excitedly, until, there again were the first two nurses bent in conversation. Private life, it had to be: the taller one leaning in to hear the gory details as the other one laughed her way through them. And there, scuttling along the corridor behind the nurses as the third one joined their conversation, was the woman he thought he'd seen. Limping strangely and grasping a small lumpy package to her chest, was none other than Scott Patterson's secretary. Anita Patel.

Thursday, 28th March

Thirteen days after

Overnight, the wintry half of autumn bustled in: the late guest everyone had hoped would never arrive. Morning light revealed leaves that had dried and curled unnoticed, now fallen and filling the streets, exciting themselves into whirlwinds wherever they found a corner. The sky had lost interest, turning its grey back on the earth. Down at the beach, Murdoch found the ocean equally indifferent. He stared at the dull water for over a minute before forcing himself in: the first time he'd swum without a clear view. One hundred strokes one way, one hundred strokes the other. Two hundred opportunities not to think about sharks: none of them taken.

The previous afternoon, on the way back from the swimming hole, Natalie had pulled off the road to take a call. A long call to which she responded in hums and haws, one eye on Murdoch until he got out of the car and gave her the distance she needed. Once driving again, she'd told him they wouldn't see each other again until the weekend and maybe not even then. Her 'other piece of work' – the one she couldn't tell him about – was ramping up at last and she was going to have to work all hours, starting pretty much as soon as she'd dropped him back home.

Murdoch told her not to worry, he was a big boy and he'd be fine without her for a bit – she had enough to worry about without making sure he was having fun. Then he told himself some time apart was probably a good idea – a little pause to calm things down, not to mention a much-needed opportunity to work out how to deal with Velis. But, back home, the house felt dark and empty, even after he'd turned on lights and music. An hour or so later, when Davie phoned for the second time – breathless with excitement – Murdoch had been happy to take the call. He'd let Davie rabbit on for twenty minutes about how he'd found footage the police hadn't seen. How Anita Patel had lied on her witness statement. How, once again, self-discipline, diligence and patience had shown themselves worth the effort.

Murdoch told Davie he'd done well, but he also told him he still couldn't believe an overweight woman could have pulled Patterson from his bed and hidden him somewhere all by herself. And, even if she had done, why was she then limping along a different corridor a couple of minutes later? But all the same – yes, Davie, I promise Davie – as soon as Anita Patel was back in the country, they'd go and talk to her.

'Anything else I can do to help in the meantime?'

'Are you joking, Bill?' Davie's squawk was even squeakier over the phone. 'Why would I rely on you to do anything?'

'Come on, don't be like that, mate. I'm free all day tomorrow and the next day. What can I do?'

But Davie refused to give him anything useful to do and Murdoch was left, for once, genuinely disappointed.

The next morning, after his swim in the sea, Murdoch sat at his kitchen table and made a list. At the top of it was the garden: pruning the shrubs and working out what to do with his hedge. Then, there were all the cupboards that needed wiping out, the frames he should dust, the vacuuming. People spoke about spring cleaning, but Murdoch had always thought autumn was a better time to do it. Winter was on its way and you were about to spend too much time in your cave. He'd do it proper, he told himself, get right in under the fridge. *Jesus Christ*. Hadn't there been years when he'd known how to entertain himself?

It was mid-afternoon – the man's timing was perfect – when Velis's text came in. Murdoch was halfway up a stepladder, dusting the huge mirror over his fireplace. It was never his favourite task, given how impossible it was to escape his reflection waving a duster. Now, as his phone buzzed in his pocket, he watched himself try and retrieve it without getting dirt all over himself. The text was as casual as ever. *Paragliding on Tuesday, if you want to come.* No question mark. Murdoch looked at himself in the mirror and scowled. Duster in one hand, phone in the other, he looked like some fucked-up version of the statue on the top of the Old Bailey. All he needed was a bleeding blindfold.

'That was quick.' Velis was as chirpy as ever. 'You caught me on the hop. Thought you might be playing hard to get.'

'Been busy, ain't I?'

'Oh yeah? What you up to?'

Velis sounded genuinely curious. Like a genuine mate, not the senior exec of an organisation that wanted you dead.

'This and that. What about you?'

Velis let the evasion go.

'Work, work and work,' he said. 'Boring and frustrating at the same time. Don't worry, I know you don't want to hear about it. You decided anything about my little proposal?'

Murdoch couldn't help but admire the bloke. No bullshit in him – straight to the point.

'Far as I remember it, Emre, you didn't give me a detailed proposal to decide about.'

'Well, like I said, you tell me you're up for it, I'll tell you the details. Otherwise, the less you know the better. I thought we'd agreed that much, at least.'

Murdoch looked at himself in the mirror – eye contact warning a friend to be careful.

'I ain't decided nothing,' he said. 'But don't get your hopes up.'

'All good, no rush. And, like I said, if the answer's no, then no hard feelings. By the way, just to demonstrate my goodwill, I'm going to do you a favour.'

'Oh yeah?'

'Jesus, Bill, don't sound so enthusiastic.'

'I'm not. Most blokes what ever did me a favour seemed to expect something in return.'

'Aha! Well, that's the point, isn't it? Because me doing you this favour and not expecting anything in return is a sign of how well we could work together, see?'

Murdoch could hear Velis's toothy smile. He was probably in the back of a limo or on the deck of a yacht somewhere.

'By the way, Emre, this phone of yours, d'you reckon it's safe?'

'Yeah, mate, it's the joy of pay-as-you-go. Phone company thinks I'm a fourteen-year-old girl in Ballarat. Listen, are you curious about this favour or not? It's a gift, honest.'

Murdoch closed his eyes. 'Go for it.'

'OK, that case you're on – Patterson bloke. I overheard a conversation the other day and there's someone you might want to talk to.'

Suddenly Murdoch didn't feel so safe on the ladder. He climbed down and sat heavily into the sofa, the duster dropping grey fluff on the cushions.

'So, Patterson's disappearing is Club business, is it?'

Case closed, sorry Davie.

'Jesus, Bill, half your luck. You really have retired if you've forgotten how the Club operates. Headlines in the papers and evidence for the cops to poke their noses through? Anyone of our lot leaving that mess would be next on the list. No, mate, when we get rid of people, it's all nice and tidy – a perfectly plausible little accident. The day you read about me dead in a car crash is the day they've caught me stepping out of line.'

'Which is exactly what you're proposing I help you do.'

'I'm proposing I step out of line, not that I get caught. Come on, Bill, live a little. Otherwise, what's the point of anything?'

Murdoch looked around him. The stepladder, the duster, the apron.

'Besides,' Velis went on, 'even if I did get caught, there's nothing to link me to you.'

'Apart from my number in your poxy little phone.'

There was a long silence. Murdoch was expecting for Velis to say something funny, but there were limits to everything, apparently.

'You've got me there, Bill. Stupid, sorry. Listen, go and get a disposable, a pay-as-you-go, same as me. Call me on it. Then I'll destroy this phone, get a new one and give you the number. Jesus, you're going to be so good at this.'

Outside the light died a little further, the invisible sun angled behind the hills or the clouds thickening, Murdoch couldn't tell. With the phone to his ear, he stood and turned on the fire – the first time in months. When the gas surged and the flames boomed, he flinched, as nervous as if he'd said yes to Velis.

'Nice try, Emre, but I'll let you know. So, who's this person what I want to talk to about the Patterson case?'

'Well, the chat I heard was just casual, you know. Blokes shooting the breeze. The cops reckon the secretary did it, but then they also reckon she couldn't have. You might want to talk to a bloke named Terry Hatch about that.'

'Terry Hatch? Who's that?'

Velis tutted. 'That's all I've got for you. Check Hatch out and thank me later. Or don't, no strings.'

There was no point asking for more. A name was just a name, but the more details you got, the less people there were who could have told you.

'Hang on.' Velis's tone was suddenly serious. Murdoch wasn't clear if the tall man was talking to him or someone at the other end. Then the line muted, leaving him alone to stare into the fire, until Velis returned in a whisper.

'I've got to go. Get a pay-as-you-go thing and call me on it. Let me know what you decide.'

He hung up without saying goodbye.

Later, when Murdoch picked up his phone to call Davie, he spotted Velis's text again. Only then did he realise they hadn't talked about any paragliding.

Saturday, 16th March

One day after

Anita wakes with the long-forgotten sensation of not knowing where she is. Opening her eyes, blurred blocks of colour reveal themselves slowly to be her bedside cabinet, her reading lamp on its side, her clothes on the carpet. It is the quiet that has confused her. Every morning for the last few years, Riya's voice has woken her – that or the little girl's fidgeting on the bed beside her. Other parents, Anita knows, go to lengths to ensure their children don't wake them too early, but she has always delighted in her early morning hours with Riya. There are days on end when it is the only time they spend together alone. But this morning, with both her mother and her daughter gone, Anita remembers what it is like to wake at your own rhythm. She remembers weeks backpacking around Europe – a different hostel every night – or inappropriate one-night stands, hazy memories of the evening before and who was going be there when you turned over. Staring at her clothes, creased in a compact heap beside her bed, Anita tries to work out why the house is so quiet: what night before could have caused this particular morning after.

She sits up straight and blinking. Please God, could it all have been a dream? But if it is a dream, why is the house so quiet, and why is her ankle pulsing heavy and painful? When Anita pulls the doona back and sees the mud-spattered bandage, she lets out a small noise, somewhere between a 'no' and an 'ah' – the helpless noise of woman remembering what she has done.

Or, at least, partially remembering. For only disjointed images have survived the previous twenty-four hours. As Anita swings her legs out of bed, wincing at the pain in her ankle, she has a memory of the syringe on her desk pointing at her in accusation. Then there is Scott's empty parking spot under the hammering rain, tiny splashes exploding across the bare asphalt. Anita turns to look out of her bedroom window – she has left the curtains undrawn – but the empty sky denies all knowledge of a storm. There is no humidity either, but the bandage on Anita's ankle is definitely there and, as she stares at it, further flashes of memory come.

The smell of bleach. The phone call from Alan Drummond. Terry Hatch squeezing the badly repacked injection kit. At the thought of the kit, Anita stands and, gasping at the pain and using the walls for support, checks her mother's and daughter's bedrooms really are empty, then heads downstairs to search for her handbag. She finds it – fallen onto its side, of course – on the hallway floor next to the doormat. But, when she picks up the bag roughly and looks inside, Anita finds only the replacement Central Coast Mariners mug she bought on Thursday, still unused.

In the front room, Anita collapses onto the lounge. How often has she fantasised about a moment like this, the house empty and her with nothing to do? But reality is never how you imagine it: the internal world ruining everything. Anita sits wide-eyed and staring, her jaw clenching as more memories come through. Tom Brandle angry. Her in her car lost in the streets behind the football stadium. A pedestrian waving a fist. The memories culminate in the scene at the hospital, a scene so awful she immediately tries to replace it with later memories. How did she even get back to the house?

Pulling herself to her feet once more, Anita hobbles to the window and sees her little Suzuki is parked outside. But, try as she might, she can't remember driving home. She can, she thinks, remember walking out of the hospital and, yes, she definitely remembers crossing the car park. She had to hold onto the handrail that ran alongside a walkway, struggling with the pain in her ankle and switching her handbag to the other shoulder. A memory flashes of looking inside the bag, then checking its contents and telling herself she had nothing to worry about. The lumpy red kit was in there, snug against the mug, spotting with rain as she confirmed its presence.

So where is it now?

Anita tells herself she needs time to wake up and remember she is a professional. She should shower and make a coffee before finding the injection kit and then head to the shops with a reasonable excuse for buying a replacement syringe and needle. After all, once she has returned the kit in its original state to Scott's office, there is nothing, *nothing*, to link her to what happened to her boss.

But, try as she might, Anita cannot resist finding the kit before she does anything else. It is not on the hall floor anywhere near where she found her handbag. Nor is it in her bedroom. Nor, at first glance, is it in the car or the kitchen or the lounge room. Anita hobbles around, knowing she should change her bandage if nothing else, but unable to resist looking again. The bathroom. The lounge room. All the bedrooms. The patio. The garden. The utility room. The laundry room. Even the bloody handbag again, until, back on the landing, she puts her back to the wall and lets herself sink slowly to the floor.

The events of the previous twenty-four hours, the day she— It is all too much. Anita has no idea where she left the bleach-filled syringe with her fingerprints all over it and no idea what to do. She uses her long-craved-for time alone in a quiet house to let herself weep uncontrollably, banging her fists on the carpet and the back of her head against the wall. Surely she has deserved this self-indulgence, if nothing else?

Sometime later – she has no idea how long – Anita finds she is calm at last. Wiping her eyes, she gets up and hobbles to the bathroom where she sits on the floor of the shower to unravel the filthy bandage from her ankle under the comforting warmth of water. Again, she tries to remember anything more recent than the hospital car park, but her memory refuses to offer clues as to what she might have done with the adulterated injection kit.

For the rest of the day Anita tears the house apart, hopping from room to room as she fails to suppress her panic. There is no need to rip open cushions or tear apart fittings, but everything that can move, she moves, digging into any space where she might have hidden the kit in her lost hours. By the time Riya's friend's mother calls to see what time Anita is picking up her daughter, Anita is so confused that she begs the friend to go through Riya's backpack.

'Sorry, Anita, what am I looking for again? I've emptied it out and there's just her dolly and pyjamas. Now, what time are you coming over, please? I do have things to do, you know.'

Anita makes a garbled apology that she is unable to drive, hangs up and continues her search. She doesn't come to her senses until Riya is returned home, her play-date's mother ringing the doorbell to the tune of her own frustration. The young mother, a tiny, exhausted Lebanese woman in a pink tracksuit, is clearly furious when, at last, Anita yanks open the door. But at the sight of Anita – more dishevelled than herself, blotchy with tears and clearly handicapped, the hall a bomb site behind her – the other woman's features soften into something closer to concern.

'My God, Anita, what happened to you?'

'Nothing.'

'But—'

'I mean, I've had some terrible news. From overseas. Family – I'm so sorry.' Anita blocks the doorway to prevent the woman from seeing past her. Riya, trying to push into the house, complains, so Anita lifts her up and holds her tight. 'I'm really sorry for not explaining on the phone. I'd only just heard.'

It takes a while longer to convince the mother, until recently so keen to get on with her life, that Anita really is fine. But with each passing minute, Anita grows calmer. Not that talking to this other woman, whose name she can't even remember, is in any way therapeutic. More that it reminds Anita that, if she is to survive this whole thing, she must behave like a professional. The lie about bad news was a good one, but needing a lie in the first place was amateurish. Anita slows her speech, apologises for her dishevelled state and her behaviour again and smiles her heartfelt thanks. Only once the other woman – Tina, that's her name – has turned back towards her car, does Anita put Riya down and allow her to run into the hallway. At the sight of the pulled-apart house, the little girl is amazed, her tiny mouth circling a dramatic 'O-', followed by a slow 'M-G' – obviously newly learned from the sleepover.

'What's happened, Mummy?'

'It's a game, sweetheart. I took everything out, so we can play at putting it back in the right place again. You have to tell me where it all lives. Let see if we can do it before Naniji gets home.'

That takes another few hours, Riya bored halfway through and demanding the iPad instead. As Anita continues alone, squeaky cartoons her only accompaniment, she finds herself practising excuses for the police. Reasons why her fingerprints are on Scott's injection kit and why

204

the is syringe filled with bleach. Because she wanted to clean it? Would anyone believe that? She wonders if it would be better to hand herself in now before the police can come for her. Whether that would help at all.

From this, she moves onto plans of how best to prepare for prison. Whether she wants Ma and Riya to visit her there or not. No, she decides. Better to disappear and then return untainted. But how can she condemn her daughter to growing up motherless? The arguments repeat themselves, as if on a loop, and encourage her to tidy faster than before. To get everything in order so she can sit down with Riya, the iPad hidden, and enjoy their last few hours together.

It is only when Ma returns on Sunday evening, as scratchy as ever after she's been away, that Anita believes there might be a glimmer of hope. At the dinner table, Ma explains she is upset that Anita didn't call her to tell her that her boss had gone missing. It was on the television and in the papers and Ma had to learn of it in front of Mrs Shah. Does Anita have any idea how embarrassing that was for her? Anita is trying to work out what impact this has – whether a journalist might have seen her at the hospital – when Riya interrupts loudly.

'Naniji,' says the little girl. 'Mummy took everything out and we had to put it away again.'

'I lost my wallet,' Anita explains, too tired to find a better lie. 'I had to turn the house upside down looking for it.'

Ma tuts without looking up from her food. 'I always tell you and you never listen. If you're looking for something, you should always start with the place you'd put it right now if you had it in your hand.'

This much-repeated advice normally makes Anita smile. Sandeep once whispered 'down your throat' at a volume only she could hear. Today, it makes her gasp. Of course! She must have put the injection kit back where it belongs. In the lost hours of Friday afternoon, she must have driven back to the office and returned it to Scott's desk drawer. Isn't that what a professional would have done?

Anita wants to limp around the table and hug her mother. Instead, she tells her how tired she is – no lie, this – and how she thinks she'll have an early night. Given everything that's been going on, she needs to get into the office particularly early in the morning.

Saturday, 30th March

Fifteen days after

Natalie arrived with the daylight, appearing on Murdoch's doorstep with coffee, the papers and a sweet smile. Like she'd never in her life objected to how he'd bought his house. They stood in his kitchen and swapped ideas about breakfast, managing a whole three minutes before they climbed the stairs. It was the scent of her he couldn't resist – like all of his skin could smell all of hers and wouldn't rest until they were naked. They fucked wildly, making up for lost days with no satisfaction sacrificed to speed. Murdoch had looked forward to the time in bed afterwards too – the borderless talk, the drowsy sharing of thoughts – but, still entangled and damp, Natalie fell asleep in his arms, her fourteen-hour workdays taking their toll.

Extracting himself as gently as he knew how, Murdoch made his way downstairs. Standing at the kitchen workbench, waiting for his coffee to warm in the microwave, he flipped through the weekend newspaper until Davie's name on the magazine cover caught his eye. He rifled through the pages quickly and found the relevant article, wincing at the photograph next to it and then, reading in detail, wincing again at what was written there. When the microwave pinged, he grabbed his coffee and carried the newspaper upstairs. As soon as Natalie woke up, he showed her the article, hoping vaguely there was some kind of joke he'd missed. But as he watched her sit up and read – guessing by her face which paragraph she was on – the hope faded until, in the end, she lay back heavily into the pillows with one arm across her eyes.

'What do you think?' he said.

'What do you think I think?'

'I mean, what do you think we should do? Should I call him?'

Natalie lay silently, her face still in the crook of her arm, and he thought for a second she'd gone back asleep. Then she said, 'No. There's nothing positive we can say about it, so the best thing is to pretend no one will have seen it. Play it down. Say we didn't see it, we don't know anyone who reads the magazine. Try and convince him it's no big deal.'

'Nat, love, it's *The Sydney Morning Herald*. Everyone reads—'

She unpeeled her arm and gave him a look he hadn't seen since they'd started sleeping together.

'Fair enough,' he said. 'Point taken.'

'Unless you can think of a better idea?'

Murdoch admitted he couldn't and asked her what they were going to do, then.

'Keep our phones on, be ready to go round whenever he calls and keep up the story that no one will have seen it. And, in the meantime, have ourselves a weekend.'

But the weekend, it seemed, would have to wait. Instead, they talked about the article for another half an hour before losing themselves in a diversion of how and when they were going to tell Davie that they were now an item. Murdoch thought it was no big deal – Davie had been trying to push them together for years – but Natalie wasn't so sure. She chewed her lip at the idea and looked more nervous than Murdoch had ever seen her. He was on the point of asking why – if there had ever been anything more than friendship between her and Davie – when Natalie pushed away the covers and jumped out of bed, naked.

'Seriously, Bill, let's have a weekend.'

'No problem. Come back to bed.'

But for once her appetite was different to his. She told him to jump in the shower and put some clothes on. It was time they ventured outdoors.

Holding hands was an interesting sport. Murdoch struggled at first with the different length of their arms, when to let go and when to hang on, how to walk at the same speed as someone who wanted to chat to everyone. Walking with Natalie around the Kildare farmers' market was like playing a new level in a video game, performing the role of Upstanding Citizen with more complex rules than ever before. He and Natalie looked at things they didn't need, talked about the weather with people he didn't know and bought organic vegetables from organic locals for twice what you paid in the supermarket. Murdoch smiled a lot and said little, knowing from experience that one day he'd understand.

Saturday drifted into Sunday on red wine and movies. Sunday morning slid past between the sheets. The rest of the week loomed like a sentencing and, over pizza on Sunday night, Natalie dropped the gavel.

'I should go,' she said. 'I need an early night and a good night's sleep. And you should check up on Davie. I still think we should pretend to know nothing, but you should probably make sure he's OK. Whatever it is he's doing.'

Their embargo on work talk was a game to them now, Natalie as likely as Murdoch to enforce the rule. Murdoch, for his part, didn't want the weekend to be over, but, knowing he never would, he said it made sense to visit Davie and waved Natalie off from his front door, bristling at its empty echoes as it shut behind her.

It was almost dark when he arrived in Crosley, the western sky barely less grey than the rest. Murdoch found a parking space on Macquarie Road, but decided it wasn't worth the risk: there was no profit in experience if you didn't learn your lesson. Ten dollars later, he walked out of the secure car park beside the train station and found the evening drained of heat. He hadn't thought to bring a jacket and jogged in his shirt the four blocks to the back of the library, remembering the map wrongly and doing three sides of the building.

The library was modern and no less ugly than the rest of town, its featureless red bricks turning black in the fading light, its high windows already dark. Halfway along its back wall, Murdoch spotted Davie's car and slowed to a walk while a ragged white cat glared at him from the recessed door of a fire escape.

The dirty pink Hyundai Excel matched its surroundings. The featureless library on its one side, the low-rise block across the way, leaves and litter scuttling between the two: there was nothing pretty here. Davie had put heat reflectors under his windscreen and back window and the car looked more abandoned than parked. Inside, it smelled the way a car smells when a man's been in it for two days. Davie smelled like that man. Murdoch pretended he wanted the window open so he could smoke. He couldn't see Davie clearly, but he could tell he was exhausted. When Davie spoke, the words came more slowly than normal, his voice creaking as much as his seat. Murdoch asked him how it was going.

'Slowly.'

'You seen anything?'

'Nothing.'

Not surprising really, what with this being a work address and today being Sunday. Murdoch didn't say it, not today. They'd had the conversation – out of earshot of Natalie – on and off over the weekend, Murdoch insisting the whole thing could wait till Monday, he was happy to help out then. But Davie was on some kind of mission to prove how hard he could work.

'Remind me, Bill ...'

Davie interrupted himself and sunk lower in his seat, gesturing for Murdoch to do the same. Across the road an olive-skinned man in a tracksuit, broad-shouldered with a rolling walk, strolled into view. As they watched he wiped his sleeve across his nose, scratched his ribs and continued on. Davie peered into his wing mirror, a stale minute before he was happy to talk again.

'Remind me who gave us Terry Hatch's name.'

His breath was as rank as the car.

'A contact,' said Murdoch.

'Right. I didn't know you had those kind of contacts any more.'

Tell me about it. 'Listen, Davie, this bloke of yours at the phone company, you reckon you can trust him?'

Davie knew someone whose brother's neighbour's mate could, for a hundred dollars, trace any unlisted number in Australia back to its billing address. The car wobbled and grew more pungent still as Davie shifted in his seat and shuffled his phone from his pocket.

'Hope so,' he said vaguely. 'And look at this, I googled it.'

He hit a button and Murdoch's own phone started ringing. No caller ID.

'See!' Tired or not, Davie was the only man in the world who could be chipper after two days in a car. 'I can phone you and you can't see my number or phone me back or do anything to find out who I am.'

'Genius,' said Murdoch. 'I mean, yeah, that's great.'

'Oh, by the way, you didn't see the *SMH* yesterday did you? I can't believe I forgot to buy it.'

'Nah, I don't get it much any more. Why?'

'That PR piece, the interview I did last week, it was supposed to be in there. Mentioned on the front page of the magazine, apparently.'

Murdoch shrugged and blew a plume of smoke out the window, careful for once that none drifted into the car. Davie, one eye in the mirror, signalled again and they sat in silence until a teenage couple appeared on the pavement beside Murdoch, giggling into each other as they passed.

'Anything else happening?'

'Not much. I phoned my dad on Friday, asked him if he knew anything about Patterson recruiting for Huntingdon's. That funny little man who works there, Mr, you know …'

'Hughes.'

'That's the one. I reckon he was hiding something. He looked so nervous.'

Murdoch thought the man must have looked rabid for Davie to have noticed it, but he said nothing.

'Anyway,' Davie went on, 'Dad said all he knew was that Patterson had useful contacts for cheap labour. "*Very cheap*, if you know what I mean, Davie." You know how he talks.'

'Cheap, as in illegal?'

'Crikey, I hope not, but I wouldn't put it past him. He said he'd been thinking of getting back to Patterson himself for some people to clear that land he's thinking of buying.'

Murdoch didn't have anything to say to that and they sat again in silence for a while until Murdoch nodded across the road. 'So which one is Hatch's office, then?'

'Second floor, fifth or sixth window from the right, I reckon.'

Davie gestured at the low-rise across the road. Built in the seventies – windows last washed in the nineties – it was three storeys of stippled concrete above mismatched awnings, a desolate strip of shops below; impossible to tell in the dark if any of the shops were still occupied. Above the awnings, all the windows were dark except for one where orange backlit curtains billowed in and out. Murdoch wondered what businesses could eke out a living here, who would want to live above the shop. He shivered, threw his butt out onto the pavement and wound the window shut, the handle coming off in his hand like it always did.

'There's a door halfway along,' said Davie. 'Says one of the businesses upstairs is Hamilton Enterprises.'

He turned, his smile a faint glimmer in the dark, and Murdoch could tell he was expecting a reaction.

'So?'

'Hamilton Enterprises, Bill. As in "Ham Ent" – the references on the payments into Patterson's secret bank account? No mention of it in Patterson's PPC contact list, though, I checked twice. No mention of Hatch's address either, just his telephone number. Shame, really, I could have saved a hundred bucks.'

Murdoch thought Davie could have turned up on Monday morning, rang the bell and saved himself a weekend in a car too. He didn't ask him where he'd got the hundred bucks from. Silence descended again and with it, for Murdoch, came doubt. The policy he and Natalie had agreed, pretending they hadn't seen the article and downplaying its importance, had been easy to believe when they had each other to focus on. Here, alone in a car with Davie, no one else watching, nothing else to do, it was more difficult to defend.

'You know, Davie' he said, 'About that PR piece—'

But Davie had held up a hand, five fingers blacker than the air between them. Murdoch rolled his eyes and wondered how long he was going to have to stay there, being nice and not talking about the article in the paper. He didn't want to give another ten dollars to the secure car park. Squinting past Davie, he saw a fat little man in a thick padded coat had waddled into view across the road. The man looked around, checked no one was watching, then turned to the shop fronts and put his hands to waist height.

'He's taking a leak, Davie. Listen ...'

Over Murdoch's whisper, they both heard keys worrying a lock, a creak and a door slamming shut. Murdoch blinked, trying to make sense of the darkness under the awning, but there were no two ways about it: the fat man had disappeared. The Hyundai wobbled again and Davie's face was suddenly lit by the screen of his phone. Murdoch watched him hit a number and only had time to say 'Hide your screen' before they heard a faint ringing. Across the road, behind the glass of a now visible door, another phone was found, its screen glowing blue in the darkness, first at waist height, then raised to the fat man's ear. Davie killed the call.

'Not bad,' said Murdoch. 'Not bad at all. I think we've got our man.'

'Why are you being so nice?'

'Shut it. Watch.'

The glow of Terry Hatch's phone angled and turned, illuminating the fat man's fingers as he tried, no doubt, to work out who had called him. After a few seconds, he gave up and all was dark again until, a minute later, a second-storey window flickered to life, a broken blind and a slice of ceiling stark in the night. Davie had been wrong: it was the third window from the right. Murdoch asked him which way the fat man had come – along the street towards them or up from behind?

'From behind,' said Davie. 'I think he might have crossed the road just before we saw him. Shall we go and introduce ourselves?'

He was about to say something else when the light in the office died. Without waiting for Davie to finish, Murdoch climbed out of the car, told Davie he'd call him and closed the door as quietly as he could. The threat of winter was less subtle than an hour before and Murdoch decided to jog again, back to the fire door where he'd seen the cat. As he stepped into the recess, something rustled in the leaves at his feet. The street beside him was eerily quiet, a dead part of town on a Sunday night, and it was easy enough to hear a door open and close, footsteps approaching. Then the fat man, Hatch, was there – tap, tap, tap, smart shoes on the pavement beside Murdoch, no hesitation as he passed.

Murdoch counted slowly to twenty, then stepped out onto the pavement. Hatch was further away than he'd thought, his dumpy form clear against a distant streetlight, bare branches slicing the yellow air above him. As Murdoch watched, Hatch crossed the street, turned the corner of the library and disappeared. Murdoch jogged again, his breath visible and, when he reached the brighter street lamps of the next street, catching the colour of the light. Here, Murdoch realised, his face would be visible too and he hesitated between holding back or following. Then a sharp breeze came through and made the decision for him.

Thirty metres ahead, huddled over whatever he now held in his arms, Hatch looked like he was feeling the cold, walking quickly to get somewhere warm. Murdoch, in his thin black shirt, had little sympathy. He watched Hatch cross this street too, disappearing and reappearing as he walked between the street lamps on the other side. Murdoch stuck to his own pavement, just another bloke out for a stroll – with no coat on the last night of March, the coldest night of the year so far.

They approached the tiny park in front of the library. Murdoch had driven past it a hundred times, seen it on leaflets posted through his door. It was the local council's pride and joy – square grass and palm trees, like an architect's drawing, an oversized play area for kids. The road around it was well-lit, but, as soon as Hatch got there, he crossed to enter the park itself, like he'd been sucked into its darkness. Murdoch swore and started jogging again, faster this time. Running, sprinting, anything to get warm. He too crossed the road around the park, but, instead of entering the square, he turned right, made for its first corner, then left, along its northern edge. At the next corner, he stopped to see if he could hear Hatch's footsteps, but the park wasn't that small. Taking a breath, he counted to ten, turned left again and ambled slowly towards the park entrance opposite the one Hatch had taken. The man had to be cutting straight across, why else leave the safety of the streets? Unless …

But there was no need for an 'unless'. Three street lamps ahead, Hatch's silhouette emerged belly first from the park. He barely glanced towards Murdoch before squeezing between two parked cars and starting across the road. Murdoch continued on, like he hadn't seen him, hands rubbing up and down his arms, the shivers threatening to take control. He reached the shadow of a low jacaranda, its branches reaching out like it too wanted to go home, and stood looking over the roofs of the parked cars. Nothing. Then, movement in the mid-distance, Murdoch saw the fat man had continued in a straight line. He was ten metres down the road that ran off the square towards Broadwater, the highway at the water's edge twinkling in the distance. Hatch was standing beside a row of parked cars, one hand fishing in his pocket until the BMW in front of him beeped to life. *Thank Christ.* Murdoch pulled out his phone, turned further into the shadow of the jacaranda and dialled Davie's number.

A clapped-out Hyundai Excel turned out to be the perfect car for following a BMW X5 across the centre of town. No matter how much the BMW accelerated or held tight to corners, no matter how much Davie panicked, the Excel was restrained by its own lack of power. On the motorway, they'd have lost the Beamer in seconds, but in central Crosley there were enough traffic lights to keep it in sight. Murdoch knew this from experience. He'd been in the opposite position often enough, embarrassed by the same old ladies who kept pootling up behind him after he'd raced between the lights. But north of the town centre – the traffic lights more distantly spaced – the Beamer soon left them behind. Davie kept doggedly on, pushing through two ambers and even a red, convinced he knew which set of tail lights he was after. Beside him, Murdoch studied the unfamiliar sights of North Crosley. No trees either side of the road, the buildings monotonous blocks, housing commission walk-ups over broken garages with badly parked cars in between.

'I think he's going left.'

A hundred metres ahead someone was going left – Murdoch could see that. Davie pulled into the left-hand lane and slowed until the dark profile of the BMW was clear to both of them, a big car heading into a housing estate.

'Go past!' Murdoch hissed it, convinced Davie was about to turn in after the Beamer. 'Take the next left instead.'

He pulled out his phone and found them on the map. Let Davie turn, then told him to stop at the next junction, engine off. They wound down their windows, the handle coming off in Murdoch's hand, but the hum of the main road behind them was too loud, no chance to hear the noise of a single car in the closer streets.

'Left,' said Murdoch.

Davie started the Excel again, but drove straight across the junction, deeper into the estate.

'We'll have missed him already unless he's gone straight on,' he said. 'I'll take the next left instead.'

But the next left turned out to be half a kilometre away, the tatty verge beside them interrupted only by broken driveways, garages and units in an endless six-storey block. Murdoch heard Davie gasp and felt the car swerve. Looked forward in time to see its headlights brush a shopping trolley upturned in the middle of the road. A working street lamp came into view, hooded figures gathered around it, smoke mingling with the steam of their breath. Remembering his window was down, Murdoch wound it up, careful with the handle. Davie did the same, before locking his door.

A minute later, a turning to the left appeared at last. Davie took it – like there was any point – and they found themselves in a street the same as the one before. Badly parked cars, man-sized litter, rare patches of light that offered no comfort. Only the bright windows in the blocks looked inviting, unreachable beyond their dark stairwells.

'There he is!' said Davie, braking so suddenly that the webbing of Murdoch's seatbelt pinched him through his shirt. To their right, a group of four-storey blocks stood around a patch of open grass and dirt, a circle of working street lights at its centre illuminating clean concrete. The space was eerily empty, some kind of hallowed ground – only a short fat man hurrying across it, huddled over whatever he was carrying.

'No way.'

But it was Hatch all right. They watched him disappear into the shadows again, Davie rolling the Excel quietly forward and turning into the curving street around the open ground. Hatch had been heading towards the small block that now stood on their left, almost every window lit, but as they continued forward they saw he hadn't gone inside. He was continuing on beside it, along a path of cracked paving stones, the rough ground either side of him black. Heading to a row of small terraced houses: buildings from an earlier age, a street somehow spared when the land was cleared for the estate. Davie pulled over and killed the lights. They couldn't drive after Hatch, not unless they wanted to mount the kerb and drive across the grass. In his wing mirror, Murdoch noticed a shadow detach itself from the nearest block.

'We can't stop here, Davie.'

Davie ignored him and Murdoch could hear he was counting under his breath. Ahead, two more shadows appeared, the parallel lines of their tracksuits catching the light as they advanced on the car.

'Davie, mate, we've got to go.'

215

'Four, five. I'm sure it's five, just let me check.'

A stone clattered on the bonnet, bouncing twice before repeating the pattern on the tarmac beside Murdoch's window. A second later, another hit the roof.

'Davie, for fuck's sake!'

Davie didn't need telling again. He started the Excel and swung into the road, one broad turn to take them back the way they'd come. The first shadow Murdoch had seen was in front of them now: an ancient young woman, pale as death, yellow hair pulled tight like a facelift on a corpse. She ran towards them, two fingers and blurred words, something else, thrown. There were two more at the first corner, same yellow hair, similar rip-off sweatshirts. They yelled too and Murdoch waited for them to throw their tinnies, praying they weren't carrying anything more dangerous than their smack and their slow disease. He wondered where Hatch had found to park his Beamer in this shithole; what made the man immune to the walking dead. Davie put his foot down and the Excel scratched slowly up to eighty.

'What's the name of that street?' he said hurriedly.

If he was scared he was hiding it. Murdoch watched him remember his lights, then fiddle with the heating. He was staring at the road ahead of them, ignoring what might be in the car mirrors.

'What street?'

'The one Hatch went over to.' Davie was excited. 'Look it up on your phone. This is Orange Grove, we've just passed Beryl.'

'Davie, mate, by the time we find our way round there, he'll be gone.'

Murdoch turned and looked out the back window. The stones on the car had shaken him, reminded him of where he was from. He wanted to get back to Montie. Turning to the front again, he caught the expression on Davie's face.

'What you so excited about?'

'He went into a house. Didn't you see, Bill? Terry Hatch went into a house on that street back there. The fifth one down on the far side. Just tell me the address and we'll find him again.'

Half the houses in Splendid Street still had their windows. In those that were occupied, bare bulbs lit the poverty inside: life on bad furniture open to view, proof there was nothing to nick. All except number ten. Number ten had bulbs on all right – one in every room by the look of it – but you had to stare at the tight curtains to be sure. Only the light in the hallway was clear, its melancholy blue infecting the glass of the front door so that purple roses sat amongst brown leaves. Each time the door opened, the blue light spread into the street like a gas and Davie and Murdoch heard music. It was duff-duff and a woman's voice, barely there before it was locked in again. They watched six pairs of headlights arrive, four pairs leave before Murdoch ran out of patience and asked Davie if he had a sweatshirt or something.

'You cold? There's a blanket in the back.'

'It's not that. It's just it'll look weird if I go in there with this on.'

It was his favourite black shirt, some fancy designer whose name he could never remember.

'Who says you're going in?' said Davie. 'Why can't I go?'

'Mate, if that place is what I think it is, you'll stick out more than me in this shirt. Odds on, you wouldn't get past the front door.'

They heard the music again and watched a man with lank grey hair emerge from the house and start down the pavement towards them. He adjusted his crotch, hoiked loudly and sent a gob of shiny phlegm to the gutter. Davie sighed, one hand in his floppy blond hair.

'So what do I do?'

'Wait here. Ten minutes tops or till things look dodgy. Any longer than that, or at any sign of trouble, clear off. I'll call you when I'm out, so you can pick me up.'

Davie reached behind his seat and, after some rummaging, pulled out a thick woollen sweater, red with white stripes. He handed it over like a precious gift.

'It's all right,' said Murdoch. 'I'll be fine in the shirt.'

The house's front garden was strangely tidy. Leafy dwarf bushes ran in neat lines around grass so perfect it had to be AstroTurf. Catching himself thinking what the little bushes might be, whether he should get

217

some for his garden, Murdoch swore and told himself he'd be fine. In and out in a jiffy, nothing to worry about.

He was looking for the doorbell, shivering in the cruel breeze, when the door was opened by a dark giant in a pale blue turban. He had a dominant brow, sticking out over his nose, thick woolly eyebrows that matched his beard, eyes like a baddy in a Bollywood movie. Like Murdoch, he was wearing a black shirt and jeans.

'Yeah?'

Murdoch rubbed his hands together, shifting his weight from foot to foot. It was easy to act nervous when you were shitting yourself.

'Yeah,' he said. 'Mate told me to come here. Said it was fifty bucks.'

White wires trailed from each of the giant's ears to the heavy breast pocket of his shirt. He smiled briefly – at what he was listening to, not at Murdoch – stepped back and let him in. A thick patterned carpet, yellow and brown, ran wall-to-wall and up the stairs. To the left of the front door, vivid against the unpatterned wall, hung a painting of a woman with a green face. Opposite, on the wall behind the door, a gilt-framed mirror hung above a half-moon table holding a vase of plastic tulips. The tulips were wobbling in time to the duff-duff upstairs, the music louder than out on the street, but no easier to understand. It was bass mostly, the woman's voice coming and going – bad karaoke, or maybe just someone singing along. It was disturbing, a woman having fun in this kind of place, and Murdoch struggled to ignore it. More difficult to ignore was the smell: a sharp sweet odour like someone had dropped a bottle of perfume or used one to hide something else.

'Seventy bucks,' the heavy said mechanically. 'And you give me your keys, your wallet and your phone.'

He sat down on the stairs, the hallway doubling in size, and leaned forward to pull an envelope from a plastic tub under the half-moon table. Like he was collecting money for rides at Luna Park. Murdoch remembered all the animals he'd ever worked with. And a quote he'd learned off the internet: 'The only thing necessary for the triumph of evil is for good men to do nothing.' But that wasn't true. It took morons like this to do the leg work. The idea of going further inside washed over him like nausea.

'My phone?' he said. 'I'm not giving you my phone.'

The heavy looked up with his soft brown eyes. *Why did there always have to be one?*

'It stays here in an envelope with me, bud. We don't hack into it or rip you off or blackmail you or nothing. It's just security, in case you do any damage. Seventy bucks, wallet, keys, phone.'

Murdoch took a deep breath. He'd come this far and he needed to change his phone anyway. He handed it over together with his keys, took seventy bucks out of his wallet, counted what was left there and handed the wallet over too. A door opened somewhere above them and the smell in the hallway grew stronger, the duff-duff louder.

'Number four,' said the heavy in the turban. He threw the envelope back in the tub, the money into the drawer of the half-moon table, stood out of the way and raised his thumb. 'Upstairs.'

There was no reason Murdoch shouldn't go ahead with it. He'd paid for it after all.

'You got any blondes?' he said. 'Tall, big knockers?'

The heavy sighed again. Whatever he was listening to, he wanted to listen undisturbed. He stared at Murdoch.

'You taking the piss? What d'you think this is, Misty's? Get up the stairs or fuck off.'

Murdoch did the whole wide-eyed act – hesitating like Davie would have done, rubbing his hands and trying a smile. But he did it slowly, full eye contact.

'Is the boss in?'

'What do you care?'

'The boss, Terry Hatch, is he here? Can I have a word?'

It was a gamble – Hatch could be a punter – but the odds weren't bad and Murdoch saw straight away he'd picked a winner. The Sikh scratched his beard, pulled the wires from his ears and shrank. That was the thing about living amongst animals: you never knew who was a predator.

'What do you care?' he said again, more quietly this time.

'Tell Terry that Smithy's here. Wants a word. Now.'

'I've not done nothing wrong but,' said the heavy. 'Wasn't being funny. We don't have any blonde girls; them's all slopes.'

'Really. What's your name?'

The big man hesitated.

'Singho,' he said.

'Tell you what, Singho. You seem like a nice lad, so let's not worry about it, eh? No reason for you to know who I am; no need for Hatch to know you was rude. Tell him Smithy was here and he sends his regards. Tell him to call me, yeah?'

Murdoch stuck out his hand, his flat palm as blue as the air, and watched Singho stare again until he caught on. Watched him bend to the tub under the half-moon table and find the envelope with his belongings. Then, after another stare, seventy bucks from the loose notes in the drawer. The Sikh moved so quickly, in short jerky movements, that Murdoch almost felt sorry for him. Except you couldn't come to a place like this, let alone work in one, without putting yourself beyond the limits.

'Thanks, Singho, there's a good lad. Remember, you tell Terry to call Smithy, yeah?'

'No worries. I'll do it now.'

Outside, in the cold night air, Murdoch found he was sweating. He walked back down the street the way he'd come, as slowly as he knew how. Davie and his car were gone.

Monday, 18th March

Three days after

Anita races up to the office at seven thirty on Monday morning. She has been awake since four and up since six, moving slowly around the house at first and telling herself not get to work *too* early. It is only while brushing her teeth the she realises the horrible error she has made. For even if, in the lost hours of Friday, she did return the injection kit to Scott's office – far more importantly – she has no way of knowing if she removed the drug-tainted Central Coast Mariners mug from his desk. Given the clean replacement mug is still in her handbag, it seems unlikely. Toothpaste dribbling down her chin, Anita races to the bottom of the stairs to find her handbag lying on its side on the hall floor. She grabs it and stares inside. The pristine mug is there and, of course, the injection kit is not.

The fact that she normally starts work at nine is now irrelevant. Anita suspects the police will have already visited the PPC offices but, on the off-chance they haven't, she is more determined than ever to get in before them. Dressing as quickly as she can, she drives to Bungaree distractedly, nearly colliding with a car at the end of her street and then racing through the lack of rush hour traffic to arrive at the industrial estate earlier than ever before. The mismatched buildings loom ominously. With their forecourts empty and their windows dark, they seem like ruins from an earlier age, as desolate as the wasteland across the road. The only signs of life are from the PPC warehouse, its roller door half-open and – once Anita has parked in a skid and wound down the Suzuki's windows – voices echoing from inside.

Taking deep breaths to calm herself, Anita realises she needs an excuse for being in so early in case any of the men in the warehouse ask. But her mind is a blank. Closing her eyes and trying another deep breath, hoping to summon the professional, she wishes she were anywhere but here, in any other life. The whispers of the distant highway, invisible from this angle, come to her on the breeze and she thinks how beautiful it would be to go away somewhere. To travel far and remember what it is like to relax. There is a dull thud from the warehouse, men's laughter rising in echoes and, remembering with a jolt where she is, Anita undoes her seatbelt, winds up her window and climbs quickly out of the car. If any of the men from the warehouse ask she will tell them she is getting things in order so that she can give the police as much information as possible. Or she will say that she wanted to get in before any journalists turn up. *Did you see the papers? Those nosey parkers are bound to visit.* Or she'll say she wanted to check if anyone one else was snooping around.

At the idea of 'anyone else' Anita freezes – car keys in one hand, handbag in the other – and stares at her reflection in the Suzuki's driver's side window. It is the sound of her own rapid breathing that wakes her. Giving her reflection a frown – meant to convey professionalism, but looking more like terror – she hobbles around to the back of the car. There she yanks open the hatch and rummages around in the detritus behind the back seat – chamois leathers, toys, an upturned toolbox – until she finds a screwdriver and then, better still, an oversized spanner. She throws the spanner roughly into her handbag and almost immediately gasps out an obscenity as she hears the crack of heavy metal meeting cheap ceramic. Praying to any god that might still exist, she rips the bag from her shoulder and, resting it on the edge of the car boot, looks inside. The majority of the replacement Central Coast Mariners mug is in three neat pieces, the largest still bearing its undamaged handle. The rest is in tiny shards. Anita wonders if maybe she should just give up. Sit there and cry until the police arrive, tell them everything and show them the evidence. But somehow no – not yet. Not while there is still a chance. She must channel this frustration into anger, in case there is anyone in the office. Arranging her handbag in such a way that she can easily reach the spanner, she walks slowly towards the door to the metal stairs.

There is no obvious sign the police have yet been. The door to the stairwell is Chubbed as normal and there is no response to Anita's loud unlocking, to her deliberate mumbling as she hurries inside to deactivate the alarm. After limping her way loudly up the metal stairs – no one can accuse her of sneaking in – she finds the door to the opening locked for once and struggles in the dim light to find the right key. Only when she has found it, and the door between the opening and the stairwell has swung closed behind her, does she wonder who locked it in the first place. She grabs the spanner from her handbag and pushes her back along the wall towards the bathroom calling out, 'Hello?'

The offices feel different, as if – just as in her home – someone has moved everything and put it back again. Anita takes this as a positive sign, a clue that she really did come back on Friday, and tries to resist the thought that maybe it's someone else who has been in there. She tells herself to take more deep breaths. If the police come, *when* the police come, she must not only appear calm, she must *be* calm. She forces herself slowly from room to room, the spanner heavy and poised. There is no one in the opening, no one in the bathroom, no one in the sales office.

Anita doesn't allow herself to think before finding the key to Scott's office, struggling with the lock and then – spanner raised high – forcing the door open with a bang. But there is no one in there either.

Anita finds she is trembling and, annoyed at her weakness, limps across the room to check she really did return the injection kit to the place where it belongs. She is desperate to believe there is some small part of her that really is that professional. But, halfway there, the office door bangs behind her, the venetian blind adding its laugh and Anita gives a little scream and turns, screaming again as her bad ankle twists in her shoe. Before she knows it, she is down on the ground, the heavy spanner hurting her knuckles against the carpet and half her hair falling across her face. Scrabbling to her hands and knees, she crawls quickly around Scott's desk and yanks open the top drawer, sitting up on her knees to stare at the paper and pens neatly arranged in there. There is no sign of the injection kit.

Crawling around the room, Anita confirms the kit isn't in the credenza either or in Scott's other desk drawers or anywhere in the room. Then, standing again but dispensing of her shoes, she limps back into the opening, searching in and under her own desk and through the cleaning cupboard. She searches in the sales office, even in the bathroom, a reversal of her earlier path, until she has confirmed beyond doubt that the injection kit did not make it back here after all.

The search feels like fakery – Anita isn't even sure she came back here on Friday afternoon, but strangely, as she progresses, she manages to find the calm that has eluded her for days. If the injection kit isn't in her house, and it isn't in the office, then she must have dumped it somewhere. With nothing on it to identify it as Scott's, what does it matter? The relief of this feels wrong, a temptation into laziness, and Anita forces herself to look again in all the places she has already looked until, back in Scott's office, she finds her shoes. They remind her of her appearance, of how she must seem to the police when they arrive.

In the opening, she clicks on the radio that sits on the fridge, pleased at the sense of normality it gives to the scene. Then she returns to the bathroom, tidying her hair and her clothes in the mirror and, once that is done, practising the responses she will give to police. She isn't used to

223

lying and has no idea how good she might be at it. She remembers once hearing the most plausible answer to any question – the easiest to pull off – is 'I don't know'. She rehearses wide innocent eyes and three different ways of saying 'Oh, honestly, officer, I've no idea.'

She is tidying Scott's office, checking she has closed all his drawers and left the credenza as she found it, feeling professional once more, when she spots his Central Coast Mariners mug sitting on his desk, full of coffee stains and traces of her sleeping tablets. Anita curses herself and grabs the damned thing, carrying it with a quick limp into the opening. Throwing it into her handbag, she takes another random cup from the top of the fridge and flicks on the kettle. 'Calm down,' she tells herself, before scalding her wrist with a splash from the kettle and hurriedly making coffee in the new mug. *Calm down, calm down, calm down!!!* She throws the newly-made coffee down the sink, waves the mug around to make the coffee stains dry more quickly and, too impatient to wait any longer, rushes with it back into Scott's office. She spends several minutes arranging it on his desk in what she thinks was the same position as the original mug, then hears cars pull up on the forecourt outside. She is barely back at her desk, her handbag firm next to her feet, the heavy spanner in her top drawer, when she hears heavy feet start up the stairs.

The police who suddenly fill the opening don't look like police at all, although they certainly don't fail to act like them. The woman in charge, after introducing herself as Detective Sergeant Natalie Something, starts by crossing to the fridge and, without consulting Anita – the opening chords of 'Manic Monday' by The Bangles are starting up – turns the radio off. She then looks around for a chair, before asking one of her colleagues – a sour-faced man with a heavy beard – to wheel one in from the sales office. As soon as he has done so, the detective sergeant turns the chair and straddles it, before fixing her surly green eyes on Anita's. The woman is in jeans and a white T-shirt and Anita wonders if she shouldn't ask for some means of identification until, as if reading her mind – a horrific idea! – the policewoman hands her a card. *Detective Sergeant Natalie Conquest.* Conquest! It is clearly a sign, but whether it means she or the police will win in the end, Anita has no idea. She stares at the name, the black letters sharp against the white card, then –

remembering to widen her innocent eyes – back up at the detective sergeant.

The questions go on for almost an hour. Detective Sergeant Conquest phrases every one as if she knows exactly what Anita has done and is annoyed she won't admit it. *Where was Mr Patterson going if his nephew was to attend the meeting alone? Why would he have been phoning hospitals in the Southern Highlands? Was he behaving strangely before he left?* With her short hair and mannish clothes, Natalie Conquest is, presumably, a lesbian and Anita finds she wants to tell the woman she has nothing against lesbians, that she herself has no current fondness for men. Anything to stop the policewoman being so aggressive. But at no point does Anita consider telling her the truth. For, staring out from her computer screen, is the photograph of Riya on the swings in the park. All Anita has to do is avoid the policewoman's gaze and look at her screensaver (well named!) and she remembers why she must lie until the cows come home. It turns out there are endless ways of saying 'I don't know.' She must remember the trick in case she ever is questioned again.

The colleagues DS Conquest has brought with her stand murmuring in Scott's office. One of them has wedged the door open and, once the detective sergeant has finished with her at last, Anita studies them from behind her desk. There is a surprisingly young man, piggy eyes and fashionable hair, taking endless photographs with an overbright flash. A round-shouldered woman, pale and prematurely grey, dusting for fingerprints (Anita presumes) as she sings quietly under her breath. Directing them both and taking notes is an old Tamil man in a suit. After a while, the police start boxing up items from the office. They take Scott's computer, the contents of his desk drawers, the files from the credenza and, of course, the cups sitting on top of his desk: the two blue ones she and Alan drank from and the replacement one she so recently placed there. This last one, Anita sees to her horror, is Alan's Canterbury Bulldogs mug. As the Bulldogs mug is lifted carefully into a plastic bag, she forces herself to look away. It is a horrible error – no one will believe Scott would drink from a Bulldogs mug – but at least, she tells herself, it will not be found to contain any sedatives. She cannot resist moving her good foot to reassure herself that her handbag, and Scott's Central Coast

Mariners mug, are safely under her desk. Realising she is sweating, she tells herself to breathe and hits Control + Alt + Delete to bring up her screensaver again.

'Are you all right, Anita?'

The detective sergeant is looking out from Scott's office with a new frown. Anita stares back and understands slowly this is an expression of concern.

'It's all a bit much,' she hears herself saying slowly. 'Poor Scott, what do you think could have happened to him?'

Detective Sergeant Conquest comes and sits on the side of her desk.

'You really can't think of anyone who might want to harm him?'

Anita allows tears to form – no idea if that old trick will work on a woman. 'No, none at all. He's such a lovely man.'

It is less than half an hour later that the detective sergeant convinces Anita she might as well run along home. Detective Constable Burran – she gestures to the sour-faced man with a beard – will call her if they have any more questions.

Anita drives home with the Suzuki's windows open, the newly cool air buffeting her and keeping her calm. She remembers the idea of travelling far away and learning how to relax again. The thought grows, a seed in a crack of dirt, until, when she hits the traffic of the highway, she says, 'Fiji' aloud, her voice strangely jubilant in the rattling car. 'Fiji!' she says again, struggling not laugh. 'We'll all go to Fiji!'

The red tail lights of the car in front of her bring her back to her senses. The car is slowing for some reason and, as Anita continues to approach at speed, she realises it is actually stopping. Ahead of it, a traffic jam appears around the bend in the highway. Anita gasps and stamps too hard on the brake, her bandaged ankle painful as the clutch resists the foot below it. Everything in the Suzuki continues forward faster than the car itself, a coat of Riya's flying between the front seats and landing on the gearstick. On the back seat, Anita's handbag topples forward and Anita herself is pressed painfully against her seatbelt. She hears her tyres singing against the asphalt and smells burning rubber, but still the car in front grows in her windscreen.

'No! No, no, no!'

Anita swerves into the outer lane – no time to check her blind spot – and gasps again as a second scream from her tyres is drowned out by a far louder noise. A monstrous truck is filling her rear-view mirror, so close she can see no more than the grille of its radiator. The screech of its tyres, the stench of their burning, are a mockery of what the Suzuki has done. Its horns bellow long and loud.

'No!!!'

Anita rips Riya's coat out of the way and gears down into second, pushing at the accelerator so hard that the Suzuki's little engine screams under the bonnet, pulling her away from a second roar of horns from the lorry. But this noise is complaint, not warning. Anita tears forwards, blurring past an accident on the inside lane, hazard lights flashing behind men inspecting damage, cars indicating impatiently.

Glancing back at the lorry, Anita sees it is a cab with no trailer and realises with horror that otherwise it would have jack-knifed and surely killed them both.

'Oh my God, I'm … unbreakable.'

Anita says the words aloud and repeats them all the way home, keeping at bay the horror of what she has nearly done. Even parked outside her house, she won't let herself give in to it. She simply undoes her seatbelt and grabs her handbag from the back seat before limping weak-legged away from the car. *I am unbreakable. I am unbreakable. I am unbreakable.* She doesn't notice her handbag is slightly lighter. That Scott's drug-tainted Central Coast Mariners mug has toppled out and rolled under the passenger seat of her car. Nor, of course, that it remains there, jammed tight against the adulterated injection kit.

Part 2: April

1

On April Fool's Day Davie woke with a jolt, his back arched from the effort of dragging air through a snore. He lay blinking, trying to remember why he wasn't in bed and what he had to feel so bad about. He'd been dreaming of a toilet lid slamming and now wondered if it had been the stink of his own breath that had woken him. Closing his mouth, he turned with a groan onto one side and tried to work out what he was looking at. Blinking again, he pushed himself upright and saw it was an empty wine bottle, the off-white label invisible against his off-white front door. He could taste the wine, at least the next day's version of it, and was getting up to fetch a glass of water when his front door shook: the same noise as the toilet lid slamming.

'Davie!'

Bill's voice was as harsh as it had been the night before.

'Davie, you all right?'

'Go away.'

But Bill didn't go away. Davie knew because the stairs down to the driveway didn't creak and, besides, Bill never did what you wanted him to do. He shuffled to the kitchen and ran the tap.

'Davie, let me in. I've got something for you.'

Davie pulled open the dishwasher and wondered how long he would own the thing before he ever remembered to turn it on. He chose the least dirty glass, filled it from the tap and drank it half empty. The front door shook again. Davie looked around to check the magazine from the weekend newspaper was out of sight and spotted it balled on the floor near the lounge.

'Davie!'

'Coming, coming.'

Because what was the point? No one ever cared what he wanted. He finished the rest of the water and shuffled to the living room, shivering in the cold air. Even after the renos the shack was always either too cold or too hot, Davie promising himself he wouldn't use his new air con unit until he got green electricity. But, today, he remembered, the world didn't deserve saving. Flicking the locks on the front door, he gave it a tug and carried on towards the dining table, pulling open its drawer to search for the air con's remote control.

'Morning.'

'Whatever.'

The drawer was full of pens and packets of tissues, bulldog clips and unpaid bills, but sometimes, if Davie rummaged long enough and remembered what he was looking for, he could find things in there. He dug deeper and, feeling a sharp jab, withdrew his hand to find a staple stuck in the end of his finger. Behind him, Bill gave an awkward cough.

'What do you want, Bill?'

'Wanted to say sorry, didn't I? And, look, I got you a gift.'

Bill closed the front door with one hand and held out a flat plastic pack with the other. Even in the diminished grey light between them, Davie could see what it was.

'Very funny. Point taken.'

The Englishman rolled his eyes and threw the gift onto the coffee table. 'I'm not being funny, mate. It's a peace offering, innit, to stop it happening again. Bleeding hell, what's got into you?'

Davie slammed the drawer shut, walked across to the bifolds and rested his forehead against the cold glass. The view was calmer than it had been in days, trees and scrub defeated, mismatched clouds flat and still. Bill never apologised unless he wanted something. The trick was to find out what it was before you gave it to him or, more likely, promised you would. Safest of all was to say nothing. At a crackling of thick paper, Davie straightened and turned. Bill, now sitting on the lounge, had picked up the newspaper supplement and was flattening it on his lap.

'What's this, then?'

It was strange: in so many situations, Bill was a fantastic liar, but, at other times, Davie could see straight through him.

'You've seen it!' Davie hadn't meant to shout. He took a deep breath and started again. 'Oh, of course, you've seen it. The whole world's seen it, haven't they? I'm sure copies of it are being passed around town in case anyone's missed out on the joke. You … oh, my God, you must have seen it on Saturday! You always get the *SMH*. Well, thanks for warning me.'

Bill gave an exaggerated sigh.

'Mate, I was going to tell you. That's what I came out for last night, but then Hatch turned up, didn't he? And, then, well, your phone wasn't working, was it?'

'Are you going to start that again?' Davie didn't care if he was shouting now – it was his turn, after all. 'Are you going to yell at me again for not charging my phone after spending two days in a car when you couldn't be bothered? Are you going to call me an *idiot* again?'

Bill had held up his hands.

'My fault, Davie. I'm sorry I was angry. It's just running miles across the wrong part of town on the coldest night of the year isn't fun. Not in my best shirt. And, like I said, it was an hour and half before I could find a taxi.'

'You said to wait ten minutes then go.'

'I did say that. You did nothing wrong. I was angry. Come on, Davie, mate. I'm sorry. Here, take this.'

Bill raised a foot and nudged the unopened phone charger across the coffee table towards him. 'It goes in your cigarette lighter.'

'I know how it works, Bill. Thanks, you can go now.'

'This isn't that bad, is it?'

He meant the article. He was flattening the magazine again, searching the text for something good. Davie walked around the table and snatched it from his lap. He turned to the photograph of himself and held it up in Bill's face. Even undoctored it would have been an unkind shot, one hand in his hair and his mouth in an idiotic smile. With the added graphics of a Sherlock Holmes hat and a magnifying glass, he looked deranged. The image covered two thirds of a page, the main photograph of an article entitled 'What Happens After The One Hit Wonder?'

'I thought you had three hits?'

'Nice try.' Davie snapped the magazine back around and read aloud. '*Of all the careers in the history of pop, Davie Wonder's must have been the briefest. But rather than admit he really is a has-been, this strange One-Hit-Wonder boy refuses to give up. He now styles himself as a modern-day Sherlock Holmes – or, perhaps, Inspector Gadget? – using his faded good looks and his unmatched experience in how to go unnoticed to solve crimes from a backwater of the Central Coast.'*

Bill winced. 'No such thing as bad publicity?'

Davie tried to ball the magazine again, but the feeling was less than satisfying. He tore at it instead, managing three uneven pieces before he opened his eyes to find Bill standing in front of him.

'Davie, listen to me.'

'I'm a bloody laughing stock! Apart from my family, of course! No one's laughing there, oh no! My dad phoned me and asked me to change my surname if I was going to continue to make a fool of myself. Everyone gave up on me years ago, apparently, but there's no need to drag him down too.'

'Davie, shut the fuck up and listen to me. You listening?'

Why shouldn't he cry? It wasn't like he could go down further in anyone's opinion. He put the heels of his hands into his eyes but found no relief in the darkness. The section of the article that covered him had gone on for five hundred and sixty-eight words, each paragraph more mocking than the one before. The word 'sad' had been used twice, no mention of his real name or anything that might drive business to the agency.

'Davie, listen to me. You listening? When I was inside, everyone I knew – *everyone* – had had bad shit happen to them. Else they wouldn't of been in there, right? And, then, once you're in, things get worse; at least, for most of us they did. But you know what, Davie? When shit happens, you've got a choice. You either lie down and let it kill you or you stand up and fight. You got me?'

Davie felt a pain in his chest. Lowering his hands, he saw Bill had poked him. Then, as he watched, he poked him again, no less gently than before.

'What you going to do, Davie? Lie down or stand up and fight?'

Davie stepped backwards, out of reach.

'Leave me alone. You were miserable yourself all of last year.'

'Yeah, I was and you wouldn't leave me alone, so now I won't leave you alone neither. Specially not with what we found out last night. Cause with that, mate, even if we don't solve this case, we're going to expose something very nasty. Well, you are.'

Bill added the last three words quickly and, despite himself, Davie wondered why. He dried his eyes with the back of his hand, and bent to pick up the wine bottle. The sound of ripping paper made him look up. Bill was tearing the article into smaller pieces than he had managed.

'So let's forget this shit,' he said, 'and work out exactly what we know.'

Green tea and raisin toast didn't help, but a shower and clean clothes did. Davie came out of the bathroom to an unfamiliar chugging that turned out to be his dishwasher. His underused surfboards were propped behind the front door, the bedclothes had disappeared from the lounge and there was no sign of the torn magazine. Bill had even got the air con working. Davie nearly asked him why he was being so nice, then remembered, bitterly, he'd asked the question the previous night in the car.

They sat at the kitchen table, Bill doing most of the talking for once, Davie struggling to focus. He kept thinking of friends who'd have seen the article. Only one had phoned, good old Guy, saying he was going to kill his brother himself and also send a letter about libel.

'So,' Bill was saying, 'our friend, Mr Scott Patterson, is not a nice fella after all.'

'Yeah. No. Why not?'

The sour look on Bill's face was the most honest thing Davie had seen there all morning. He watched him swallow it away, grimacing at the taste before finding a gentler voice.

'Well, let's join the dots. Patterson puts ads into Asian papers about jobs at some fancy country club in Australia with a PO box address and all. That'd be irresistible to all them poor locals desperate for a bit of cash – not to mention an escape from the poverty trap they live in. Then Patterson gets regular payments from a company calling itself Hamilton Enterprises. Hamilton Enterprises is run by a certain Terry Hatch, who is the boss of an illegal knocking shop what only has Asian girls. Get it?'

Davie wasn't quite sure he did get it.

'That place you went to was a brothel?'

'What d'you think it was, a bleeding McDonald's?'

'I don't know, Bill. You didn't tell me, remember? Last night on the phone, all you did was shout at me about what an idiot I was for driving off like you told me to and then for not being able to charge my phone until I got back here. Or don't you remember that?'

Bill held his hands up in surrender again until, at a shrill ringing, he used them to struggle a cheap phone from his pocket and hold it below the table to kill the call.

'What's that?'

'Nothing.'

'Yes, it is, Bill. Why have you got a new phone?'

'I haven't.'

'Yes, you have.'

'Davie, listen to me. D'you know what this means with Patterson and Hatch? It means the look on your dad's face when you uncover a human trafficking ring.'

'At Huntingdon's?'

Bill hesitated. 'Nah. Well, maybe, I dunno. Can't see that place working as a whorehouse, not unless it's only the old blokes what know about it. But anyway, listen to me, will you? Even if not up there, definitely at Hatch's joint. Think about it, Davie. You expose that and you'll get police commendations, medals or whatever they give out these days. You got it? That's front page of the proper paper that is – not some stupid weekend thingy what no one bothers reading.'

'Everyone reads it.'

'Nah, no one does. They just do the Quick Quiz and chuck it away.'

There were limits. 'Bill, why are you being so nice? What's going on?'

Watching the Englishman's blush, Davie immediately knew what it was. As an excuse to hide his face, he stood quickly and walked over to the kitchen. Hilarious. Bill's visit had cheered him up after all. He flicked on the kettle and shouted back over his shoulder.

'Go on then. Is there something else you want you want to tell me?'

'Jesus, mate, no flies on you, Davie. You see right through me.'

'Cut the suck-up and tell me, would you?'

He turned and watched Bill wipe a hand across his scalp. He needed a haircut, you could see the red in the lengthening stubble.

'Well, the thing is mate, we've not really talked about … Well, since me and, you know, Natalie. Since Natalie and me started, you know.'

'What?'

'Seeing each other. Going out. Thought I should clear it with you, official like. I know she's like a sister to you.'

'Yeah, she is. But it's all right, no stress. The only thing is …'

This time it was Davie's phone that tried to interrupt, buzzing softly on the table and trying to turn, like it wanted to rev donuts in the crumbs.

Reminder: Wendy Skellen.

Davie grabbed the phone before Bill could read the screen.

'The only thing is what, Davie?'

'Bill, did you mean it, about the look on my dad's face and all that? Do you think we really could expose a people trafficking ring?'

'Said so, didn't I?' Bill looked as honest as he ever did, his hand on his scalp again. 'But about Natalie, the only thing is what?'

'But you'll still help me with the Patterson case too?'

'Er, yeah sure.'

'Promise?'

'Promise.'

'Good. Then you have to come out with me this afternoon. There's someone we have to meet.'

Bill sat back heavily, his face struggling to still be nice.

'Fine,' he said. 'No problem. But only if you tell me what you was going to say about me and Natalie. The only thing is what?"

Davie checked his watch and leaned in quickly before he could chicken out.

'The only thing is, Bill, if you hurt her, I will go to my friend, Guy – you know, the lawyer? And I'll ask him to introduce me to every crook he can find and I'll tell them all that you're alive and where you live.'

Davie braced himself for a snarl, maybe even another poke in the chest. What he got was a sight he'd never seen before: Bill's English skin drawn and translucent.

Montagne Road, once it had looped from the lagoon and run between the shops and the beach, crossed a tiny roundabout – ignoring the turn-off out of town – and quickly became a second-gear gradient. Two minutes later, you were on top of the world. The climb was so sudden there was a lookout at the top – a renovated platform and a plaque about Captain Cook. Two hundred and seventy degrees of bumpy blue horizon. Murdoch and Davie ignored the view and drove on, peering instead at the properties on the other side of the road, ugly McMansions set back from the cliffs.

'There.'

Davie pointed at a drive between two of the houses. To its right was a home-made sign: a black wooden arrow with *Nos 24 to 36* in neat white brush strokes. Turning in, they had a brief view of the lagoon – a puddle, low and far away. Then they turned again and followed the drive downhill under thick tree cover, grevillea and bottlebrush reaching out to tickle the sides of the Merc. Above them, to the left, steep land climbed to the back of the McMansions on Montagne Road. To their right, wooden stilt houses interrupted the canopy of trees further down the hill.

'Jesus,' said Murdoch. 'Every time I think I know Montie, I find somewhere new.'

Wendy Skellen was a large, good-looking woman with flawless skin, soft brown eyes and a broad full-lipped mouth. Her husky voice came as a surprise, the voice of a woman who'd just finished smoking a cigar, not one who had been hanging her sheets on the line, her hands still full of pegs. She showed them into her kitchen and sat them at a table beside wide glass doors, the tops of eucalypts and turpentine pressing against the deck outside, lorikeets squabbling on the railing.

'Nice place,' said Murdoch.

He meant hidden from the main road, no way in but through the front door. That morning he'd spoken to Velis again. Wendy Skellen gave a forced smile, thanked him and sat down. The house smelled of coffee, but she didn't offer them one.

'Anne Lincoln said you wanted to know about my time at PPC,' she said. 'I'm more than happy to help, but I'm afraid I have to go out in a few minutes.'

Murdoch let Davie respond to that. The chances of Anne Lincoln's cousin's neighbour having any useful information were slim. Her home was more interesting. It was like a tree-house with all mod cons. A kitchen open to the living room, a pot-bellied stove by the sofas glowing with barely burnt logs. Outside, the lorikeets took flight, bullied away by a pair of king parrots, blazing red replacing green on the railing. There was a bird feeder out there, Murdoch saw, a small tray hanging off the far side.

'Did Scott have any, er, unusual clients?'

Davie, subtle as a brick, was too subtle for Wendy Skellen.

'Unusual?'

'Unsavoury.'

Murdoch wondered what words Davie would use to describe Emre Velis. Unusual, unsavoury, unpalatable? Un-everything Murdoch wanted to be involved with. And yet Murdoch had phoned him back as soon as he could, the little phone, so small and weightless, making the whole thing feel like a game. Velis, of course, had had an invitation and Murdoch still wasn't sure why he'd accepted.

'What about Scott's personal life?' Davie was saying. 'Sorry to be forward, but do you think he was ever unfaithful to his wife?'

Wendy Skellen's face, the real one beneath the fixed smile, froze for a tiny second, the way it had when Davie mentioned 'unsavoury connections'. Murdoch watched her look at her watch for longer than she needed to.

'Oof, I wouldn't know.'

She gave a know-nothing shrug, physical sarcasm at the idea she should be expected to know. The gesture appeared again, in different versions, as she answered Davie's next few questions. Soon, it was accompanied by the drumming of her fingers on the table between them.

'Now, look,' she said eventually, 'I really should be running along.'

'You live alone,' said Murdoch.

It was the first time he'd spoken since complimenting the house and both Wendy and Davie turned in surprise. When Wendy responded, her voice was calm.

'And what's that got to do with anything?'

239

'If you're about to go out, why have you put a new log on the fire? That one in there's hardly burnt.'

'Bill!'

Murdoch held up a hand to silence Davie.

'The thing is, Wendy, we know that Patterson was not a very nice man. I think you know that too and I think you should tell us about it.'

Davie opened his mouth again, silenced this time by the changing colour of Wendy Skellen's face.

'I don't ... I don't think ...'

'Please,' said Davie. 'Please tell us. We don't want to intrude, but anything you say could help us find him.'

There it was again, the hardening of the jaw, the sharpening of her cheekbones.

'Or,' said Murdoch, 'it could help us put him behind bars for a very, very long time. Maybe forever. Would you like that? Scott Patterson rotting in jail where he deserves to be?'

He'd hit the money spot. Even Davie saw it and, together, they watched Wendy Skellen's perfect skin flush again, this time into ugly blotches, the confident mouth not so confident any more. It was another ten minutes before she started telling them anything useful.

'It started so subtly. And he seemed so nice, so gentle, I thought maybe I was imagining it. He'd say something and I'd think, "Ooh, that sounds a bit rude," but then you'd look at him and he'd act so innocently you'd think it was *you*, not him, with the filthy mind.'

They were still at her kitchen table, each with a coffee now. Murdoch thought Wendy Skellen could do with something stronger, but no, she insisted, what she needed was to toughen up. She didn't offer them coffee, just made them a cup each – milk, no sugar – when she made one for herself, moving efficiently around the kitchen as they waited in silence. Outside, the king parrots had given way to a kookaburra. It sat, ignoring the seeds on the tray and staring in with its head on one side, like it wanted to hear the story too.

'My desk was in a space between his office and another one at the back. He called the space "the opening" and I suppose I just got used to

240

it. "I've left something in your opening" and "I'll meet you at your opening," all wide eyes, you know, so I'd think it was me not him. That's how it started, anyway. Then he had these horrible practical jokes. He'd pretend he was calling to me from inside his office, getting annoyed that I wasn't responding quickly enough. But it was just a stupid recording – he wasn't even in there. Then, on other days he really would call out to me and I had no idea if I was supposed to answer or not. It sounds ridiculous but it was so unnerving – always perfectly timed for when no one else was around. Then he started getting physical. I'm not going to go into details, I'm sorry. Suffice to say he …' she struggled with the words, '… he raped me. Forced himself on me, on more than one occasion.'

'Why didn't you tell anyone?'

Wendy Skellen glared at Davie, started to say something and cut herself short.

'Was there a reason you couldn't tell anyone?' Murdoch tried. 'I reckon there must have been a good reason.'

She'd never heard of good cop, bad cop.

'Thank you. I didn't tell anyone because I knew no one would believe me. You know, I can sit here now and see how he planned the whole thing, the evil bastard. He approached me with the offer of the job, I should have told you that. Said he thought it was disgusting the way I'd been treated and he'd be happy to help out however he could. He needed a PA, would I be interested? Arsehole.'

Murdoch waited, but Davie was too busy taking notes, so he had to ask himself.

'Sorry, love, what do you mean about the way you'd been treated? What had happened?'

Wendy Skellen sought courage in another slug of coffee. 'At my previous employment, I had been sexually harassed. I know what you're thinking, but it's true. I'd been the victim of an ongoing campaign by the marketing manager – little toad. Nothing as bad as what happened at PPC, but I complained. They ignored my complaints and it went to court. Front page news of the local rag, thank you very much; me coming out of court looking like a mad woman. The verdict went against me and suddenly I've no job, no income and friends pretending they believe me but not pretending very well. Then Scott Patterson comes along like a knight in shining armour.' Her eyes shone, but she blinked the tears into submission. 'Later, when he was … on me, Scott told me if I left PPC I'd never work again. He'd tell people I was dangerously insane, they only had to look at the paper for proof. He'd get off on those threats almost as much as he did on … the other stuff. It's the fear, he liked. The …'

She stood and turned to the windows. Outside, the kookaburra continued to stare.

'You survived,' said Davie. 'You got away.'

'Ha!' She barked it out, harsh in the quiet house, and for a few minutes said nothing more. Then she wiped her eyes and turned again. 'Got away with HIV, thank you very much. And yes, before you ask, I'm *sure* it was from him. And he was right about me not finding work again. I tried a few places, but even temping agencies wouldn't touch me – he saw to that. In the end, I changed my name and got a job in a florist's. Worked my arse off and I own three of them now. You know Moments in the mall? That's me. His wife came in once.'

Davie was nodding slowly: a toy dog on a dashboard with an understanding smile. Then the smile disappeared.

'Oh, crikey,' he said turning to Murdoch. 'Oh wow!'

'What?'

'Nothing.'

'You what?'

Davie pushed a hand through his blond mop and turned back to Wendy Skellen.

'Well, thank you very much for talking to us. We'd better be going.'

He scraped his chair back and stood, frowning at Murdoch to do the same. Murdoch ignored him.

'Would you be willing to testify against Patterson?' he said. 'Now that some time has passed? You know, to stop him doing it to anyone else?'

Wendy Skellen gave a dry sigh. 'I don't think so, no. I've spent the last five years leaving all of that behind me. I've done well, I own this place.' She looked around the kitchen like she'd forgotten where they were. 'I've got a nice life now. I've been to court before, remember; it was a nightmare. And I lost. So I've Buckley's of winning a second time round. Besides, he's been kidnapped, hasn't he? So let him rot. I hope whoever's got him bloody well kills him. I hope they torture him to death, dick first.'

'Let me guess,' said Murdoch, back in the car. 'You went to one of her flower shops once?'

'What? No, listen. Anita Patel once took an employer to court for sexual harassment. The last place she worked before she started at PPC – some company in Sacramento. It comes up if you google her name. And she lost. Patterson must have offered her a job the same way he did to Wendy Skellen and he must have been sexually abusing her too.'

Murdoch thought about it as he rolled the Merc down the narrow drive, no option but to continue the same way as before. Behind them, Wendy Skellen was standing in her doorway, hugging herself as if the day was cold, watching to make sure they left.

'I told you Anita was involved, Bill. That's why she's on the CCTV at the hospital, why she acted so strangely with the police. It's her, I'm sure of it. All we need now is proof!'

That evening Murdoch drove north. The journey was shorter than his phone had predicted and, sitting in the car park of McDonald's in Tamborine, he was tempted to grab a burger. He was halfway out of the car when Velis's DB9 sidled up beside him. Velis turned on his inside light, cracked his huge smile and signalled for Murdoch to come on in. They were taking his motor, apparently.

Murdoch let Velis do the talking. His own voice, he thought, would betray him, reveal how nervous he was in the tall man's presence now, knowing what he was. He stared out at the passing KFCs, Red Roosters and petrol stations, half-listening as Velis told them they were going to a dinner – probably a barbie, but the food would be great – in Green Bay. It was the last beach before The Inway.

Hearing Velis say 'The Inway' made Murdoch think of 'the opening'; he'd never think of the place the same way again. Not that he'd ever understood why it was such a drawcard. Surrounded by three sides on water – Lake Nura to the left; the ocean to the right; the channel between the two to the north – The Inway should have been beautiful. But the town was made of brick and asbestos, full of traffic and mismatched businesses, more tattoo parlours than restaurants. Everyone on the Coast loved the place, took weeks off to go on holiday there. Green Bay, he had never heard of.

'It's nice,' Velis said vaguely. 'Listen, I was thinking we should find a name for you this evening. Don't worry, no Clubbies there or anything, but no need to advertise I'm running around with a Bill Murdoch either. Didn't you ever think of changing your name?'

Like he was asking if Murdoch had ever been to Brisbane or wanted sugar or milk in his tea. Murdoch didn't want to talk about it, not on the way to a nice evening out. He could easily have changed his name: the NSW Witness Protection Program had given him a shiny new one, a real ID to go with it. But he'd decided he didn't need them. After all, the Club thought he was dead.

'Any preferences?' Velis was focusing on the traffic. 'Barry? Brian?'

'Tony.'

It had been a nickname at a borstal for a while; he couldn't remember why.

'Tony, great. And an equally forgettable surname?'

'Simms?'

'Perfect!' Velis's teeth caught the headlights of the oncoming traffic. 'I'll introduce you as Simmo; up to them if they think it's your first or your last name or something in between. Hang on.'

He was negotiating a junction, picking the right lane for the purring car. A highway sign pointed left to The Inway, but, when the lights changed, Velis drove straight on and, suddenly, they were in flat suburbia: bungalows lit better than the streets; neat lawns separated by driveways; no trees along the road. Velis turned and turned again as he mumbled quietly to himself, a man who'd been here before but had to concentrate to remember the route. After climbing a hill, they turned into a cul-de-sac, the houses bigger here, the older ones less showy, but all of them stretching back on long blocks of land: those on the right to reach the beach, those on the left to climb the hill and look over the houses opposite. On both sides of the road, they were built to within inches of the property next door.

'Aussies don't like gardens,' said Murdoch.

'Wogs don't.' Velis caught the look on Murdoch's face and laughed. 'I'm allowed to say it because I am one.'

Murdoch told him the word meant something different where he came from and Velis said, yeah, he knew, but out here it was OK. Sort of. Might be best not to use it tonight but.

'Oh, and listen,' he said, slowing the car outside a half-built house, then turning into the driveway opposite as he rummaged in the door beside him. 'Be nice to our hostess, yeah? And don't win the card game. This is for you.' A fat envelope of fifties landed in Murdoch's lap. 'That's your stake. Lose as slowly as you can.'

'I don't want your money.'

'Aw hish, I make twice that off her in a week. It's a business expense.'

'I don't do Club business.'

Velis turned at the tone and stopped the car abruptly. They were in front of a huge double garage, the bow of a boat silhouetted in there next to what looked like a Jaguar. Beyond the car, a man and a woman were talking. Velis checked his windows were closed.

'This is not Club business, Bill. This is fun. But let's not play silly buggers about who pays the bills. Your name's Simmo, you lose at cards, you keep your eyes open in the downstairs dunny. Do you trust me?'

Murdoch didn't have time to answer that. The two in the garage were approaching, squeezing their way between the low car and the boat.

'Well, whether you do or you don't, I won't let you down.' Velis had pulled on a fixed grin for the couple outside. 'I promise. Just have a good look in the dunny, yeah?'

Then he opened the door and got out with a cry of 'Angie!', leaving Murdoch to shove the money into his trouser pocket.

Angie Anathassiou was tall and athletic with an easy smile and a deep tan. Her thick hair was dyed black above suspiciously tight skin, but it was her bright eyes and enthusiasm that disguised her age. Murdoch put her at over fifty, still more kitten than cat.

'Simmo!' she said, pumping his hand before deciding on a kiss on the cheek after all. 'Great to meet you! I'd like to say I've heard all about you, but Emre here never tells me a thing, does he? This is my mate, Pete.'

Murdoch shook hands with the man who'd followed Anathassiou out of the garage. He had a shot of grey through his red hair, a round and freckled face that seemed to smooth straight through his shoulders and into his upper arms.

'Peter Branagan,' he said, proudly. 'Nice place this, isn't it?'

Murdoch looked around him. They were still in front of the garage, no light to see anything but the boat and the car, but he gave a smile and said yeah, lovely, nice, etc.

Velis had been right about the barbecue. When Anathassiou locked the garage and led them through the house, Murdoch barely had time to take in the double-height hallway before they were through a huge living room and onto the deck. Beyond was darkness and the sound of waves. Anathassiou stood beside her quietly smoking Weber, arms folded and smiling. Murdoch smiled back until he felt Velis prod him in the back.

'Wow,' he said. 'Nice place, Ange. Amazing. Is that the beach?'

'Sure is. That's what you get when you pay three and a half million for a house.' She walked to the edge of the deck and gestured down to the ocean like she'd bought that too. 'Have a swim, if you want. Seriously, feel free. The water's great this time of year and I've got spare shorts, towels, whatever you want.'

Murdoch wasn't tempted. He could see the waves now, crests coming out of nowhere and exploding with soft booms into foam. Everything else was black, even the sand between them and the water, only its closest edges catching the lights of the deck.

'What's for dinner?' he said. 'Smells good.'

'Seafood, hope you like it. I didn't know you could do lobster on a barbie, but we were in the Caribbean a few weeks ago and it's the only way they do it. Got the recipe from the chef, eventually – me and my powers of persuasion. But no promises, eh? This is the first time I've done it.'

Murdoch told her it smelled good again and there was an awkward silence, only the waves knowing what to say, until Velis came up with some bullshit about how lobsters mate. Murdoch listened politely, smiling at the right bits, wondering what the hell he was doing there. The ocean breeze was uncompromising and he looked with dismay at the outdoor table laid for four, perfect for a view of dinner if you were walking along the beach. Velis reached his punchline and they all laughed, until Peter Branagan started a story about whales. Anathassiou swore and ran to the barbecue.

'Pete! Drinks! You know where they are.'

Murdoch said he'd help. He was in his best black shirt again; the damned thing was cursed: he was cold whenever he wore it. In the over-lit living room, mottled leather sofas and a beige Ezyboy were angled around a stone fireplace. Apart from a flat-screen television, the only thing on the walls was a printed canvas, the words '*RELAX, LAUGH, BREATHE, GO TO THE BEACH*' shouting in assorted colours. No signs of any security. At the drinks trolley, Murdoch asked Peter how he knew their hostess.

'Neighbours.' Apparently, this was some kind of achievement, Peter pausing until Murdoch looked impressed. 'We met on the beach, would you believe it? I was admiring the boat bobbing around offshore and Angie told me it was hers. Impressive girl. I had no idea there was so much money in lingerie.'

He looked up from the bottles with a knowing glance. Murdoch didn't know if he'd made a joke or if they were both supposed to know Anathassiou didn't make her money in lingerie. He was reminded of the brothel in North Crosley, the heavy at the door doing the dirty work.

'So what business you in then, Peter?'

He didn't care, but that's what you did: asked people about the most boring part of their lives.

'I buy insurance.' Peter straightened and waddled around the trolley to hand Murdoch a weak whisky.

'You buy it?'

'Yes. I can buy you some if you want.'

He laughed at his own joke and Murdoch realised slowly there was no hidden message. When Peter Branagan said insurance, he meant it. Probably thought it was interesting too.

'Listen, Peter, I'm busting. Do you know if there's a toilet on this floor?'

'No, there isn't.' The other man leaned forward conspiratorially, the lingerie expression on his face again. 'Well, I think there is, but Angie doesn't let people use it. No idea why. So you want to go upstairs, first on the right.'

He accompanied Murdoch into the hallway and watched him climb the stairs with another proud smile. Murdoch played along, telling him how amazed he was by the gigantic chandelier hanging above.

'See,' said Peter, beaming. 'Impressive girl!'

The food was as good as Velis had promised. Large portions of smoky lobster and endless side dishes, all of them explained in detail. Fennel, celeriac, beetroot, eggplant. Braised, charred, parboiled. Anathassiou really was like a kitten: interesting for the first ten minutes. After that, Murdoch gave up trying to answer her questions or pass comment on anything she said. She had learned to cook in Seville, but took her mum back to Greece every year, at least once, and, of course, that affected her tastes. The Jaguar was new, she'd traded her Maserati for it. Her daughters, Demi and Desree, were worse than her husband. Men!

Velis, like Murdoch, listened in silence, but Peter Branagan gasped and laughed on cue.

'Fat fuck,' Anathassiou said, when her neighbour went to the bathroom. 'Bet you he's gone to stick his fingers down his throat so he can shovel some more in. Simmo! More lobster? Your plate's empty.'

Murdoch glanced at Velis more than once, but the look was never acknowledged. Once Peter had returned from the bathroom, he forced himself to wait ten minutes, Anathassiou now onto the evils of immigration – just look at Europe! – before excusing himself and walking inside. There was less light in the corridor than at the back of the house, easy to check no one had followed him. The first door he tried was a laundry room – a washing machine and dryer gleaming like an advert, empty drying rails above them. The second was the downstairs toilet – what Velis had called the 'dunny'. Murdoch locked the door behind him, sat on the toilet lid and looked around. He'd expected a few fat lines of coke, chopped and ready to go – Christ, the evening needed it – but the marble around the sink was clear. In the cupboard underneath, there was nothing but cleaning fluids, expensive toilet paper, a dead cockroach on its back. Nothing else to look at apart from a painting on the wall behind the door, a few lines for trees and people without faces. No safe behind it – Murdoch was grasping at straws – no loose tiles on the floor or walls. The panel above the toilet knocked hollow, but when he prised it loose, he found nothing but the cistern. He spent a good five minutes pushing the panel back into place, checking it was smooth, before his bladder responded to the surroundings. He took a leak, washed his hands – no towel – looked around again and left.

The others were still on the deck, but they had stood and were clearing the table. Murdoch thanked Anathassiou for the amazing food – what a great evening, blah, blah, blah. But no, no, no, they were just heading inside for the game.

'I guess that's the downside of living right on the beach,' she said. 'And of having so many bank notes that can blow away.'

Peter laughed nervously and Murdoch knew the man had brought more money than he could afford to lose. He wondered aloud if they shouldn't call it a night, but Anathassiou wouldn't hear of it.

'That's what we're here for, the cards. Isn't it, Emre? No-one would come all the way up here just for a bit of tucker. Well, Pete might!'

She crossed the room and patted the man hard on the stomach, only Peter himself laughing at the gesture.

Murdoch had spent most of his life in one sort of prison or another and had passed a lot of that time playing cards. He could count what had gone down without thinking about it, read faces more easily than books. At Anathassiou's that night they played Texas Hold 'Em – easy to work the odds and lose, nice and slowly. Of the others around the table, Peter Branagan was the most difficult to read. It was like fighting an amateur, the punches not coming where they should, the feet telling you nothing. Peter bluffed wildly on middling cards, folded when he could probably have won. Murdoch knew because, outside of play, the man hid nothing, puffing with frustration, guffawing when he won a hundred or two no matter how the cash in front of him dwindled. The more he lost, the more he drank, and before midnight he was out of the game, sitting back from the table, sleepy and sad.

'How you getting home?' Anathassiou snapped at him. 'You're not staying here. And look at you, you can't drive.'

Peter frowned, confused at what he'd done wrong.

'But it's ten kays at least and you know what taxis are like round here. It's not like I can walk.'

'Bit of exercise'll do you good.' She grinned at Murdoch and Velis for support. 'I reckon I could sell tickets to watch him try and walk that far.'

'I'll take him home,' said Velis quietly. 'We'll be done here soon, anyway, Angie. Any more luck and you'll have cleaned us out, you old bitch.'

Anathassiou guffawed.

'Less of the old!'

Murdoch and Velis stood at the front door watching Peter Branagan squeeze himself into the DB9. Anathassiou was inside somewhere, stashing her winnings.

'Thought you said this was going to be fun?'

Velis smiled wearily. 'It will be. More than you can imagine.'

'Your mate Angie's a right cow.'

'That's what's going to make it so much fun. Just let me get this idiot home and I'll explain.'

Murdoch followed him to the car, leaning down to look in at Peter wrestling with the seatbelt.

'Thought you said you was a neighbour?'

'Well, neighbouring suburb.' He was pale and wide-eyed, a man sobering up to how much he'd lost. 'Same bit of coast, really.'

Behind him, Murdoch heard Velis grumble, 'Melbourne's on the same bit of coast, if you go far enough.' He grinned, stood straight and found the other man looking nervous.

'Listen, Bi—Simmo,' he said, 'I'll be back straightaway. I won't come in, so wait out here. Don't say—'

'Angie, love!' called Murdoch. Their hostess had reappeared in her doorway, out of Velis's line of sight. 'I reckon this is an excuse for another whisky, what do you reckon? Chance for us to get to know each other.'

Velis grimaced and got into his car.

Inside, Murdoch made more nice noises about the house, about how nice it must be to have a private beach. It wasn't private, they'd passed a sign to it down the street, but Anathassiou didn't correct him. Out on the deck, the breeze had turned damp.

'So, Simmo, how do you know Emre then? You a work colleague?'

Murdoch took a slow sip. None of Anathassiou's other questions that evening had waited for an answer, but thirty seconds later they were still standing in silence.

'Nah, not really,' Murdoch said to the ocean.

'But you're in the business, I can tell. Not a civvy like that idiot Peter.'

Anathassiou's eyes were bright above her smile. First, she'd won at cards, now she could see through people.

'What business would that be then, Ange, love?'

'Aw, come on, darl. You can't fool me. The business that dare not speak its name, that's what Emre calls it. The business for people who know there's only one way to get ahead in life – i.e. do the things other people aren't willing to do.'

'I'm retired,' said Murdoch. 'But I used to be in waste disposal.'

He said it slowly and unsmiling.

'Yeah, right. And, like Peter, I'm in insurance. Pay my boys enough money and I'll make sure your shop doesn't burn down.'

She laughed – something else she was proud of – until they both heard the DB9's engine and Murdoch forced himself in for a hug.

2

The next night, another house – less impressive to the Peter Branagans of the world, but Murdoch liked it well enough. Even in the dark, you could tell it was a home, more comfortable than the shiny mansion on the beach. There was a vague smell of foreign cooking, books on shelves, toys jumbled in a huge crate. Once inside, Murdoch confirmed he could open the front door and went room to room closing the curtains, fussing them tight. Then he turned on all the lights and texted Davie. Four minutes later the doorbell rang.

'Are you sure this makes sense?'

Davie was wide-eyed and talking too loudly. Murdoch pulled him in and shut the door behind him.

'It was your idea, mate. I wasn't sure, remember?'

'No, I mean turning all the lights on. What if the neighbours know she's gone away?'

'If they notice and if they remember, they'll think she's got someone staying. Better than noticing a pair of flashlights moving around. You start in the living room, I'll go upstairs. Pretend it's a game.'

Murdoch took the stairs two at a time, fizzy with excitement. The word 'naughty' came into his head and he cursed Velis for putting it there when explaining the visit to Anathassiou's. He shook the memory away and started in the kid's room – always the worst bit of a break and enter, every burglar's nightmare to find a kid inside. Looking through the toys and a drawer of tiny clothes, he had to remind himself they were doing nothing wrong. It wasn't like they were stealing, was it? At least, not stealing anything that hadn't already been stolen. He remembered Velis's proposal again, swore out loud and started on a new drawer.

He and Davie searched Anita Patel's house for an hour, not a word between them, difficult when they didn't know what they were looking for. Davie had convinced himself the evidence they needed had to be in there somewhere: documents belonging to Patterson, a half-written ransom note, body parts in the freezer. Murdoch had been less convinced, but he was keen to help: no one in Montie was talking about anything but the article in the paper. But it wasn't just that. A part of him was also beginning to see that Davie's detailed approach to things tended to pay dividends. Now, though, conferring in whispers at the bottom of the stairs, the two of them confirmed they had found nothing.

'It's all right, Davie. It was a long shot, mate, but like you said, cover all leads, eh? Do the stuff other people aren't willing to do.'

Was it Davie had said that? Murdoch had a weird feeling that it wasn't. He told Davie to stay where he was and walked around the house turning off the lights. Upstairs in the dark, he felt the fizz again. Being somewhere you shouldn't be – it was like taking your first pill, as big a rush as canyoning or a smash at the net. Was that what all the stuff with Velis had been? A test he was up for it? Or worse, a reminder of what fun could be? Murdoch walked into the front bedroom and pulled open the curtains. He was halfway back to the bedroom door when a powerful car rolled up outside and blue light flashed around him.

His first thought was for Davie, that he'd either freeze where a copper's torch could find him or panic and run out the front door. Or try and force himself through the back window that Murdoch had jimmied. He took the stairs two at a time again, stumbling as much as running, but found Davie was where he'd left him, back against the hall wall. Even in the dark, the flashing blue from the police car not reaching this far, he could see Davie's eyes were staring.

'Where's the door to the garage?'

Davie said nothing and Murdoch gave him a little slap.

'Mate, don't worry. I've been in this situation a hundred times. There's a garage, I checked. Just tell me where the door to it is.'

'Garage?'

Murdoch sighed, closed his eyes and remembered where it had to be. He hadn't heard a car door yet, but that didn't mean the coppers hadn't opened one. He turned and blinked into the darkness, stepped across to a door on the other side of the hallway, pulled it open and smelled oil in the cold air beyond. Then he pulled Davie slowly by the shoulders and told him to get under the car.

'What?'

'Get under the fucking car, Davie. Even if they come inside, they never look there.'

Murdoch left him to it and hurried to the kitchen to check on himself. But, of course, he'd shut the window again, locked it the way Anita Patel should have done. He was fine, he was a pro, he was good at this. Just like Velis had said.

It was an hour and half before they stood again, more than enough for the cold from the concrete under the Suzuki to infect their bones. At least the car hadn't been dripping oil; that had happened to Murdoch once as a kid, flammable jeans by the end of the night. The talk outside hadn't lasted long. Between the two coppers; between them and the neighbour who'd called them; between them and the crackle on the end of their radio. The whole thing took less than half an hour. But rozzers always circled back, Murdoch told Davie – normally more than once. Just in case they saw a bloke in a black-and-white striped top and a bag with '*SWAG*' written on it. When Davie whispered furiously, 'You're enjoying this,' Murdoch smiled and tried to deny it.

Once they were standing – still in the garage – he made them listen again, anything close to silence not enough. He closed his eyes and concentrated on everything he could hear, how close it was, what explained it. Opened them again to find Davie peering into the car, hands around his eyes like there was light to block out.

'What you doing?'

'We should look in here too.'

'We should get going, mate, that's what we should do.'

But Davie had already opened the rear passenger door of Anita Patel's little car and was feeling around inside, one hand on the back seat, the other on the floor.

The Senior Constable behind the desk at Crosley police station – a round-faced Aboriginal woman, hair tight and high in a ponytail – was smilier than Murdoch had ever seen her before. Most times he'd met her, she'd been angry before he'd opened his mouth. Now, she gave him all her beautiful teeth and a glint in her eye as she told him he'd have to wait. He replied that he didn't mind and, for once, he meant it. Maybe enough time on a nick's wooden bench would drill some sense into him arse-first.

'She could be another hour,' the Senior Constable warned him through the glass, standing on tiptoe so she could peer down at him. 'She's in with the boss.'

'That's OK.'

'You're her new fella, aren't you? Bill, is it?'

'Guilty as charged.'

Murdoch winced at his choice of words and made a hurried remark about the weather outside. He had barely finished it when the Senior Constable was off. The weather in Crosley was awful, she much preferred Queensland, her husband worked here too, they'd not made many friends. Murdoch let her talk, smiling and nodding, determined not to let Natalie down. Not even when the Senior Constable nodded at the plastic bag he was holding and asked if it was a gift for Nat. He ignored the question and asked her about what she'd told him. Whereabouts in Queensland, how long had she worked here, didn't it get *very busy*? The Senior Constable didn't get the hint, telling him instead about her bunions. Eventually, when a phone rang, she struggled to prioritise before stomping off to answer it.

A few minutes later, the street door opened with a sucking noise – waves on stones – and Murdoch looked up hopefully. But it was just a pair of uniforms who glanced at him, then glanced at each other, before crossing the grubby floor to the security door. There, one of them tapped in a six-digit code and they disappeared into the back of the building, the door banging heavily behind them. The process was repeated three times – another uniform, a plain-clothes guy, an older gent in a suit – before, at last, the security door opened from the inside and there she was: Natalie looking worried.

'Bethany said you needed to see me. What's wrong?'

'Nothing's wrong. Just a bit of an update on the case. Wanted to tell you personal, like.'

Her frown barely softened as she checked her watch.

'Fine. I need to be quick, though. I'm sorry, but it's all a bit crazy at the moment.'

She remembered to kiss him, to ask how he was. Turned back to the door and told him to follow.

'658906,' he said. 'You should tell people to be more careful when they're entering the code.'

She turned with a scowl, her sense of humour left upstairs somewhere.

'Just saying,' he said, hands up in defence, the plastic bag dangling between them. 'Look, I brought you some evidence.'

Because he had to bring her something.

There were no meeting rooms free, so she took him to her desk, one of several dozen on the sixth floor, rows of mess in a long low space with square windows at the end. He knew this part of the building from the outside, the seventies extension off the back of the nick. A monument to the days of police corruption. Half the desks were empty, but the place was buzzy with activity, groups bent around shared screens, hunched backs one-finger typing, blokes with phones jammed into their necks while both hands looked for the right bit of paper.

'Jesus,' he said. 'I know Crosley's a hole, but do you really need all these coppers?'

'It's not just Crosley. This is the Local Area Command for all of Broadwater.'

She said it like he should know. Wherever her mind was, it wasn't on him. She wheeled a chair over and sat him at the end of her desk – a patch of calm in the middle of chaos, the floor beneath it clear, the papers beside her computer neatly stacked.

'We're looking at the secretary,' he told her. 'Anita Patel.'

Natalie nodded at someone across the floor and raised a hand – two fingers to mean two minutes.

'I'll be quick,' said Murdoch. 'But this is important.'

She looked at him properly for the first time that day.

'Bill, I'm so sorry, it's … you know, that other piece of work I can't tell you about. We're on the hook – I did say it'd be crazy. What is it you want to tell me?'

Murdoch unravelled the plastic bag, turning it inside out so he could put the Central Coast Mariners mug on her desk without touching it.

'We found this in Anita Patel's car. It's in a bunch of photos Davie took in Scott Patterson's office the day before you lot got there.'

Natalie shook her head slowly, the colour rising in her cheeks. Before she could talk, Murdoch went on.

'I know, love, I know. I would of told you we'd gone in there, but it was before you and me … well, you know, and after that we promised not to talk about work.' It was no defence and he hurried on, knowing he was talking too fast. It was supposed to sound like a confession. 'Anyway, listen. This mug here, it's one of the three what Davie got pictures of sitting on Patterson's desk; the other two are plain blue. In the photos you lot took, the next day, the blue ones are still there, but this one had been swapped for a Canterbury Bulldogs mug. You check your evidence lists, you probably took it away with you. But this one here is definitely Patterson's. Davie called Patterson's nephew, Alan Drummond, this morning and checked. Drummond said Patterson would never drink out of anything with a rugby league logo on it. Anyway, we found this one here, the Mariners mug, under the passenger seat of Anita's car. I was thinking maybe you could get it checked, you know, for the sedatives they found in his system? It's got Davie's prints on it, but otherwise it should be all right.'

Natalie used a pen to pull the mug towards her.

'In her car? Really?' She shook her head slowly. 'I knew it. Local patrol got a call to a suspected break-in at her address last night. DC Burran got alerted because Patel's a person of interest, but we thought nothing of it. At least, I tried to.'

'I figured if you found traces of the sedative, her car could get nicked and abandoned and then you could find the mug in there. Then it would be admissible evidence.'

Natalie bent forward, her frown back on full volume. 'Bill, this is the police, not some dodgy detective agency. We don't go around rearranging things so we can get admissible evidence.'

That wasn't how Murdoch remembered it, but he said nothing. Natalie was still talking.

'You guys are supposed to be working with us on this, not breaking the law because we can't. If we have strong enough suspicions against the Patel woman we'll get a search warrant for her house.'

This was why he hadn't brought the injection kit. A syringe full of what smelled like bleach would have had the case taken off them in minutes, police all over the secretary and them unable to talk her. Murdoch watched Natalie pick up the mug with a tissue, look inside and sniff it.

'Can you get traces off it?'

Her face creased back and forth, not clear where to start explaining. She said a few words, something about TV shows and reality, but was interrupted by a call from across the room. She raised another hand – *coming, coming* – and looked at Murdoch in exasperation.

'Anything else?'

'Can I run some names by you? Just to see if they register?'

She thought about it, then dragged her keyboard over and angled her screen so he couldn't see.

'Hatch,' he said. 'Terry Hatch.'

He gave her the address behind the library and she typed quickly. Beside her, the telephone rang, but she ignored it.

'Nothing at that address,' she said, typing again. 'But, yeah, I've got a Terence Hatch, resident in Warriwul. He's got some nasty friends and we've pulled him in a few times to talk to him about them, but we've never had anything on him directly.'

'He's not the guy you're working on that "other piece of work" about?'

'No.'

'What about Angie Anathassiou? Or Angela maybe?'

This time Natalie didn't type. Instead, she looked around, half-standing to see over her monitor, hesitating once back in her seat.

'What about her?'

'Dunno. Maybe nothing. You know her?'

'How strong a lead is this?'

She was whispering, the mug forgotten.

'No idea, yet. Just a name. Why?'

'Stay here.'

Natalie stood and walked quickly to the far end of the room, just another bee in the hive, until she reached a group of figures blurred by the bright windows behind them. Less than a minute later, she was on the way back. Murdoch watched her approach and wondered how the hell he'd ended up in love with a copper. What Amanda would have to say about that.

'Let's go for a walk,' said Natalie.

Outside, the air was blinking and bright. Murdoch remembered those days in prison where you dreaded leaving the yard before you'd even got out into it, the only crime being inside. It was colder again today than the day before, but the soft autumn sunshine was back, even Macquarie Road looking good for once. Mothers and toddlers shared the pavements with shoppers and suits, the whole scene like something from a kid's book – A is for Accountant and B for is Butcher. Too early in the day for Z is for Zombie Smackhead. Natalie was walking fast, talking faster.

'Tell me about Angie Anathassiou. What's she got to do with the Scott Patterson case?'

'Nat, love, I'm not going to bullshit you. She's just one of a list of names. People what we're thinking of checking out because they look a bit dodgy. Obviously, given the way you're reacting, she's now at the top of that list.'

That slowed her down. She let him take her hand, although with less interest than at the weekend.

'If you find anything about her, you come to me.' Her eyes were checking his to be sure he was listening. 'Just me. No one else, got it?'

'Go on.'

She didn't want to go on. She looked into the empty window beside them, a shoe shop once, now dusty and forlorn. This was where they'd stood the evening she'd invited him round to dinner. It felt like a different life. Retracting her hand, Natalie put it up to her brow, squinting against the sun. Murdoch found his sunglasses and put them on her.

'Angie Anathassiou is a nasty piece of work, Bill. What *you* would call an animal – king of the jungle, in her case. Or queen, I suppose. If it can make money Angie's in it, no worries about who gets hurt. Drugs, bit of smuggling, bit of pimping. Protection seems to be her main racket.'

'So?'

Natalie looked back the way they'd come. 'This is confidential, Bill. This is me telling you this because we're in a relationship; me, trusting you a hundred per cent. You got it?'

'Got what? What's the big deal?'

'There's something rotten high up in the LAC. Or someone, I should say. A few maybe, who knows? The point is, the Command's had its sights on Anathassiou for years, she's so obviously the kingpin for the whole coast – or queenpin, I suppose. It's not like she tries to hide it. She's got all these boats and customised cars, a huge house down in Sydney. And her weekender up here. You should see the place Bill, it's huge – right on the water over at … Well, I can't tell you anything specific. But the worst thing is, this woman is smart. She might flash her money in our faces, but we're struggling to pin anything on her. Every time we do a raid on her property, she's cleared out – everything and everyone gone before we get there. We get reliable information there's a meet going to happen, or one of her famous parties, and at the last minute the whole thing moves. Drugs, whores, funny money, half a dozen individuals we'd like to talk to – the whole lot cancelled or shifted. But only the ones we know about in advance. All the others, we find out afterwards, have gone ahead as normal. It's the same news with busts on her businesses, everything squeaky clean by the time we get there. Which means to persuade the DPP to prosecute, me and my team have got to write a sufficiency of evidence document based on not much more than circumstantial stuff. You have no idea how difficult that is; how many hundreds of pages …'

Natalie seemed to realise she was ranting. She took a deep breath and checked her watch before carrying on. 'The point is, Bill, someone on our side is talking. You asked me why we were giving you the Patterson case, asked if it was something we didn't want to do internally? It was because I thought Patterson might have a link to Anathassiou. There's a money trail there somehow. And now it sounds like you've found it.'

Shit.

Natalie carried on, mumbling about the corruption in her Local Area Command like it was a confession; like she was personally to blame.

There were a hundred jokes Murdoch could have made, but now wasn't the time. He knew how Natalie felt about the force. He'd never feel the same way – he still remembered the injustices – but he liked the fact she believed in it. It meant he could separate her from the bad ones.

'So, anything you hear, or want to know—'

'I'll come to you,' he said. 'Got it. But, sweetheart, it might be nothing. She was just a name on a list, nothing more.'

'Who else was on it?'

'Terry Hatch, I told you. James Butterfin, Harry Peel.'

Making up names was too dangerous without his sunglasses on.

'I'll look them up too.'

She reached for her pocket, pulled out her buzzing mobile, and bit her lip before answering. Then she handed him back his glasses, gave an apologetic wave and took the call back to the station.

3.

Davie's Wednesday started well, a cheque made out to '*Cash*' arriving in the mail. Fran Patterson had responded to his request to pay him this way with the same mild questioning she gave all his news. It wasn't that she didn't believe him – at least, not as far as Davie could tell – more that she didn't understand, so that he had to pile lie upon lie, twisting her world into something better than it really was. He didn't have the heart to tell Fran they had found her husband's injection kit or that it seemed to be filled with bleach. Nor did he tell her he had no idea how soon they'd be able to find Scott. Nor, of course, that he had no idea how he himself had spent the money from her previous payment. It had gone, it seemed, the same way as all money went with him: one minute in his bank account, the next minute evaporated, as if he could make it disappear just by knowing it was there.

So, on Wednesday morning, when a lavender envelope appeared in his mailbox amongst the white ones he'd learned not to open, Davie tore at it feverishly and whooped with joy. Down at the general store, Anne Lincoln was less enthusiastic.

'What's wrong with it?' she said, turning the cheque and holding it up to the light. 'Why can't you cash it yourself?'

'Because my bank would swallow it into the money I owe them and never let me see it again.'

Honesty or nothing was the best policy with Anne – only Murdoch knew how to lie to her.

'I see,' she said slowly. 'Well, just this once. I'll do it when I'm next at the bank.'

'Oh. I was kind of hoping you could do it today?'

Anne raised her hands, either beseeching heaven or signalling the work of the shop around her. He never discovered which because, just then, Brian Yeow walked in. Davie mumbled uncertain thanks, an even more uncertain greeting to the pharmacist, and hurried out to the brightness of the day.

Murdoch had agreed they had more than enough evidence to pressure a confession from Anita Patel. The prescription fulfilled by Yeow compared to the drugs in Patterson's bloodstream, the missing mug, the bleach-filled injection kit in her car. And even if she didn't confess to them, they could probably get the police to give it a go, which meant everything now was a waiting game. There was no point in alerting the secretary to their suspicions, they just had to wait for her to come home from her holiday. That, apparently, was only two days away and an extradition from Fiji would take far longer. If Patterson was still alive, the best thing they could do for him was to be patient. It was still four or five days before they needed to start worrying about his health declining because of the lack of an ARV injection. When Murdoch had said that maybe, knowing now what they knew about the bloke, they shouldn't worry too much about that either, even Davie had struggled to look outraged.

Davie was crossing the road to look at the surf, wondering what else he could do to try and find Patterson and when Anne might go to the bank, when his phone beeped with a text message.

Looking forward to lunch! See you there 12.30. g

Davie closed his eyes and sighed. He had forgotten about lunch with Guy Hawthorne. Worse, he had no idea whose turn it was to pay. He typed a cancellation message in return – a long one, promising Guy his cancellation had nothing to do with the article his brother, Glenn, had organised – and promised himself he'd make it up to Guy soon. But when he hit Send, an error message popped up immediately, the phone bristling in his hand.

Sorry your service is deactivated. Please call 13 22 00 to make a payment.

An hour and a half later, at the best table in Brown's, Davie was working hard on his optimism. Wasn't it supposed to be its own reward? Anita Patel would return from holiday soon, she'd reveal where Patterson was and Davie would receive his full fee plus some publicity for uncovering a human trafficking ring. And, more immediately, it might not be his turn to pay for lunch and he was pretty sure he had enough petrol in the Hyundai to get himself back home. Who knew, maybe Guy would even quell any doubts Davie still had about the evidence they had against the secretary – he was a lawyer, after all.

Davie watched the restaurant fill around him, the diners increasingly sure of themselves as they became a crowd and wine was poured. Bill had said something about this place recently and Davie tried to remember what it was. Brown's was on Matilda Bay, inside the southern tip of the peninsula that held Broadwater back from the ocean, the boats outside the restaurant floating or muddily tipped depending on the tide. Today they were bobbing cheerily, the sun glinting on the water as much as on the cutlery; a scene from a movie depicting how the other half lived: everyone rich and happy.

'Are you sure you don't want a drink while you're waiting for your friend? A glass of white wine?'

There was an edge to the waitress's perkiness. She was young and pretty, with long brown hair, a smile not to be messed with. Davie was at her best table and not ordering.

'Tap water's fine,' he told her with a smile to match her own. Because it would be just his luck if for some reason Guy couldn't make it. Ignoring the smells from the kitchen and the rumbles from his stomach, Davie checked his watch and realised he'd left it at home. 'I'm sure he'll be here soon.'

'He's here now.'

Even if he hadn't recognised Guy's voice, Davie would have known from the waitress's face who was standing behind him. Her eyes lit up over a genuine smile, teeth parting to reveal a tiny tip of tongue. Davie pretended the smile was for him and said, on second thoughts, they'd start with a dozen oysters and a bottle of the Riesling.

It wasn't that Guy Hawthorne, Davie's oldest friend, was that good-looking, at least not as far as Davie could tell. He was below average height, narrowly built and, as a result of all the hours he spent in his office or court, always pale. When they had first known each other at school, and later, of course, in his music years, Davie had always got more attention from girls. But then, as they left youth behind, it was his friend who women lit up for. Guy said they liked the Italian in him. He didn't mean his complexion or his big blue eyes. He meant his hair – kept as long as the legal profession could stand – expensive shirts and well-cut suits, boundless infectious energy.

'Hey, man!' Guy grasped Davie's hand and pulled him into a hug over the sponsored barrier that stood between the table and the pavement. 'It's been too long. How perfect is this place? Good pick.'

Which meant Davie had chosen the restaurant and, according to ancient rules, it was his turn to pay. Composing a worried face, he leaned forward, elbows on the table, and, as soon as Guy was sitting opposite him, whispered a full confession of his finances, interrupted only by the arrival of the Riesling. They sat in silence as the waitress poured, good old Guy declining to flirt in deference to the seriousness of the situation. Once she was gone again, he whispered harshly in return.

'Davie, man, are you joking? Today is absolutely on me. Or, I should say, on my stupid bloody brother. Trust me, I'll be sending Glenn the bill as soon as I've paid it. He promised me he'd see you right with a good piece of PR and … have I apologised enough on his behalf already? I was worried you'd be so pissed off, you'd bail on me for lunch today.'

Davie, so relieved about the bill he actually wanted to cry, reminded Guy he'd been apologising for Glenn half his life. It was his own fault, Davie insisted, that he'd forgotten what an dil Guy's brother could be; he'd let his ego blind him.

'Besides,' he went on, 'it's not that bad. Maybe no one saw the stupid article.'

'Yeah, right!' Guy seemed to realise he wasn't joking. 'I mean, yeah, right. Anyway, the point is, man, lunch is on me. So, let's change the subject, eh? Look at this place!'

He gestured with one hand towards the sparkling bay, with the other to the restaurant, shiny with glassware and the glow of tans. But Davie – reminded of Anne Lincoln's similar gesture in the shop earlier that morning – didn't want to change the subject. He wanted to be told his worries would soon be over, his case about to come good. He laid the facts out carefully for Guy, enjoying how solid it all sounded: the motive, the means, the evidence. He trusted Guy implicitly and knew his friend would tell him if he was sharing more than was good for him. More than that, he was keen to hear his verdict.

At first, 'poor woman' was Guy's only response. Apparently, the menu was far more interesting and Davie remembered how vague Guy always was if you spoke to him socially about anything legal. He couldn't blame him. Davie remembered a time when he himself had been asked about house prices at every barbeque. But maybe today Guy remembered he owed him because, after a sip of his wine, he carried on. 'You can't really blame her if that's what the bastard had been doing. If I was a woman and someone put me in that situation, I reckon I'd kill him too. But she'll still go to jail for it.'

A red motorbike swung into view onto the road behind Guy, the rider clenched over its bars as the bike cracked into gear and roared between the restaurant and the water, its engine greedy for all available air. Now behind Davie, it paused, then cracked loud again, exploding up the hill and away from the bay. Guy raised one hand and wiggled a little finger, raising laughter from the other tables.

'As long as you're happy,' he said to fading motorbike. 'Who cares about anyone else?'

They ordered slowly and ate more slowly still, swapping regrets they couldn't drink through the afternoon. They emailed often enough for there to be no news, just a more languid analysis of their lives. Why they

were both still single, who disliked his family more. With dessert, Davie brought them back to the case, picking at Guy's legal expertise.

'You said the secretary will have to go to jail if she killed him? Is that always the case? I thought if a woman could show she'd been subjected to, you know, long-term harassment?'

'Years of emotional and physical abuse? An ongoing regime of persistent mental torture? Restricting her freedom and options for wellbeing to the point where she felt she feared for her life and her children's lives?'

'You're quoting at me.'

Guy held up his hands in innocence. 'I'm quoting from unsuccessful defences of women who killed the husbands who tortured them, and sometimes their children, for years. There's a thing called "reasonableness". A woman has to prove she tried all reasonable alternatives to escape from her situation and, I'm telling you man, they hardly ever manage it. Basically, the guy has to be on ice with a knife to her throat at the safe house she escaped to with her kids. Unavoidable self-defence, she's sorry about afterwards. And, of course, she needs a bloody good lawyer.'

'To work against the one who's prosecuting her.'

The Italian hands went up again. 'Don't look at me, man. It's why I didn't go into criminal law. I don't know what's worse, defending someone you know is guilty or prosecuting someone who shouldn't go to jail.'

'What about if she's got a little kid? And an elderly mother she supports?'

'Who doesn't? Davie, man, don't worry. If you can convince a jury this woman murdered your client's husband, she's going to jail for a very long time. Plus, you'll get your success fee. Cheers.' Guy raised a glass then frowned at the new expression Davie had on his face. 'Aw, man, now what?'

Murdoch was in the sea again. That morning, on his way to see Natalie, he'd noticed the waves off Montauban and felt his stomach shrink. But later, up at Green Bay – between outshoots of rock that shaped the beach

into scallops - he'd found the water reassuringly flat. Wading through the shallows, ignoring everything in his head, he crossed paths with an older man coming out of the water, peeling off his cap and goggles as Murdoch was peeling on his.

'Another day in paradise!' the older man said. 'Water's crystal – good old Greeny, eh? Anything with east in it and she's fierce, but on a day like today, she's like a row of Olympic pools.'

The words sank in slowly as Murdoch stroked out past the rocks. He hadn't known some beaches were more protected than others and made a mental note to ask Davie about it, immediately looking forward to the conversation. At last he could talk about the water like every other fucker on the coast. Vis, temp, swell – he couldn't wait.

Out past the rocks there were some waves after all and Murdoch turned quickly to swim into the next pool north. Beneath him, the ocean floor had dropped away, but, even at its deepest, he could still see the sand. Above it, were fish, blue and white, dark grey – more stuff to learn the names of – and there was even a short period, while he was treading water and staring at the biggest house on the beach, that he forgot to worry he was too far out.

Back in Montie, buoyant at his bravery and tight with salt, he ran up Davie's stairs and hammered on his front door louder than he'd meant to. But Davie wasn't home. He didn't seem to be in his office either, Murdoch nearly breaking the door between the chip shop and the bakery as he gave it three strong tugs. It was only when the frame complained with a worrying crack that he realised it was actually locked. Standing back and wondering why he was so surprised, Murdoch noticed a piece of notepaper sellotaped inside the glass: *For Sale, $1,000 for both.* Below was a photograph of the fat leather armchairs that sat at the top of the stairs.

Viewed from the whale-watching platform, Davie's office windows were as dark as the corridor below. More tellingly, the office window was closed. Murdoch took out his phone and dialled Davie's number, but the call went straight through to voicemail, the first time he could remember it happening. You could call Davie at three in the morning and he'd answer; he didn't know how to turn his bleeding phone off. Murdoch

267

hung up without leaving a message and was crossing towards the general store when he spotted Davie's car parked further along the street, outside the estate agency. Then the man himself appeared, coming out of the agency with his old boss, Jacqui Russell. Murdoch remembered her name because it suited her so well: she was small and fierce with a patchy tan. As Murdoch watched, she stopped chewing gum long enough to give Davie a vicious smile. In reply, Davie turned, head down, and sloped away from her in the direction of home.

'Oi, Davie!' Murdoch hurried after him. 'Here, mate, hang on.'

Davie stopped and, after a small hesitation, turned with a strange look on his face.

'What?'

'Guess where I've been!'

'Later, Bill, yeah? Tell me later.'

Davie walked on again, Murdoch jogging to keep up with his long strides.

'Go on, guess. Actually, don't guess, I'll tell you. I've been out in the sea again, but further out, real deep.'

'Fantastic. Very happy for you.'

'What's wrong with you?'

'Who says anything's wrong?'

'I do.' Murdoch jogged forwards, then turned so he was blocking Davie's path. The muppet's face was a picture of misery. 'What's wrong.'

'Leave me alone, Bill. Please?'

'Come down the beach with me and then I'll leave you alone. Ten minutes. I just want to show you something. Then you can go and be by yourself for as long as you want.'

They looked at each other for a few seconds and Murdoch had an image of them tussling in the street, him taking Davie down as he struggled to get past. From a physical point of view, Davie could have made a good fighter: he had the long arms and the natural strength, good reflexes. It was the attitude that was the problem. Murdoch had seen fourteen-year-old girls who could kick the shit out of him. He blinked the idea away and watched Davie sigh and shrug before turning to shuffle across the road.

Neither of them spoke as they kicked off their flip-flops and walked down the path between the dunes, nor as they carried on to the water's edge. High above, a sea eagle was balancing on the thermals – life at an easy distance. Murdoch knew the bird well: it nested with its mate in a brittle gum across the lagoon from his garden. Every time he saw it he felt at home.

'What did you want to show me?' said Davie.

Murdoch pointed at the ocean.

'That. I went swimming in it today. I reckon it was about twenty degrees, you could see for miles. How come it's all wavy here and flat and harmless up at … well, other places?'

Davie scowled. 'It's not harmless, Bill. Wherever you go its full of rips and sharks and jellyfish. You just happened to survive.'

In two swift motions Davie threw his flip-flops out to the waves, their dirty white plastic too light against the ocean breeze. Murdoch remembered the day he'd met Natalie here, the bat he'd tried to throw.

'You want to tell me about it, Davie?'

'Nothing to tell. Just I won't be needing my thongs for a while. It's formal shoes for me; that's all estate agents wear.'

'Go on.'

Davie shook his head in silence, then gave up on that idea too.

'The phone company have cut me off, the bank's after me and I've started getting letters from the people I financed the computer through. Any day now, someone's going to come and take it back. I'm scared to be at the office in case they turn up.'

'But you're sorted, mate. Soon as Anita Patel gets back, we can pressure her into a confession or get the cops to do it. Then you get your big fat pay cheque. Not to mention your fame and glory for—'

'For putting a woman in prison, who, for the last few years, has been at the mercy of a sadistic rapist. A man who, for extra cash, smuggles vulnerable girls into prostitution.'

'So you'll get recognition for uncovering a trafficking ring too.'

Davie sat heavily, elbows on knees, chin in his hands. His flip-flops bobbed in the shallows like evidence of a distant wreck.

'Uncovering a trafficking ring doesn't pay the bills, though, does it? The only way to pay the bills is to prove Anita Patel is guilty of defending herself. She's got that little girl and that old lady who depend on her. What about them?'

'So what you're saying is, you know she did it, and you can prove it, but you're not going to do anything about it because you feel sorry for her?'

Davie looked up angrily. 'I'm not going to sell my soul, Bill. What's the point in being successful if I have to do that?'

'Davie, you nutter, that's the only way to be successful. You have to do stuff what nobody else is willing to do.'

It was Angie Anathassiou who'd said it, Murdoch remembered now. He spat into the sand and tried again.

'Look,' he said. 'Do you think your dad never trod on anyone else to get where he is today?'

'Please don't compare me to my dad.'

'But that's what you're doing. You're wanting to be some big shot high-earning detective just so you can impress him. But if success means money, mate, then you have to prioritise making money. Do you honestly reckon you're gonna get anywhere without being ruthless? Getting all gushy about some secretary's reasons for knocking off her boss?'

Davie pushed his hair back from his forehead. 'You heard what Wendy Skellen said. Patterson deliberately chose her because she was helpless. He'll have done the same with Anita Patel.'

Murdoch rolled his eyes. He pulled off his trousers, waded into the water for the second time that day and slowly retrieved the flip-flops. The strength of the waves, their power to frighten him even now, came as a surprise and by the time he'd clambered back up the steep sand, he was breathing heavily. Still though: Murdoch–2, Sea–0. He dropped into the sand next to Davie, rubbing his legs dry with his hands as he explained there was a third way. A way to get the success fee and keep Anita Patel out of jail.

4

Early the next morning, Murdoch cleaned out his gutters. After that, he weeded the lawn. At lunchtime he went to the supermarket and found it deserted, as empty as a church now that no one believed. Forcing himself up and down the aisles, he tried to kindle some interest in cooking, but even the fruit and vegetables seemed lifeless: no smell in the tomatoes, the apples so perfect it was difficult to believe they grew on trees. Back in Montie, there was no sign of Davie and Murdoch had no way of knowing if he was following up on his promise to contact everyone who was after him for money or just off borrowing more of the stuff. In the general store, dust in the dirty rays pouring through the lottery posters, Anne Lincoln told him she was too busy to chat.

'I've got to clean every one of these shelves. And it's double-delivery day and they need watching let me tell you. You going to buy one of those magazines or what?'

Murdoch was staring at the rack of monthlies, trying to find something interesting.

'You're like me,' Anne told him, 'you need a project. If you're bored, you should read a book. Go to the library. Or a bookshop. It's not like you can't afford to buy something to read.'

Murdoch did go to the library, but not for the books. He took the ID he rarely used, the one the Witness Protection Program had given him – Jim Young, born in Ulladulla, aged thirty-five. The library was deserted – maybe there was a party on somewhere and he was the only one not invited? – and he let the librarian talk to him about lending limits and additional services, her voice the only noise in the low-ceilinged room.

Strolling slowly between the tightly-packed bookshelves, he stopped at the row of public computers: dusty PCs only a few years old and already looking dated. Following the log-in instructions and bringing up Google, he typed 'Congregation Leaving the Reformed Church in Nuenen.' It was like when you gave in and looked at porn. You could be deciding in your head you didn't want to do it, but your fingers had a life of their own. He angled the monitor so the librarian couldn't see, clicked on the first image offered and stared at it intently.

For the next hour and half, Murdoch read so many articles and excerpts that soon he found himself referred to sources he'd already seen. Velis had told him no word of a lie. The history, the reward, the conflicting stories. Murdoch wanted to read more – there was gossip in forums – but he'd already stayed on the computer too long.

Crosley only had one bookshop, an open-fronted space in the mall squeezed between a butcher's and a wool shop. Garish red letters spelling *Crosley Books* were peeling off the base of the front most display: a pile of *Harry Potter* jigsaws. Inside were more colours, yellow and purple and blue, cartoon letters shouting *Cooking* or *Health*. Murdoch knew he was in the wrong place – it was like when you wandered into a lingerie department or a shop that only sold women's clothes – but before he could escape, a shop assistant appeared. He was young and eager with bad skin and dry hair, wearing a once-black shirt made for someone broader. When he spoke, his voice was surprisingly deep: a grown man trapped in a skinny kid's body.

'Can I help you? Looking for anything specific?'

Murdoch shook his head. 'You're all right, mate. I think I'm in the wrong place. I was looking for a book on Van Gogh. It's called *Van Gogh: The Life and Works*.'

The kid's smile flickered and Murdoch knew he'd pronounced it wrong.

'Yeah, sorry,' the kid said. 'We don't have many art books. Mostly just introductions to art for kids, that kind of thing.'

Murdoch told him no worries, he'd look somewhere else, but the shop assistant wasn't going to let him get away that easily.

'I'll look it up,' he said eagerly. 'Find out who's got it. It's really easy.'

His enthusiasm was infectious and Murdoch decided what the hell, it wasn't like he had to give a name or anything. He watched the spotty kid run behind his counter and start tapping at a keyboard, an opportunity to prove he was better than the place he worked in. Murdoch swallowed his pride.

'How do you pronounce it then?'

The shop assistant looked up and smiled. 'Most people pronounce it "Van *Goff*". Least, in Oz we do. The Americans say "Van *Go*". But Van

Gogh was Dutch, and in Dutch you say it from the back of the throat, at the beginning and the end.' He coughed out a new version of the name.

'You taking the piss?'

The kid looked up and smiled again, then went back to his computer screen, searching for quiet minutes while Murdoch tried to work out how he could leave without being rude.

'Oh, I think I've found one.' The shop assistant sounded surprised at his success. 'It looks like they have it at the Art Gallery of New South Wales bookshop. Shall we call them? Or, you know, we could probably order it online?'

He was like a puppy bringing back a bone and Murdoch had to insist, no really, he could take it from there.

On the freeway south, the afternoon sky gave way to thickening clouds and, by the time Murdoch arrived in Sydney, it was raining hard. He sat indicating on Art Gallery Road waiting for an elderly Saab to free up a parking spot, wondering if it was raining in Montie too now, filling up the lagoon at last, or if he'd just driven into this. In front of him the rain was coming in sheets across the open fields of the Domain, the CBD just vague grey shapes beyond. There had been a time when it had been life-threatening for Murdoch to even visit the city – too many people around wanting him dead. Now most of *them* were dead and the rest thought *he* was. All apart from Velis. A car horn woke him from his thoughts, a green Volvo wanting to know if he was going to take that parking spot or not.

The gallery was pretty much as Murdoch had expected. A three-storey high ceiling over an echoing lobby, arches to rooms full of paintings, better scenery than most parts of the city. What he hadn't expected was to find it full. Maybe this was the party everyone had been invited to? In the main hall, gangs of children followed their teachers and screamed and laughed at each other. Pensioners and tourists strolled in pairs under banners advertising a fundraising drive. The rooms with the paintings were busier but quieter, people of all ages walking slowly or chatting in low voices about what they were looking at, none of them embarrassed to be there. Murdoch stopped in front of a huge picture, by far the biggest

273

in sight. Four metres by five, it showed a thousand men charging life-sized horses across rocky ground, swords in the air.

'Fantastic, isn't it?'

A woman with damp grey hair and half-steamed glasses was at his elbow, no one else near.

'You what?'

'Look at the fear in that horse's face. The sense of thousands of men you get from those tiny blobs of colour there. Just like the artist was there. No photograph to work off, of course.'

Murdoch didn't know what to say. He smiled awkwardly and grunted something that sounded like agreement. The old woman smiled back and doddered off across the echoing room. Murdoch looked at the painting again, more closely this time, then went to find the information desk.

'Are you here for the fundraiser?'

The man behind the counter looked like a prison warden. He was well-built, with short grey hair the same shade as his cardigan and shirt, grey skin around his grey eyes. Murdoch wanted to lean over and check if his trousers and shoes were grey too.

'No, mate, just the bookshop.'

'It's just that the three o'clock tour for the fundraiser was supposed to meet at the bookshop, but now it's meeting outside the café.'

'I just wanna buy a book.'

'It's a free tour. Good all-round introduction to art, if you're interested?'

'You gonna tell me where the bookshop is or what?'

The man wasn't a prison warden after all. He shrank a little and apologised, pointed Murdoch across the hall – standing and leaning across the counter so there could be no confusion: his trousers were black – and apologised again.

Ten minutes later Murdoch had his book, so shiny he didn't want to open it, but the rain outside was heavier than ever and, besides, he'd paid for two hours parking. He found the gallery café, but it was busier than anywhere else in the building with a wait to get in – like most people had missed the point and thought the rooms with the paintings were just a nice entrance hall. Deciding if he wanted to queue or not, Murdoch spotted the grey man from the information desk. He was on a small platform, a head's height above the dozen or so people around him, his voice raised to compete with the echoes. Murdoch walked over.

'Because in *those* days, if you think about it, art was exclusively for the very *wealthy*. *Hundreds* of people were engaged in *making* art – stonemasons, painters, weavers and all the people who supplied them. But outside of *churches*, the vast majority of people never got to *see* much art. It sat underappreciated in the villas and chateaux of the *super*-rich. *Today*, of course, things are very different, although – as we *all* know – art doesn't cost any less. So as we *start* this tour, and indeed *every* time you visit a gallery, please remember how much it costs to ensure *everybody* gets to share in the world's art and it doesn't sit in the hands of the privileged *few*. And, please, remember it's up to *all* of us to contribute to that.'

The grey man smiled at his audience, flicking his eyes across their heads as he counted them. He noticed Murdoch.

'Oh,' he said, cautiously hopeful. 'Are you joining us after all?'

For days the rain owned the world. Conversations, plans, the radio news, the land, the ocean, the refilling lagoon. There was nothing to do but hurry home through it, then stand in an empty house and look out at it. By Friday night, Murdoch had had enough. A final brief phone call to make sure nothing had changed, no clear idea why he was doing this, and he drove north to Green Bay, parking three streets from the beach.

Even through the clean wool of a new balaclava, the mansion smelled of its recent party. Cigarette smoke, alcohol, sweat. The floors were sticky, other surfaces clouded in ring marks, the house tidied but not yet clean. Compared to the fresh earthy smells of the rain outside, the grime felt unnaturally oppressive. Why would you wait for so long before cleaning up after a party? Murdoch thought about it hard, but couldn't make it an excuse for turning back. Instead he took a deep breath and closed the door behind him, the endless ocean silenced by a single pane of glass.

At the end of the dark corridor, near the front door, he found the downstairs toilet firmly locked. Expecting this, he had gone out and bought a few tools, traipsing around Bunnings in a pretence he might not use them. The lock was nothing complicated – you could get through it with a knife if you had to – but Murdoch had always believed in tidy burglary, leaving places the same way you found them. Apart from the obvious exception.

He locked the door behind him again, turned off his head torch and stared at the digits on his watch. The balaclava was as itchy as hell, but he left it on, a constant reminder to do everything by the book. Slowing his breath, he listened to the house and the rain outside, two minutes of nothing under muted water. No splashing steps from a curious neighbour, no rumbling in the damp driveway, no creaking floorboard upstairs. He flicked on the bathroom light, let the inside of his eyelids dull from red to black, then slowly opened his eyes. Here was the house as he'd last seen it. The floor clean and white, the marble surface around the sink bare, the picture on the wall behind the door. Like the ocean, it looked different now that he knew what it was. He'd read so much about it over the previous few days, so much about Van Gogh in general, that it was difficult to believe he was alone with it. He still couldn't see what the fuss was about. It was like diamonds or gold – they were nice enough, but not worth dying for. *Congregation* was reckoned at somewhere between ten and twenty million, depending on what you read. The reward was a measly million.

'Lack of insurance,' Velis had told him. 'If a painting's insured, then the reward gets interesting because otherwise the insurance company has to pay up. They don't mind passing over a small fortune to get a picture back, if it stops them having to pay the museum the full amount insured. Most museums can't afford the insurance but. And it doesn't matter who pays, they never admit it. Our little picture will be "found as part of a seizure of assets", or some bullshit like that. Bundled in with other stuff they've recovered over the last few years.'

This had been on their return to the car park of Tamborine McDonald's, Velis's face reflecting the light from the golden arches. He had abandoned his policy of not sharing the details of his proposal, sensing perhaps Murdoch's resistance beginning to weaken. Murdoch, for his part, had been keen to get home, to shower off the shitty evening at Anathassiou's. He'd already decided he was going to say no to whatever Velis proposed, but there was no harm in listening to what the man had to say.

'So your idea is, Angie meets me for the first time, lets me in her house and then, a week later, her most valuable possession goes missing. And she's not supposed to suspect me?'

Velis had an answer for everything.

'On Thursday she's having a party; the house will be full. Clients, employees, good-time girls. Lots of people she's never met before and a fair few who know what she's got in there. One or two who even think it should belong to them; I might have helped with that. Picture goes missing a few days later, it could have been anyone.'

'So why don't you just invite me to the party?'

'Because there'll be about a dozen Club employees there.'

Murdoch had sighed heavily, desperate for reasons to disapprove.

'Security?'

'You tell me.'

Of course, he'd looked. One thing he had in common with Davie, he couldn't go in a house without knowing what he could get from it.

'So you're telling me that fuzzy old picture in Ange's downstairs lav is worth a million in reward money and she's not got no cameras or alarms or nothing around it?'

'That's what she tells me.'

Velis had said something about the power of fear, about how anyone who knew it was there, also knew better than to do anything about it.

'Easy pickings, mate,' he'd said.

It made even less sense now that Murdoch knew what *Congregation* was, standing alone with it after two simple locks. Deep down, he knew he should have spent hours casing Anathassiou's house, working out what other security there might be. But he also knew that wasn't in his nature. He'd always done best when flying by the seat of his pants, in and out while everyone else was still thinking about it. Besides, you could be as careful as you want and still get caught. In 2002 Octave Durham and Henk Bieslijn had beaten infrared systems and top-end cameras to get to

Congregation Leaving the Reformed Church in Nuenen. At least, that's what the courts had decided. Murdoch had forced himself to learn the men's names, spellings and all. Two blokes smart enough to do all that and dumb enough to leave behind the evidence needed to convict them. They got four years each, they'd be out and about by now. If he was that careless, he wouldn't be so lucky.

'I have to warn you,' Velis had told him. 'If you do this, Bill, there are dangers involved. Angie Anathassiou is an evil bitch. She gets a whiff of this and we're both dead men.'

Murdoch had rolled his eyes and made to get out of the car.

'I mean it, Bill. She likes to be talked about. Like I said, the "power of fear" and all that. She has this henchman, Marco, some kind of psycho that likes to fuck people up. His predecessor was too soft for her, apparently – let someone off with broken legs. Angie invited the rest of the team around and set the dogs on him. Dogs, Bill, dogs – I'm not joking. They tore him apart. I heard about it from a bloke who was there, too scared to look away.'

Murdoch lifted the painting off the wall, testing its weight, tempted to carry it out like that. Anathassiou, or whoever she'd got it from, had hung *Congregation* in a white box frame: Van Gogh's thick brush strokes two inches behind the glass. Murdoch turned the box over and found it sealed at the back by a thin piece of hardboard stapled into the frame. He shrugged off his backpack, chose a flat screwdriver and, sitting on the closed lid of the toilet, started prising off the hardboard. He'd allocated twenty minutes for this, plenty of time, but he was unnerved by the splinting and cracking of the hardboard, the squeaking of the industrial staples as they clung to the frame. Four times he stopped to check the rest of the house was silent, nothing but the muted rain. By the time the hardboard came away, his hands were aching, the balaclava uncomfortable against his face. Again, he waited, but there was no new noise. Nothing but his rapid breath, below that, the painful thump of his heart. Behind the board, attached to the thickness of frame, thin white paper stretched from one side to the other. Murdoch turned the box again in case he'd missed it, but the paper wasn't visible from the front;

the painting and the canvas ended where the wood began – whoever had stuck it to the paper had done a precise job. Murdoch tried using the flat screwdriver to cut through from the back, but, turning the box again, he saw the blade had come through in Van Gogh's blue sky – a hole in a twenty-million-dollar painting. He swore, threw the screwdriver into his backpack and leaned forward to see what else was in there. Nothing he could use. Sitting up again, he plucked the balaclava away from his forehead and told himself he was fine. There was another eight minutes for this. He stood, the hardboard clattering to the cold tiles at his feet, and pulled his wallet from his pocket. But a credit card was no good either, he needed something with a sharper corner. His fingers found an expensive business card: *Davie Simms Detection Services.* Sweating in tight wool, hands shaking in their gloves, Murdoch managed a smile. Davie Simms would be delighted to contribute to great art remaining available to the public. He sat again, laid the box frame on his lap and pushed the business card hard against the inside of the white wooden frame, then down into the paper at an angle. Turning the box, tilting it so the glass no longer caught the LEDs above, he saw the business card's corner had pushed through between the brush strokes and the wood of the frame.

He worked as slowly as he could. This was nothing like the fizz he'd felt in Anita Patel's house: the naughty fun Velis had promised. This was fear and genuine danger, playing Robin Hood with loaded guns. Cutting the paper with the business card, progress was painfully slow. It was like chopping coke under untrusting eyes when you're too conscious of what could go wrong. There were four minutes left to get around the full frame and he was determined to stick to that, but the thought of the damage he'd done with the screwdriver sickened him. He swore aloud and told himself to focus. Was adjusting the frame to turn a corner, when a sound from the hallway made him stop. Angie Anathassiou's front door was being rattled against its frame.

In the car park in Tamborine, Murdoch had tried Natalie's arguments on Velis, a little speech he'd rehearsed.

'I don't want to have nothing to with crime no more—'

'Really? How did my Terry Hatch tip-off go?'

He tried again. 'I'm not a crim no more, Emre. You know, once you get out of it, the world's lovely. People trust you, even when they don't know you. Like when you go in a shop and there's no cages over the windows, or alarms under the doormats, no one checking you don't nick nothing. It's a nice world and I don't want to make it bad.'

Velis had managed not to laugh.

'What are you talking about, Bill? I'm not proposing you run a shoplifting gang. What are we, twelve? I'm asking you to steal from a thief. You've seen her. You recognised her for what she is straight away, I saw you. Taking from that woman wouldn't be immoral if we kept the picture ourselves. But we're not, we're going to put it back where it belongs. We'll take the reward and everyone's happy. Everyone but Angie Anathassiou, so it has to be right.'

'So why don't you do it through the Club?'

A group of four middle-aged women had wobbled out through the doors of the McDonald's, hunching their shoulders against the cold. One of them spotted Velis and Murdoch sitting in the Aston Martin and pointed, shouting something inaudible until her friends laughed and pulled her away. Velis hadn't found it funny.

'The Club?' he spat. 'Have you been listening to anything I said since we were out fishing? Bill, the Club is why I'm doing this. I want something they know nothing about. They make me keep receipts, do you know that?'

Murdoch hadn't seen him angry before. Without the toothy smile and the flashing eyes, Velis was just another middle-aged man, disappointed by the past and scared of the future.

'Don't do it if you're frightened, Bill.' Velis was watching the four women waiting at the lights, any view better than Murdoch. 'It's fine, I understand. I'll find someone else.'

Murdoch had spat back that he wasn't frightened, knowing as he said it that neither of them believed that to be true, nor that it mattered either way. If Velis had been worried about Murdoch being scared, he wouldn't have shared the story of the dogs.

Was that why he was here now? To prove to himself that, despite all the dangers, he still had the guts to do this kind of thing? Or was it because of his hatred of the Anathassious of the world? Or because he was on some kind of crusade to return art to its rightful place? Each reason seemed less likely than the one before and Murdoch realised he had no idea. He knew only that he was terrified. Grabbing the box frame with one hand, he avoided the hardboard at his feet, stepped over his backpack and hit the bathroom light switch. Whoever had opened the front door was whispering.

'Hurry up! Stop that, come on, you'll get a soaking.'

A woman's voice, struggling to speak through laughter. A line of light appeared at the bottom of the bathroom door, interrupted by shadows. There was a surprising bang as the front door shut, followed by a new silence as the shadows came together.

'Mmm, that's nice.'

She wasn't whispering now, but her voice was soft with intimacy. She laughed again and Murdoch knew she was young. Then a male voice, horribly close to his ear, said, 'Show us around then, Dem.'

Their footsteps headed to the back of the house, their echoing voices punctuated by the clicking of flicked switches.

'Sorry it's in such a state, Zac. Mum had a gathering last night, but the cleaners won't be here till tomorrow. Want a gin?'

She was putting on a voice – the accent different from a minute before. Murdoch listened to her and the boy discussing the view, then agreeing to turn off the lights so no one could see in from the beach. There was no more talk after that for a while, just irregular clunks as shoes and what sounded like a belt were dropped to the floor. Furniture scraped against the tiles and sighed under human weight. Soon Murdoch thought he could hear soft moaning – from the boy as much as from the girl – and, once or twice, a smack of saliva or maybe skin against skin. Murdoch gave them three minutes by his watch, then reached up and turned on his head torch. The yellow tunnel of light felt claustrophobic, no knowing what was in the darkness pressing in from every side. Squatting down, he laid the box frame onto the tiles as slowly as he knew how. Then, the floor hard on his knees, he crawled slowly towards the hardboard. It had fallen with the points of its staples upmost, a square spike strip waiting for him. Picking it up carefully, Murdoch sat back on his arse and turned to the wooden frame. Five minutes, he decided. Five minutes to press this fucker back into place, abort the mission and walk out the front door. Even young Zac ought to last that long. But then another idea occurred to him. What about five minutes to finish cutting the painting out of the frame as per his original plan? Or why not just walk out with the whole thing, box frame and all, under his arm? Murdoch sat in indecision, his mind frozen until a digit on his watch changed. Follow the rules. That was always the answer and the rule was to get out fast and empty-handed. He laid the hardboard down and, picking up the wooden frame, moved his head around so the torch could find the business card stuck in the paper. He went around again, slowly in the opposite direction, then a third time.

'No!' Murdoch whispered it aloud before he could stop himself. *No, no, no, no, no!*

There was the thin rip through the paper between the canvas and the frame, that was clear enough. But there was no sign of the cutter. Murdoch spun the box frame in his hands until at last his torch found the business card. It had fallen through the slit it had been cutting and was lying face up inside the frame – as proud as a kid in a lion enclosure. Shaking the frame hard, Murdoch managed to nudge the business card towards the rip it had made, but he knew it was no good. It had only cut the paper with pressure; no way was it coming back out now.

Murdoch dropped the frame into his lap and hit himself hard on the head. Twice, three times, before he remembered to breathe. To dedicate a minute, timed by his watch, to breathing. He hated himself and the evil gods no less by the end of it, but at least now he could think. Lying the frame onto the floor again – *slowly, carefully, take your fucking time!* – he crawled to his rucksack to retrieve his screwdriver. A piercing scream filled the house, interrupted only by Demi Anathassiou's need to inhale before screaming again.

'Oh my God, oh my God, oh my God!'

Murdoch's heart and lungs protested at the pressure as his skin and muscles shrank around them. Wheeling around, he confirmed the bathroom door was still shut behind him, harmless in his sweeping torchlight.

Another door was opening though – the one that led to the deck and the beach, he thought – and he heard a shout of male protest and one last scream before Demi's voice yelled instead: 'Oh my God! You frightened the life out of me! What the hell?'

Thick beads of sweat were making their way slowly down Murdoch's ribs. He put his left hand across his body and pushed his black pullover against them, shocked to feel his heartbeat even over there. In the living room, a deep voice was raised in anger.

'Who's this?'

Zac's voice protested, his turn to demand who the other man was until Demi told him to shut up.

'Uncle George,' she said. 'It's just ... He's just ... Why shouldn't we? The house was empty. Desree said no one would be here.'

She was crying now or trying to. Murdoch could hear her feet on the hard tiles of the living room, slapping around as she looked for something.

'You deserve a hiding, my girl. Your mum finds out about this—'

'You can't tell Mum, you can't ...'

It was like listening to a radio show, sitting in the dark while someone else got into trouble. Murdoch remembered the screwdriver in his hand, put it carefully into the backpack and picked up the box instead. He shook it slightly until Davie's business card was face down on the floor of the frame between the glass and the picture, white cardboard on white wood. Then he picked up the hardboard and started pushing the thick staples back into their original holes. Moving slowly was a struggle, a silent fight against adrenalin and sweat and the mounting drama in the living room.

'Don't talk to her that way.'

Zac was playing the hero, Uncle George, the thug.

'I'll talk to her anyway I want.' The older man's voice was louder than before, no rein on his rage now. 'So you'll sit down you little shit and shut the fuck up, if you know what's good for you.'

'Leave him alone.' Demi's voice was more cautious than Zac's. 'Mum said we could come here. She went to Melbourne this afternoon; she'll be away till after the weekend.'

'Really? She said you could use the place? Then she tells me and Marco the motion sensors are on and we're to get here straight off if anything beeps? So she forgot, did she? Accidentally ruined my one night of the week with your Aunty Vic and the kids just so I could sit in the rain until you two turned the lights on? Meanwhile, Marco's out the front and not at home with his new baby. Which is lucky, really, otherwise he'd have been the one to see you being fucked by Romeo here. I said, *sit down!* Let's ring up your mum, will we, Demi? Tell her what a stupid mistake she made?'

Demi had nothing to say to that, the sudden silence interrupted in the bathroom by the squeak of a staple finding its home. Murdoch closed his eyes and thought he was going to be sick, but no one in the living room seemed to have heard. Demi was trying to cry again, pleading with Uncle George not to tell Mum. Murdoch gave another push, struggling in his exhaustion to care about the noise, and found his job was finished. The hardboard was fully attached to the back of the frame. He picked the whole thing up and realised the minute he'd wasted before. Shook the frame until again Davie's business card was lying face down at the bottom once more, then hung it on the wall. He forced himself to inspect it in the yellow light of his head torch. Forced himself to admit there was nothing he could do to improve it. There was the sound of a scuffle in the living room, the dull thud of a punch, an exhalation of air and furniture scraping on the floor again.

'It's never you what gets hurt, is it, Demi?' Always the poor bloke you get caught with. "Oh, I've learnt my lesson, Uncle Georgie." Remember that? Remember you saying you wouldn't—'

It was Uncle George's turn to exhale, a cough of rage and surprise. Glass broke, Demi gave another little scream and something heavy clattered onto the living room floor.

'Go and get Marco!' Uncle George was struggling with something, his voice choked and breathless. 'He's out the front; go and get him now. Now!'

'Leave him alone!'

Murdoch tore the balaclava from his head, the head torch blinkered and bundled inside the wool. Flicking on the bathroom light, he threw everything into his rucksack, then rummaged past it again to pull out his baseball cap. In the living room, Anathassiou's brother and daughter were still screaming at each other, Zac unable to do more than grunt and gargle.

'Don't hurt him!'

Murdoch took a deep breath and opened the bathroom door. The voices were surprisingly loud and, for a panicked second, he thought he'd misjudged – that the fight was in the hallway. But, twisting towards the living room, he saw no one until the silhouette of a teenage girl appeared, naked but for a black thong, her hands to her face as she screamed at the floor in front of her.

Outside the heavy front door, the air was full of water, a welcome disguise for his sweat-soaked face.

'Help!' Murdoch shouted, not too loud. 'Someone call the police!'

He shouted it again and again as he walked down the driveway, trying to sound pathetic. Halfway to the gate, a man appeared from the shining bushes. He was small and tightly built, thick cords in his neck and wrists, his shape clear through his rain-soaked jacket. Above his boxer's nose, his head was shorn, the bottom half of his face covered by a thick black beard.

'Oh, thank God,' said Murdoch. 'Can you call the police? People are fighting in there.'

'Who the fuck are you?'

'I was just passing by and I heard a noise. The door was open and … can you call the police?'

'I didn't see you go inside.'

Murdoch knew he couldn't fight this man. Lumbering gorillas hired for their size, no problem, but this guy was a pro. Even at his peak, he'd have struggled. Nowadays, even if he could get past him, the man called Marco would easily run him down.

'I'm a neighbour …'

Murdoch had left the front door open and they both heard a smash breaking through the rain, Demi's latest scream mingling with her uncle's repeated yell to get Marco in here, *now*. Murdoch grunted as the solid block of Marco shoved him out the way before running to the front door and disappearing inside. Murdoch walked on towards the gate. Only when he was through it and on the street, did he start to sprint, pausing twice to bend and throw up into the gutter.

5.

Natalie only seemed to exhale; even that, the tiniest whisper of life. There was no evidence of her breathing in at all, no discernible movement – the rain outside louder than her need for air. Murdoch listened jealously. Sleep was like another room for her, all she had to do was take a step inside. They'd been talking about the day ahead, how, even though it was Saturday, she still had to go into work, and – just like that – she was gone, her mouth open, her body still. Murdoch closed his eyes and told himself how tired he was, how little sleep he'd had the night before, how early it had been that morning when Natalie had come round. He just needed to rest, everything was fine.

The memory that it wasn't chased away any chance of sleep for good. Suddenly bored of being in bed awake, a heavy ache of worry like wind in his chest, Murdoch adjusted his weight and got up carefully, found a pair of boxers and headed downstairs. He had one foot on the hall floor when, upstairs in the bedroom, his phone started ringing.

Natalie didn't do groggy reawakenings. He found her propped up on one elbow, looking towards his phone and asking who it was, like they'd never stopped talking. Murdoch told her it was no one and reached in for a kiss, but the doorbell sounded before he'd reached her lips.

'Oh, *that* no one.' She fell back into her pillow with a worried smile. 'I suppose you better let him in. It's about time I talked to him about us.'

Outside the front door, beneath his dripping umbrella, Davie seemed surprised.

'Oh, I thought maybe you weren't in.'

'But you rang the bell anyway?'

'I'm never convinced it works. I can't hear it.'

'You don't need to hear it. You're not in the house. I am in the house. I can hear it.'

Davie smiled, this was a fun game. Murdoch reminded himself that the least he could do was be nice. All night he'd been troubled by images of what Anathassiou might have Marco do to Davie. He'd pictured Davie screaming, torn at by dogs until he couldn't scream any more. Murdoch blinked the idea away for the hundredth time. Davie was talking to him.

'Sorry, mate,' he said. 'What was that? You all right?'

'I said are you going to let me in?'

Aware his voice could be heard upstairs, Murdoch said yeah, of course, sorry, come on in – how are you, mate? Earlier that morning, Natalie had made it clear once again that she wouldn't believe Davie was cool about them being an item until she'd spoken with him about it one-on-one. Wracking his brain for an excuse to leave them to it, Murdoch took Davie's dripping umbrella and stashed it in the cloakroom. Davie still managed to drip water the length of the hall.

'Smells funny in your house,' he said. 'Sort of fusty.'

'Tea?'

They'd reached the living room, Davie in the doorway trying to remember why he was here, Murdoch trying to get in first and check there was no obvious evidence of how he and Natalie had spent the first half of the morning.

'Guess what,' said Davie. 'I've got awesome news.'

Murdoch spotted Natalie's jeans splayed across the sofa, a scrunch of underwear clinging to one leg.

'Go make yourself a cup of tea,' he said, pushing Davie towards the kitchen. 'Give me a second, I only just woke up.'

Christ, if only that was true. Davie's innocent excitement was like the DREGS of a hangover: Disappointment, Regret, Embarrassment, Guilt, Shame. Murdoch rushed into the living room, grabbed Natalie's jeans and underwear and threw them behind the sofa. Looking around, he spotted his own strewn clothes: jeans kicked inside out, boxers on the coffee table. He threw them after Natalie's and wandered into the kitchen.

'So what did you get up to last night?' Davie was trying to work the kettle. 'You seen Nat at all?'

'Yeah.' Murdoch said it like it needed thinking about. 'Yeah, I did. I mean, well, she's upstairs, actually. What's your news?'

Davie blushed and the lid of the kettle flew into the air between them. Murdoch caught it with a smirk.

'That all right, Davie?'

'Er, yeah, sure. But it means we can't talk about *my news*.'

Davie's version of whispering was either not a whisper at all or – on days like this – so quiet you could hardly hear it. Murdoch forced a smile and handed over the lid to the kettle.

'Let's talk later then,' he whispered back. 'Now make the tea.'

'Oh, no, I need to tell you now. We need to get going, actually. There's not a moment to lose.'

'Get going?'

'We have to – oh, hi Nat!'

She was standing in the kitchen doorway, the bed sheet twisted like a toga. *Interesting choice*, thought Murdoch. Natalie glanced at him, stepped in, reached up and gave Davie a kiss on the cheek.

'Nice to see you,' she said determinedly. 'What you up to?'

'Oh,' said Davie blushing. 'Nothing. Not much.'

'You making tea?'

'Yeah, no. I mean, yeah.'

As Davie fumbled the lid onto the kettle and turned to plug it in, Natalie looked at Murdoch again. He frowned and nodded everything was OK, then asked her if it was OK if he used the shower first. Natalie said absolutely. She hadn't seen Davie in ages and it would be good to catch up. They probably needed to talk.

In the bathroom, Murdoch studied the grouting while the shower steamed beside him. Demi Anathassiou had said her parents were away until after the weekend. He hadn't locked the bathroom door behind him when he'd left. The cleaners would have been in. The hole in the painting was a small one. The business card was face down – white on a white frame. There were motion sensors. He left the shower running and went back to the bedroom to grab his Luckys from the bedside cabinet. But, opening the window and leaning out, the cigarette got as wet as if he'd smoked in the shower. He managed two unsatisfactory drags, then threw the thing down to the patio. Took the shower cold in the end – anything to stop his mind chasing in circles. In the living room, Natalie and Davie were silent on opposing sofas.

'Davie doesn't want to go out for lunch,' said Natalie, smiling too hard. 'And he doesn't much want to talk. He won't tell me why, but everything's fine, apparently.'

Davie's smile was less successful.

'I just popped in. I can't stay. In fact, we both have to go. Don't we, Bill?'

'Davie!'

'It's about the case,' said Murdoch wearily, ignoring Davie's sudden expression. 'Not about us. So it's fair enough. House rules, remember? We never discuss work when we're at home?'

The words 'at home' hung awkwardly between them, like a confession they'd lived this way for years. Murdoch sighed and walked over to the window. The cigarette he'd thrown lay disembowelled on the pavers.

'What do you mean "it's not about us"?' Davie squeaked behind him. 'Why would you think it's about you two? I'm really happy this has happened, I keep telling you both. I thought you'd never get round to it.'

Turning back, Murdoch saw Natalie had changed shape, the tension released from her face, her whole body relaxing into the sofa. When she spoke, there was laughter in her voice, at herself or at them, it wasn't clear.

'Oh, well, don't let me stop you. I've got a bit of work to do myself, actually. Ooh, but don't ask me what it is.'

She raised her hands in scary monster mode and stood too quickly, so that her makeshift toga fell to the floor. Murdoch barked out a laugh, but Natalie screamed and grabbed uselessly at the bed sheet while Davie recoiled in blushes. Just to make sure there was no awkwardness.

At night, the house in Kildare had seemed welcoming, a cosy refuge. On a drowned grey Saturday it turned out to be just another sad brick house in just another sad brick estate. Murdoch asked Davie how he knew the secretary was back.

'Denise Bentley saw her shopping in Coles last night.'

'Denise?'

'You know, works on the checkout?'

Murdoch nodded and let smoke out through his nostrils. They had taken the Merc, no chance of the rain coming in when the windows were shut and, more importantly, no chance for Davie's nonsense about smoking.

'Anyone on the Central Coast *not* know we want to talk to her?'

'It was just general gossip,' Davie said vaguely. 'I wasn't asking about her specifically. Just chit-chat, you know?'

Murdoch knew. It was the reason he avoided Kildare Coles.

'And how do you know she's home now?'

Davie rubbed his hands together hopefully. 'Because there's a light on? Because it's raining?'

The umbrella was more trouble than it was worth, threatening to break in both directions while Davie wrestled with it uselessly. In the house's front garden, a hedge of lilly-pillies was having a similar fight, leaves pulled out by the hissing wind, the plants bending tight, then rearing up to take a deep breath before bending down again. There was no answer to their first press of the bell. Murdoch – shoulders hunched, neck wet, fingers cold around the plastic bag – asked Davie why he didn't lean on the thing 'like you do at my house'. Davie scowled and pressed the buzzer again, slightly longer this time, until the door was opened by Anita Patel. She was darker and plumper than Murdoch had expected and he remembered she was just off her holidays.

'Can I help you?' she said politely, then recognised Davie. 'Oh, no. It's you. You can't. I mean, you need an appointment. Sorry. Sorry!'

She tried shutting the door less timidly than she'd opened it, then looked down to see what was in her way. Murdoch kept his foot where it was.

'You want to talk to us, Anita.'

'What? No, I don't. Who are you?'

'This is my partner, Bill Murdoch.' Davie had given up on the umbrella and was wiping rain from his eyes. 'It's either us or the police, Anita, and Bill's right, you want to talk to us. We're here to help you.'

She wasn't convinced, but Davie gave her his Little-Boy-Lost look, shivering against the weather and saying, 'Please let us in,' until she stood back like she didn't have a choice. The timid action bothered Murdoch; he couldn't imagine Anita Patel harming anyone.

In the lounge room, a kid was playing in the corner, while an old woman in a bright green sari watched regally from a sofa. The kid barely glanced up, but Murdoch could see she was the spit of her mother, those huge brown eyes, a small pout of a mouth. She was like a kid in a cartoon: drawn to be loved. Her grandmother stood when Davie and Murdoch walked in and looked down her long nose as she shook hands with them. She was faded and quiet, almost transparently grey, obviously used to being in charge. Anita asked them all to sit, no offer of tea, and Murdoch realised it was the same scene Davie had described. Three generations of Anita Patel, a show-and-tell of how people aged. He wondered how often the three women sat like this, safe in female company. He smelled the familiar smell of the house, sweet and exotic, a perfume or a joss stick, and it sickened him. It wasn't that it was wrong to be here – these women unaware of how recently he and Davie had fingered their belongings. It was the memory he was a housebreaker again; that there was another house he'd recently cracked.

'We was hoping to talk to you alone,' he said to Anita. 'Private, like.'

'No.' They were in her territory now. 'No, I think I'd rather there were other people here.'

There was something annoying about her confidence. Like she knew they had nothing; no matter what she'd done, they couldn't touch her. She wasn't the same woman as at the front door – the nervous secretary he'd heard described. She was stiff-spined with rigid eye contact, a woman possessed, something more than an act. Murdoch reached down to the bag between his feet and slowly lifted out the red nylon pouch containing the injection kit. He held it between his knees so only the secretary could see, but, looking up, found she was smiling rigidly at his face, refusing to play his game. In the end, he raised the kit into the air between them. Even then she took a while to look at it. When she did, the reaction was immediate. She stood with a gasp, turned to the corner and grabbed her shocked daughter, the little girl erupting immediately into howls. Turning back, the secretary almost threw the child at its grandmother, bubbling at them both in urgent Indian. The older lady stood too and shouted back, but Anita was already bustling her out of the room, one hand on the small of her mother's back, the other on her daughter, all three of them protesting noisily. But, even now, there was something harmless in the secretary's gestures: a gentleness in the urgency. Murdoch sat back to keep out of the way and looked through the confusion of bodies at Davie. He was rubbing his hands on his trousers, blinking under his damp hair, a man about to confess everything. *We're the guilty ones. We were here the other night. There's a hairbrush stuck under the sofa!*

The fight between the three generations lasted a few moments, Anita squeezing the door on her mother and daughter and leaning heavily against it, the weight of her body her only strength left. There was a final shout from the old lady, now shut in the hall, a single bang on the lounge door, before they heard her lead the screaming child away to the back of the house. The silence would have been deafening, if Davie had let it.

'We're here to help you,' he said.

It sounded ridiculous given the scene they'd caused, the fear and exhaustion in the secretary's face as she stood against the door. She was pretty in a way, Murdoch thought, huge eyes rich with lashes, beautifully even teeth, clear brown skin. On her third attempt at speaking – too many options of where to start – she told them she'd done nothing wrong. She didn't know what they were talking about. Why had they come? Murdoch spoke slowly.

'Anita, love, this thing stinks of bleach and I bet your bleeding fingerprints are all over it. There's footage of you at the hospital on the day Scott Patterson disappeared. There's Patterson's Central Coast Mariners mug what you swapped with the Bulldogs one and there's traces of your sleeping pills in his bloodstream. I think you know what we're talking about.'

It was like letting down a car tyre – a slow and steady collapse. Anita Patel slid down her living room door until she was sitting on the garish carpet, her knees level with her chin. Her mouth hung open and she stared straight ahead, the straight-spined woman long gone.

'But it's all right, see. We know all about Scott Patterson. We know what a nasty piece of work he was. We know what he was doing to you; he done it to other women too. Anita, you listening?'

'Let me say goodbye to Riya.' She coughed, wiped her mouth with the back of her hand and forced her huge dark eyes towards him. 'I just need some time with her and my mum before I go.'

'No, Anita, you're not listening.'

'Bill, wait.'

Davie stood and crossed the room in two strides, then sat cross-legged on the floor in front of her. He took her hands in his and held his face close to hers.

'Anita?'

'Yes.'

'We don't want you to go to prison. We're not going to tell the police what you did. Do you understand?'

She didn't. She pulled her head back so it banged against the door, then let it rest there, before turning it slowly to Murdoch again.

'Scott Patterson had it coming,' he said.

'He did it to at least one other woman,' Davie told her gently. 'He targeted women who had lost sexual harassment claims. He was involved in … other things too. We're not going to tell the police what you did.'

Fat tears appeared on her lower lashes, hovering and refusing to fall. Anita sniffed and knuckled them away.

'Why not?'

The question was a challenge. She asked it again, demanding an answer, stood quickly and brushed down her skirt, stepping past Davie and across to the window. Outside was no calmer, rain throwing itself against the glass, desperate to get in. Murdoch spoke to Anita's back.

'We don't need to, love. Patterson's wife hired us to find him and we do that, we get rewarded, no matter what. The contract is clear. We just need the body.'

She said nothing. Murdoch held up a hand before Davie could even think about it and they waited in silence. Anita Patel stood shaking softly at the window until she suddenly turned and half-sat, half-fell onto the sofa beside Murdoch. She looked up at them desperately.

'What do you want?'

'We want to keep you out of prison. We want to hide what you did from the police. But we need to know what you did with Scott Patterson.' Davie said it like he was talking to a child. 'We need to know where he is.'

Anita looked at Murdoch, her head on one side. She'd missed the point and maybe he could explain.

'The body,' he said. 'Where is Scott Patterson's body?'

'But I don't know!' The statement erupted from her, spittle landing on Murdoch's thigh and mingling with the damp from the rain. 'I don't know what happened to him! I went to the hospital and he wasn't there! There was a mess, the bed all undone and things broken on the floor. I didn't know what to do. I thought maybe he'd escaped, maybe he was coming after me. Then, suddenly, there were police everywhere and I ... I left before they could talk to me.' She broke down, sobs wracking her body. There was a box of tissues beside him, but when Murdoch passed it she knocked it away. 'I don't know where he is! I lie awake at night worrying he's out there, coming for me. I didn't want to come back here at all, but Ma and Riya hated Fiji. Every time I close my eyes, I see him. And now the police are after me again!'

'The police?'

'A Detective Constable Burran keeps calling me. They've got new evidence, questions about the mug. They want to talk to me again. I think they're going to arrest me soon.'

It was over an hour before they left the house. Thirty minutes for them to convince Anita they wouldn't tell the police. Thirty minutes for Anita to convince them she'd understood. Outside the rain hammered on regardless, soaking them again before they'd reached the car. They were halfway to Montauban before either of them spoke.

'Awesome,' said Davie. 'I don't get to send a victimised woman to prison.'

Murdoch turned at Davie's tone. 'Jesus Christ, isn't that what you wanted? What's wrong with you now?'

'What do you think's wrong with me? Today's the sixth – it's the last possible day to get Patterson his shot without his health deteriorating. I

294

thought we'd be driving on the way to give it to him now. Either that or to his body – I'm not sure I care which any more. Sorry, that's not true, of course, it isn't. But the point is we've got nothing and Patterson could be anywhere. That was our last lead, Bill.'

Murdoch snorted and shook his head. 'No, it wasn't, you muppet. That was the lead what never made sense. Which means now we can concentrate on the one what always did.'

There was no let-up in the rain that weekend and none forecast for the coming days either. It was going to be one of those fortnights that explains how eastern Australia is so green when the sky above is normally so blue. Murdoch and Davie agreed a plan, but that didn't stop Davie phoning regularly, outraged Murdoch wasn't doing more to help. Murdoch, for his part, knew Davie had every reason to be upset – if he only knew the half of it – but still, he snapped in the end.

'What d'you mean, not helping? Whose bleeding car you sitting in?'

But the loan of the Merc had only increased Davie's suspicions. Why was Bill being so nice? What had he done this time? What was wrong with the Merc? Murdoch didn't explain it was Davie's car he was worried about – who might have researched the rego and be looking for it even now.

The phone calls with Natalie were worse. Her strange schedule suddenly freed her two afternoons in a row, the first opportunities he'd not taken to be with her, and she'd started using a tone he'd not heard since before they were a couple.

'Sorry, where are you, then?'

'I'm not going to lie to you, Nat, but I can't tell you.'

'Can't or won't. Hello, Bill?'

Murdoch was sitting in Davie's Hyundai Excel, as far as possible from the house he was watching. It wasn't the ideal car to be using, but if anyone was going to be found in it, it was only fair it was him. Around him, the mismatched McMansions were eerily quiet, the only movement a delivery of sand to a half-built house. The only noise the rain.

'I'm here,' he said. 'I'm thinking about it. But I can't tell you, Nat. It's to do with the case.'

'Really? Is that so? Because Davie tells me he's working all hours and you're not helping.'

A white Range Rover pulled up at the other end of the street. The man called Marco climbed out, looked around and let himself in through Anathassiou's gate. Murdoch told Natalie he'd call her back, hung up and drove off before Marco could come out again. Four blocks inland, parked at a hurried angle, he spent the next call promising Natalie he'd never hang up on her again. She told him she'd stopped sleeping with other people.

'Oh.' Murdoch didn't know what to say. 'Right.'

'Well, don't sound so pleased about it.'

'I'm not. I mean, I am. I'm just ...'

He wanted to say surprised, as in surprised she thought this was news. Instead, he said, 'Stopped when?' and let her tease him about being jealous, anything to keep the peace.

Back in Montauban, the street door to Davie's office was locked again. Here, the rain was mixing with ocean spray at the perfect angle to come under the awning and run down the back of Murdoch's collar. All the same, he struggled with the office's lock for longer than he had done with the one to Anathassiou's bathroom. The frame was so loose there was nothing to lever against; it would have been easier to take the whole thing off.

'What you doing?'

Hattie Thornton was in the doorway of the chip shop in a flowery plastic housecoat, her pockmarked arms visible to the shoulder. She was giving him her vacant smile and wiping her hands on a Chux.

'Locked myself out,' said Murdoch.

He could probably have said, 'Breaking in to steal the computer' and she'd have forgotten about it before she was back at the fryer. Bending over the lock again, Murdoch could feel her watching, nothing else to do on a wet midweek morning.

'Davie's always doing that,' she said. 'He leaves a spare key with me, just in case. Do you want to borrow it?'

Murdoch didn't know what was more annoying– the offer, or the fact she'd not offered earlier. He wanted to say no, no lock ever beat him, but

296

even Hattie would have to think that was strange, which meant Anne Lincoln would soon hear about it. He followed her into the stinking chip shop and watched her reach to a hook beside the drinks machine.

'Just because it's you, mind.' She handed over the key on its green plastic fob. 'I wouldn't give it to anyone, you know.'

Murdoch didn't tell her she wouldn't need to, that anyone could take it while her back was turned. Instead, he smiled a quick thanks and got out before he stank of the place.

Outside Davie's office window, the scene on the street was as he'd left it: the asphalt empty but for the car; the sand beyond it pitted like an overused sponge. Squatting down, Murdoch pulled Davie's three-bar heater from under the shelves, plugged it in and tried the switches, but the thing remained dead at his feet. He tried the kettle with the same result, then the lights. Davie answered on the second ring.

'Let me guess; you're calling to say you're going to come and help. Or to tell me what you're up to.'

'Don't start.'

'You've seen the error of your ways and you've remembered how you promised this time you'd get involved.'

'Davie, are you eating? Stinking up my car? What did I tell you about that?'

Davie protested it was a salad sandwich and Murdoch remembered it was himself he could smell: a mixture of chip fat and sweat. He sat on Davie's desk and looked out at the Excel parked across the road. In the rain, the little car looked worse than ever, the rust breaking through the paintwork like lesions. But anyone asking would be told Davie couldn't be far away.

'So. What's news?'

'Nothing.' Davie sounded like Murdoch felt: days of boredom and worry. 'He does the same thing every day.'

'How did you go with all your bills? Get the bank off your back?'

'Well, I sorted the phone, obviously. Appointment with the bank's next week, Guy's going to come with me. Should be fine.'

'Electricity bills?'

'The one at home's fine for a few weeks. The one at the office can wait. Seeing as I'm on the case alone and I have to sit in a car twenty-four hours a day, I can't get there anyway, can I?'

'No phone calls from strangers?'

'No. Why do you keep asking that?'

'Nothing. Tell me more about our man. What's he been up to?'

But Davie only repeated what he already knew. Terry Hatch seemed to live in Warriwul, took his wife to work and the kids to school every day, visited the office behind the library sometimes but never for very long. He'd been back to the brothel only once. Murdoch didn't like the idea of Davie following Hatch in the Merc, but he knew it was only fair. Hatch was no more likely to notice the Merc than Marco was to notice the Excel. Or Anathassiou the business card. He had a sudden vision of Davie being tortured by Marco, keeping his mouth shut because he didn't know what to confess until the man killed him in frustration. Tuning back in to the real-life Davie, he heard Fran Patterson was still phoning every other day, DC Burran sounded strangely excited and Anita Patel had called too. The police had been to her house apparently, interviewing her for longer than before.

'I think they're going to charge her,' Davie told him. 'I advised her to get a good lawyer. As if she could afford one of those.'

Down on the street a movement caught Murdoch's eye, a red Honda 4x4 pulling up behind Davie's car. Murdoch let Davie rabbit on, barely listening until Ruby from the bakery climbed out and ran through the rain towards the chip shop.

'So Hatch hasn't been out of your sight once, unless he's at home or in the office?'

A tiny silence at the other end of the phone. 'Well, no. So either he's got Patterson in one of those two places, or he doesn't have him at all.'

Murdoch said nothing for a second, listening to Davie munch on bread like that's why he'd stopped talking.

'And where are you now?'

'Down the road from his house. I'm tempted to just go and knock on the door. Anything to get out of this car. He drove up about half an hour ago and unless he's nipped out the back, he must be in there. Maybe Patterson will answer the door.'

Murdoch rolled his eyes, but kept his voice nice as he walked over to the six-thousand-dollar armchairs. They were as uncomfortable as they looked.

'Davie.'

'What?'

'When did you lose him?'

'What?'

'You said he just drove up. Which means you were following him home and then you lost him and now you've found him again. So where exactly did you lose him?'

Davie would have one hand in his hair, like maybe he'd left the answer in there.

'I don't really lose him,' he said huffily. 'It's just he always takes the scenic route home to Warriwul, avoiding the worst of the traffic, I guess. I always keep two or three cars back like you told me to, but it's the Old Friendship Road – it's really bendy and then, when I get to his house, I'm always there first. He must know some shortcut. It's only like thirty minutes of the entire day when he's actually out of sight.'

'Really?'

'Well, forty-five. Or maybe a bit more. You don't think—?'

'Don't I?' Murdoch heard the penny drop. 'Davie, look at your phone, look at the map of where you lose him and see there are any side-roads or—'

'Yes, yes! I get it. I'm not stupid. I'm just tired from the being the only one watching.'

'And Davie, make me a promise, yeah? Even if you find a place what looks likely, don't go there by yourself.'

'Oh, I just call you to come in for the moment of glory, do I?'

'I'm serious, Davie. If you do manage to find the right place and Hatch gets a wind of anyone near it—'

'He'll have cleared it out before we can get in and prove a thing, I know, I know.'

Murdoch shook his head slowly, looking at the cold office around him. He remembered catching Emre Velis there. The way Velis had been apologetic but not too much, strong and then friendly so you couldn't mind. Pitch fucking perfect.

'Actually, I was going to say he'll kill you without a— Hang on, Davie, what did you just say?'

'Which bit?'

'Oh, Davie, you're a genius. Do you know that? You are a bleeding genius! I'll call you back. Don't move.'

'But—'

But Murdoch had already hung up and was running down the stairs to the street.

6.

Murdoch couldn't remember where he'd learned Parkinson's Law. It was the kind of thing Amanda would have told him about, but he didn't reckon he'd heard it from her. Maybe he'd found it in the first weeks of his grief, when he'd thought memorising everything on the internet would leave no room for anything else. He knew it off by heart, that was for sure. 'Work expands so as to fill the time available for its completion.' Which meant if you've got five minutes, buying a stamp takes five minutes. If you've got ten minutes, it takes ten. During the long months when he could plan a whole day around buying a stamp, he had come to hate the mocking phrase.

Three hours after hanging up on Davie, he thought of the law again, the first time in months. Work didn't just expand to fill the time available, it squashed together tiny when you had no time at all. In the hours after leaving the freezing office, he'd bought yet another cheap phone with yet another pre-paid SIM, driven halfway to Newcastle, hired a grey Toyota Corolla, loaded it with supplies and had a detailed conversation with Natalie's boss. The last of these had been the most difficult. His first attempt at calling had been from the car park of Crosley Mall, keen to use his new phone and dump it as soon as he could.

'Is Detective Inspector Ian Mackintosh there? I want to talk to him please.'

'*Oy wunt te tok tim, ploys*'. Murdoch's attempt at a Birmingham accent sounded ridiculous, but then so did the genuine article. The copper on the end of the phone didn't like it.

'Oh yeah? What kind of information would that be then, sir?'

'I'm only willing to speak to Mackintosh. It's about that Scott Patterson, who's gone missing.'

'And you are?'

'It's an anonymous tip-off.'

'I can't pass you on without a name.'

Murdoch rubbed his hand across his scalp. How quickly could they trace the location of a mobile phone? Pretending to give in, he gave his name as Adam Mansfield, and was told to hang on. Four slow minutes later – the rental car steaming around him, the Mall's car park invisible – a familiar voice came on the line.

'My name is Detective Sergeant Natalie Conquest. I understand you think you might have some information for us?'

Murdoch hung up and swore, tempted to smash the phone already. Fifteen minutes later, when he tried again, DC Burran answered. Murdoch told him he knew where Patterson was, but he was only willing to speak to Detective Inspector Ian Mackintosh.

'Aw, it's you!' said Burran. 'Hang on, just ... hang on.'

Burran forgot to put him on hold and Murdoch listened to the echoes and cracks of Broadwater Local Area Command. Somewhere in there, Natalie would be running around, feeling extra stress because of him. He closed his eyes and waited.

'Yeah.' DC Burran again. 'I mean, we're trying to get hold of him. Do you want to give me a number where we can reach you?'

Murdoch told him he'd call back in fifteen minutes before remembering his Birmingham accent. Would they be taping yet? He tried again.

'Make sure he's there if you want to find Patterson.'

He was tempted to wait in the car park, the rain trying different rhythms on the roof, but realised he had no idea how fast things would move once he pulled the trigger. Blinking away his exhaustion, he started the car and drove in the general direction of Green Bay. Natalie's voice had thrown him and he struggled to concentrate on driving, indicating when he wanted to slow the wipers, turning them off or up at every corner. After half an hour or so, no real idea where he was, he pulled into a side street, parked and tried Mackintosh again. The phone was answered on the first ring, DC Burran again, and Murdoch could tell he wasn't alone. The detective's voice was louder and calmer than before – a man talking while people listened. He called Murdoch 'Adam' and said he was putting him through. Thirty or forty seconds before Mackintosh came on the line and Murdoch wondered what technology was pointing at him now. Nothing? Everything? One day he'd ask Natalie. Wouldn't that be nice, a life where he could be honest with her?

'Detective Inspector Ian Mackintosh.'

It was him all right. Murdoch remembered how tired the man looked, the skin hanging heavy from his face. He wondered what more important business he'd pulled him from.

'I've got some information about Scott Patterson.'

Now, at last, he had the Brummie accent. Flat and nasal, somewhere between bored and thick. Mackintosh wasn't impressed.

'Oh yeah?'

'I know where he is. But if you want to get him while he's still alive, you might want to hurry up.'

'And where is he then, Mr ...?'

There was a smile in Mackintosh's voice. This was a wind-up and they both knew it.

'Does the name Angie Anathassiou mean anything to you? She's the one what's got him.'

'Excuse me?'

'You heard me. Angie Anathassiou's got a big beach house in Green Bay. 215 Werona Parade. Patterson's in the downstairs toilet. And there's drugs in the house too and some fancy pictures, so you might want to have a good look round.'

'And why should I believe you?'

302

But Mackintosh was curious now and Murdoch could tell he didn't completely disbelieve him. The detective inspector's voice had changed – no smile any more – the question only there to buy time.

'Because if you don't and the papers find out you knew and did nothing about it, it's going to look pretty stupid, innit?'

His accent had slipped again. Murdoch banged the heel of his hand against his forehead.

'Listen to me,' he said in full Brummie. 'I'm recording this call and this recording is going to be sent to *The Daily Telegraph* tomorrow. So you might want to do something about it. Patterson's life is in your hands.'

'But what—'

Murdoch hung up. With the door of the Corolla open, the rain heavier than ever, his thigh was wet in seconds. He leaned out optimistically, tried to stretch again and swore. All this planning and he hadn't thought of an umbrella. He was outside for less than fifteen seconds, bending down to push the phone under the front tyre, but in that time his neck and the back of his shoulders were soaked. He rolled the car forward and back, continuing to reverse until he was sure the smashed plastic had swum into the gutter to mix in the sewers and flow into the ocean with all the dog shit and litter and everything else that stopped people swimming after rain. Christ, he was sick of it all.

In Green Bay he stayed inside the rental car at first. There was something comforting about the smell of its new leather, the cleanliness of the dashboard and carpets. A little reminder there were still things unspoiled in the world. But while a new grey Corolla – the second most popular car in Australia in the second most popular colour – was less memorable than Davie's old pink Excel, someone sitting inside it wouldn't be. The men, when they arrived, would be nervous. They'd look up and down the street more than normal, have a good nose around and check if anyone was watching. Even upstairs in the half-built McMansion, peering through a thick piece of plastic sheeting that breathed and snapped in the rain-sodden wind, Murdoch felt exposed. He didn't smoke and he didn't read his phone. Only when it got dark would he allow himself to return to the warmth of the car, until then this was safer and, today, safety was everything. He pulled out the phone he'd bought for talking to Velis and gave the man a quick call, no idea why. They had a vague argument about what Murdoch was planning to do.

'You're cracked,' Velis told him. 'We thought it was going to be easy, but we were wrong. Best leave it alone, mate.'

Murdoch told him leaving it alone wasn't an option, but he didn't tell him why. They tussled back and forth until Murdoch's other phone – his normal one – buzzed and he used it as an excuse to hang up on Velis.

'Davie, what's happening?'

'You were going to call me back, remember? Don't move, you said.'

A small knot formed in Murdoch's stomach.

'What did you do, Davie?'

'I moved. See, I looked at Google Earth on my phone and found the stretch of the Old Friendship Road where I kept losing Hatch.'

'Kept losing? Davie—'

'Yes, I know, it was your idea. You were right and I was wrong. Anyway, there was only one real turn-off it could have been, a single lane track over an old wooden bridge. But it was a dead end, nothing but a few farm buildings.'

'Just get straight to the end of the story.'

'So I was at a bit of a loss but then I noticed, across the main road, off to the other side, there was this track. You can barely see it, it's not on the map even. But it goes downhill and around this paddock and, at the bottom, there's a bunch of trees around what looks like a shed.'

'Davie, where are you?'

The wind turned and the plastic sheeting between Murdoch and the rain billowed towards him.

'Don't worry, Hatch isn't here. But he *was* here. On the way to him picking up the kids from school, I followed him again and lost him again. But, instead of continuing on, I parked up and walked back this way. Along the road, a bit from where the track turns off, you can see down across the paddock to the shed and I saw the roof of his car! Bill, if Hatch is our man then I think this is the place. He—'

'Davie, where are you? You don't go anywhere near that shed, you got me?'

The sheeting surged out again, its fight against the weather drowned by the engine of a powerful car. Squinting through the plastic, Murdoch could see only that the vehicle was big and white and pulling up outside Anathassiou's gate.

'Davie, hang on.'

Murdoch pulled a pen-knife from his pocket, leaned slowly forward and made a cut in the plastic sheeting. He had to get the car's rego. His plan was not to let it out of his sight, but, if it did, he'd need to find it again fast. He needn't have worried. The car was the same white Range Rover as he'd seen before and, from this improved angle, he could see it had been heavily customised. Its radiator, the casing of its wing mirrors, and even the thick spokes of its hubcaps were as shiny and reflective as mirrors. As if that wasn't enough, the car had been turned into a convertible, the soft black roof matching the dark windows. The Range Rover was parked at an arrogant angle and, as Murdoch watched, Marco climbed out of the passenger side, his thin features immediately shiny with rain as he looked up and down the street, then signalled to the driver. Then the bastardised car rocked slightly as Angie Anathassiou appeared, shoulders hunched against the weather, black hair soaked to her head in seconds. Murdoch swore under his breath.

'Mate,' he said to Davie, 'promise me you won't go in till I get there.'

'And when's that going to be?'

'Not now.'

Davie sighed loudly and Murdoch told him one last time – '*Don't. Go. In!*' – and hung up. Standing slowly, he forced himself to look around and be sure he'd left nothing behind. Then he walked slowly down the stairs and out to the street.

Davie sat in the Mercedes, staring at the rain on the windscreen and thinking about his divorce. He remembered the relief he'd felt years before, the release from endless worry, when he'd accepted his relationship with Hannah was over. It was like when you stopped banging your head against a brick wall. Could he make the marriage work? Would he ever be happy? Would one day he know what do to and how before Hannah nagged him to do it? He had no longer had to worry about any of those things. Discovering Bill had hung up on him again, he experienced a similar sensation. He was on his own and, as frustrating as that might be, it meant he could do whatever he wanted.

Grabbing his phone from where he'd thrown it, Davie started to call Bill back. *Don't bother, I'll sort it out myself.* But as soon as he hit the first button, the thing died in his hand. The recharge cable Bill had given him was in the Excel. That would be his fault too – Davie could see the expression on Bill's face. Throwing the phone down again, he leaned across and wiped the inside of the passenger window. He wanted a last look down to Hatch's shed but at this angle there was nothing to see. You had to stand at the top of the slope – it was invisible from the road. Indicating to no one, he pulled out in the direction of Warriwul.

The rain was lighter than it had been in days, drifting a little before it hit the ground. Far to his left, across the dip that held the shed, there were tiny blue rips in the clouds. Lost in thought, eyes on the sky as much as the road, Davie didn't register the car approaching in the opposite lane until it had almost passed him. As soon as it had, he blinked and let the Mercedes slow while he stared in the rear-view mirror. The other car had been a black BMW; the man driving it, Terry Hatch. Davie drifted slower still, careful not to flare his brake lights until Hatch had disappeared around the bend behind him, then he pulled over, tyres into the mud at the side of the road, and slowly turned the Mercedes.

The track down to the shed was steeper than it had looked and Davie walked with legs bent, convinced he was going to slip and fall. To his right, across a narrow ditch, ran an unruly line of bushes and trees, some ancient boundary between this land and the next. To his left – between him and Hatch's car – there was nothing but a bulge of paddock to hide him from view, the tops of the trees that stood around the shed peeking over the top. At first, Davie kept to the track's centre, above the wet tyre tracks and pockmarked puddles, until he realised this only made him more visible. He bent further, stepped to the right and edged along the brink of the ditch. Progress was slower here, the slippiness of the mud threatening to slide him into the running water, lantana and brambles

306

reaching out of the bushes and wiping across his chest – beggars demanding attention. Then the ditch ran louder, more water pouring in from somewhere, and ahead, where the land levelled and the track turned, Davie saw a huge brown puddle blocking his path. He paddled through it, his trainers submerged, until he could peer around the corner. Hatch's black X5 was less than twenty metres away, glistening and ready to pounce. Beyond it was the patch of trees, glistening ash and oaks, dripping lightly onto, not a shed, after all, but a faded red shipping container. One of the doors in its nearest end was open, the space inside black. Davie blinked against the remains of the rain and approached the BMW. Halfway there, the wet air was filled by a full-throated scream. It was the scream of a man, hoarse and horrified and suddenly gone, leaving the rain to pitter-patter onto Davie's hood and the water to run in the ditch, the only other sound the faint tearing of tyres along the Old Friendship Road. Davie found he was in a tense half-crouch, staring over the bonnet of the BMW at the open end of the container. He forced himself on, the squelch of his footsteps horribly loud, the rustling of his jacket unbearable until he lifted his arms from his sides. A metre from the container door, he heard a murmur of voices and had the horrible idea that there was someone still in Hatch's car. He swung round and stared at its dark windows, his reflection bobbing as he stepped towards it. Only when his hands were cupped around his eyes and his nose was pressed against the glass was he convinced the BMW was empty. Catching the fear in his reflection, he took a deep breath and turned back to the container.

Brown cardboard boxes. Davie hadn't known what he'd find, but he hadn't expected this. Leaning in through the open door, the container was full of them. From one metre in they stretched wall to wall and ceiling to floor, each the size of a washing machine. The murmur of voices came again and, avoiding the metal door, Davie trod a careful foot inside, gave it his weight, held his breath, then brought the other one in. The container smelled of disinfectant, something sweet and putrid under that, something bad. Taking a few steps to the left, Davie squinted in the dark until he was certain the wall of boxes didn't fully stretch across the container after all. It stopped just before the left-hand side, cardboard on the container wall creating an optical illusion. Stepping into the gap, Davie found a second cardboard wall, this one stopping short of the right-hand side of the container. The gap there, at the far end of the narrowness between the two walls of boxes, was glowing softly. The voices were clearer now, men's voices back and forth, but still only voices, no words he could make out.

Outside again, under the rain, Davie stripped off his crunching jacket, then stood uncertainly until he spotted a giant tyre in the mud at the bottom of the paddock. He ran over and found it full of water but stuffed his jacket in anyway, then made his way back to the container.

'Money' was the first word he understood. He thought the two men were arguing, but then one of them laughed.

'… money, then, you bastard!'

That was Terry Hatch. From the gap in the second cardboard wall, Davie could see the man's shoulders and the back of his head moving with the effort of shouting his words before they echoed around the container. He, and whoever he was shouting at, were at the far end of a makeshift dormitory. Six or seven metal beds in an uneven row, thin mattresses stained or not there at all, a metal chest of drawers next to each. Davie's view of the scene was broken by strange shapes of material hanging from the roof: black curtains bunched or stretched or hanging half-torn. A bare light bulb cast long shadows.

'*Our* money,' said the second voice. '*Our* investment. We both lost the shipment, Terry.'

This was the man who'd laughed and there was laughter in his voice now until Hatch bent forward out of Davie's view and the scream came again. It was like nails on a blackboard, no clear difference between the noise and the pain itself. Davie covered his ears and stepped further into the container, walking quickly around the foot of the closest bed and stepping into the shadow of a stretched curtain. Hatch's broad back was bent over a bed four or five metres away from Davie, the fat man's frame wobbling with effort. Then he stood suddenly to look down at his work, a pair of pliers visible in his right hand, something dark and shiny between the prongs.

'Not laughing now, are you?' Hatch said. 'Well, are you?'

But the man on the bed did laugh. It was forced and laboured and gurgling but it was a laugh all the same, the noise no less grating to Davie than the scream. It clearly bothered Hatch too. The fat man threw the pliers at the floor and gave a yell of such desperate frustration that, at first, Davie assumed the noise was not from him. But then Hatch turned, his face clear, and yelled again before stomping out of sight and leaving Davie with a clear view of the man on the bed. It was Scott Patterson. He was paler than in his photographs: cut up, unshaven, wild-haired and covered in sweat. But it was definitely him. Both of his wrists were handcuffed to the metal frame of the bed, like a crooked crucifix in a hospital gown. At the bed's other end, his feet were tied to the metal uprights, the one closest to Davie bleeding heavily from the toes. As Davie watched, a dark line of blood made its way down the side of Patterson's foot and dripped onto the floor. Hatch lurched back into view, grabbing Patterson by his hair.

'Why are you making me do this? Why don't you just pay up?'

Patterson grimaced. 'Business is business, Terry. We made an investment and we both lost. You took your risk, why should I cover you for it?'

'Bullshit. You act like you don't know who you're dealing with. A hundred grand disappears and I'm supposed to take it on the chin like some loser?'

Patterson sighed, a man dealing with a child who isn't trying hard enough. 'I've shown you the papers. The girls were put in the truck like normal. It's not my fault if the slopes forgot to open the vents. What am I supposed to do? Get the bodies off the bottom of the ocean and—'

Hatch slapped Patterson hard and bent to shout into his face. 'I don't give a shit. Just tell me how you're going to get me my money back, or you're going to die in here, you understand?'

'I'm hungry.'

'What?!'

Patterson coughed and said he needed some food. Davie watched Hatch raise his fists imploringly to heaven.

'You know what?' said Hatch. 'No. I'm not fucking feeding you any more. I told you when I brought you here, I'll keep you alive for a month

309

and then that's it. Today's three weeks, did you know that? So you better pay up or in seven days, you'll be dead. And if that's from starvation, then it'll save me the bother of putting a bullet in your head. Might be a nice warning to others when they write about that in the papers. Maybe it'll scare your missus into giving me what I'm owed.'

Patterson's face seemed to flinch at the mention of his wife, but within seconds he had croaked out a laugh again. 'It takes more than seven days to starve to death, you moron.'

'Not if you don't get no water.'

Hatch turned, pulled a bunch of keys from his jacket pocket and made his way along the foot the beds, only the curtain blocking his view of Davie.

'Seven days,' he shouted over his shoulder. 'Then we'll see who's laughing.'

'Ha ha ha!'

Patterson's voice was hoarse and, again, the noise was nothing like a laugh. But it was more than enough for Hatch. The fat man shoved his fingers in his ears and continued towards the open end of the container. It wasn't too late. If he would just turn back to the bed, take a few steps towards Patterson, Davie could get out and away. But Hatch didn't turn. Instead, he waddled on, fingers in his ears, past Davie to the inside wall of cardboard boxes. Davie stared at the oval of his back, the only noise from Davie's own heart. A few seconds later he heard a click and all was dark, the sound of his heart replaced by the heavy slam of the container door and the slow deliberate sound of locks and chains.

If Murdoch had kept his head down he might have gotten away unnoticed. His face and hair were hidden by a baseball cap, his plain jacket could have made him anyone. The cold and damp gave him every reason to hunch his shoulders and keep his chin down as he scurried away. But it was this feeling of scurrying that undid him, running away like a frightened mouse when he'd spent his life being strong. He took a final brazen look at the white Range Rover and there he met the gaze of Marco, grimacing at the rain or maybe the weight of the black Adidas holdalls he was carrying. Did Murdoch stare too long or look away too quickly? Just in case, he held up a hand to say hello, the way he might to Mr Minter in Montauban, the neighbour he never wanted to talk to.

'Scuse me!'

Marco's voice was clear in the rain-spattered street. When Murdoch ignored it, the grey Corolla only six cars away, Marco's footsteps smacked across the tarmac towards him.

'Scuse me, mate. Wait up.'

Murdoch prepared a face and looked up, focusing first on Anathassiou's empty driveway, then on the man running towards him.

'Oh,' he said, walking on slowly so Marco could fall in beside him. 'Hello. How did you go the other night? Did you call the police?'

In the light of day Marco had piercing green eyes. They examined Murdoch closely as he played the game too.

'Yeah,' he said. 'We sorted it. So, which house you in then?'

Murdoch nodded behind him, unable to turn in case Anathassiou had come outside, standing in her driveway to look at them.

'The one that's never going to be finished, not in this weather.' He realised he was still using the Birmingham accent, didn't know whether to ditch it or to carry on. He nodded at the holdalls in Marco's hands. 'You off on holiday again?'

'Again?'

Marco's keen eyes were fixed on his, his wiry frame tense with the effort of the bags.

'Angie told me she travels a lot. You a relative?'

They had reached the Corolla and Murdoch stopped, one hand on the frame above the driver's door, a man unafraid of his car being noted. Marco walked around him and stopped where it would be difficult for him to open the door. What did a friendly neighbour do now? Tell the other man to fuck off? Marco saved him the bother. He looked over Murdoch's shoulder and raised his chin at someone down the street.

'Come and ask her yourself,' he said. 'You got a minute?'

Murdoch gave his best smile yet.

'It's not really the best time for me. I'll wind the window down and say a quick hello as I drive past. I'm curious to hear what happened with the police the other night.'

Marco thought about it, nodded and stepped out of his way, watching Murdoch get into the Corolla like they both knew who'd won. Looking slowly for nothing in the glovebox, Murdoch raised the brim of his cap just enough to get a view down the street. Anathassiou was outside her gate, a rectangular object awkward in her hands, wrapped in what looked like red material. Something in Murdoch knew it was the painting, just like he knew Davie's business card had tumbled around in the frame as Anathassiou had wrapped it. His view was blocked for a second by Marco jogging his tight frame and the two holdalls down the tarmac, shouting answers to his boss's rough questions. Murdoch started the Corolla and swung it into the street. The wasn't enough space to turn around in one go and, as he looked in his rear-view mirror and reversed into the three-point turn, he saw Marco swing round, drop the bags and start running towards him. Taking a deep breath, Murdoch changed gear again and drove slowly away, ignoring the surprisingly persistent sprinting of the man in his rear-view mirror and then, when he gradually put more distance between them, the fury of his yells.

Davie found the light switch easily enough, just inside the container doors. He had a little torch on his key ring: five bucks from the hardware store, the best money he'd ever spent. But Patterson heard him before he'd flicked the switch and started yelling from his bed, a new attempt at dry laughter in his voice.

'Very funny, Hatch, but I'm no more scared of you in the dark than I am in the light. Less, in fact, because I don't have to see your ugly face.'

The loud and croaking mockery was unnerving and Davie was grateful he'd let Hatch drive away before moving around himself. Back amongst the beds, the bare bulb lit the columns of dark material like a burnt-out forest. He made his way slowly towards Patterson's bed.

'Oh, he's sent a henchman!' Patterson was trying a fake laugh again. 'Get squeamish, did he? Hope you're not, mate, because he's made a right mess of that foot there.'

He moved the tortured foot and Davie saw parts of the second and fourth toes were missing, the wound from the latter still pumping confidently, the blood on the floor a small pool. The smell below the disinfectant was stronger here, a covered bucket further along the container. Patterson caught him looking at it.

'Don't like the shit? Well, the next lot's going to be in the bed, mate, I've had my visiting rights rescinded.'

Davie forced himself forward. He wanted to hold himself steady but couldn't bear to put his hand near Patterson's foot. He coughed his voice into confidence.

'I'm here to help you actually. My name is Davie Simms, I'm a private detective.'

Patterson pulled a sarcastic face. Handcuffed to a bed, dehydrated and sweating with pain, he made Davie feel small. There was a hard confidence in his brown eyes and his scornful mouth, a lack of fear Davie couldn't compete with.

'Oh, you're doing the old "*make them feel there's a chance and then rip it away*" trick! I know that one. I crumble and promise you everything if only you'll let me go.'

The last words came out weaker than the rest, as if he'd seen something in Davie's face.

'No,' said Davie. 'I mean, I really am. I've been following Hatch for days. I snuck in while you were talking and hid behind that curtain. I … we need to get out of here.'

On the metal drawers next to Patterson's bed was an open bottle of water. Davie stepped towards it and felt something under his foot. Stared at it for seconds before he realised it was the end of a toe. He gasped, turned and made it to the dark end of the container before the contents of his stomach filled his mouth. He spat them onto the floor, studying the small pile of clothes they splashed, anything to erase his memory. There was a ripped T-shirt with a sequinned logo, a pair of denim shorts, a gold high heel, all of them tiny. Returning to Patterson's bedside, carefully avoiding the toe on the ground, Davie picked up the bottle and put it to the man's lips.

'Sorry,' he said as Patterson drank. 'I'm not very good with blood. I just need some fresh air.'

It was a standard phrase, but Davie heard the words as if for the first time, looking around at the container walls searching for ventilation holes. Patterson gargled and coughed and Davie remembered what he was doing. The man in the bed rolled his eyes and gave him another sour look, but Davie could see there were cracks in the armour, his damaged face struggling to keep up the game. He stared at Davie almost hopefully, his lips twitching, then flicked back to cynical.

'A private detective?'

'Yes, I was hired to find you.'

'Really.'

Davie found one of his business cards and held it up to Patterson's face. 'I live in Montauban. We thought for a while you were dead, but, well … anyway, I'm here now. We've just got to find a way out.'

He forced himself to the bottom of the bed and started untying Patterson's undamaged foot, the red stumps of the other one hovering on the edge of his vision. In the end, he shut one eye, forcing the first knot until his fingers hurt. Behind him, gargling sobs exploded from Patterson as the man believed him at last, the whole bed shaking and pulling the knot from Davie's fingers. The smell of him grew stronger and Davie realised that, naked beneath his blue hospital gown, Patterson had already soiled himself. He blinked the knowledge of that away too, focusing on nothing but the rope, remembering his mum telling him to push knots not pull them, that was the secret. He tried to shut down his senses – the rich stink from the bed, the pain in his fingers, the sound of Patterson's crying – and to focus only on how to untie rope. But it was a while before the first knot began to slide undone, suddenly gone. There were another seven on each foot. Patterson had calmed by then, his body still again, his breathing something close to normal. Davie made him drink more water and Patterson looked at him with narrowed eyes.

'Maybe you should try the handcuffs? This one on the left's a bit looser. You got something you can pick it with?'

Davie patted his pockets uselessly.

'Really?' Patterson was annoyed. 'You're not a very good rescuer, are you? Just my luck to get the one with no means of actually rescuing me.'

In the drawers beside the bed, Davie found nothing but an elasticated bracelet, a broken watch and a hairclip with a plastic flower. He grabbed the hairclip and tried it in the lock of the handcuffs.

'So who the hell are you again?'

'My name is Davie Simms, I'm a private investigator. Your wife, Fran, hired me to find you.'

There was a jerk in the arm. Patterson was staring at him, his breath strangely shallow.

'My Frannie? How is she? Is she coping?' Patterson pulled against the handcuff so it slipped from Davie's grasp and clanked against the metal bed frame. 'Shit, does she know about Hatch?'

The last question was the most fevered, something like despair cracking his voice.

'She's fine.' Davie picked up the handcuff and started working with the pliant metal of the hairclip again. 'She's absolutely fine. She just misses you. And she hired me, so she obviously wants you back.'

Davie realised Patterson hadn't asked about that. He stood straight, walked around the bed and poured some more water into the man's mouth. He was suddenly cold and tired, wanted to curl up on one of the other beds and close his eyes for half an hour. Looking at the nearest one, he saw it too had a handcuff hanging from a corner. He walked down the row, studying the assorted clothes and shoes on the floor beneath the beds, the cuffs dangling from them like earrings. Studying the black material more closely, he saw it hung from rails between the beds. Drawn closed it would create rooms and a corridor.

'Is she eating enough?' Patterson's voice had softened.

Davie remembered what he was supposed to be doing, blinked at the hairpin in his hand and returned to Patterson's bed.

'What? Yeah, yeah, she's fine. What is this place? Were other people held in here with you?'

He knew the answer but wanted to hear Patterson confess to it.

'Whorehouse,' said Patterson proudly. It was a new voice again, a new face. A bloke at a barbie about to share too much. 'Designed for the mines and construction sites.'

Something clicked in the cuff that hadn't clicked before, the curve of metal holding Patterson's wrist shifting to a new angle. Davie wiggled the hairclip harder, almost hoping the softer metal would break. He could sense Patterson looking up at him.

'Let me guess, Mr Private Detective, you're too clean-cut for that kind of thing? Wouldn't want to get your hands dirty with a whore?'

Davie remembered the elastic bracelet on the floor, the size of the clothes.

'I'm going to check on the doors,' he said, walking towards the cardboard wall. 'It might be easier if I went and found help.'

'Aw, don't be like that, mate. Davie, is it? Just talking man to man.'

It was the sound of yet another new voice that made Davie stop and turn, a version of Patterson he'd not yet met. Surrounded by shadows and harsh white light, it was like being in a dream, characters appearing from nowhere and then gone again. Davie continued on to the container doors, Patterson's voice muted by the giant boxes. He took his time using the little torch again, trying not to think of the shipment Patterson had lost, but he found nothing. As soon as he was back amongst the beds, Patterson started talking again.

'Don't take it the wrong way, mate. It's just I like to be in charge, it's what I'm used to.'

Davie started checking the metal drawers beside each bedframe, talking to them, not wanting to look at Patterson or the stained mattresses.

'I'd have thought Hatch had taught you something about that. He left you without access to food or water.'

'Hatch.' Patterson gave the word his first genuine laugh. 'He's pathetic. Here's me, chained to a bed, and I can control his every move. Were you here when I made him throw down the pliers? It's like pulling the strings on a puppet.'

'A puppet that's going to kill you?'

'Just as long as he's a puppet.'

Davie said nothing, the only noise, the rasping of the drawers. When he reached the bed next to Patterson's, he saw the man was studying him.

'You don't approve, Mr Detective?'

Davie shrugged his shoulders. 'Nothing to do with me. I just want my reward money for bringing you home.'

'You think you're better than blokes who deal with whores.'

'Not at all.' Davie was determined not to let his feelings show. 'Prostitution is a vital part of society.'

In these surroundings the words were wrong, a contribution to the misery. He wondered if he shouldn't leave Patterson here – whether torture or starving to death were no more than the man deserved. It amazed him to think there had been a time so recently that he'd been racing to get Patterson a life-saving injection. Slamming the drawer shut and giving the man a wide arc, Davie moved on to the next bed. Patterson called after him.

'Well put, Mr Detective! Prostitution's a vital service all right. Fucking's a part of a man's nature, like eating and drinking and shitting. True the world over, rich and poor alike.'

'Even up at Huntingdon's, apparently.'

Patterson had been projecting his voice, like a man on a podium in front of an adoring audience, and he seemed annoyed at being interrupted. He corrected Davie hurriedly in something close to whisper.

'What, that stuck-up place? No, no – that's just a little front. Win-win that one. They get cheapos to clean the shitters, I get a few girls writing home and telling their family everything's fine. That way no one comes sniffing after me. Anyway, where was I? Oh, yeah.' He raised his voice again, a man who'd forgotten he was handcuffed to a bed. 'Prostitution's a vital part of society all right. Wives don't let you in 'em, not once they've got a ring on their finger. The fucking courts guarantee them half of what you own, why would they bother? They've got it and we want it so, so it's only natural we've got to pay for it. No wonder, I make so much money.'

Davie looked up. Patterson was looking at him eagerly, clearly expecting a reaction.

'I think you'll find,' said Davie through gritted teeth, 'that women like sex when they can decide …'

'Women like sex when they're whores! Even then, they give and take it when they feel like it. Most men are pathetic. They spend their whole lives pretending to be something better than what they really are, but at the end of the day, we're all animals, mate, all of us. Me and my little import business, even Hatch, we're more honest than the lot of them.'

Davie shook his head and moved on to the last set of drawers. The stench of urine was strongest here and he was afraid to look beyond it, to see what was in the shadows. He tugged the top drawer open, keen to drown out Patterson's voice, and saw a small ring with two keys slide to the front. He'd spent enough time staring at Patterson's handcuffs to know what they were for. He turned and saw the man was still looking at him.

'What is it? What's in there?'

'Nothing. Listen, Scott, we need a Plan B. What are we going to do if Hatch comes back and I haven't got you off that bed?'

'You got a weapon? No, of course, you haven't, bloody useless. Hatch has, he carries a little automatic everywhere he goes, matches his little shoes and his little fucking dick. He doesn't mind using it either.' Patterson banged the back of his head against the bed frame, the handcuffs rattling. 'Fuck! It's going to take two of us to overpower him. He looks fat but he's like a Mallee bull. Just come and get me off this bed.'

Davie turned so his body blocked Patterson's view and, returning to the bed with only the hairpin visible in his hand, started worrying the lock again. A minute later, when Patterson closed his eyes, he used the key on it, immediately pulling it free again and only then letting the cuff fall open. Patterson snapped his head round, eyes wide and excited, another new face for the world. Swinging his newly free hand to his mouth, he licked the wounds around his wrist, his tongue wild around the scratches. Davie looked away. Walking to a nearby bed, he grabbed its dirty yellow sheet and threw it over Patterson's injured foot. The man in the bed jolted, pain twisting his voice.

'Fuck. Be careful, won't you?'

Davie went to work on the ropes around the other foot again. He could feel the tiny keys in his trouser pocket, thought he could hear them jingling there and wondered if Patterson would notice the noise too. His fingers slipped and he heard Patterson swear. Looking round, he found the man had yet another face on.

'What?'

Patterson raised his free hand to silence him and then Davie heard it too. A car approaching, the splashing of tyres in puddles, then the engine as it came closer to the container. Davie ran around the foot of the bed, one hand in his pocket to grab the keys. Before he had either of them in the locked cuff, Patterson had reached across himself to grab Davie by the belt of his trousers.

'Don't leave me here,' he croaked. 'Don't leave me!'

A car door slammed.

'I'm going to uncuff you,' Davie whispered quickly. 'I'll hide, then we'll take him together.'

'Don't go!' Patterson was pulling at his belt, not listening. 'I need medication. I can't—'

He was interrupted by the rattle of chains against the container door, then the slow creak of the locking mechanism. Davie gave up on the handcuff and pulled away from the man in the bed, but he couldn't get him to loosen his grip. Patterson's eyes were furious now, his words accompanied by phlegm.

'You were hired to rescue me, so rescue me! Don't leave me here, you cunt!'

The full weight of his body pulled Davie's waistband towards the bed, releasing only when Davies stumbled and put out a hand against Patterson's injured foot. Patterson grunted and turned white, his eyes fluttering and then closing, small groans from deep in his throat. Prising Patterson's hand loose from his waist band, Davie righted himself, staring around the container desperately, choosing the best curtain to hide behind. But all he saw was the fat frame of Terry Hatch filling the gap in the cardboard wall, a confused expression on his pudgy face as he reached into his jacket and produced a gleaming gun.

7.

There were three routes the Range Rover could take from Werona Parade. Turn around and go back the way it had come, continue on and take the next left, or drive to the end of the street and turn left there like

319

Murdoch had done. The first of these options seemed the least likely. Anathassiou and Marco had been in a hurry, they wouldn't waste time turning in a narrow street. So, once he was happy they weren't coming after him – *Marco, you've gone and scared the neighbours again* – Murdoch doubled back. He drove to Harbour Road, the street parallel to Werona, and parked halfway between the two most likely routes.

In the days when Davie had been spending too much money, he'd bought himself a fancy new rain jacket, a precious thing he hardly ever wore. He'd given his old one, a dark green shell, fusty with mildew, to Murdoch. Now Murdoch put it on, pulling up the hood more for disguise than shelter from the weakening rain. All he had to do was stand here, staring up at one street, then down to the next, twitching back and forth like a giant green bird until the white Range Rover appeared. Any coppers stopping to ask what he was up to wouldn't even have to get out their car.

The Range Rover appeared after fifteen minutes on the same road Murdoch had taken. Head down, as if against the rain, he turned and walked slowly towards it, knees wide apart and limping. Even if they noticed him, they'd see a different man, and he didn't need to glance up to see which way they turned; the Range Rover's doctored engine passed him along Harbour Road, his first bit of luck all day. Unless, of course, the people inside noticed the grey Corolla they passed. Marco had chased him long enough to make a note of its plates, might even be on the lookout for it, while Anathassiou drove. But Murdoch had pulled both tyres onto the kerb and parked close to the car behind; even if they noticed a grey Corolla, they'd have to stop to check it was the same car. But the Range Rover didn't stop. It just growled away through the rain and the slowly building traffic. When it was two hundred yards further down the road, Murdoch pulled out after it.

The ideal in traffic, he reckoned, was an average of six cars back. That way you could move up and down the line as others joined and left without the driver up front catching on. But that was on a clear day following a normal car, not a souped-up Range Rover faster than everything else on the road, visibility half of what it should be. As the rain fell doggedly, most vehicles around him with their headlights on,

Murdoch reduced his average to four. He hadn't even seen if the painting had been loaded into the Range Rover and, he realised now, he had no idea what to do if he didn't get the business card back. Get Davie to shut the office and change his name? Confess everything to Natalie and see her walk away? He felt a sudden need to hear her voice, worried for a second, he really meant Amanda's, and told himself to concentrate and calm the fuck down. It didn't matter that his shoulders were concrete, the tension in his neck steering the car, he just had to keep his eyes on the Range Rover and stop Marco and Anathassiou from spotting him.

Two roundabouts were enough to convince him they weren't heading for the freeway and he remembered at last to breathe. He hated this, hated it mattering so much. They never told you about this when they were tempting you in. It was all naughty excitement and 'easy pickings', never the pain between your eyebrows and your throat closing on every breath. Murdoch thought again of what Anathassiou would do to Davie, slammed the steering wheel and cursed Velis's name. The car in front of him braked unexpectedly and he nearly went into the back of it, so close, the other car's brake lights disappeared. *Breathe.* He turned on the radio and focused on the road, blinking past the wipers and the endless rain.

Forty minutes they drove, long enough for Murdoch to start smelling himself and make promises to a god who was unreliable at best. Then they were in Crosley, the streets overlooking Broadwater crowding around them. Murdoch had no choice but to keep just one car between him and the Range Rover far ahead. When it indicated, then turned uphill, he accelerated, parked illegally just before the corner and ran the last few metres on foot. It was his second bit of luck for the day. The Range Rover had stopped less than a hundred metres up the steep side street. As he watched, it turned under one of the tall buildings built to look over the inlet, the pink brick blocks on thick white pillars the locals called 'The Schoolgirls'. Murdoch forced himself back to the Toyota, parking it far enough away to keep the odds on his side.

The rain had almost stopped, the weather refusing to make up its mind, but he kept his hood up and tight as he walked back to the steep street, peeking out only to check directions. There was a siren in the distant traffic, the urban echo of rain, and he took it as a warning. Letting

Marco see him in Green Bay was only forgivable if he learned from the mistake. He'd give the building a single glance on his first walk past and only approach when the coast was clear. Stomping up the hill on the far side of the road, a man angry to be in the rain, he kept his head down and almost collided with a woman coming down the other way. It was Anathassiou, black hair flat on her head, a garish bomber jacket zipped to her chin. In the rain, her tan looked out of place. Murdoch flinched, then carried on without a word.

'Simmo!'

It took him two more steps to realise she meant him. She knew, he was sure. She'd recognised him in the street at Green Bay and let herself and Marco be followed here. He nearly ran, blind fear would give him speed, but forced himself to turn, to confirm Anathassiou was alone. Across the road, in the shadows beyond the white pillars, the Range Rover was parked at an open garage, someone moving around in its orange light.

'It is you!' Anathassiou took a step forward and pumped his hand. 'What you doing around here?'

For seconds Murdoch was lost for words, struggling to focus on the woman in front of him, instead of wondering where the hell Marco was. Anathassiou misread his confusion.

'Angie?' she said. 'You came to my place in Green Bay for cards with Emre Velis?'

'Oh, yeah.' Murdoch had no choice but to play along. If she thought that he thought that she thought … 'Sorry, Angie, love. Didn't recognise you out of context, know what I mean? What you doing in this neck of the woods?'

He was piling on the 'Landan' accent, anything to separate him from any description Marco might have given. Twisting awkwardly, he hid his face from the other side of the road, struggling to turn his back on what might be already approaching.

'Got some business here. Isn't it a shithole?' Anathassiou turned up her satin collar like it could keep out more than the rain. 'What about you?'

'Come to see a girl I know what lives here.'

'Oh. Well, excusez my French, nothing personal. Listen, I gotta go, but do me a favour, I wasn't here. Not now, not ever, you got it?'

'Me neither,' said Murdoch. 'Not today.'

There was a second of eye-contact, a tiny understanding, and Murdoch remembered what it was like to be so far in you could ask a man to forget he'd seen you and not think he might find it strange. He put his head down and carried on up the hill. This is when Marco would take him. Maybe he was up ahead, maybe it was someone else in the garage. At the top of the street, his torso bathed in sweat, he turned onto the path to the last block of flats and thought, no, this was when they'd do it. But he was alone, the steep street below him empty, nothing to look at but the greyness of Broadwater, half of that lost in the rain. He walked on until the pink brick porch around the block's front door hid him from view. He waited there, five minutes, ten, the shakes coming with the understanding that he'd had his third stroke of luck. Eventually an engine growled down the hill. Leaning out, he saw the Range Rover pull onto the street. At the bottom corner, where he'd been tempted to leave the Toyota, it stopped to pick up Anathassiou, a mobile phone pinned to her ear. Then it turned and roared out of sight.

How much do you recognise a man from a description? Enough for the suspect neighbour in a baseball cap to be the same guy you met at cards two weeks ago? What about when they both reappear on the same day? Both Poms. Squatting in front of the locked garage, his rucksack retrieved from the Corolla, Murdoch tried again and again to focus. To forget his worries and concentrate on opening the industrial padlock that held the garage's roller door to a bar cemented in the ground. There were situations where nerves could help – running fast, hitting hard – but this wasn't one of them. The padlock wasn't enough security for a twenty-million-dollar painting, but it wasn't child's play either. He had to return to the Corolla, grateful at least he'd stocked it well, and return with smaller tools. The alternative would be bigger ones, a sledgehammer to smash the lock from the bar, but what was he supposed to do if someone saw him? Pretend he was practising his golf swing?

On his third trip to the Corolla he brought the car back with him, parking it so he was invisible to the street, hunched in a squat over the padlock. If anyone came from the back of the building he could be doing his shoelaces, any bullshit story. He checked his watch and bent again, his nostrils full of his armpits. Stayed like that for twenty minutes, feeling his way, until the mechanism clicked and gave way in his hands.

It was like every other garage in the world, ownership's last purgatory before the junkyard, maybe this one tidier than most. At the top of its back wall, every second brick was missing so that the space remained dimly lit even after Murdoch had rumbled the roller door down again. Blinking in the half-light, he had a patchwork view of tyres and the bottom of a car that was parked beneath the next block up the hill. Beside him raw wooden shelves ran the length of the garage, the kind of thing you bought from Ikea knowing no one would ever see them. They were empty but for some plastic boxes and, on the bottom shelf, a full set of dumb-bells, a dozen dusty sizes or more, arranged in pairs along the wood, like their only purpose was to weigh the shelves down. Near the opposite wall was an exercise bike with its saddle missing, behind that a yellowed mosquito screen slashed across the middle. The two holdalls Marco had carried were in the middle of the floor, on top of them the red-wrapped rectangle Anathassiou herself had carried. The wrapping was paper, not material, and Murdoch tore at it like a kid at Christmas time, worrying it wasn't going to be the painting until Van Gogh's *Congregation* lay in his hands – Davie's business card flipped up and waving in the foreground. There was no way of knowing if Anathassiou had seen it or not, not until Davie's body was found. Murdoch blinked the idea away, stood and reached for his rucksack. This time, he'd brought a scalpel.

Unworried by noise, the task of ripping the hardwood from the back of the frame took seconds. Cutting out the picture took longer, even if he gave it less care than the first time around, and, when at last he picked out Davie's business card, it felt like a triumph. He ripped the thing into tiny pieces, swearing as he distributed them between his pockets and his rucksack, reminding himself it was why he was here. Not because of anything a dirty crook thought was valuable.

When he'd broken into Anathassiou's house, he'd brought a thick cardboard tube with him, thinking he'd use that to carry the painting home. So maybe he was lucky he'd hadn't got it that day after all, cracking the thick oils as he rolled the canvas. Today he had a flat plastic carrier, what the man in the shop had called a portfolio case. Even in that the painting crunched slightly, every crumb of colour a hundred dollars. Noticing the two holdalls again, Murdoch bent and unzipped them. Seeing what they held, he squatted down to rummage inside and confirm the unlikely amount of cash, nothing but green hundreds. He was zipping the second bag closed again, unsure whether to take them or not, when the familiar growl of a souped-up Range Rover sounded beyond the garage door. It grew loud quickly, louder still and then suddenly silent as it pulled up outside the garage.

Murdoch had read on the internet once why things went into slow motion in times of stress. Something about how the brain records stuff, or maybe how the eye sees. He thought of this now, not how to survive, as the walls around him squeezed the air from the garage. He forced himself towards the shelves, then, changing his mind, grabbed his rucksack and tore at its insides until he found his balaclava. He was reaching for the shelves again when the roller door roared open. Marco was standing a metre away, out of the way of any potential attack. His green eyes were panicked, his face white, the man who'd forgotten to put the lock on or arrived too late to do anything about it. Seeing someone was still inside the garage, he immediately ran forward and pulled open the passenger door of the Range Rover, reaching inside towards the glovebox. Murdoch ran too, throwing himself against the car door, rewarded with a pained exhalation from Marco, who twisted and elbowed back hard. Murdoch hadn't thought the passenger window might be open and the flash of pain across his face confused him. He used the bonnet of the car to hold himself upright and found it was his turn to be smashed by the door as Marco shoved it open with both hands. Stumbling backwards until his spine and skull hit the corner of the garage wall, he blinked and saw Marco was at the glovebox again, struggling with it and swearing. Again, Murdoch ran at the door, ignoring the pain pulsing through his head and shoulders, his imperfect vision. Using his whole body, he slammed the car door shut on nothing. Marco had pulled his legs fully inside and was tugging at the glovebox again. Murdoch leaned back and put a side kick through the open window, but Marco rolled and took it, the kick worse than useless as Murdoch's unpractised hamstrings screamed with the effort. As he pulled his kicking leg back and turned to run, he felt something in his standing leg tear, the pain weaker than the fear spurring him on. Would Marco abandon the millions in the garage to chase down a man the street? The answer was so heavy and solid that for a second Murdoch lost consciousness, coming to with his face against the tarmac, his entire body focused on getting air into his lungs. A knee in the ribs didn't help. He tried to roll away from the weight on his back, the street reeling near the top of his vision, white pillars hanging from the car park towards the building far below, but there was another knee into his side and he knew he would never take breath for granted again. He was drowning on dry land, the balaclava a tenth of its previous size, suckered to his head and clinging at his neck, the pain in his back and sides so complete that it weighed him down rather than helping him to his feet. He felt himself turned and found he was looking up at Marco's sharp features, the thin nose and jagged cheekbones red with the effort of dragging him towards the garage. Murdoch punched upwards, but his fist was irrelevant in the air between them as they continued across the tarmac, Marco pulling him slowly to death. Murdoch reached for his own throat instead and found nothing there, no belt or noose tight beyond hope, just the collar of his jumper pulled against his Adam's apple. He just needed to breathe and think. Breathe and be calm. But before he had time, Marco dumped him heavily, his head making contact with the concrete floor of the garage, the balaclava no protection at all. The wooden shelves to his right swam in the patchwork light from the back wall, the parallel lines hypnotic until they darkened under the rumble of the roller door. A sharp kick into his thigh brought him back to his senses and he saw Marco above him, a dimly lit smile creasing his face. He spat and Murdoch felt the gob land on his lips. With it came a strange settling, something like acceptance. Or maybe the solid strength of hatred rather than the compromised angles of fear. Nothing that allowed him to push himself more than halfway to seated. Marco reached down to grab at his head and Murdoch closed his eyes against the pain of having it banged against the concrete floor. Then, when Marco grabbed only the balaclava, Murdoch pushed himself further upright, fully seated now, one hand reached to the shelves, like it would do him any good to steady himself. Above him, Marco stared with the black wool limp in his hand, looking like he'd pulled Murdoch's face off, horrified and delighted by what he'd found beneath.

'I knew it,' Marco said. 'I don't fucking believe it.'

With no wool over his ears, every noise was amplified to Murdoch. The exertion from his own lungs as he swung the dumb-bell from the shelf; the cracks and pops of Marco's right knee as it exploded towards the left; the restrained chords of Marco's yell and the moist crack of his head meeting the floor. Murdoch rolled himself over, ignoring how his head swam, and crawled forwards to swing again, looking away at the last second so he could remember the furious expression of Marco's pain and not the inside of the man's skull.

Confusion was Davie's only constant. He was awake, then waking up, deep in nightmares then slipping into unconsciousness. He had been sucked through the looking glass, Patterson's turn to move around the room, while he was crucified on the bed. Except Patterson was tied up too, looming in and out of view to his right as someone else walked around. Strange creatures rushed in from the darkness, leaping forwards to bite or slap until the slaps were real and he was awake again, the pain from his leg so intense it was difficult to know where it ended and began. The nightmarish creatures focused on his wound, their fangs in the flesh of his thigh, pulling it open until the bed jolted across the floor. But, opening his eyes, the bed hadn't moved at all. It stood solidly next to Patterson's, Davie's wrists pinched to its corners, Hatch's face closing in.

In his mind, there was an image of Hatch pointing the gun at him as he vaulted across the beds, racing for the gap in the cardboard wall. Then the air had exploded and Davie was on the floor, vaguely aware he couldn't stand. He had no memory of being moved or restrained. Between the desperate need for escape and the waking horror of the handcuffs, only the ringing in his ears stayed with him, shadows in the corners howling. He could see a black hole in his leg, the fabric of his jeans curved into his flesh, and smell his own vomit on his chest. The smell of Hatch's breath was worse.

'I said, who the fuck are you?'

Davie began to tell him again and felt the world crack apart as Hatch slapped him angrily on the thigh. After that, all was black for a while, too dark even for nightmares. '*My name is Davie Simms,*' he could hear his own voice, or at least the intention to talk. '*I'm a private detective. Fran Patterson hired me.*' Hatch slapped his face, the stinging in his cheek a blessed release.

'How did you find me?' His voice had a twist of fear to it, a feverish urgency. 'How did you fucking find me?'

Davie heard himself babbling, his words struggling past each other, anything to keep the monster away from his leg. He had followed him home, seen him drive down here, snuck in while the door was open. But he had no idea if truth was what the man wanted. Hatch's face was close again, dark and angry, blemishes and veins competing in ugliness against the twisted mouth.

'I mean, how'd you know to look for me? How did you get my name?'

In the corner of his eye, Davie caught the look on Patterson's face. He was curious to know the answer too. Davie stared at him until Hatch's hand appeared and he closed his eyes against a slap that didn't come. Instead, he felt his cheeks clamped between fingers and a thumb, his head pulled away from Patterson.

'How did you get my name?'

'What?'

Now the slap came. Cuffed awkwardly he was unable to let his head roll and he felt something in his neck give way, pain swallowed down his back to spark and burn with the rest. Davie gasped and, seeing Hatch looking at his leg, said, 'Wait, wait.' Five … Giving Bill's name wasn't an option. Four … He couldn't mention Anita Patel. Three … He knew he was going to die in here so what was the point? Two …

'Patterson's desk.' The words came out of his mouth before he knew he was going to say them. 'The pad on top of his desk. Your name was written on there with a phone number.'

Davie heard himself crying. Then, for a while, he was alone in the open ocean, giving into its strength with grace. All he needed to do was wait and the pain of drowning would pass; it was the way he'd always wanted to go. But even here, Hatch and Patterson were with him. And Patterson was laughing, of course. Not his dry and desperate croak, but a full-throated cackle, the movement of his body coming into view through the murky depths until Hatch turned and drove a fist into the middle of his bed. A wave broke, like a man exhaling in pain, Patterson suddenly clear with spittle on his chin, the colour drained from face, his breath in short sharp gasps. Hatch was the shark, curving into the half-distance, then suddenly close again, unsure who to bite first. Beds stretched in each direction, Wendy Skellen chained to one, Anita Patel to another. At others still, were faceless women, too many to count, all of them struggling or crying until, suddenly, Davie was awake again. In the bed beside him, Patterson was at a new angle, trying to sit himself up, and wearing a new mask. There was a new alertness about him, his eyes fixed on the cardboard wall at the far end of the container. Then he disappeared from view behind Terry Hatch's belly, chest and face.

'You work alone?'

With the bare bulb behind him, Hatch wore a small white halo, an angel of this confusing hell. Davie closed his eyes: he had to talk, but he mustn't – opened them and saw Hatch reaching his fist towards his wound.

'Hands in the air.'

It was death: a woman's voice loud and harsh, but fair. Except Hatch heard it too, confusion pulling at his features as he swung around, wobbling the mattress close to Davie's leg. If pain came this time, Davie didn't notice. He was definitely still in the container, the harsh light horribly real, Hatch beside him staring over Patterson's bed towards the cardboard wall. But Natalie was there too, and, behind her, a man in a police uniform pointing a gun, both of them approaching cautiously. Then Bill appeared behind another policeman, a crutch under one armpit, his left eye closed by purple swelling. Davie wanted to be in the ocean again, alone with the waves, not in this twisted knot of people. But opening his eyes, they were all still there, silent as they stared at each other, even Patterson mute for once. Then Hatch made a fast movement and again the container exploded in noise. He was awake, Davie realised, this was real, the sounds and colour of it filling him with hope until Hatch tumbled backwards and fell across his legs so that again he was sucked into the dark well of pain.

Part 3: May

8.

By now the staff were wary of Murdoch. On previous visits, he'd learned you can't lie to nurses about injuries and the nurses had learned not to tease him for the truth. Today, as he approached their work station with a start-again smile, the younger of the two on the afternoon shift – olive-skinned with spiky dark hair – blushed and turned her back on him to concentrate on an overbright monitor. Her older colleague, Sigourney Weaver in a tight uniform, just stared until it was Murdoch's turn to look away. In doing so, he noticed the clock on the wall behind her. He swore, apologised for swearing, swore again and hobbled along the corridor, his crutch uneven on the tiles as he struggled with the newspapers under his arm and his still-closed left eye making navigation difficult.

Davie was in a two-bed room, the other bed empty, its sheets and blankets so tightly tucked it was difficult to believe anyone would get in there again. It wasn't a bad room as hospital rooms went. No flowers or pictures, but no rows of old men coughing their guts out either. There were two windows, matching oblongs opposite each other, one looking into the corridor, the other filled by cloudless sky. Murdoch found Davie sitting up, staring out at the empty blue, one hand picking at the tube in his nose, the other on the blanket holding his phone. He sighed when he saw Murdoch, his face creased around a problem.

'I've been trying to work out what makes hospitals so depressing. So … third world, do you know what I mean? This room's not that bad. It's clean, it's nice and quiet now they've kept the journos away, but it's still … horrible.'

Murdoch crutched his way over to the scratched green wing chair that stood between the beds, collapsed into it and rubbed his armpit hard. Davie barely missed a beat.

'And I've decided it's everything. The curtains, the smell, the lack of privacy, this horrible gown, the fake cheeriness. I never liked hospitals before, but, now, everything reminds me of the container. Which is good, I suppose – exposure therapy, you know. But sometimes when I wake up in the night, I worry I'm still there.'

Murdoch threw the papers onto the bed and sneaked a look at his watch. Davie was still sleeping a lot, maybe he'd drift off. Davie nodded at the newspapers, unsure if they were friend or foe.

'What have you brought them in for?'

'To show you, me old china, the headlines about Davie Simms, superstar. You did it, mate, congratulations! Phone'll be ringing off the hook.'

But Davie was looking out the window again.

'You know, Bill, I always wondered how people who were tortured ever got over it. How they even left the house, you know? But for some reason, I think I'll be fine. I actually feel all right.'

Murdoch didn't tell Davie it was because his experience of torture was limited to one end of the scale. Instead, he said it was too early to know how he'd feel; all sorts of stuff might still come up. In the meantime, he should have a squiz at the papers – see all the nice names they'd called Davie Wonder and what bits they'd manage to get right.

'C'mon, mate, you've deserved this—'

But Davie spoke over him, today of all days opening up about what had happened in the container. The clothes on the floor, the smell. Murdoch sat back to listen, his watch retreating under his cuff, like it was afraid to tell him the time. He didn't think he'd ever been so tired.

'It was like Patterson was proud of it,' Davie was saying. '*Is* proud of it.'

'He's locked up, mate. Another man in prison with HIV, no big news there, although I don't fancy his chances of staying on a fancy ARV trial. Anyway, point is, him and Hatch both are inside and they will be for a very long time.'

'Yes, I know. But Guy tells me there's a thing called the McNaughton Rules and I think Patterson might try and use them to be sent to a mental institution and not go to prison at all. Or maybe his wife or his lawyers will – the man is clearly insane. He wasn't ashamed of any of it, you know. Not even about those poor women who died. It's as if he honestly thinks that treating women badly is somehow … I don't know … the right thing to do and it's the rest of us who are denying how the world should be. But I'm not sure if that makes him nuts or just evil. I've never really believed in evil before, but now … And how did you find me, Bill?'

Murdoch opened his eyes. 'You what?'

'How did you know where I was? I mean, what if you hadn't come just then? He'd have killed me, you know that.'

'Davie, do you remember what that counsellor lady said? She said what you've got to keep remembering is that we did come just then. We walked in and you're safe and Hatch and Patterson are going down.'

'But how? How did you find me?'

Murdoch rubbed his scalp. The conversation could only go one way.

'Well, you told me about where you'd seen Hatch, remember? That curve of road, opposite the only turn-off. You even left my car up there. I bleeding well knew you'd break in.'

Davie sighed and looked away and Murdoch thought maybe he'd got away with it. He checked his watch and shifted forward to the front of the wing chair.

'Listen, Davie, I can't hang about. I've got an appointment …'

'But where *were* you? If you knew I was going to break in, and you knew what might happen, where were you? Why didn't you come and help me?'

'I did. We just went through that. I turned up in the nick of time, remember?'

'Before that!'

Davie let go of his phone and used the steel supports either side of the bed to pull himself upright, pain marking his face and making Murdoch look away.

'Where were you, Bill, that was so bloody important?'

Murdoch struggled to his feet and swore as the crutch clattered noisily to the floor. Without looking at Davie, he used the back of the armchair, the empty bed, the wall to get him across the room. Closing the door to the corridor, he turned and leaned against it out of breath.

'I bleeding well told you not to break in,' he said. 'I told you whatever you do, don't go in there.'

'So why have you been looking so guilty ever since? Because you knew I would! You knew I couldn't stop myself even if I wanted to. We don't have a lot in common, Bill, but we're both bloody-minded, that's just how we are. So where were you?'

Murdoch heaved himself back across the room until he was sitting on the foot of Davie's bed. When he spoke it was as quietly as he knew how, the words repellent to him.

'Last week I took something from someone very nasty. Hatch and Patterson are amateurs compared to this one, Davie. A big-shot gangster, well-connected. Anyway, I took something of … theirs, but I left one of your business cards behind by mistake. It fell out of my wallet. That day, when you called and I knew you was going down there, I was in the process of getting it back. That's what happened to my face and my leg, thanks for asking.'

Neither of them spoke for a minute or more, nothing to hear but the ticking of the little plastic clock on the drawers beside Davie's bed. When Murdoch looked up, Davie was staring at him.

'I thought you got injured when you were breaking into the container,' he said. 'I didn't think … I didn't think you did that kind of thing any more. You know, criminal stuff or—'

'Yeah, well, you and me both, mate. And just for the record, I don't. It was a one-off mistake. Do us a favour, though, don't tell Nat, eh?'

Davie was back again, his laugh filling the quiet room.

'Crikey, Bill, of course, I won't! Think I'm stupid or something?

'Well, you don't look too clever right now.'

'Don't look so crash-hot yourself.'

They smiled at each other until Murdoch staggered quickly to his feet, afraid Davie was about to say something soppy. He hopped towards the wing chair and reached down for the fallen crutch.

'Well, then,' he wheezed. 'I've got this appointment, see—'

'Oh no.'

Davie was staring at the window looking out onto the corridor, pain in his face again. 'Talking about dysfunctional relationships. Bill, don't leave me with them. Just stick with me through this and all is forgiven.'

'Here he is! Cooee, brave soldier.'

Penny Simms's perfume was first through the door, the woman herself following fast behind to plant a kiss on Davie's cheek. John

Simms followed in a slow march, uneasy about where to stand. He decided on the foot of the bed, grabbing at the records that hung there and squinting at them critically.

'So much for overcrowded hospitals,' he said, nodding at the other bed in the room. 'Waste of my taxes.'

'Oh, hush now.' Davie's mother had sat herself in the green wing chair and was fussing with the lap of her dress. 'You were in a room by yourself when you had your tonsils out.'

'That was a private hospital. Not like this place.'

John Simms took his time over the last word, a man who'd promised to behave but didn't know how. Murdoch steadied himself with one hand on the back of the wing chair, shifting his weight awkwardly from one foot to the other, rubbing his bad leg heavily.

'Nice to see you both,' he said.

Penny Simms simpered up from the comfort of the chair, but her husband coughed disapprovingly.

'I see you've been in the wars too,' he said. 'I bet detectiving doesn't feel so clever now, does it?'

'Now, John …'

'Did you not see the papers, then?' Murdoch stepped awkwardly to the bed and picked up *The Australian*. 'I thought a bloke like you would read this one every day.'

John Simms accepted the comment like it was a compliment but refused to take the newspaper. 'I do, actually. And, yes, I did.' He turned back to Davie, an attempt to salvage family business. 'But enough is enough, son, just look at you. This nonsense has got to stop. I'll help you get a job if that's what you need.'

Murdoch snorted, trying to persuade himself that was enough. But the part of him that might have accepted that was buried beneath pain and exhaustion. What the hell.

'Are you having a laugh?!' he shouted. 'Jesus Christ, mate, your son is on the front page of every newspaper in the bleeding country. They're all calling him a hero. One of 'em's suggesting a medal or something and it's still not good enough?'

'I'm sorry, but—'

'It's not me you should be saying sorry to, it's Davie there. The only reason he does all this stupid stuff is to try and impress you. And all you've ever done is tell him he's not good enough. But when were you ever called a hero, eh? When did you ever do anything to help anyone but yourself, you miserable ...'

'Bill!'

Davie was pulling himself seated again, but Murdoch ignored him, the forefinger of his free hand jabbing the air between him and John Simms.

'You're a twat, do you know that, mate? A self-important twat. You think you're shit-hot just because you made a load of money. You've got your big ugly house and too much land – what you're happy to get cleared for less than minimum wage by people who struggle to feed themselves – and you think that makes you something. But do you know what, mate? It don't make you nothing. You're a crap father. You think you're a big success with your big bleeding business and being busy all the time, but you see him? Davie does what he wants. He's free and you can't stand it, can you? Cos you're jealous. I reckon, you're jealous that everyone respects him and no one will ever really respect you. Not even your own kids!'

'Bill! What the hell?' Davie's hands were on the steel supports again, his face the same red as his father's. 'Who do you think you are?'

'C'mon, Davie, you know it's true.'

'You need to go, Bill.'

'You what? But—'

'Get out!'

In the corridor, Murdoch found Jane Simms leaning against the doorframe. She was in a sensible skirt and matching jacket, looking at him the way he'd wanted her to look the previous time they'd met.

'Well done,' she said, 'someone had to say it.'

'Yeah. You did. You're the only one what he listens to, so you should try sticking up for your brother occasionally. But you never will. What you worried about, the inheritance?'

She laughed at that and put a hand on his forearm, but Murdoch turned suddenly and stomped away, desperate to be somewhere else.

9

The traffic lights that had allowed Murdoch and Davie to follow Hatch across Crosley were working their magic again, the Mercedes revving north in tiny spurts of speed. Even on the highway, Murdoch was frustrated – dawdlers in the right-hand lane, traffic jams building and dwindling for no apparent reason. It wasn't until the meandering road towards the state forest that he could really put his foot down. He sped between open fields and sprawling properties, telegraph poles and two bar fences, the road barely wider than the car. Knuckles white on the steering wheel, he told himself he was late and wanted this over and done with. Told himself Davie didn't deserve his help, the muppet only had himself to blame.

Beside Murdoch, on the passenger seat, his phone jangled and he turned his head tight so his open eye could see it. Natalie's face was flashing on the screen – an image of her at the waterfall. Back on the road, a lump in the asphalt appeared, growing so quickly that, before he knew it, Murdoch was on a tiny bridge over a creek. Then he was flying, all four wheels of the Merc clear of the tarmac. The weightlessness of the fall – the complete lack of control over steering, speed, his own voice – brought him back to his senses. He landed with a thump and braked too hard, his tyres screaming. After a small waver, the car straightened, the only harm a skid mark in the middle of nowhere. Looking around to see who might have heard, Murdoch spotted away to his right two men on the veranda of a flat farmhouse, hands shielding their eyes as they squinted towards him. He gave them two fingers, pushed on another kilometre and heard the phone beside him complaining again. It stopped more quickly this time, its noise replaced by a message: *Pick up. Immediately!*

But, of course, the bush was thick around him now, no space beside the road for him to park. Murdoch continued on for five minutes, ten, fifteen, none of them improving his mood. At the turn-off into the state forest proper, he gave up and parked in the middle of an unsealed track. Its surface had recently been creviced by streaming water, but all that lay there now was yellow dust. Murdoch opened his window and yelled at the top of his lungs. It didn't make him feel any better, so he yelled again. Then, noticing the quiet, he tried listening instead. To the bellbirds chipping at the silence, to the eucalypts rustling like rushing water, to the nothing behind it all. It never failed to amaze him how quickly you could find wilderness in Australia. All this life going on regardless, you'd think it would give you perspective. Natalie answered on the first ring.

'Where are you, Bill?'

'People used to ask "*How are you?*" Now it's always "Where are you?" You ever noticed that?'

She asked him how he was and he told her he was fine. Told her what had happened in the hospital and she said yes, she knew. She'd arrived a few minutes after he'd left and had had to pick up the pieces, thank you very much. What the hell had he been thinking? Murdoch took a deep breath.

'In all honesty, Nat, I dunno. I really don't. It's just, you know, looking at Davie, the idiot, lying there all broken and taking their shit, it just got to me.'

'Yeah, well, get in the queue. I've had to put up with his nightmare family half my life. Davie and I grew up together, remember?'

'They're arseholes, specially his dad.'

'I know.'

'And as for his mum …'

'I know.'

'But it was his reaction what got to me the most. He was standing up for them, like he thinks they're the bees' knees or something.'

'I know, Bill, I know. But what's the point of shouting at parents? By the time you're old enough to speak to them on equal terms, it's too late to make them any better. And besides, they're *his* family, not yours. Have you never heard of "blood is thicker than water?" Families screw you up, they're dysfunctional and horrible, but they're still family. It's natural to defend them when they're under attack.'

Murdoch had no way of knowing if that was true. He changed hands on the phone, pushed in the lighter on the dash and started rummaging around in the glovebox for a fag.

'Dare I ask again where you are?' said Natalie.

'Seeing a man about a dog. You?'

'At the station, where I always am. Which reminds me, I need to find out from you the link between Scott Patterson and Angie Anathassiou.'

But Murdoch had had time to think this through. 'If there was one, love, we didn't find it. Like I said at the time, all we had was the name. We found it scribbled on a piece of paper. Nothing else anywhere. Maybe there was a connection, but, like you said, Ana-thingybob's too smart to leave a trail.'

Natalie wasn't put off that easily, but, hating himself for being the cause of her disappointment, Murdoch stonewalled her further questions. Nothing, no idea, no way of knowing. Sorry, love. Eventually the conversation moved on, Murdoch asking Natalie what she was up to that night.

'Well, depending on how we go here, I might be free. Want to come round my place and I can play nursey?'

He told her to come to his place instead, he'd cook first. Anything to take his mind off things.

Driving through the forest, the low sun through the trees like a projector through film, Murdoch couldn't remember why he'd been so angry. The fury had drifted away with the dust from the road and the words he'd spoken to Natalie. The sky was blue, the air warm, the scene in the hospital a story he'd heard. He stopped again, looking forward to a bit of time alone, but immediately heard a car approaching from the opposite direction. Four minutes later, they were bumper to bumper on the pitted road, the Aston Martin so close Murdoch could see Velis's smile through their windscreens, then the shocked look that replaced it.

'Jesus!' In seconds, Velis was beside Murdoch's door, huge in a T-shirt and jeans, then squatting down so he was the shorter man for once. 'Mate, are you all right?'

Murdoch gestured him out of the way so he could shove the door open, then make a show of struggling out and reaching back in for the crutch.

'Easy pickings,' he said.

'Excuse me?'

'Easy pickings. That's what you said to me when we first talked about the painting. This is what "easy pickings" looks like, Emre, up close, it does. Course you're not used to close-ups are you? You normally like to manage things from a nice safe distance, being an executive and all.'

It was a chain of accusations: Davie in the hospital blaming him; him in the dusty road blaming Velis. He wondered who Velis would blame.

'It's your own stupid fault, Bill, don't try and pin this on me. I told you to leave it, not to go back. I couldn't have made it any clearer.' He paused, regretting his tone. 'Seriously, are you OK?'

Murdoch pushed past him and hobbled around to the boot of the Mercedes. He'd already clicked it open from inside the car; now he pulled out the portfolio case, still rippled with Marco's blood.

'This is for you,' he said, throwing it onto the corrugated ground between them. 'You get the money?'

He'd left the two holdalls in the Toyota on a suburban street in Warriwul.

'I did, Bill, and there were no tracking devices on it or in the bags, so there's no need for all this cloak-and-dagger stuff. We could have met over a beer or something. Talk about how you're going to spend your half of the money.'

'I don't want any fucking money.'

They stared at each other, Velis looking away first to study the portfolio case lying in the dust. He rolled his eyes and bent slowly to lift it, curling his lip into a scowl as he wiped it clean. Murdoch realised how rarely he'd seen Velis with anything but a smile on his face. He had no idea which expression revealed the truth of the man, the smile or the scowl, or something else he'd never seen.

'The thing is, Emre, I don't want to be seen with you in public. Not worth the danger, if you know what I mean.'

Velis opened the case and examined the picture slowly, still no smile. 'We both knew there was a risk of you getting hurt when we first discussed it. But, honestly, Bill, I didn't think it was going to happen. And I did try and stop you going back.'

'It's crime, Emre. That's what happens in crime, people get hurt. But don't worry about me, you should see the state of the other guy.'

Velis winced, eyes still on the painting. 'Yeah, I heard. Listen, don't forget, Marco was a nasty piece of work.'

'I didn't mean him. I meant a mate of mine what's got nothing to do with this and is in hospital with a bullet wound thanks to me. Blood's thicker than water, you know. I want to be around people I care about.'

Murdoch pushed roughly past again, not wanting to explain, and climbed awkwardly into the Mercedes. The engine complained as he reversed too quickly along the yellow dirt, the twist required to see behind him pulling painfully on his leg. He had turned the car and was back at the junction with the sealed road when the Aston Martin appeared in his rear-view mirror. Suddenly close in its cloud of grit, its headlights were flashing. Murdoch stopped and let Velis pull alongside. Watched him get out of his car and walk slowly round until he was leaning on the door again.

'Here's the thing, Bill. We've got a lot in common you and me. I don't like many people and I don't think you do either, so we're mates no matter what you feel about that right now. And when this has all died down, when your bruises have gone and you're stuck at home watching the paint dry, you're gonna want to call me. It's not easy being a man of leisure without getting bored, and you don't do boredom well, Bill, it's not in your blood. So do me a favour and don't back yourself into a corner where your pride won't let you have some fun. OK, I fucked up and I'm sorry, right? But wasn't it fun until then? Didn't it feel good to be what you really are, instead of pretending to be something else?'

Murdoch stared through the windscreen at the dust that had followed and then passed them. It hung over the start of the tarmac road, marking the angles of the light. Beside him, Velis sighed heavily.

'They say blood is thicker than water, Bill. But me, I'm not so sure. Either way, you don't have any blood, remember? Water is all you've got, mate. So, call me, yeah? Use the money as an excuse. Remind me I owe you seven hundred grand and let's see what happens then.'

Murdoch started the engine and the big man stepped back from the car. When he glanced in the mirror Velis was still standing there, hands by his sides, less confident than Murdoch had ever seen him.

Murdoch visited the hospital every day after that, finding comfort in its environment and, eventually admitting it, not wanting to be home alone. Davie had told the medical staff Murdoch was next of kin and the nurses, drawing their own conclusions, began to warm to him. Murdoch, in turn, let them look at his eye and give him advice on how to walk with the crutch. The bed next to Davie's was filled by a large and loud Lebanese patient with a larger and louder family, then by an ancient and pale man whose equally ancient wife visited once a day to shout at him in a strange and guttural language. On the day Davie was due to be discharged, he and the pale man were both snoring softly when Murdoch was disturbed from his paper by another, similar noise. The metal drawers on the other side of Davie's bed were vibrating.

'Leave it,' said Davie, waking slowly. 'It's just my phone. I charged it last night and it's been going off non-stop. It'll go to voicemail.'

But Murdoch was up and around the foot of the bed by then and he wasn't wasting the pain of that journey. 'Leave it? What you talking about? If you want to grow the agency this is prime time, mate. Them headlines was the best publicity you'll ever get.' He pulled open the metal drawer, Davie wincing at the noise, and took out the phone. 'Twenty-six missed calls! Davie, you muppet, that's money right there. What's your security code?'

Davie told him reluctantly and Murdoch dialled into voicemail.

'Twenty voicemails,' he said. 'How do you put it onto loudspeaker?'

'You can't. Not in here, it's not allowed. You'll wake up the old man.'

'Davie, his wife struggles to wake him and she could wake the dead.'

Davie winced again. There was something about the man in the other bed, his breathing or the colour of him, you knew he wasn't long for the world. Moving to close the drawer, Murdoch noticed a twist of wires in there, ear buds at one end, mini-jack at the other.

'Budge up,' he said. 'We'll listen with these in one ear each. Come on, what you waiting for, move over. You got a pen and paper?'

Davie sighed huffily but made space for Murdoch to squeeze onto the bed beside him. A short while later, when the nurse arrived, they were looking at the beginnings of a list, discussing why an unidentified caller had rung so often but refused to leave a message.

'Look at you two,' she said. 'Cute.'

Her name was Sally; she was the attractive older nurse Murdoch had clashed with on early visits. He preferred her when she was scowling.

'My husband and I used to share music like that. But you two need to get a move on, you know. I just need to change Mr Moyhal's dressing and then I'll be over. Big day today, Davie.'

She disappeared out to the corridor, admiring them again as she walked past the window. Murdoch looked at Davie.

'Here, she ever give you any bed baths then?'

'No!'

Davie blushed and Murdoch knew she had.

'What about her little friend with the ponytail and the tits?'

Davie hit the screen of his phone and the next voicemail sounded in their ears.

'Hello, Davie, this is Max Ringman and I think you might want to give me a call. Give the receptionist your name and she'll put you straight through. Looking forward to it!'

Max Ringman didn't leave a number which, Murdoch thought, took a certain amount of balls. But then balls were probably how you got to be the biggest press agent in town. He turned to Davie with a smile so broad it hurt where it creased his eye. Davie didn't return it. Instead, as Murdoch watched, he wrote Ringman's name on the pad on his lap and hit the screen on his phone again. Murdoch grabbed the phone before Davie could stop him and stopped the next voicemail in its tracks.

'Davie, mate, I reckon you should call him right now.'

'Yeah, I don't know. Maybe later, when I get home.'

He went to take the phone, but Murdoch snatched it out of the way.

'What do you mean? What don't you know, you muppet?'

'I don't know if I want to do a load of PR. I don't know if I want to take on a load of cases. You know, I keep thinking about what Patterson said, about how we all repress ourselves.'

'I don't seem to remember him doing much repressing of himself.'

'No, but it made me think. You know, sitting here day after day, all I've missed is my surfing ...'

The nurse called Sally walked in on this comment and laughed. 'Sorry,' she said, bending over the foot of the man in the other bed and starting to unwrap his bandaged foot. 'I forgot to tell you. The water temperature today is nineteen degrees. There's a two-foot swell with forty second intervals and an offshore breeze.'

Murdoch rolled his eyes as Davie carried on talking.

'The physio says it's important to have a goal, it will help me heal quicker if I do. And I do want to get back to work, take a new case. But it's the surfing that's really driving me on. It's not like I want to sit in an office running a big business.'

Murdoch sighed. 'Are you joking?'

'No. That's just not who I am. And I don't care what you or anyone thinks, I have to be true to myself.'

'And what about when I told you that two months ago? What about when I said, "Keep the agency small so you can surf whenever you like?" Or when I said, "Ignore your dad and live your own life?" That was all bollocks was it? But now that some nutter chained to a bed says it, it makes complete fucking sense!'

'Language,' said Sally sternly, nodding towards her patient's head in case he could sleep through her unwrapping his foot but be disturbed by a bit of swearing.

'This one's an idiot,' Murdoch told her, pulling himself off the bed and throwing the phone back behind him. 'Unbelievable.'

'Enough of that.' Sally was frowning at her handiwork. 'Don't you boys fight, not when you're not even home yet.'

'Men,' said Murdoch sourly. 'We are men, not boys. And, for your information, we don't live together and at least one of us likes women.'

There was a queue of staff who insisted on saying goodbye. Murdoch recognised a few of the nurses, a doctor who looked like Davie's dad, but he'd never seen any of the others. It reminded him how many people it had taken to get Davie well again. The hospital offered an ambulance, but Davie said there'd be enough fuss as it was, he didn't need to advertise the fact he was arriving home. So the nurses helped him into Murdoch's Merc, shoving the wheelchair into the back with scant regard for the leather interiors.

In Montauban, they drove straight to the north end of the beach, the best view down the surf line. The sun had started to set and the spray was catching pink and gold, four or five guys out off the point. As Davie talked about the water quality and his rehab plan and how soon he wanted to get out there, Murdoch realised he wanted to be in the water too, swimming himself better and clean.

Above them, at a point on the hill with a good view of the beach and the road to its north, another car sat and watched. It too caught the light of the sunset, the golds of the dying sky reflecting brightly in the mirrored casing of its wing mirrors. But only when the air had grown dark, and Murdoch had driven Davie home and helped him up the stairs into his house, did this car, a customised white Range Rover, make its move.

The End

THE MURDOCH SERIES

Have you read the other books in the
'Bill Murdoch Mysteries' series?

 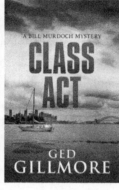 

Murdoch will be back for more Australian adventures soon. To be the first to hear about upcoming new releases (and special price promotions) sign up for book news at: www.gedgillmore.com

Ged always loves to hear from his readers, so if you'd like to ask him anything relating to his books, or give him feedback, then drop him a line at info@gedgillmore.com

P.S. If you enjoyed BASE NATURE, please take a moment to rate it – or even better – leave a quick review online. Reviews are incredibly helpful for emerging authors.

Many thanks,
GG